Mastering Python

Machine Learning, Data Structures, Django, Object Oriented Programming and Software Engineering

(Including Programming Interview Questions) [2nd Edition]

Table of Contents

Introduction

Welcome to my guide to learning Python. Unlike some guides that give you just the basics that you need to get started, my aim is to teach you everything you need to know about using Python including what you can use it for. Python is a diverse language and is the foundation of much of what we use in the world today. Most data applications, many websites, machine learning, are all powered by Python and you'll be pleased to learn that it really isn't difficult to learn. I have divided this book into five sections to make it easier for you:

- Part 1 – Data Structures and Algorithms
- Part 2 – Machine Learning
- Part 3 – Django
- Part 4 – ArcGIS Programming
- Part 5 – Software Development and Testing

Each part is comprehensive and complex; work through the sections one at a time and ensure that you understand it thoroughly before you move on to the next one. Below, is an overview of each part:

Part 1 – Data Structures and Algorithms

If you want to be successful building data applications that work, you need to have a good working knowledge of Python data structures along with algorithms that give those structures life. With this understanding, the secrets that lie within data can be unlocked. This is a skill that is becoming incredibly important in a world that is saturated with data, such a vast amount of data that we simply don't have the ability to analyze it all. What we do have are the tools, and in the first part of this guide, you will learn about the Python data structures and the algorithms, along with the basics of Python programming. Some of the algorithms we will look at are those that give us the solutions to common data analysis problems, such as searching data, sorting it, extracting statistics and more. You will learn about complex data structures and how to create stacks, lists, and queues. You will learn how to sort algorithms using techniques, such as insertion sort and bubble sort. You will learn the common structures and some of the techniques required to preprocess data, to model it, and transform it. You will learn how your code should be paganized for efficiency, manageability, and readability. And you will learn how you can build components that are easily understandable that can be used in multiple applications and can easily be debugged.

Part 2 – Machine Learning

We use machine learning more in our daily lives now than we ever have before and most of us don't realize it. In brief, machine learning is a subset of artificial intelligence, of using algorithms to improve how the machines learn autonomously. We do this by providing information and data in several formats, notably real-world interactions and observations. In short, we are teaching computers to think and act, to make decisions as humans do.

Most of Part Two will cover how machine learning works. We will talk about how the data should be processed so that the algorithms can make informed decisions and how to choose the correct algorithm for the problem we need to solve. We'll cover the why as well, such as why correct measurements are important, why one algorithm might work better than another in a certain scenario and so on.

This is the tip of the iceberg as far as machine learning goes and research is ongoing. Hopefully, by the end of this section, you will have enough information at your fingertips to continue as quickly and as painlessly as possible.

Part 3 – Django

This part looks at Django, the most popular framework for web development. With Django, it is possible to build top-quality web apps and maintain them with the least amount of fuss. Django is an exciting development and it takes the repetitiveness out of web development leaving you to concentrate on the fun side of creating a website. It gives you shortcuts for some of the tasks you do more frequently in programming and provides you with clear problem-solving conventions, all while staying as far out of the way as it can.

In this section, while I can't make you into a Django expert, I can tell you how it all works and walk you through building an application, the easiest way to learn the concepts behind it along with the skills you need.

Part 4 – ArcGIS Programming

ArcGIS is geographical software provided by ESRI, an industry leader that allows geospatial data to be analyzed and presented. The fact that Python has been integrated into ArcGIS means that the arcpy module is now one of the most important tools for anyone studying Geographical Information Systems (GIS). ArcPY has proven very powerful in geospatial analysis, especially to improve productivity. From basic scripts to the most advanced methods and properties from arcpy, the speed of any GIS workflow, as well as its repeatability, all seem set to vastly improve.

In this part of the guide, I will take you through basic scripts and the tools for advanced scripts. I will focus primarily on scripts for geospatial analysis with a look at how to automate cartographic output.

By the end of this section, you will have learned to create modules that you can reuse, add repeatable analyses in ArcToolBox as a scripting tool, and automatically export maps. You will also see just how efficient ArcGIS and arcpy are together, how one professional can have the power of an entire GIS team.

Part 5 – Software Development and Testing

In Part Five, the last part of the book, we take a look mainly at testing in Python. Testing is a requisite part of Python programming, particularly to build software and web apps. We will look at Test-Driven Development (TDT), Behavior-Driven Development (BDD), the Principles of Automated Testing and what the purpose is. We will look at the difference between unit and integration testing, how tests should be prioritized, and the testing of DSLs. We finish by looking at Python Mocking, a way of replacing bits of the system and making your unit tests far more efficient.

The Python programming language has led to more people learning to appreciate computer programming and what can be achieved with it. It is a fun language; it is concise in its problem descriptions and it makes learning easy.

We start the guide with an in-depth look at the language; you do not need to have any prior experience with Python.

The Zen of Python

Taken from https/python.org

"Beautiful is better than ugly.

Explicit is better than implicit.

Simple is better than complex.

Complex is better than complicated.

Flat is better than nested.

Sparse is better than dense.

Readability counts.

Special cases aren't special enough to break the rules.

Although practicality beats purity.

Errors should never pass silently.

Unless explicitly silenced.

In the face of ambiguity, refuse the temptation to guess.

There should be one-- and preferably only one --obvious way to do it.

Although that way may not be obvious at first unless you're Dutch.

Now is better than never.

Although never is often better than *right* now.

If the implementation is hard to explain, it's a bad idea.

If the implementation is easy to explain, it may be a good idea.

Namespaces are one honking great idea -- let's do more of those!"

Setting Up Your Environment

Before you can even start thinking about anything in this guide, you should set up your environment so there are no interruptions later. We'll start with Python itself.

You will need Python 2.7 or earlier; it's best to go for 3.6 if you can – the later the version, the more chance you have of everything being compatible.

Linux/Mac OS

You should already have Python installed on your computer; to check, open a terminal and type python 3 at the command prompt. You will see immediately if it is installed because you will see a version number.

Windows

You will need to download Python to your computer; go to https://www.python.org/downloads and download the latest version (3, not 2). Once the download has finished, open your computer's downloads folder and double-click the python.msi file and the installer will run.

Now, by default, the executable file for Python does NOT get added to the statement for Windows PATH – you need to add it, but this is simple. Wait for the installer screen to load and then check the box that says "Add Python 3.x to PATH" before you hit the Install button. Click Install and wait; when it has finished, open a command window and type python – you should see confirmation of the version you installed. If it doesn't show up, reboot your computer and try again. Once you see the confirmation, there is one last thing to do – close Python and then go to the command prompt in the command window – type the following:

python -m pip install -U pip

You will now see a message that tells you pip is up-to-date or you will see a message telling you that the latest version is being downloaded – the old version will be uninstalled first.

Pip is the package manager for Python and is what you will use to install the packages you need. Next, we 'll install a virtual environment. It's best to work inside a virtual environment so that you don't inadvertently write something that can change the variables and dependencies on which other software on your computer depend. The virtual environment wraps up environment variables and dependencies that your new software uses into one file system that is kept separate from anything else running on your computer.

To install the Python virtual environment, open your terminal or command prompt and type the following:

pip install virtualenv

You should now see a message in the window telling you that virtualenv is now installed.

This sets you up with Python; as we go through the guide, I will tell you, at the start of each section, what other packages you need to install.

Chapter 1: An Overview of Data Structures and Algorithms

Python is the chosen programming language for many different data tasks and there is a good reason for that. It is an easy programming language to learn and the addition of intuitive structures means that it is one of the most straightforward languages for a whole range of different data tasks. Python is not just for scripting; it is a fully featured object-oriented programming language (OOP).

One of the most useful features of Python is the fact that it has many built-in data structures and algorithms. Because it is object-based, creating custom data objects is relatively simple. We're going to be looking at the internal Python libraries, some external libraries, and we will be learning how to use first principles to build data objects.

I am assuming that you have some knowledge of Python but, just in case you need a refresher, this first section will go over the basics. If you still need a refresher, take a look at the tutorials at https://docs.python.org.

In this section, we will be:

- Looking at and learning about data structures and algorithms
- Learning the fundamental data types and what they do
- Looking into the object-oriented side of Python

Data Structures and Algorithms

Data Structures and Algorithms are perhaps the most basic of all computing concepts because they are the building blocks that we use to build software. Understanding these concepts is vital to software design and, for that, you will need to learn the following:

- How data inside a data structure is manipulated by algorithms
- How data is organized in memory
- The performance characteristic of certain data structures

Some of this will be addressed in Part Two when we discuss machine learning but we will be looking at the basics of Python from several perspectives, first and foremost from the perspective of the algorithms and data structures. We also need to make sure that we have the mathematical tools we need to understand the basic computer science concepts. For this, we need an understanding of mathematics, but, by developing a few guiding principles, understanding the key principles won't require anything more than high-school math.

Evaluation is also vital. To measure the performance of an algorithm, you must understand how the increases in the size of the data affect data operations. With real-world applications or large datasets, we must ensure that the data structures and the algorithms are working efficiently.

To understand a little about algorithmic thinking, we'll look at a quick real-world example. Let's say that we are in a marketplace that is not familiar to us. We have been asked to buy a specific list of items. Assume that the market has been randomly laid out and that each of the vendors will sell a random subset of the items, and some of these might just be on our list. What we want to do is minimize how long we are there, so we would start with an algorithm like this:

- Does the first vendor sell any of the items I want, and do they cost less than the predicted cost?
- If yes, buy the items and remove them from the list. If no, proceed to the next vendor.
- If there are no more vendors, we're finished.

Repeat for every vendor.

This is, in programming terms, nothing more than an iterator; it has a decision and it has an action. If this were to be implemented, we would need to define the item list that we have and the items that each vendor sells, and this is done through data structures. We would need to find the best way to match the items in each of the lists and we need a little logic to determine whether to buy or not.

We can see several things here. First, the cost calculation is prediction-based. We have no idea of the average cost. If we go with an underprediction we will leave the market with items left to buy so we need a way to go back to the vendor that has the lowest cost.

We also need an understanding of the time needed to compare the items on the list with what each vendor sells – either our list will increase or the number of items sold by a vendor will increase. The time it takes to search will depend on in what order we search and the data structure shapes. Clearly, it would be better to have the list structured in such a way that it matches the order of the vendors, thus cutting down the search time.

Still with me? Good, because next, we need to think about the effect if we were to change our purchase condition so that we bought at the lowest price and at the price that is just under the average. This makes the problem entirely different; instead of visiting the vendors in sequence, we need to go through the market once and then order the list as to the vendors we need to visit.

Clearly, there is more to turning a real-world problem into a programming language. As we go through the market, for example, we expand our knowledge of product costs so the variable we have for the predicted average price will improve; by the time we get to the end of the market, we can look at our whole strategy and review it. Adding in conditions like data structure shape, the variability of prices, backtrack cost, and so on, help us to work out the best solution.

Python for Data

Python very helpfully contains a number of built-in structures including dictionaries, lists, and sets and we can use these to build customized objects. There are also libraries, like collections and a math object; these let us create structures that are a bit more advanced and we can perform calculations on them. Lastly, there are external libraries, like those in the SciPy packages and it is these that let us do some of the more advanced data tasks that pertain to machine learning. However, while these external libraries are useful, there are penalties to pay in terms of performance compared to ground-up customized objects. If we can learn to code the objects, they can be targeted at particular tasks and this will make them far more efficient.

Chapter 2: Python Variables and Expressions

There are two associated tasks involved in translating real-world problems into those that an algorithm can solve. First, the variables must be selected and second, we need the expressions that are related to the variables. A variable is a label that is attached to an object. They are neither the object nor are they the object containers. Variables do not contain objects; they are pointers to objects. Look at this code:

a=[2, 4, 6]

b=a

a.append(8)

print(b)

[2, 4, 6, 8]

A variable has been created and this references a list object. Another variable is created, and this references the same object. When an element is appended, we see that both a and b reflect the change.

Python is known as a dynamically-typed language. We can bind a variable name to different types and values during execution; each of the values is of a specific type, perhaps an integer or a string but the name that references the value will not have a particular type. What this means is whenever a variable is initialized in Python, there is no need to declare a type. The object that a variable points to can also change type.

Variable Scope

One of the most important things to understand is the rules of scope surrounding a variable in a function. New local namespaces are created whenever a function is executed. These namespaces represent environments in which you will find the names of each parameter and each variable that the function assigned. When a function is called the namespace needs to be resolved and, to do this, the Python interpreter will search the function; if it can't find a match, it will then search the module in which the function is defined – this is the global namespace. If the name is still not there, the built-in namespace is searched and, if this doesn't work, the interpreter will raise a NameError exception. Look at this code:

```
a=20; b=30
def my_function():
    global a
    a=21; b=31
my_function()
print(a) #prints 21
print(b) #prints 30
```

We have defined a pair of global variables and the interpreter needs to be told that, within the function, we are using the global keyword to refer to a global variable. When the variable gets changed to 11 the global scope will reflect the changes. However, where the variable called b is set to 21, it is actually a local variable and, if we make any changes within the function, there is no reflection of them in the global scope. If you run that function and print that variable, you would see that b keeps its global value.

Iteration and Flow Control

All Python programs are made up of sequences of statements. Each statement is executed in order until all are done. All the statements have an equal status, regardless of whether they are function definitions, variable assignments, module imports or class definitions. None of the statement types have a priority that is higher than another and any statement can be placed anywhere within the program. Program exaction flow can be controlled in two ways – using loops and using conditional statements.

The conditional statements are:

- if
- else
- elif

Generally, a series of the if and elif statements end with an else statement:

```
x='two'
if x==1:
    print('False')
elif x==2:
    print('True')
else:
    print('Another value')
#prints 'Another value'
```

Did you spot the == operator? We use that to test for equal values and, if they are equal, it will return True, and False if otherwise. Also note that when x is set as a string, the return will not be a type error as you would expect; instead, it will be *something else*.

Loops are the other way of controlling program flow and we create this using two more statements:

- while
- for

Look at this example:

```
x=0
while x < 3: print (x); x += 1
```

0

1

2

Chapter 3: Overview of Data Types And Objects

Built into Python are no less than 12 data types including four that are numeric:

- int
- float
- complex
- bool

There are four that are sequence types:

- str
- list
- tuple
- range

A mapping type called dict and two of type set are also included. You may also create your own user-defined objects like classes or functions. First, we'll look at lists and strings and move onto the rest of the data types later.

Every Python data type is an object, as are functions, classes, modules, and pretty much anything else in Python – and that includes string and integer literals. Each Python object has its own type, identity, and value. For example, when you write *greeting = "hello world"* you are creating an instance. This instance is a string object that has an identity of *greet* and a value of *"hello world"*. The object identity is a reference to where the object is located in memory. The object type, otherwise known as its class, is a description of the internal representation of the object along with any operations and methods supported by it. When an object instance has been created, you cannot change either the type or the identity.

There is a function built into Python called id() and this can be used to find an object's identity. It will return an integer that identifies it, and this may refer to the location in memory – do not rely on this though. We can also compare objects in several ways:

if a== b: #a and b have identical values
if a is b: # if a and b are identical object types
if type(a) is type(b): # a and b are identical types

Before we go any further, we need to distinguish between objects that are mutable and immutable. With a mutable object, like a list, you can change their values using methods like append() or insert(). With an immutable object, like a string, you cannot change the values. When their methods are run, a value is returned; there is no change to the value of any underlying object. However, you can use the returned value – simply use it as a function argument or assign it to a variable.

Strings

A string is a sequence object that is immutable. Each character is representative of one element in that sequence. Operations are performed on the objects using methods. Because a string is immutable, the instances are not changed; each method will do nothing more than return a value. We can store this value as a variable or we can pass it to a method or a function as an argument. Below are the most common string methods along with a description:

s.count(substring, [start, end])

Will count the number of substrings that have optional start and end
parameters

s.expandtabs([tabsize])

Will replace any tab with a space

s.find(substring, [start, end])

Will return the index of the first substring; -1 is returned if the substring can't
be found

s.isalnum()

Will return True if every character is alphanumeric; False if not

s.isalpha()

Will return True if every character is alphabetic; False if not

s.isdigit()

Will return True if every character is a digit; False if not

s.join(t)

Will join together the strings in the given sequence (t, in this case)

s.lower()

Will convert the string to be lowercase

s.replace(old, new [maxreplace])

Will replace a substring (old) with another (new)

s.strip([characters])

Will remove any optional characters or whitespace

s.split([separator], [maxsplit])

Will split a string that is separated with an optional separator or whitespace and will return a list

Like every type of sequence, a string has support for both indexing and slicing. We use the index s[i] to retrieve a given character from the string and we can use s[i:j] to get a slice from the string – i and j indicate the start point and the end point of the slice. We can add a stride to get an extended slice s[i:j:stride]. Let's make this a little clearer with a piece of code:

greet = 'hello world'
print(greet[1])

Running this code will return:

[e]

print(greet [0:8])

Running this code will return:

'hello wo'

print(greet [0:8:2])

Running this code will return:

'hlow'

print(greet [0::2])

Running this code will return:

'hlowrd'

Example 1 and 2 are easy; we asked for and got the character located at the first index and the initial 7 letters from the string. Example 3 includes a stride of 2 which gives us every 2nd character while, in the last example, we left out the end index; the slice we got was every 2nd character from the whole string.

Any variable, expression or operator can be used for the index so long as it has an integer for the value:

print(greet [1+2])

Running this code will return:

'l'

print(greet[len(greet)-1])

Running this code will return:

'd'

As we know, strings are immutable so one of the most common questions is, how do we do operations like inserting a value? Instead of changing the string, we must come up with other ways of building new objects that give us the results we need. For example, let's say that we wanted to add a word to the greeting; we would assign variables like this:

print(greet[:5] + ' wonderful ' + greet[5:])

Running this code will return:

'hello wonderful world'

We split the string using the slice operator and we did this at index 5. The + operator is used to concatenate the strings. The string contents are never interpreted by Python as numbers. If we needed to do a math operation on a string, we would have to convert the string to type numeric:

```
x='3'; y = '2'
print(x + y) #concatenation
```

Running this code will return:

'32'

```
print(int(x) + int (y)) #addition
```

Running this code will return:

5

Lists

The list is the most common data structure and is used the most often because they can be made up of any data type. A list, like a string, is indexed using integers that begin with a zero. Below are the common list methods and a description of each:

list(s)

Will return a list of the given sequence (s)

s.append(x)

Will append the element called x to s (at the end)

s.extend(x)

Will append the list called x to s

s.count(x)

Will count how many times x is in s

s.index(x, [start], [stop])

Will return the index that is the smallest and may include an optional start, stop index

s.insert(i,e)

Will insert x at the given index (i)

s.pop(i)

Will return the element called i and take it out of the list

s.remove(x)

Will take x out of s

s.reverse()

Will reverse the order of s

s.sort(key,[reverse])

Will sort s using reverse and optional key

When we work with any list or any container object, we must understand what mechanism Python employs to copy them. Python will only create a real copy if it has no alternative. When a variable value is assigned to another variable, both of them will go to the same location in memory. We only get a new memory slot if a variable is changed. This has consequences for lists and other mutable compound objects. Look at this code:

```
x=1; y=2; z=3
list1 =[x, y, z]
list2 = list1
list2[1] = 4
print(list1)
```

Running this code will return:

```
[1, 4, 3]
```

The variables called list1 and list2 both point to the same memory slot; when the y variable is changed to 4, the y variable that list1 points to is changed as it is the same variable.

One other important thing about lists is that you can have nested structures in them. This means they can contain other lists, like this:

```
items = [ ["rice", 2.4, 8], ["flour", 1.8, 5], ["corn", 4.7, 6] ]
```

The brackets operator is used to access the values in the lists and, because the list is mutable, they are copied where they are. The next code example shows you how to update an element using this fact. We are going to raise the flour price by 20%:

```
items[1][1] = items [1][1] * 1.2
print(items[1][1])
```

Running this code will return:

2.16

We can also use list comprehensions to create a list from some expressions. We write one expression into the list and create a list:

```
l= [2, 4, 8, 16]
print([i**3 for i in l])
```

Running this code will return:

[8, 64, 512, 4096]

List comprehensions are flexible. Look at the next code; it is showing two ways that you can do a function composition applying one function to another. The code will print 2 lists that represent the compositions of f1 and f2, using a for loop and then a list comprehension to calculate them:

```
def f1(x): return x*2
def f2(x): return x*4

lst = []
for i in range(16):
    lst.append(f1(f2(i)))

print(lst)

print([f1(x) for x in range(64) if x in [f2(j) for j in range(16)]])
```

The first output line comes from the construct of the for loop while the second comes from the expression for the list comprehension.

We can also use a list comprehension to provide a more compact replication of the action of the nested loops. Each element is multiplied with each other within the list:

```
list1= [[1, 2, 3], [4, 5, 6]]
print([i * j for i in list1[0] for j in list1[1]])
```

Running this code will return:

[4, 5, 6, 8, 10, 12, 15, 18]

Lastly, list comprehensions can also be used together with objects to build other structures. The last code example shows a list of words created along with the word count:

```
words = 'here is a sentence'.split()
print([[word, len(word) ] for word in words])
```

Running this code will return:

[['here', 4], ['is', 2], ['a', 1], ['sentence', 8]]

As we continue, you will see that lists are a fundamental basis for a wide range of data structures. They are versatile, very easy to create, and we can use them to build highly complex and specialized data structures.

First-Class Objects – Functions

It isn't just the data types in Python that are treated as objects; both classes and functions are too, and they come under the heading of 'first-class' objects. They can be manipulated the same as any of the data types built-in. The definition of a first-class object is:

- That creation takes place at runtime
- That they are assigned in a data structure or as a variable
- That they are passed to functions as arguments
- That they are returned as a function result

The term, 'first-class object' is somewhat a misnomer because it gives the impression that there is some kind of hierarchy but, in Python, every object is first-class.

Look at the following function definition to see how this works:

```
def greeting(language):
```

```
if language== 'eng':
    return 'hello world'
if language  == 'fr':
    return 'Bonjour le monde'
else: return 'language not supported'
```

Because any user-defined function is an object, we can add it into another object, like a list:

```
l=[greeting('eng'), greeting('fr'), greeting('ger')]
print(l[1])
```

Running this code will return:

' Bonjour le monde'

We can also use a function as an argument for another function. Look at this example:

```
def callf(f) :
  lang='eng'
  return  (f(lang))
```

```
print(callf(greeting))
```

Running this code will return:

'hello world'

In this code, callf() has a function as an argument; the language variable is then set to 'eng' and the function is called and takes the language variable as its argument. It's easy to see how this could be useful, especially if we wanted to build a program that would return given sentences in different languages, a language application program perhaps. Here we have a place to set up the language and alongside the greeting, we could have other functions that would return other sentences. By having a single point where the language is set, the rest of the logic in the program is ignored. If we wanted a different language, we would just set the language variable and leave everything else alone.

Higher-Order Functions

If a function takes a function as an argument or it returns a function, it is known as a higher-order function. There are two of these built into Python 3 – map() and filter(). In earlier Python versions, these functions would have returned lists, but in Python 3 we get an iterator. This makes them highly efficient. With the map() function, we can easily transform items into iterable objects. Look at this example of a neat and efficient way of carrying out an operation on a sequence. Note that we use the lambda function (anonymous):

lst=[1,2,3,4]

print(list(map(lambda x: x**3, lst)))

Running this code will return:

[1, 8, 27, 64]

In much the same way, the filter() function can be used for filtering list items:

print(list(filter((lambda x: x<3), lst)))

Running this code will return:

[1, 2]

The map() and the filter() functions both do exactly the same as what we can achieve with a list comprehension. In fact, there is little difference in terms of performance with the exception of using the built-in functions without using lambda provides a slight advantage over list comprehensions. In spite of this, list comprehensions are the preferred way of doing things as they can be read much easier.

The functional style of Python means that we can easily create higher-order functions. In the next example, we pass len to the sort function as the key, allowing us to sort a word list by word length:

words=str.split('The longest word in this sentence')
print(sorted(words, key=len))

Running this code will return:

['in', 'The', 'this', 'longest', 'sentence']

Let's have a look at another example, this time for case-insensitive sorting:

```
sl=['A', 'b', 'a', 'C', 'c']
sl.sort(key=str.lower)
print(sl)
```

Running this code will return:

['A', 'a', 'b', 'C', 'c']


```
sl.sort()
```

```
print(sl)
```

Running this code will return:

['A', 'C', 'a', 'b', 'c']

There is a difference between the method list.sort() and the built-in function sorted; list.sort() is a method of the object called list and it is used to sort an instance of a list without actually copying it. It will change the target object and the return will be None. One of the more important Python conventions is that methods or functions that can change an object will return None, and as such makes it clear that there haven't been any new objects created and that the object was changed.

On the other hand, the built-in function called sorted will return a brand-new list. It will take iterable objects as arguments but a list will always be returned. Both functions can take up to two optional arguments (keyword) as key.

A very easy way to sort complex structures is by using the element index to sort with lambda, like this:

items.sort(key=lambda item: item[1])

print(items)

Running this code will return:

[['flour', 1.8, 5], ['rice', 2.4, 8], ['corn', 4.7, 6]]

We sorted all the items in price order.

Recursive Functions

Recursion is a basic computer science concept and in Python, there is an easy way to implement recursive functions. All we do is call the function inside the body of the function. However, if we just use a recursive function, we run the risk of it turning into an infinite loop. To stop this, we require a minimum of one argument that will test for a terminating case that will finish the recursion. This is known as the "base case".

It is worth remembering that recursion is not the same as iteration. Although both revolve around repetition, an iteration will loop through an operation sequence whereas recursion will call a function repeatedly. Both can only end with a selection statement. In technical terms, recursion is actually a version of iteration called "tail iteration". It is nearly always possible for a recursive function to be converted to an iterative function and vice versa.

The next code will show the difference between the two. Both functions will print the numbers in between low and high – the first function uses iteration while the second uses recursion:

```
def iterTest(low, high):
    while low <= high:
        print (low)
        low=low+1

def recurTest(low, high):
    if low <= high:
        print(low)
        recurTest(low+1, high)
```

Note that in iterTest, we have used a while statement for testing the condition, then the print method is called, and the low value incremented. In recurTest, an if statement is used to test the condition, the print method called, and the low variable is incremented in the argument. Generally, iteration is far more efficient, but recursive functions tend to be easier to read and to write. Recursive functions are also good to manipulate data structures that are recursive, like trees and linked lists.

Generators and Co-Routines

Functions that return sequences of results rather than a single result can also be created and we do this with the yield statement. We call these functions 'generators' and, in Python you will see that there are some generator functions already built-in. These provide us with an easy and efficient way of creating iterators and they are a useful replacement for lists that are long and unworkable. Generators yield items; they don't build lists.

Have a look at the code example; this shows you why generators are a better option than creating lists:

```
# the running time of the list is compared to the generator
import time
# an iterator containing odd numbers between the letters n and m is created
by the generator function
def oddGen(n, m):
    while n < m:
        yield n
        n += 2
#a list of odd numbers from n to m is built
def oddLst(n,m):
    lst=[]
    while n<m:
        lst.append(n)
        n +=2
    return lst
#the length of time taken for a sum to be performed on an iterator
t1=time.time()
sum(oddGen(1,1000000))
print("Time to sum an iterator: %f" % (time.time() - t1))
```

```
#the length of time taken to build a list and sum it
t1=time.time()
sum(oddLst(1,1000000))
print("Time to build and sum a list: %f" % (time.time() - t1))
```

As you can see, it takes quite a bit longer to build a list for this calculation. The significant improvement in performance using a generator comes from the values being generated on demand instead of saving the list in memory. The calculation can start before the elements have all been generated and they will only be generated as and when they are required.

In the last example, the sum method is loading the numbers into memory when they are required for the calculation. This is done by the generator object; it calls the _next_() special method repeatedly. A generator is not able to return any value aside from None.

Usually, a generator object is used in a for loop. For example, the oddGen generator function that we generated in the last code can be used to print odd integers from 1 to 10:

```
for i in oddGen(1,10):print(i)
```

A generator expression can also be created. These use the exact same syntax as a list comprehension with the exception that we replace the square brackets with a set of parentheses. These create generator objects, not lists. The object will not create any data until it is demanded. What this means is that there is no support for sequence methods, such as insert() and append() but we can use the list() function to convert a generator to a list:

```
lst1= [1, 2, 3, 4]

gen1 = (10**i for i in lst1)

print(gen1)
```

Running this code will return:

```
<generator object <genexpr> at 0x000001B981504C50>
```

```
for x in gen1: print(x)
```

10

100

1000

10000

Chapter 4: Classes - Object Programming

We can use classes to create all kinds of objects and they are a central point of OOP. Classes define sets of attributes that may be shared over all instances of the class. A typical class is a set of properties, variables, and functions.

OOP is somewhat compelling because it gives us a good basis for thinking about the core functionality of any program that we write. Because we can organize those programs around data and objects and not logic and actions, we have a strong but flexible way of building algorithms, particularly complex ones. Of course, we still have the logic and the actions, but because we have them embodied in objects, we have a method of encapsulating the functionality so that we can change objects in highly specific ways. Because of this, our code is less prone to errors, we can extend it and maintain it much easier, and we can model real-world objects.

We create a class in python by using the class statement; this results in a shared attributes set being defined and this is associated with a class instance collection. Classes usually have several methods, computed properties, and class variables. It needs to be understood that, when you define a class, you do not create any class instances. For an instance to be created, you must assign a variable to the class. Inside the body of the class are several statements that will execute during the definition. The functions that are defined in the class are known as instance methods; they are used to apply operations to the instance of the class and this is done by an instance of the class being passed as the initial argument. By convention, the argument is known as self, but any legal identifier can be used for it. Look at an example:

```
class Employee(object):
    numEmployee = 0
    def __init__(self, name, rate):
        self.owed = 0
        self.name = name
        self.rate=rate
        Employee.numEmployee += 1

    def __del__(self):
```

```
        Employee.numEmployee -= 1

    def hours(self, numHours):
        self.owed += numHours * self.rate
        return("%.2f hours worked" % numHours)

    def pay(self):
        self.owed = 0
        return("payed %s " % self.name)
```

A class variable, like numEmployee, will share its values with all the class instances. In the example, we used numEmployee to count how many employee instances there are. Note: the class called Employee will implement the special methods calls _init_ and _del_ and we'll talk more about those shortly. First, let's look at an example to create an instance of the Employee object, how to run the methods, and how to return the class and the instance variables:

```
emp1=Employee("Jill", 15.50)
emp2=Employee("Jack", 15.50)
print(Employee.numEmployee)
```

Running this code will return:

2


```
print(emp1.hours(20))
```

Running this code will return:

'20.00 hours worked'


```
print(emp1.owed)
```

Running this code will return:

print(emp1.pay())

Running this code will return:

'paid Jill '

Methods: Special

The function called dir(object) can be used to get the attributes list for a specified object. If a method starts with an underscore and ends with one, it is called a special method. With one exception, a special method tends to be called by the interpreter and not the programmer: let's say that you use the + operator; what you are doing is calling _add_(). For example, instead of my_object_len_(), we could use len(my_object). It is a good deal faster using len() on string objects because the returned value is representative of the size of the object in memory. The exception mentioned earlier is the method called _init_. This is the only method that a programmer can call in a program and it is used for invoking the superclass initializer in the class definitions. One thing that must be made clear is that you should NOT use the double underscore for objects that you create because it could cause a conflict, either now or in the future, with the special methods built into Python.

However, there may come a time when you want special methods implemented into custom objects; you would do this if you wanted the object to have some of the built-in type behaviors. In the next code, we are going to create a class that will implement the method called _repr_. This method is used to create string representations of the object and this is good for the purpose of an inspection:

```
class my_class():
    def __init__(self, greet):
        self.greet = greet
    def __repr__(self):
        return 'a custom object (%r)' % (self.greet)
```

When an instance of that object is created and inspected, the custom string representation is present. Note that the %r format placeholder is used so the object's standard representation is returned. This is classed as best practice and is very useful because the object called greet is surrounded by quotation marks, indicating that is it a string:

a=my_class("gday")
print(a)

Running this code will return:

a custom object ('gday')

Inheritance

We can also create a class that will modify how an existing class behaves using inheritance. To do this, the inherited class is passed inside the class definition as an argument. We tend to use this when we want the behavior of an existing method to be modified. An example:

class specialEmployee(Employee):
  def hours(self, numHours):
    *self.owed += numHours * self.rate * 2*
    return("%.2f hours worked" % numHours)

Note that one instance of the class specialEmployee is exactly the same as an Employee instance with the exception of the change to the hours() method.

If we want to define a new class variable using a subclass, the _init_() method must be defined by the subclass, like this:

class specialEmployee(Employee):
  def __init__(self,name,rate, bonus):
    Employee.__init__(self, name, rate) #the base classes are called
    self.bonus = bonus

  def hours(self, numHours):

```
    self.owed += numHours * self.rate + self.bonus
    return("%.2f hours worked" % numHours)
```

The methods in the base class are not invoked automatically and, as such, the derived class must call them. Class membership can be tested if we use the isinstance(obj1, obj2) function built into Python. If obj1 belongs to the obj2 class or any class that has been derived from it, this function returns True.

It tends to be assumed that all methods in a class definition will operate on the class instance. This is not required, but there are some other method types – class methods and static methods. Static methods are ordinary functions that are defined inside a class; they do not do any operation on instances and we use the class decorator called @staticmethod to define them. A static method is not able to access any instance attributes so they tend to be used more as a convenient way of grouping together the utility functions.

Within a class definition, it is assumed that all methods operate on the instance, but this is not a requirement. There are, however, other types of methods: **static methods** and **class methods**. A static method is just an ordinary function that just happens to be defined in a class. It does not perform any operations on the instance and it is defined using the @staticmethod class decorator. Static methods cannot access the attributes of an instance, so their most common usage is as a convenience to group utility functions together.

A class method, on the other hand, performs operations on the class in much the same way that class variables are associated with the class and not the class instances. We use the decorator called @classmethod to define them and the differentiation between the two methods is that, in this one, the class gets passed as the initial argument. By convention, this has a name of cls.

```
class Aexp(object):
    base=2
    @classmethod
    def exp(cls,x):
        return(cls.base**x)
```

class Bexp(Aexp):
    base=3

The class called Bexp will inherit from the class called Aexp and the base class variable is changed to 3. The exp() method from the parent class is run like this:

BxSqr = Bexp()
print(BxSqr.exp(3))

Running this code will return:

27

There are a few reasons why a class method could be useful. For example, subclasses will inherit the same features that the parent class has and that means it can potentially break an inherited method. The class method can be used as a way of defining the methods that need to be run.

Data Encapsulation and Properties

Unless it is specified otherwise, methods and attributes can all be accessed without any restrictions. What this means is anything that has been defined inside the base class can be accessed from the derived class. When OOP applications are built, it can cause a few problems, especially if the internal implementation of the object is wanted to be hidden. This leads to conflicts in the namespace between the objects that were defined inside a derived class and the base class. To stop this happening, where we have defined private attributes in a method, that method has the double underscore, for example, __privateMethod(). This name would be changed automatically to _Classname__privateMethod() to stop the conflicts with the base class defined methods. This doesn't actually hide the private attributes; instead, it just stops the name conflicts.

The recommendation is that the private attributes should be used when a class property for defining attributes that are mutable are used. Properties are attributes that, when called, compute the value instead of returning a value that has been stored. As an example, we could do the following to redefine the property called exp():

```
class Bexp(Aexp):
    __base=3
    def __exp(self):
        return(x**cls.base)
```

Next, we are going to look at the data structures built into Python.

Chapter 5: Python Structures and Data Types

We'll start by looking at data types in some detail. The two that we have already used are str() and list(), the string and the list. In Python, you will often want to represent your data using specialized objects and, as well as the data types built into Python, there are some internal modules that provide the tools to correct common problems with data structures. First, we'll look at the common expressions and operations used for all data types.

Operations and Expressions

There are quite a few common operations; for example, the truth value operators can be used for just about all data types and objects. The values below are those that Python considers as False values:

- The data type 'None'
- False
- Any float, integer or complex zero
- Empty sequences or mapping
- Any instance of a class defined by a user that defines a _bool_() or _len_() method that returns False or zero

Python considers any other value to be True.

Booleans

Boolean operations return one of two values – True or False. They are in priority order, therefore, if there are two or more in one expression, the highest priority Boolean operation will happen first. Below are all three of the Boolean operators in order of priority, with the operator and an example.

not x

If x is False, this returns True; False is returned otherwise

x and y

If x and y are both True, this returns True; False is returned otherwise

x or y

if x or y is True, this returns True; False is returned otherwise

When they evaluate expressions, the 'and' and 'or' operators use something called short-circuiting. With this, Python evaluates an operator only if it is required. For example, let's say that x is True; in the expression, 'x or y', y isn't evaluated because it is obvious the expression is True. With the expression, 'x and y', where x is false, the Python interpreter will evaluate x, return a value of False, and ignore y.

Comparison and Arithmetic Operators

There are four basic arithmetic operators (as well as a few others):

- Addition (+)
- Subtraction (-)
- Multiplication (*)
- Division (/)

The other arithmetic operators are the //, which provides an integer quotient (3//2 will return 1, for example), **, which is the exponent operator and %, the modulus operator, returning the remainder of a division. The comparison operators, which are (<, <=, >, >=, == and!=) all work with numbers, lists, strings, and any collection object and, provided the given condition holds, they will return True. For a collection object, the operators make a comparison of how many elements there are and ==, which is the equivalence operator, will check to see if each of the objects is structurally equivalent and that each element has an identical value, return True if they are, False if otherwise.

Membership Operators, Identity and Logical Operations

The membership operators are 'in' and 'not in' and they are used to test for variables in given sequences; for example, x in y will return True should the variable x be in y. The identity operator, 'is', compares the identity of objects. For example, the next code snippet demonstrates object identity and contrast equivalence:

x =[1,2,3]; y=[1, 2, 3]

print(x == y) #equivalence

Running this code will return:

True

print(x is y) # object identity

Running this code will return:

False

x = y #assignment

print(x is y)

Running this code will return:

True

Built-In Data Types

The data types built into Python can be separated into three categories: Numeric, Sequence, and Mapping. There is also the object called 'None', which is representative of a Null or when there is no value. Do not forget, objects like files, classes, and exceptions are also considered as types, but we won't be discussing those here.

Every single Python value has a data type, but unlike other computer programming languages, Python does not require explicit declaration of a variable type because Python internally tracks the types. The following shows the built-in data types with the category, name and description:

Category	Name	Description
None	None	Null Object
Numeric	int	Integer
	float	Floating point number
	complex	Complex number
	bool	Boolean
Sequences	str	Character string
	list	Lists arbitrary objects
	tuple	Groups arbitrary
Objects	range	Creates ramges of integers
Mapping	dict	Ditionary containing key-value pairs
	set	Mutable collection of unordered, unique items
	frozenset	Immutable set

None

The type None is an immutable type and it has a single value of 'None'. It is used as a representation of no value and is returned by any object that doesn't explicitly return a value and in Boolean expressions, will evaluate as False. None tends to be used as a default value for optional arguments so that the function can determine whether a value has been passed by the caller or not.

Numeric

With the exception of the bool, all of the numeric types are signed and are immutable. The Booleans will return one of two values – True or False – and these are mapped, respectively, to 0 and 1. The int is used to represent whole numbers of an unlimited range while floats are represented by the double precision machine representation. Two floating point numbers represent the complex numbers, and these are assigned through the j operator signifying the 'imaginary' bit of a complex number, like this:

a = 2+3j

Accessing the real part and the imaginary part are done through a.real and a.imag respectively.

Sequences

A sequence is an ordered set containing objects indexed by integers that are non-negative. Tuples and lists are sequences containing arbitrary objects while a string is a character sequence. Tuple, string, and range objects are immutable. Every sequence type has some operations in common; index and slice operators apply to all sequences. For any immutable type, an operation will return a value; it will NOT change the value.

The following methods are common to all sequences:

len(s)

how many elements are in (s)

min(s, [,default=obj, key=func])

minimum value found in (s) – alphabetically if a string

max(s, [,default=obj, key=func])

maximum value found in (s) – alphabetically if a string

sum(s,[,start=0])

sum of all elements – if (s) isn't numeric, TypeError is returned

all(s)

if all elements in (s) are True, True is returned – they cannot be 0, Null or False

any(s)

Checks to see if any of the items in (s) are True

Sequences also all support these operations:

s + r

concatenation of two sequences of the same type

s * n

will make n copies of s (where n is an int)

v1, v2..., vn = s

unpacks n variables from s to v1, v2, etc.

s[i]

Indexing – this returns element i from s

s[i:j:stride]

Slicing – will return elements from i to j with an optional stride

x in s

if element x is in s, this will return True

x not in s

if element x is not in s, this will return True

Tuples

A tuple is an immutable sequence that contains arbitrary objects and are indexed by ints that are greater than zero. A tuple is hashable, meaning we can sort lists of tuples and they can also be used as dictionary keys. In syntax, a tuple is a sequence of values, each separated by a comma. Common practice has then enclosed in a set of parentheses:

tpl= ('a', 'b', 'c')

A trailing comma must be used when a tuple is created with just one element:

t = ('a',)

If you omit the trailing comma, the interpreter would see this as a string.

We can also use the built-in tuple() function to create a tuple. Without an argument, we get an empty tuple; if the argument was a sequence, a tuple of elements of the given sequence would be created.

Most of the operators, like those for indexing and slicing, work the same way on a tuple as they do on a list. However, the immutability of a tuple means that attempting to modify a tuple element will return a TypeError. We can use the ==, < and > operators to compare tuples the same as any other sequence.

One of the most important uses of a tuple is to assign multiple variables in one hit by putting a tuple on the left side of an assignment:

l=('one', 'two')
x, y = l # x and y are assigned respectively to 'one' and 'two'

We could use multiple assignments for swapping tuple values, like this:

x, y = y, x # x = 'two' and y = 'one'

If the number of values on either side of the assignment is not the same, we will get a ValueError.

Dictionaries

A dictionary is an arbitrary collection of objects that are indexed by immutable objects, such as strings or numbers. However, while a dictionary is mutable, its index keys must be immutable. Below is a list of the dictionary methods and what they do:

len(d)

tells us how many items are in (d)

d.clear()

will remove all items from (d)

d.copy()

will make a shallow copy of (d)

d.fromkeys(s [,value])

will return a dictionary that has keys from the sequence (s) and values all set to value

d.get(k [,v])

will return d[k] if it is found; otherwise v is returned or, if v is not given, None is returned

d.items()

will return a sequence of the key:value pairs from (d)

d.keys()

will return a sequence of the keys in (d)

d.pop(k [,default])

will return d[k] and take it out of (d). if d[k] cannot be found, the default is returned or KeyError raised

d.popitem()

will remove a random key:value pair from (d) and then return it as a tuple

d.setdefault(k [,v])

d[k] is returned; if not found, v is returned and d[k] is set to v

d.update(b)

all objects from b to d are added

d.values()

a sequence of the values in (d) are returned

Dictionaries are the only built-in mapping type in Python and they are much like the associative arrays or hash tables in other languages. We can think of it as a mapping from a key set to a value set. We use the syntax {key:value} to create them; the following example shows a dictionary that maps words to numbers being created:

d ={'one': 1, 'two': 2, 'three': 3 } # a dictionary is created

Keys and values can be added like this:

d['four']=4 # an item is added

Or we can do the following to update multiple values:

d.update({'five': 5, 'six': 6}) # multiple items are added

When d is inspected, we see the following:

print(d)

Running this code will return:

{'five' : 5, 'four' : 4, one' : 1, 'six' : 6, 'three' : 3, 'two' : 2}

And we can use the in operator for testing for a value occurrence, like this:

print('five' in d)

Running this code will return:

True

Be aware that the in operator doesn't work the same way for lists and dictionaries. With a list, we have a linear relationship between the time taken to locate an element and to list size. By this, we mean the bigger a list is, the time taken to find the element will grow linearly. In contrast, when we use the in operator on a dictionary, a hashing algorithm is used. This makes the time increase in looking up elements pretty much independent to the dictionary size.

When the key:value pairs are printed from the dictionary, they are done so in no specific order. Because we are using specified keys for looking up the values, this isn't an issue; it would be if we used a sequence of ordered integers, as we do with lists and strings.

Sorting Dictionaries

We can easily do a sort on the values or the keys of a dictionary, like this:

print(sorted(list(d))) # sorts keys

Running this code will return:

['five', 'four', 'one', 'six', 'three', 'two']

print(sorted(list(d.values()))) # sorts values

Running this code will return:

[1, 2, 3, 4, 5]

Line one of this code does the sorting in alphabetical order while the next one does it in integer value order. The method called sorted() has two interesting optional arguments – reverse and key. The key is nothing at all to do with the dictionary keys; it is a way to pass the sort algorithm a function that determines the sort order. Here's an example where we use a special method called ___getitem___ to sort the keys as per the values in dictionary:

print(sorted (list(d), key = d.___getitem___))

['one', 'two', 'three', 'four', 'five', 'six']

What we have done here is, for each key in d, the corresponding value has been used to sort. The values can also be sorted as per the sorted order of the keys in the dictionary. However, because a dictionary does not contain any method that will return a key using its value, it becomes a little tricky to use the optional key argument. Another way of doing this would be to use list comprehension as in the next example:

print([value for (key, value) in sorted(d.items())])

Running this code will return:

[5, 4, 1, 6, 3, 2]

There is also an optional reverse argument in the sorted() method and, as expected, it does exactly what it says on the tin – reverses the sorted list order. An example:

print(sorted(list(d), key = d.___getitem___, reverse=True))

Running this code will return:

['six', 'five', 'four', 'three', 'two' 'one']

Look at the following dictionary. We have the keys written as English words and the values as French words. What we want to do is put the values into the right numerical order.

d2 ={'one':'uno', 'two':'deux', 'three':'trois', 'four': 'quatre', 'five': 'cinq', 'six':'six'}

When this dictionary is printed, it won't print in the right order, not as it is. The reason for this is both the values and the keys are strings, so we don't have any proper context to put them in numerical order. To do this, we must go back to the first dictionary we made; the words need to be mapped to the numerals so that English to French dictionary can be placed in order:

print(sorted(d2, key=d.___getitem___))

Running this code will return:

['one', 'two', 'three', 'four', 'five', 'six']

We've used the values from our first dictionary called d to sort the keys in the second dictionary called d2. Because the keys are the same in both of the dictionaries, we can make use of list comprehension to sort the English to French dictionary values.

print([d2[i] for i in sorted(d2, key=d.___getitem___)])

Running this code will return:

['uno', 'deux', 'trois', 'quatre', 'cinq', 'six']

We can, if we want, define a custom method for the key argument used in the sorted() method. In the next example, a function is defined to return the final letter in a string:

def corder(string):

  return(string[len(string)-1])

Now we can use this as the key to the sorted() function so that each element can be sorted by its final letter:

print(sorted(d2.values(), key=corder))

['quatre', 'uno', 'cinq', 'trois', 'six', 'deux']

Using Dictionaries for Text Analysis

One of the most common uses for a dictionary is to count the occurrences of similar items in a sequence, for example, how many times words appear in a specified body of text. The next piece of code will create a dictionary where each of the words in the given text is used as keys and the value of each key is how many times that word occurs. We are using nested loops here, a common loop in Python, to go through each line in the file using an outer loop with the dictionary keys in the inner loop.

```
def wordcount(fname):
    try:
        fhand=open(fname)
    except:
        print('File cannot be opened')
        exit()

    count= dict()
    for line in fhand:
        words = line.split()
        for word in words:
            if word not in count:
                count[word] = 1
            else:
                count[word] += 1
    return(count)
```

What will result will be a dictionary containing one element for each of the unique words within the file.

Sets

A Python set is an unordered collection containing unique items. While sets are mutable, meaning that we can add items to them and remove items, each item must itself be immutable. One important thing about sets is that you cannot have any duplicate items in them. We usually use sets to do mathematical operations, like union, intersection, complement, and difference.

Unlike a sequence type, a set type doesn't provide any slicing or indexing operations. The values do not have any keys associated with them as the dictionaries do. Python contains two types of sets – mutable set and immutable frozenset. Each type of set is created the same way with a set of curly braces containing values each separated by a comma. An empty set using the curly braces cannot be created though as a={} will create a dictionary! Empty sets are created by using a=set() or a=frozenset().

Below are the methods and the operations for sets:

len(s)

will return how many elements are in (s)

s.copy()

will return a shallow copy of (s)

s.difference(t)

will return a set containing the items in (s) but not (t)

s.intersection(t)

will return a set containing the items in both (s) and (t)

s.isdisjoint(t)

will return True if there are no common items between (s) and (t)

s.issubset(t)

will return True if the contents of (s) are in (t)

s.issuperset(t)

will return True if the contents of (t) are in (s)

s.symmetric_difference

will return a set of the items from (s) or (t) but not those in both

s.union(t)

will return a set containing the items in (s) or (t)

The parameter of (t) may be any object in Python that will support iteration and any method that is available to the objects set and frozenset. Be aware, if you need to use an operator version of these methods, you must set the arguments – the methods themselves will accept any type that is iterable. Below are the operator versions of the methods:

Operator Methods:

s.difference(t)

s − t − t2 - ...

s.issubset(t)

s<=t

s<(t(s!=t)

s.issuperset(t)

s>=t

s>t(s!=t)

s.symmetric_difference(t)

s∧t

s.union(t)

s | t1 | t2 | ...

For the mutable set objects, there are some extra methods:

s.add(item)

will add the item to (s) – if the item is already there, nothing will happen

s.clear()

all items are removed from (s)

s.difference_update(t)

will remove items in (s) that are also in (t)

s.discard(item)

will remove the specified item from (s)

s.intersection_update(t)

will remove items from (s) that do not appear in the intersection of (s) and (t)

s.pop()

will return and remove a given arbitrary item from (s)

s.remove(item)

will remove the specified item from (s)

s.symmetric_difference_update(t)

will remove items from (S) that cannot be found in the symmetric difference of (s) and (t)

s.update(t)

will add the items from iterable (t) to (s)

The next example will show you a couple of set operations and the results:

s1={'ab', 3, 4, (5, 6)}
s2={'ab', 7, (7, 6)}
print(s1-s2) # identical to s1.difference (s2)

Running this code will return:

{(5, 6), 3, 4}

print(s1.intersection(s2))

Running this code will return:

{'ab'}

print(s1.union(s2))

Running this code will return:

{ 'ab', 3, 4, 7, (5, 6), (7, 6)}

The set object is not bothered if its members are of different types; they just have to all be immutable. If you were to try using mutable objects, like a list or a dictionary, in your set, an unhashable type error will be thrown. All hashable types have got a hash value that remains the same through the entire lifecycle of the instance and all of the built-in immutable types are of a hashable type. The built-in mutable types are not of a hashable type so cannot be included in sets as elements or as dictionary keys.

Note, when the s1 and the s2 union is printed, there is just one 'ab' value. Remember, sets do not include any duplicates. As well as the built-in methods, there are several other operations that can be performed on a set. For example, if you wanted to test a set for membership, you would do the following:

print('ab' in s1)

Running this code will return:

True

print('ab' not in s1)

Running this code will return:

False

Looping through the elements of a set would look like this:

for element in s1: print(element)

(5, 6)

ab

3

4

Immutable Sets

As mentioned earlier, Python has an immutable set type known as frozenset. It works much the same as set does but with one difference – you cannot use any operation or method that can change values, such as the clear() or add() methods. Immutability can be quite useful in a number of ways. For example, a normal set is mutable, which means it is not hashable and that, in turn, means that it cannot be a member of another set. On the other hand, frozenset can be a member of another set because it is immutable. Plus, this immutability of frozenset means that it can be used as a dictionary key, like this:

fs1 = frozenset(s1)

fs2 = frozenset(s2)

print({fs1: 'fs1', fs2: 'fs2'})

Running this code will return:

{ frozenset({(5, 6), 3, 4, 'ab'}): 'fs1', frozenset({(7, 6), 'ab', 7}); 'fs2'}

Modules for Algorithms and Data Structures

As well as these built-in types, Python has a few modules that can be used for extending those built-in functions and types. Much of the time, the modules may be more efficient and may offer advantages in programming terms that let us make our code simpler.

Up to now, we have examined the built-in types for dictionaries, lists, sets, and strings. These are often termed as ADTs or abstract data types and may be considered to be mathematical specifications for the operations that may be performed on the data. Their behavior is what defines them, not their implementation. Besides the ADTs we already looked at, there are a few Python libraries that include extensions for the built-in datatypes and we'll be looking at these next.

Collections

The module called collections contains alternatives for these data types, high-performance specialized alternatives, in addition to a utility function for the creation of named tuples. Below are the datatypes, the operations, and what they do:

namedtuple()

will create a tuple subclass with the given fields

deque

provides lists that have fast appends and that pop at either end

ChainMap

a class much like a dictionary that creates a single view showing multiple mappings

Counter

a dictionary subclass used for counting the hashable objects

OrderedDict

a dictionary subclass that will remember the order of entries

defaultdict

a dictionary subclass that will call a function that can supply the missing values

- UserDict
- UserList
- UserString

These datatypes are used as wrappers for the base class that underlies each one. We don't tend to use these very much now but subclass the base classes instead. They can, however, be used for accessing the underlying objects as attributes.

Deques

A deque (pronounced deck) is a double-ended queue. These objects are similar to lists with support for appends that are thread-safe and memory-efficient. A deque is mutable and has support for some of the list operations, like indexing. You can assign a deque by index, but you cannot slice one directly. For example, if you tried dq[1:2], you would get a Type Error; there is a way to do it though and we'll look at that later.

The biggest advantage of using a deque and not a list is that it is much faster to insert an item at the start of a deque than it is as the start of a list. That said, it isn't always faster to insert items at the end of a deque. All deques are thread-safe and we can serialize them using a module called pickle.

Perhaps one of the most useful ways to use a deque is for the population and consummation of items. Population and consummation of deque items happen sequentially from each end.

from collections import deque

dq = deque('abc') #the deque is created

dq.append('d') #value 'd' is added on the right

dq.appendleft('z') # value 'z' is added on the left

dq.extend('efg') # multiple items are added on the right

dq.extendleft('yxw') # multiple items are added on the left

print(dq)

Running this code will return:

deque(['w', 'x', 'y', 'z', 'a', 'b', 'c', 'd', 'e', 'f', 'g'])

To consume items in our deque, we can use the pop() and popleft() methods:

print(dq.pop()) #item on the right is returned and removed

Running this code will return:

'g'

print(dq.popleft()) # item on the left is returned and removed

Running this code will return:

'w'

print(dq)

Running this code will return:

deque(['x', 'y', 'z', 'a', 'b', 'c', 'd', 'e', 'f'])

We also have a method called rotate(n) which moves and rotates any item of n steps right for positive n integer values and left for negative n integer values, with positive integers used for the argument:

dq.rotate(2) #all the items are moved 2 steps to the right

print(dq)

Running this code will return:

deque(['e', 'f', 'x', 'y', 'z', 'a', 'b', 'c', 'd'])

dq.rotate(-2) # all the items are moved 2 steps to the left

print(dq)

Running this code will return:

deque(['x', 'y', 'z', 'a', 'b', 'c', 'd', 'e', 'f'])

We can also use these pop() and rotate() methods to delete elements too. The way to return a slice as a list is this:

print(dq)

Running this code will return:

deque(['x', 'y', 'z', 'a', 'b', 'c', 'd', 'e', 'f'])

import itertools

print(list(itertools.islice(dq, 3, 9)))

Running this code will return:

['a', 'b', 'c', 'd', 'e', 'f']

The itertools.islice() method is the same as a slice on a list, but instead of the argument being a list, it is an iterable and selected values are returned as a list, using start and stop indices.

One of the more useful deque features is that a maxlen parameter is supported as optional and used for restricting the deque size. This is ideal for circular buffers, a type of data structure which is fixed in size and is connected end-to-end. These tend to be used when data streams are to be buffered. Here is an example:

```
dq2=deque([],maxlen=3)
for i in range(6):
    dq2.append(i)
    print(dq2)
```

We have populated from the right and consumed from the left. As soon as the buffer has been filled, the older values are consumed, and new values come in from the right.

ChainMaps

The class called collections. chainmap was not added to Python until v3.2. It is used to link several dictionaries or mappings together so that they are, to all intents and purposes, a single object. There is also a new_child() method, a maps attribute, and a parents property. The mappings for the ChainMaps object are stored in lists and we use the maps[i] attribute to access them by retrieving the ith dictionary. Note: although a dictionary is unordered, the dictionaries in the ChainMap are in order.

We can use ChainMap in applications where multiple dictionaries contain data that is related. The application that is doing the consuming wants data in terms of priority, for example, a key found in two dictionaries is given the priority if it happens at the start of the underlying list. A typical use for ChainMap is to simulate nested contexts, for example, where you have several configuration settings that override one another.

This example shows one possible ChainMap use:

```
from collections import ChainMap

defaults={'theme':'Default', 'language':'eng', 'showIndex':True,
'showFooter':True}
```

cm=ChainMap(defaults) # ChainMap with default configuration created

cm2 =cm.new_child({'theme':'bluesky'}) # new ChainMap with a child for overriding the parent is created

print(cm2['theme']) # overridden theme is returned

Running this code will return:

'bluesky'

print(cm2.pop('theme')) # value for the child theme is returned and removed

Running this code will return:

'bluesky'

print(cm2['theme']) # default theme is returned

Running this code will return:

'Default'

Using a ChainMap instead of a dictionary has the advantage that we can hang on to values set previously. When you add a child context, it will override the values for the same key but will not take it out of the data structure. This can prove useful when we need a record of changes kept allowing us to go back to a previous setting very easily.

We can give the map() method the appropriate index to retrieve any value from any of the dictionaries and change the value. The index will represent a dictionary contained in the ChainMap. We can also retrieve parent or default settings with the parents() method.

Counter Objects

Counters are subclasses of dictionaries where each of the keys in the dictionary is a hashable object and the value associated with the key is an integer count. We can initialize a counter in three ways:

First, we can pass the counter to a sequence object, a tuple of format {object=value, ...}, or to a dictionary that has key:value pairs:

cm2.maps[0] ={'theme':'desert', 'showIndex': False} # root context that is identical to new_child is added

print(cm2['showIndex']) # overridden showIndex value is returned

Running this code will return:

False

print(cm2.parents) # returns defaults

Running this code will return:

ChainMap({'theme': 'Default', 'language': 'eng', showIndex': True, 'showFooter': True, })

Empty counter objects can also be created and then populated. This is done by passing an iterable or dictionary to the update() method:

from collections import Counter

print(Counter('anysequence'))

Running this code will return:

Counter({'a': 1, 'c': 1, 'e': 3, 'n;: 2, 'q': 1, 's': 1, 'u': 1, 'y': 1})

Note the update() adds counts; it doesn't replace them with a new value. When the counter has been populated, the stored values can be accessed the same as for a dictionary.

The biggest difference between the dictionary and counter object is that the latter will return a zero count for a missing item, where a dictionary will raise a key error.

It is possible to create iterators from Counter objects by using the elements() method. An iterator will be returned where any counts lower than 1 are not included and there is no guarantee of order. Below is an example of some updates being done, an iterator being created from the Counter elements, and the leys alphabetically sorted using sorted():

ct = Counter('anysequence')

for item in ct:

   print('%s : %d' % (item, ct[item]))

a : 1

n : 2

y : 1

s : 1

e : 3

q : 1

u : 1

c : 1

We can also use two more Counter methods – most_common(), which takes an integer argument which will determine how many of the common elements to return as a list of tuples in (key, value) format, and subtract(). The subtract()

method works in the same way as update except it subtracts values rather than adding them.

Ordered Dictionaries

The most important thing to remember about ordered dictionaries is that they will remember the order of insertion. When they are iterated over, the values are returned in the order in which they were inserted. By contrast, a normal dictionary has an arbitrary order. When we want to test if two dictionaries are equal, the equality will only be based on the keys and values. However, with OrderedDict, the order of insertion is also taken into account. If we were to run a test for equality between a pair of OrderedDicts that have the same keys and values but with different orders of insertion, the return would be False.

In the same way, if we use the update() method to add in values from a list, OrderedDict will keep the same order that the list has. This order is what is returned when we iterate over the values:

print(ct.most_common())

Running this code will return:

[('e', 3), ('n', 2), ('u', 1), ('c', 1), ('y', 1), ('s', 1), ('a', 1), ('q', 1)]

ct.subtract({'a':2})

print(ct)

Running this code will return:

Counter({'e': 3, 'n': 2, 'u': 1, 'c': 1, 'y': 1, 's': 1, 'q': 1, 'a': -1})

OrderedDict is often used together with sorted() to create sorted dictionaries. We can use the lambda function to sort the values and the following example is a numerical expression to sort the integer values:

from collections import OrderedDict

```
od1 = OrderedDict()

od1['one'] = 1

od1['two'] = 2

od2 = OrderedDict()

od2['two'] = 2

od2['one'] = 1

print(od1 == od2)
```

Running this code will return:

False

Defaultdict

Defaultdict is a dict subclass sharing operations and methods. Defaultdict is a convenient way of initializing dictionaries. If you try accessing a key that is not in the dictionary with dict, Python throws a KeyError. Defaultdict will override the __missing__(key) method and will create default_factory, a new instance variable. Instead of throwing errors, defaultdict will run the function, which will be supplied as the argument to default_factory and will generate a value. One of the easiest uses for defaultdict is to add item counts in the dictionary by setting the default_factory to int:

```
kvs = [('three', 3), ('four', 4), ('five', 5), ('six', 6)]

od1.update(kvs)

for k, v in od1.items(): print(k,v)
```

Running this code will return:

one 1

two 2

three 3

four 4

five 5

six 6

If we were to do this with a normal dictionary, a KeyError would be raised when we attempted to put the first key in. The int supplied as the dict argument is the int() function that returns only a zero. We could create a custom function to determine the values in the dictionary, such as the following one that returns True if the argument supplied is a primary color (red, blue or green); False is returned if not:

```
def isprimary(c):
    if (c == 'red') or (c == 'blue') or (c == 'green'):
        return True
    else:
        return False
```

Named Tuples

namedtuple() will return an object much like a tuple with fields that can be accessed through named indexes and through normal tuple integer indexes. This makes our code somewhat more readable and self-documenting. This is useful when we have an application with lots of tuples and we need to keep track of what each one is representing; namedtuple() will inherit its methods from and is backward compatible with tuple.

We pass the field names to namedtuple() as values separated by whitespace or commas, or they can be passed as a string sequence. Each field name is one string and they may be any Python identifier that is legal and does not start with an underscore or a digit.

namedtuple() can take two Boolean arguments, both optional – verbose and rename. Setting verbose=True will result in the class definition being printed when built. Setting rename=True will result in positional arguments being used to replace invalid field names. If we try to use def as the field name, normally an error would be generated, but because rename=True, the interpreter will let it pass. However, if you try to look def up, a syntax error is thrown because def is actually one of the reserved keywords. The field name is illegal, and it is replaced by a new name created by an underscore added to the positional value.

As well as the tuple methods inherited, namedtuple() will also define three of its own methods - _make(), _replace() and _asdict(). The underscore is used to stop conflict with field names. Below is an example of _make() and the method will take an argument of an iterable and convert it to a named tuple object:

from collections import namedtuple

space = namedtuple('space', 'x y z')

s1 = space(x = 2.0, y = 4.0, z = 10)

*print(s1.x * s1.y * s1.z)   #calculates volume*

Running this code will return:

80.0

_asdict() will return an OrderedDict, mapping the field names to index keys and the values to dictionary values. An example:

from collections import namedtuple

space = namedtuple('space', 'x y z')

s1 = space(x = 2.0, y = 4.0, z = 10)

*print(s1.x * s1.y * s1.z)   #calculates volume*

Running this code will return:

File "<ipython-input-79-75c7c11b4596>", line 1

    sl.def

$\wedge$

SyntaxError: invalid syntax

print(s1._1)

Running this code will return:

4

Lastly, _replace() will return a new tuple instance with the specified values replaced:

s1 = [4, 5, 6]

print(space._make(s1))

Running this code will return:

Space(x=4, y=5, z=6)

Arrays

The module, array, will define an array datatype that is much like the list datatype with one constraint – the array contents must be a single type of the representation that underlies it – this is determined by the machine architecture or C implementation.

Array types are determined when they are created and are indicated by one of these codes:

Code	C-Type	Python Type
'b'	signed char	int
'B'	unsigned char	int
'u'	Py_UNICODE	Unicode character
'h'	signed short	int
'H'	unsigned short	int
'i'	signed int	int
'I'	unsigned int	int
'l'	signed long	int
'L'	unsigned long	int
'q'	signed long	int
'Q'	unsigned long	int
'f'	float	float
'd'	double	float

Array objects have support for these methods and attributes:

a.typecode

typecode character for creating the array

a.itemsize

byte size of items that are stored in the array

a.append(x)

appends the item (x) to the array end

a.buffer_info()

returns length and memory location of the buffer used for storing the array

a.byteswap()

swaps the byte order for each item. Used when writing to a file or machine that has a different byte order

a.count(x)

returns how many times x appears

a.extend(b)

will append any iterable to the end of the array

a.frombytes(s)

will append string items as a machine value array

a.fromfile(f, n)

will read n items from a file object as machine values, appending them to a. An EOFError is raised if n has fewer items than n

a.fromlist(l)

will append from list l

a.fromunicode(s)

will use an Unicode string to extend a. Array a has to be type u or ValueError will be raised

index(x)

will return the first smallest index item

a.insert(i, x)

will insert the item before the specified index

a.pop([i])

will remove and return items with the specified index but, if none specified, the last item will be defaulted

a.remove(x)

will remove the first occurrence of the specified item

a.reverse()

reverses the item order

a.tobytes()

will convert the array into machine values and return the byte representation

a.tofile(f)

will write all items to the file object as machine values

a.tolist()

will convert the array into a list

a.tounicode()

will convert the array to a Unicode string; array type must be 'of U' type or ValueError will be raised

Array objects also support all the usual sequence operations like concatenation, slicing, indexing and multiplication.

It is more efficient to use arrays instead of lists to store data of identical types. The next code will show you an integer array containing digits from 0 to 1 million minus 1 along with an identical list. To store a million integers in an array will use about 45% of the memory an equivalent list would use:

print(s1._1)

Running this code will return:

4

print(s1._asdict())

Running this code will return:

OrderedDict([('x', 3). ('_1', 4), ('z', 5)])

To save space when dealing with big datasets and a limit on memory size, in-place operations are done on arrays and copies only created when necessary. Typically, we would use enumerate when an operation is performed on each element; the next example shows 1 being added to each array item:

print(s1._replace(x = 7, z = 9))

Running this code will return:

Space2(x=7, _1=4, z=9)

In the next part, we look at basic algorithm theory and design techniques.

Chapter 6: The Principles of Algorithm Design

Algorithms are all-important; they are the very foundation of computers and computer science. Your computer may be constructed of hardware items, but without algorithms, it's all a waste of space. The Turing Machine is the theoretical foundation of all algorithms and this was established many years before we even thought about implementing a machine like that using digital logic circuits. The Turing Machine is a model that can translate a set of given inputs into outputs, working to a set of pre-defined rules, much like today's Machine Learning.

Algorithms affect our lives in more ways than we realize. Take page ranking on search engines for example. These are based on algorithms and these allow anyone to search quickly through huge amounts of information. This, in turn, hastens the rate at which new research can be done, new discoveries can be found, and with which innovative technologies can be developed.

Studying algorithms is also essential because it makes us think about problems in specific ways. Our mental abilities sharpen, and we can improve our problem-solving abilities by learning to find and isolate the core components of a problem and define the relationship between them.

In its simplest form, an algorithm is nothing more than a list of instructions to be carried out in sequence. Think of it, in Python terms, as a linear form of do x, then do y, and then do z. However, we can change things and make these algorithms do more by adding if-else statements. By doing that, the direction the action takes then depends on conditions being met, and then we add operations, while statements, for statements, and iteration. To expand our algorithm a bit more, we add recursion which often provides the same result that iteration does even though they are very different. Recursive functions apply the function to inputs that get progressively smaller. The input of one recursive step is the output of the previous one.

Paradigms of Algorithm Design

There are three main paradigms to algorithm design:

- Divide and Conquer
- Greedy
- Dynamic programming

Let's take these one at a time. Divide and conquer is self-explanatory – the problem is broken down into small subproblems and the results of each one combined into an overall solution. This has to be one of the most common techniques to solve problems and is perhaps the most common approach to the design of algorithms.

Greedy algorithms involve optimizing and combining. In short, it means to take the shortest path to the most useful solution for local problems, all the while hoping that somewhere it will all lead to the global solution.

Dynamic programming is most useful when the subproblems start to overlap. This is not the same as the divide and conquers paradigm. Instead of breaking the problem down into individual subproblems, intermediate solutions get cached and then used in a later operation. It does use recursion like divide and conquers but, with dynamic programming, we compare the results at different times. This provides a boost in terms of performance for some types of problems; it can be quicker to retrieve a previous result than it is to go through recalculating it.

Backtracking and Recursion

Recursion is incredibly useful in terms of divide and conquer but it can be hard to see exactly what is going on; each of the recursive calls spins off another recursive call. There are two types of cases at the heart of a recursive function:

- Base case – this tells recursion when it should terminate
- Recursive case – this calls the function the case is in

The calculation of factorials is one of the simplest examples of a problem that results in a recursive solution. The factorial algorithm is responsible for defining 2 cases:

- the base case where n is equal to zero
- the recursive case where n is more than zero. Here is an example of an implementation:

```
def factorial(n):
  #test for a base case
  if n==0:
    return 1
  # a calculation and a recursive call are made
  f= n*factorial(n-1)
  print(f)
  return(f)


factorial(4)
```

When this code is printed, we get 1, 2, 6, 24. For 24 to be calculated, we need the parent call and four recursive calls. On each of the recursions, a copy is made of the method variables and it is stored in memory. When the method has returned, that copy is removed.

It isn't always going to be clear whether iteration or recursion is the best result for a problem. Both repeat sets of operations and both work well with divide and conquer. Iteration keeps on going until the problem has been solved and recursion breaks it down into ever smaller chunks combining the results from each one. Iteration does tend to be better for programmers because control tends to remain local to the loop; with recursion, you get a closer representation to factorials and other like mathematical concepts. Recursive calls are stored in the memory; iterations aren't. All of this leads to trade-offs between memory use and processor cycles, so determination may come down to whether your task is memory or processor intensive.

Backtracking

Backtracking is a type of recursion that tends to be used more for problems like the traversal of tree structures. In these problems, each node presents us with several options and we need to choose one of them. Doing that leads to more options; dependent on the options chosen throughout, we either reach a dead end or a goal state. If the former, we need to backtrack to an earlier node and go down a different route. Backtracking is also a kind of divide and conquers method when we need to do exhaustive searches. More importantly, when we backtrack, we prune off the branches that don't provide any results. Look at this example of backtracking; a recursive approach has been used to generate all the permutations that are possible for a given strength of a given length:

def bitStr(n, s):

   if n == 1: return s

   return [digit + bits for digit in bitStr(1,s)for bits in bitStr(n - 1,s)]

print (bitStr(3,'abc'))

Notice that we have two recursive calls and a 'double list' compression. This results in all the elements of the first sequence being concatenated recursively with the return when n=1. Each of the string elements was generated in the recursive call that came before.

Divide and Conquer - Long Multiplication

Recursion isn't just a clever little trick, but to understand what it can do, we need to compare it to approaches like iteration and we need to be able to understand when to use it for a faster algorithm. In primary math, we all learned an iterative algorithm used for the multiplication of a pair of large numbers. That algorithm was long multiplication involving iterative multiplication and carrying, followed by shifting and addition.

What we want to do is work out whether this procedure really is all that efficient for the multiplication of the numbers. When you multiply two numbers each four digits long, it takes no less than 16 multiplication operations. This method of algorithm analysis, in terms of how many computational primitives are needed, is vital because it provides us with a way of understanding what the relationship is between the time taken to do the computation and the input size to the computation. What we really want to know is, what will happen when the input is massive? We call this topic asymptomatic analysis, otherwise known as time complexity, and it is important when studying algorithms; we will talk about it quite a bit through the course of this section of the book.

A Recursive Approach

As far as long multiplication goes, there is a better way; several algorithms exist for the more efficient operation of multiplying large numbers. The Karatsuba algorithm is one of the best-known long multiplication alternatives and it dates back to 1962. This algorithm takes a very different approach instead of iterative multiplication of single digits, it does recursive multiplication on inputs that progressively get smaller. A recursive program will call itself on each small subset of the parent input.

To build an algorithm, we need to take a large number and decompose it into smaller numbers. The easiest way is to split it into two – one half with important digits and one with less important digits. For example, a number with 4 digits of 2345 would become 2 sets of numbers, each with 2 digits, 23 and 45.

Let's take 2 n digit numbers and write a general decomposition for them. The numbers are x and y and m is a positive integer with a lower value than n:

$x = 10^m a + b$

$y = 10^m c + d$

We can now write the x and y multiplication problem like this:

$(10^m a + b)(10^m c + d)$

If we were to expand it and gather in like terms, we would get this:

$10^m ac + 10^{2m}(ad + bc) + bd$

A more convenient way of writing it would be:

$10^{2m} z_2 + 10^m z_1 + z_0$

Where:

$z_2 = ac; \quad z_1 = ad + bc; \quad z_0 = bd$

This does suggest that we are using recursion to multiply the numbers because the process involves multiplication. More specifically, ac, ad, bc, and bd all have smaller numbers than the input making it not inconceivable that the same operation could be applied as a partial solution to the bigger problem. So far, the algorithm has four recursive steps (all multiplication) and it is not yet clear whether this would be more efficient than traditional long multiplication.

So far, we have looked at nothing more than what mathematicians have known for years. However, the Karatsuba algorithm goes a step further and observes that we only really need to know three of the quantities to solve the equation. Those quantities are $z_2 = ac$; $z_1 = ad + bc$ and $z_0 = bd$. We only need to know what the values of a, b, c, and d are in as much as they make a contribution to the overall sum and the products required to calculate z_2, z_1, and z_0. This brings about the possibility that we could reduce how many recursive steps are needed and, as it turns out, we can do that.

Because ac and bd have already been reduced to their simplest form, we can't really take these calculations out. What we can do is this:

$(a+b)(c+d) = ac + bd + ad + bc$

When ac and bd, calculated previously, are taken away, we are left with the quantity that we need $- (ad + bc)$:

$ac + bd + ad + bc - ac - bc = ad + bc$

What this shows is that it is perfectly possible to compute ad+bc without having to compute the individual quantities separately. Below is the Karatsuba algorithm in a Python implementation:

```python
from math import log10, ceil
def karatsuba(x,y):

    # The base case for recursion
    if x < 10 or y < 10:
        return x*y

    #sets n, which is the number of digits in the highest input number
```

$$n = max(int(log10(x)+1), int(log10(y)+1))$$

```
# rounds up n/2
n_2 = int(ceil(n / 2.0))
#adds 1 if n is uneven
n = n if n % 2 == 0 else n + 1

#splits the input numbers
a, b = divmod(x, 10**n_2)
c, d = divmod(y, 10**n_2)

#applies the three recursive steps
ac = karatsuba(a,c)
bd = karatsuba(b,d)
ad_bc = karatsuba((a+b),(c+d)) - ac - bd

#performs the multiplication
return (((10**n)*ac) + bd + ((10**n_2)*(ad_bc)))
```

Just to satisfy ourselves that this really works, there is a test function we can run:

```
import random
def test():
    for i in range(1000):
        x = random.randint(1,10**5)
        y = random.randint(1,10**5)
        expected = x * y
        result = karatsuba(x, y)
        if result != expected:
            return("failed")
    return('ok')
```

Runtime Analysis

By now, it should be clear that one of the more important sides of algorithm design is gauging how efficient it is in terms of time, or how many operations, and memory. The analysis of the number of operations is called Runtime Analysis. There are several ways to run this and the most obvious is nothing more than a measurement of the time taken for the algorithm to finish. There are problems with this approach; how long it takes depends on what hardware it is run, for a start. Another way, independent of the platform, is to count how many operations it takes, but this also causes problems in that we don't have any definitive way of quantifying operations. This would depend on the programming language used, the style of coding, and how we opt to count the operations. However, we could use this way if we were to combine it with an expectation that the runtime increases as the input size increases and it does it in a specific way. In other words, that there is a relationship mathematically between the input size (n) and the time the algorithm takes to run. There are three principles that guide this, and their importance will become clear as we go on. First, the principles:

- Making no assumptions about the input data giving us a worst-case analysis
- Ignoring or suppressing lower order terms and constant factors – with larger inputs, the higher-order terms will be dominant
- Focus only on those problems with the large inputs.

The first one is very useful because it provides us with an upper bound that is tight – the algorithm is guaranteed to fail. The second is just about ignoring anything that doesn't contribute majorly to the runtime making work easier and letting us focus on what impacts performance more.

With the Karatsuba algorithm, the square of the input size increased, and so did the number of operations used for multiplication. With a four-digit number, we use 16 operations and with an eight-digit number, we need 64. However, we're not so interested in how an algorithm with small n values behaves so we ignore the factors that only increase linearly or lowly. At the higher n values, the operations that increase fast as n is increased will be the dominant ones.

We'll talk briefly about the merge-sort algorithm here because it is useful to learn about performance at runtime. This is one of the classic algorithms from more than 60 years ago and it is still used today in some of the highly popular sorting libraries. Merge-sort is recursive and uses divide and conquer, which, as you know, means breaking a problem down, sorting the parts recursively, and putting the results together. Merge-sort is an obvious demonstration of this algorithm design paradigm.

Merge-sort has just three steps:

1. Sorts the left side of the input array recursively
2. Sorts the right side of the input array recursively
3. Merges the sorted arrays into one

One typical use is to sort numbers into numerical order. Merge-sort will divide the list in two and work on each side in parallel. Here is the Python code for the algorithm:

```
def mergeSort(A):
    #base case if the input array is one or zero just return.
    if len(A) > 1:
        # splitting input array
        print('splitting ', A )
        mid = len(A)//2
        left = A[:mid]
        right = A[mid:]
        #recursive calls to mergeSort for left and right subarrays
        mergeSort(left)
        mergeSort(right)
        #initializes pointers for left (i) right (j) and output array (k)
        # 3 initialization operations
        i = j = k = 0
        #Traverse and merges the sorted arrays
        while i <len(left) and j<len(right):
            # if left < right comparison operation
            if left[i] < right[j]:
                # if left < right Assignment operation
                A[k]=left[i]
                i=i+1
```

```
    else:
        #if right <= left assignment
        A[k]= right[j]
         j=j+1
      k=k+1


    while i<len(left):
        #Assignment operation
        A[k]=left[i]
        i=i+1
        k=k+1


    while j<len(right):
        #Assignment operation
        A[k]=right[j]
        j=j+1
        k=k+1
   print('merging ', A)
   return(A)
```

The easiest way to determine the running time performance is to start by mapping the recursive calls onto a tree structure with each tree node being a call that works on an ever smaller subprogram. Each time we invoke merge-sort, we get two recursive calls, so we can use a binary tree to represent this, with each child node getting an input subset. To work out the time the algorithm takes to finish relative to n, we start by working out how much work there is and how many operations are on each tree level.

Keeping our focus on the runtime analysis, on the first level we have two $n/2$ subproblems; level two gives us four, and so on. So, when does the recursion get to its base case? Simply, when the array is one or zero. To get to a number that is nearly one, we take the number of recursive levels and divide n by 2 that many times. This is the definition of log2 and, as the first recursive level is 0, the number of levels is $\log_2 n + 1$.

Let's refine the definitions. Up to now, we have used n to represent the number of elements in an input, referring to how many elements are in the first recursive level, or the length of the first input. What we need to do is be able to know the difference between the initial input length and the input length at each recursive level. For this, we use m i.e. m_j for the input length at recursive level j.

Using recursion trees for algorithm analysis has the advantage of being able to know what is done at each recursive level. Defining the work is the number of operations in relation to the input size. We must measure the performance of an algorithm in a way that is independent of the platform although runtime will depend on the hardware. It is important to count how many operations there are because this is our metric related directly to the performance of our algorithm.

Generally, because we get two recursive calls each time merge-sort is invoked, each level has double the number of calls of the previous one. At the same time, each call is working on an input that is half the size of its parent. To work out how many operations there are, we must know how many operations are used by one merge of two sub-arrays. Look at the Python code above. After the first two recursive calls, we can count the operations – three assignments followed by three while loops. The first loop has an if-else statement and within each is a comparison and an assignment – two operations. This is counted as a set and there is only one set in an if-else, so this set was carried out m times. The last two while loops each have an assignment operation, making for a total of 4m+3 operations for each merge-sort recursion.

Because m has to be at least 1, the number of operations has an upper bound of 7m. This is not an exact science; it all depends on how the operations are counted. We haven't included any increment or housekeeping operations as we are only interested in the runtime growth rate related to n at the high n values.

All this may seem a bit daunting because every call from a recursive call spins off to even more recursive calls and things look as if they exponentially explode. What makes this manageable is as the recursive calls double, the subproblem size halves. These cancel each other out very nicely as we will demonstrate.

To work out the max number of the operations on each tree level, the number of subproblems are multiplied by the number of operations in each of those subproblems, like this:

$2^j \times 7(n/2^j) = 7n$

What we see here is 2^j cancels out how the number of operations there are on each level independently of the level, giving us an upper bound to work with. In our example, it is 7n. This number includes the operations that each recursive call performs on that level only, not on any other. From this, as we get a doubling of the recursive calls for each level, and this is counter-balanced by the subproblem input size halving on each level.

If we wanted to know how many operations there were for one complete merge-sort, we would take the number of operations per level and multiply that by the total number of levels, like this:

$7n(\log_2 n + 1)$

Expanding that gives us:

$7n\log_2 n + 7$

The key to take from this is that the relationship between input size and running time has a logarithmic component and, if you remember your high-school math, logarithm functions flatten off fast. As x, an input variable, increases in size, so y, the output variable, will increase by progressively smaller amounts.

Asymptotic Analysis

Runtime performance of an algorithm can be characterized in one of three ways:

- Worst-case – using an input that is slow to perform
- Best case – using an input that gives us the best results
- Average case – assuming the input is random

To calculate each one, we must know what the lower and upper bounds are. We looked at using mathematical expressions to represent runtime using multiplication and addition operators. For asymptotic analysis, we need two expressions, one for the best and one for the worst-case.

Big O Notation

The "O" stands for order and denotes that the growth rates are defined as orders of functions. We could say that a function, $T(n)$, is a big O of $F(n)$ and this is defined like this:

$T(n)=O(F(n))$ if there are constants, n_0, and C in a way that:

$T(n) \leq C(F(n))$ for all $n \geq n_0$

The function of the input size n is $g(n)$ and this is based on all large enough values of n, $g(n)$ being upper bound by a constant multiple of $f(n)$. What we want to do is find the smallest growth rate equal to less than $f(n)$. We are only interested in the higher n values; the variable, n, represents the threshold – below that, we're not interested in the growth rate. $T(n)$ is the function that represents $F(n)$, the tight upper bound.

The notation that reads $f(n) = O(g(n))$ is telling us that $O(g(n))$ is a set of functions, within which are all the functions with smaller or equal growth rates than $f(n)$. Below, are the common growth rates from low to high. These are sometimes called a function time complexity:

Complexity	Class Name	Operation Examples
$O(1)$	Constant	get item, set item, append
$O(\log n)$	Logarithmic	find an element in an array that is sorted
$O(n)$	Linear	insert, copy, iteration, delete
$n \log n$	Linear-logarithmic	merge-sort, sorting lists
n^2	Quadratic	nested loops, finding the shortest path between nodes
n^3	Cubic	Matrix multiplication
2^n	Exponential	backtracking

Complexity Classes

Normally, we would be looking for the total running time of several basic operations, but it seems that we can take simple operations and combine their complexity classes to determine the class of combined operations that are somewhat more complex. The goal is to look at the combined statements in a method or a function to find the time complexity of executing multiple operations. The easiest way of combining complexity classes is to add them and this happens when the operations are sequential.

Let's say that we have a pair of operations that insert an element in a list and then proceed to sort the list. When the item is inserted, it happens in $O(n)$ time while sorting happens in $O(nlogn)$ time. The time complexity can be written as $O(n + nlogn)$. However, because we are focusing only on the high order term, we can work with just $O(nlogn)$.

Let's then assume that we use a while loop to repeat an operation; we would take the complexity class and multiply it by how many times the operation is done. For example, an operation that has a time complexity of $O(f(n))$ is repeated $O(n)$ times; both complexities are multiplied as follows:

$O(f(n)) * O(n) = O(nf(n))$

Let's assume that a function called f(...) has $O(n^2)$ as a time complexity and it is executed in a while loop n times, like this:

```
for i n range(n):
    f(...)
```

This loop then has a time complexity of $O(n^2) * O(n) = O(n * n^2) = O(n^3)$. All we have done is multiply the operation's time complexity by the number of times that operation was executed. A loop's running time is no more than the combined running time of all the statements in the loop multiplied by the iterations. Assuming both loops will run n times, a single nested loop runs in n^2 time. For example:

```
for i in range(0,n):
    for j in range(0,n)
        #statements
```

Each of these statements is a constant (c) that is executed nn times. The running time can thus be expressed as; cn n + cn² = O(n2)

For all consecutive statements in a nested loop, the time complexity for each of the statements is added and then multiplied by the iterations of the statement. For example:

```
n = 500    #c0
#executes n times
for i in range(0,n):
    print(i)   #c1
#executes n times
for i in range(0,n):
    #executes n times
    for j in range(0,n):
        print(j)  #c2
```
We can write this as $c_0 + c_1 n + cn2 = O(n2)$.

Amortized Analysis

Sometimes we are not bothered so much about the time complexity of an individual operation; sometimes we want to know what the average running time is of a sequence of operations. This is called amortized analysis and, as you will see later, it is not the same as the average case analysis because it doesn't assume anything about the data distribution of any input values. What it does do is take the change in state of the data structures into account. For example, sorting a list should make finding operations faster in the future. The amortized analysis considers the change in the state because the sequence of operations is analyzed; it doesn't just aggregate single operations.

What amortized analysis does is determines the upper bound on runtime and it does this by imposing each operation in a sequence with an artificial cost. Each of these costs is then combined. This takes consideration of the fact that the initial expense of an operation can then make future operations much cheaper.

When there are multiple small operations that are expensive, like sorting, and multiple options that are cheaper, like lookups, using worst-case analysis can give us pessimistic results. This is because worst-case assumes that each of the lookups should compare every element until a match is found.

Up to now, we have assumed that we have random input data and we only looked at how the input size affects the runtime. There are two more common algorithm analyses we can look at:

- Average Case Analysis
- Benchmarking

Average case analysis takes some assumptions about the relative frequency of the different input values and determines the average running time. Benchmarking is when a previously agreed set of inputs is used to measure performance.

Both approaches rely on some domain knowledge. For a start, we would need to know what the expected or the typical datasets are. Ultimately, we will be trying to improve the performance by finetuning to an application setting that is highly specific.

A straightforward benchmarking approach would be to time how long the algorithm takes to finish given different input sizes. This is entirely dependent on what hardware the algorithm is run on; the faster the processor, the better the result. However, the relative growth rates that come with the increases in the input rates will retain the characteristics of the algorithm and not the platform they run on.

Let's look at an easy nested loop example. The time complexity is $O(n^2)$ because each n iteration in the external loop is matched by the same in the inner loop. In our example, we have one statement that is executed in the inner loop:

```
def nest(n):
    for i in range(n):
        for j in range(n):
            i+j
```

Next, you can see the test function required to run the nest function with n values that increase. With each iteration, we can calculate the time taken for the function to complete using the function called timeit.timeit. In this example, the function takes no less than three arguments – a string representation of the function being timed, an int parameter that indicates how many times the main statement is executed, and a setup function used for importing the nest function. All we want to know is how long, in relation to the size of the input, the nest function takes to complete. All we need to do is call that nest function one time for each iteration. The test function below will return a list of the runtimes calculated for each n value:

```
import timeit
def test2(n):
    ls=[]
    for n in range(n):
        t=timeit.timeit("nest(" + str(n) +")", setup="from __main__ import nest", number = 1)
        ls.append(t)
    return ls
```

We now run the test2 function and the results would be shown on a graph with an n^2 function scaled appropriately for comparison:

```
import matplotlib.pyplot as plt
n=1000
plt.plot(test2(n))
plt.plot([x*x/10000000 for x in range(n)])
plt.show()
```

This provides us with a result that we expect. Do keep in mind that this is representative of the algorithm performance and the way the software and hardware behave. Performance will always be subject to things like processor, constraints on memory, running processes, clock speed, and more.

Next, we will be looking at pointer structures, like linked lists.

Chapter 7: Lists and Pointer Structures

If you are familiar with Python, you are familiar with lists. Lists are powerful and they are convenient. Normally, when you want things stored in a list you would use the built-in Python list implementation, but for the purposes of this section, we are going to look at how a list works. As you will see, there is more than one type of list.

While the list implementation in Python is powerful and can be used for multiple use cases, we are going to be more stringent in the way we define a list. One concept that is vital to lists is the node.

One thing we are going to be covering is pointers so let's be reminded what a pointer is. Imagine that we are selling a house. We don't have much time, so we get an agent to find buyers for us. How do we do this? We give the agent the address of the house and directions; that is passed to prospective buyers. We might write this down several times and each time, each piece of paper we write on is called a pointer.

It is much the same in Python. Assuming we have some large resolution images that we want to pass among several functions. The images are kept in one place in memory and a variable is created for each image. Instead of passing the image to each function, we pass them a small variable instead that points to the image.

We don't directly manipulate a pointer in Python as we do in other languages and this has led to many people believing they are not used. As an example, look that the following assignment written in the Python interactive shell:

>>> s = set()

Normally we would say that s is a variable of the set type, so s is a set. However, this isn't quite true. In fact, s is a reference to a set. The constructor for the set will create a set in the memory and then returns the location of the start of the set and this is what s stores.

Arrays

Arrays are sequential lists of data. A sequence means that each of the elements is stored immediately one after the other in memory. If we have a large array and we have little memory, it may not be possible to store the array in memory.

There is an upside; arrays are fast. Because the elements are sequential, there isn't any need to search in different locations. This can be vital when we are making a choice between using a list or an array in our applications.

Pointer Structures

Unlike an array, a pointer structure is a list of items that may be spread across memory. This is because each of the items has at least one link to another structure item. The type of these links will depend on the structure type; if it was linked lists, then the links would be to the next structure item, and even the previous one. With a tree, there are sibling links and parent-child links. In a tile game where hexes are used to build a game map, each of the nodes will contain links to adjacent cells.

Pointer structures are beneficial in that sequential storage space is not required and they can begin quite small and arbitrarily grow as more nodes are added to the structure. This does come with a cost; with an integer list, each node will take the space of an integer and an extra integer to store the pointer besides the node.

Nodes

The concept of a node is at the heart of a list and some other data structures. Before we move on, let's consider an idea. We'll start with some strings:

>>> a = "eggs"
>>> b = "ham"
>>> c = "spam"

We have three variables. Each one is given a unique name, a type of its own, and a value. We don't have any way to say that these three variables are related to one another. This is where nodes come in. A node is a type of container that contains data as well as at least one link to another node; that link is a pointer.

One of the simplest types of nodes is one that has one link to the following node.

Knowing what we now know about pointers, however, it's clear that this isn't true – the string isn't stored inside the node; a pointer to the string is. As such, all we need for this kind of node is a pair of memory addresses as storage. The node data attributes are the pointers to the strings of ham and eggs.

Finding an Endpoint

So, we have three nodes, one with eggs, one with ham, and one with spam. The egg node is pointing to the ham node and this, in turn, is pointing to the spam node, which points ... where? Because spam is the final element, the next member of the list must have a value that makes it clear. By having the final element point nowhere that is made clear and, in Python, we will denote nothing by using the value of None. The last node's next point will point to None indicating that it is the final node in the node chain.

This is a simple implementation that demonstrates what we have discussed:

```
class Node:
    def __init__(self, data=None):
        self.data = data
        self.next = None
```

We have initialized the pointer called next to None. What this means is that, unless Next's value is changed, that node will be the endpoint. This means that we cannot forget to correctly terminate the list.

Other things can be added to the node class as wanted; all we need to do is ensure that we keep the distinction between data and node in mind. If our node has customer data in it, we need a Customer class to store the data.

We can also implement the _str_ method to call the same method of the contained object when the node object is passed for printing.

```
def __str__(self):
    return str(data)
```

Other Node Types

We have looked at a simple node type, one that points the next node, but we may require something a bit more complex and other node types can be created. Suppose we want to move from A to B and B to A simultaneously. To do that, we would add a next pointer and a previous pointer. The first and the last nodes would point to None showing that the boundary of the list endpoint has been reached. The previous pointer has no predecessor and the next pointer has no successor.

If we had a tile-based game and we were trying to create tiles for it, we wouldn't use previous or next; we would probably use north, east, south, and west. There are other pointer types, but the principle is that the tiles at the map's end will point to None.

Singly Linked Lists

Singly linked lists are lists that have just one pointer between successive nodes. Traversal is only possible in one direction – we may go from the first to the last node, but we can't go from the last to the first. We can implement a simple singly linked list by using the previously created node class:

```
>>> n1 = Node('eggs')
>>> n2 = Node('ham')
>>> n3 = Node('spam')
```

Net, the nodes are linked to form a chain:

```
>>> n1.next = n2
>>> n2.next = n3
```

Traversal of the list would look something like the following. The variable called current is set to the first list item:

```
current = n1
while current:
   print(current.data)
   current = current.next
```

The current element is printed in the loop after the current is set to point to the next successive list element. We continue to do this until the end of the list is reached but there are some problems with this kind of simplistic implementation:

- It takes far too much manual programming work
- It is prone to errors
- The inner list workings are exposed to the programmer

We will be looking at these in the next sections.

Singly Linked List Class

A list is clearly different from a node in terms of concept, so we will begin by creating a simple class that will contain our list. We start with a constructor; this has a reference to the initial node in the list and, because this list is empty to start with, the reference is set to None.

```
class SinglyLinkedList:
   def __init__(self):
      self.tail = None
```

Append Operation

First, items need to be appended to the list. The append operation sometimes is called the insert operation and we can use it to hide the Node class. In all truthfulness, anyone using the list class should never need to interact with Node objects because they are for internal use only.

The append() may look like this, to begin with:

```
class SinglyLinkedList:
    def __init__(self):
        self.tail = None
    def append(self, data):
        # Encapsulate the data in a Node
        node = Node(data)

        if self.tail == None:
            self.tail = node
        else:
            current = self.tail
            while current.next:
                current = current.next
            current.next = node
```

The data is encapsulated in a node and now has the attribute of the next pointer. Now we will look to see if any other nodes exist in the list – we look to see if self.tail points to any Node. If not, the new node is made into the first node. If there is another node, we traverse the list through to the last node looking for an insertion point and the next pointer for the final node is updated to the new node.

Now some items can be appended:

```
>>> words = SinglyLinkedList()
 >>> words.append('egg')
 >>> words.append('ham')
 >>> words.append('spam')
```

List traversal is much the same as before and we get the initial list element from the list:

```
>>> current = words.tail
>>> while current:
    print(current.data)
    current = current.next
```

A Faster Way to Append

The previous append method has a large problem attached to it; finding the insertion point involves traversal of the entire list. If there are few items in the list, this isn't so much of an issue but when you need thousands of items added, the append operations will get progressively slower. We can fix this by storing a reference to both the first and last nodes in the list. By doing this, a new node can be appended quickly to the end. The worst-case analysis of the append running time is reduced from O(n) to O(1). What we need to do is ensure that the previous final node is pointing to the new one that is to be appended. The new code will look like this:

```
class SinglyLinkedList:
    def __init__(self):
        self.head = None
        self.tail = None

    def append(self, data):
        node = Node(data)
        if self.head:
            self.head.next = node
            self.head = node
        else:
            self.tail = node
            self.head = node
```

Note the convention we are using. We use self.head as the point at which new nodes are appended and self-tail points to the first list node.

Obtaining the List Size

We want to be able to count the nodes to determine the size of the list. One way would be to traverse the whole list with a counter increasing as we do so:

```
def size(self):
    count = 0
    current = self.tail
    while current:
        count += 1
        current = current.next
    return count
```

This does work, but using list traversal can be quite expensive and we shouldn't do it unless we have to. So, we will rewrite the method instead. A size member is added to the class called SinglyLinkedList and it is initialized in the constructor to 1. Then the size is incremented in the append method by 1:

```
class SinglyLinkedList:
    def __init__(self):
        self.head = None
        self.tail = None
        self.size = 0
    def append(self, data):
        node = Node(data)
        if self.head:
            self.head.next = node
            self.head = node
        else:
            self.tail = node
            self.head = node
        self.size += 1
    def size(self):
        count = 0
        current = self.tail
        while current:
            count += 1
            current = current.next
        return count
```

Now we are reading only the node object's size attribute rather than using loops to count the nodes. This means the worst-case running time is reduced from O(n) to O(1).

Improve the List Traversal

Notice when we traverse the list, there is still a point at which we are exposed to node and to determine the contents of the node we need node.data and getting to the next one requires node.next. Earlier, we said that the user should not interact with the Node objects and this is achievable through a method that will return a generator, like this:

```
def iter(self):
    current = self.tail
    while current:
        val = current.data
        current = current.next
        yield val
```

List traversal is now easier and looks better. We can forget about there being anything called a Node outside the list:

```
for word in words.iter():
    print(word)
```

Note, because the method called iter() gives us the node's data member, the client code or user need not worry about it.

Deleting Nodes

Node deletion is one of the more common operations to perform on a list. This might seem to be very simple, but we must first decide how we are going to choose the node for deletion. Will we use an index number, or will we opt for the data contained in the node? For our example, we will go with the latter.

When the node we want to delete is in between two others, the previous node must be directly linked to the successor of the following node. Simply, the node for deletion is removed from the chain. The delete() method implementation may look something like this:

```
def delete(self, data):
    current = self.tail
    prev = self.tail
    while current:
        if current.data == data:
            if current == self.tail:
                self.tail = current.next
            else:
                prev.next = current.next
            self.size -= 1
            return
        prev = current
        current = current.next
```

The time taken to delete the node should be O(n).

List Search

Sometimes, we might want to see if a list contains a specific item and this is easy to implement because we can use our previously created iter() method. Each iteration over the loop looks at the current data for a match to the data being looked for. If one is found, we get True; if not, we get False.

```
def search(self, data):
    for node in self.iter():
        if data == node:
            return True
    return False
```

Clearing Lists

It is also very easy to clear a list quickly by clearing the head and tail pointers; this is done by setting them to None:

```
def clear(self):
    """ Clear the entire list. """
```

```
self.tail = None
self.head = None
```

In one hit, all the nodes at the tail and head pointers are orphaned and this has a knock-on effect of all the nodes in between being orphaned too.

Doubly Linked Lists

We know what a singly linked list is all about and what operations we can perform on it. Now we turn to doubly linked lists. These are similar to the singly linked list in that we still use the idea of stringing nodes together. In the singly linked list, there is a single link between successive nodes; in the doubly linked list, there are two pointers – one to the next and one to the last node. Because there are two pointers, doubly linked lists now have additional capabilities.

They can be traversed in either direction. Nodes can refer to previous nodes where needed without having to use a variable to track the node. And, because we have access to the last and next nodes immediately, it is much easier to delete a node.

Doubly Linked List Nodes

In the Python code for creating the class to capture what the linked list node is, we include the three instance variables in the initializing method: prev, next, and data. When a node is created, those variables are set to None by default:

```
class Node(object):

    def __init__(self, data=None, next=None, prev=None):

        self.data = data

        self.next = next

        self.prev = prev
```

Inside the prev variable is a reference to the last node; next holds the reference to the net node.

We still need a class that will capture the data on which the functions are operating:

```
class DoublyLinkedList(object):

    def __init__(self):

        self.head = None

        self.tail = None

        self.count = 0
```

To enhance the size method, the instance variable called count is set to 0; tail and head point to the tail and head of the list when we start adding nodes into the list. Contrary to the singly linked list, we will be using a new convention whereby self.tail will point the newest node and self.head points to the first node.

A doubly linked list must also provide the functions that will:

- Insert a node
- Return the list size
- Delete a node

We'll be looking at the code that does this and we'll start with the append operation.

Append Operation

When the append operation is happening, we must check that head is None. If it is, the list is empty, and head should be set to point the newly created node. The tail should also point, through the head, to the new node. By the end of the following code, head and tail should both point to the same node:

```
def append(self, data):

    """ Append an item to the list. """
```

```
new_node = Node(data, None, None)
if self.head is None:
    self.head = new_node
    self.tail = self.head
else:
    new_node.prev = self.tail
    self.tail.next = new_node
    self.tail = new_node


    self.count += 1
```

The else section will only be executed if the list isn't empty and the previous variable of the new node is set to the list tail:

new_node.prev = self.tail

The next pointer of the tail is set to the newly created node:

self.tail.next = new_node

Finally, the tail pointer is updated and it points to the newly created node:

self.tail = new_node

Because the append operation raises the node number by one, we must increase the counter by the same:

self.count += 1

Delete Operation

Contrary to the singly linked list where the previous node needed to be tracked whenever the entire list was traversed, with the doubly linked list, that entire step is avoided by using the previous pointer. The algorithm to remove a node from the doubly linked list will go through four scenarios before completing the deletion. They are:

- When the search item is not found
- When the search item is at the start of the list
- When the search item is at the tail
- When the search item is in the middle of the list

The node for removal is identified by the data variable of the node matching the search data that was passed to the method. When a matching node is located and removed, the variable called node_deleted gets set as True; anything else would result in False:

def delete(self, data):

   current = self.head

   node_deleted = False

...

The current variable in the delete method point to self.head of the list and a set of if...else statements will then look through the different bits to the list to find the node that has the given data. First, the head node is searched. Because current points to tail, if current is returned as None, it will be assumed that there are no nodes to be searched:

if current is None:

   node_deleted = False

However, if current has got the data being searched for, self.head will be set so it points to the current next node. There is now no node behind head so self.head.prev is set as None:

elif current.data == data:

    self.head = current.next

    self.head.prev = None

    node_deleted = True

We would do something similar if the node for deletion were at the end of the list. The third statement looks for that possibility:

elif self.tail.data == data:

    self.tail = self.tail.prev

    self.tail.next = None

    node_deleted = True

Finally, the algorithm will loop through the node list and, if a matching node is located, the previous node of current is connected to the next node of current. After that, the next node of current will be connected to the previous node:

else:

    while current:

        if current.data == data:

            current.prev.next = current.next

            current.next.prev = current.prev

            node_deleted = True

        current = current.next

The variable called node_delete then is checked after the if-else statements have all been evaluated. If the variable were changed by any of those statements, it would mean the node had been deleted and the count variable is decremented by 1:

if node_deleted:

   self.count -= 1

List Search

The search algorithm is much like that for the singly linked list. The internal iter() method is called to return the data from all the nodes and, as the data is looped through, it is matched against the data that went into the method called contain. If a match is found, True is returned; if not, False is returned:

def contain(self, data):

  for node_data in self.iter():

    if data == node_data:

      return True

    return False

The doubly linked list has a running time for the append operation of O(1) and O(n) for delete.

Circular Lists

Circular lists are special types of linked list and they are lists that have the endpoints connected. In other words, the last node points to the first node. Circular lists may be based on singly linked and doubly linked lists; with the latter, the first node must also point to the last.

We're going to look at a singly linked circular list and is a straightforward implementation once you understand the basic concept. The node class we created for the singly linked lists can be reused; in fact, we can reuse much of the SinglyLinkedList class. What we will focus on are the methods where the implementation differs from a standard singly linked list.

Appending an Element

When an element is appended to a circular list, the new node must point back to the tail. We can see this in the next code. There is also an extra line above the singly linked implementation:

```
def append(self, data):
    node = Node(data)
    if self.head:
        self.head.next = node
        self.head = node
    else:
        self.head = node
        self.tail = node
    self.head.next = self.tail
    self.size += 1
```

Element Deletion

You might think the same applies as that of the append method and that the head must point to the tail. Doing that would give us this implementation:

```
def delete(self, data):
    current = self.tail
    prev = self.tail
    while current:
        if current.data == data:
            if current == self.tail:
```

```
        self.tail = current.next

        self.head.next = self.tail

    else:

        prev.next = current.next

    self.size -= 1

    return

prev = current

current = current.next
```

We only need to change one line; when the tail node is removed, we must ensure that we update the head node to point to the newly created tail node.

However, we have a problem. With a circular list, we have to wait for current to become None before we can loop and that isn't going to happen. If an existing node is deleted this would never be seen, but if we try to delete a node that is nonexistent we will have created an infinite loop.

So, we need another way of controlling our while loop. We can't check to see if current has got to head because the last node would never be checked. We can, however, use prev because it is one node behind current. There is a special case – in the initial loop iteration both current and prev point to the tail node. We need to make sure that the node is running here because the one-node list needs to be considered. Our delete method should now look like this:

```
def delete(self, data):

    current = self.tail

    prev = self.tail

    while prev == current or prev != self.head:

        if current.data == data:
```

```
        if current == self.tail:

            self.tail = current.next

            self.head.next = self.tail

        else:

            prev.next = current.next

            self.size -= 1

            return

        prev = current

        current = current.next
```

Iteration Through Circular Lists

The iter() method doesn't need modifying as it will work just fine for the circular list. However, an exit condition needs to be added when the circular list is iterated through, otherwise, the program gets caught in a loop. We could do this with a counter variable:

```
words = CircularList()


words.append('eggs')

words.append('ham')

words.append('spam')


counter = 0

for word in words.iter():

    print(word)
```

```
    counter += 1

    if counter > 1000:

        break
```

When 1000 elements have been printed, the loop can be broken out of.

Next, we are going to be examining two more data structures that we implement using a list – queues and stacks.

Chapter 8: Stacks

In this section, we will continue building on what we learned to create special implementations of lists. We will continue to use linear structures; we will consider more complex structures later. We are going to look at:

- Implementations of stacks and queues
- Some of the applications stacks and queues are used for

<u>Stacks</u>

Stacks are data structures that look, in a real-world sense, like a stack of plates. When we wash one it goes on the top. When we need one, we take it from the top. The last added is the first removed and that makes a stack a LIFO structure, which means Last In, First Out.

Stacks do two main operations – pop and push. When you add an element to the top it gets pushed to the stack; when you remove an element, it is popped out. Another operation that is occasionally used on stacks is peek, which allows a glimpse at an element without needing to pop it out of the stack.

Stacks can be used for many things and one of the more common uses is to track the return address throughout a function call. Look at this next program:

def b():

  print('b')

def a():

  b()

a()

print("done")

As the program executes, when it gets to the a() call, the address of the next instruction is pushed to the stack and then it jumps to a(). In a(), we call b(), but before that happens, we push the return address to the stack. Once it is in b() and the function is complete, that address is popped from the stack and we go right back to a(). When a() is finished, we pop the return address off the stack and go back to the print statement.

The actual use of a stack is to pass data from one function to another. Look at the following function call that might be in our code somewhere:

somefunc(14, 'eggs', 'ham', 'spam')

So, 14, eggs, ham, and spam are all going to be pushed, one at a time, onto the stack. When the function is jumped into, the a, b, c, and d values get popped from the stack. Spam pops first and gets assigned to d; ham is assigned to c, and so on:

def somefunc(a, b, c, d):

   print("function executed")

Stack Implementation

Now, we'll look at how a stack is implemented in Python. The first step is to create a node class, as we did with lists:

class Node:

   def __init__(self, data=None):

    self.data = data

    self.next = None

You should be able to do this in your sleep by now – nodes hold data together with a reference that points to the next list item. We are implementing a stack this time, but the principle remains the same – nodes are linked together.

The stack class begins in much the same way as a singly linked list. We must know what the node is at the top of the list and we also need to track how many nodes are in the stack; that means we need these fields in our class:

class Stack:

   def __init__(self):

     self.top = None

     self.size = 0

The Push Operation

We add elements to the top of a stack using the push operation, which is implemented in this way:

   def push(self, data):

     node = Node(data)

     if self.top:

       node.next = self.top

       self.top = node

     else:

       self.top = node

     self.size += 1

If, after we create a new node, there is no existing one, self.top points to the new one. This is guaranteed by the else part of the if-else statement. Where we already have an existing stack, self.top would be moved so it pointed to the new node. The next pointer of the new node must point to the node that was originally on the top of the stack.

The POP Operation

To remove the top element off the stack, we use the pop operation. At the same time, the top element needs to be returned as well. If there are no other elements the stack can be made to return None:

```
def pop(self):
    if self.top:
        data = self.top.data
        self.size -= 1
        if self.top.next:
            self.top = self.top.next
        else:
            self.top = None
        return data
    else:
        return None
```

What we need to pay special attention to here is the inner if statement. If the next attribute of the top node points to another node, the top of the stack now must also point to the same node.

The Peek Operation

As we mentioned earlier, there is another operation sometimes used on stacks, and that is the peek operation. This returns to the top without removing an element from the stack, thus allowing us to see the top element without making any changes to the stack. This operation is very simple; if there is an element at the top, its data is returned; if not, None is returned and the rest of peeks behavior will be the same as pop:

```
def peek(self):

    if self.top:

        return self.top.data

    else:

        return None
```

A Bracket-Matching Application

To learn how the stack implementation we built can be used, we will write a function that verifies whether a statement that has brackets of some description is a balanced statement. By that, we mean that the opening brackets should have a matched closing bracket and that there is the same number of opening and closing brackets. The function will also check that a pair of brackets is contained inside another:

```
def check_brackets(statement):

    stack = Stack()

    for ch in statement:

        if ch in ('{', '[', '('):

            stack.push(ch)

        if ch in ('}', ']', ')'):

            last = stack.pop()

            if last is '{' and ch is '}':

                continue

            elif last is '[' and ch is ']':

                continue

            elif last is '(' and ch is ')':
```

```
            continue
        else:
            return False
    if stack.size > 0:
        return False
    else:
        return True
```

Our little function will parse each of the characters contained in the statement. If it finds an open bracket, it is pushed to the stack. If it gets a closing bracket, it will pop the top element from the stack and compare it to see if it has a matching bracket. If not, False is returned and parsing continues. Once the end of the statement is reached, one last check is needed. If there is nothing in the stack, everything is good and True can be returned. If the stack isn't empty, False is returned because we have an opening bracket that is not matched by a closing bracket.

The following code can be used to test the application:

```
s1 = (
    "{(foo)(bar)}[hello](((this)is)a)test",
    "{(foo)(bar)}[hello](((this)is)atest",
    "{(foo)(bar)}[hello](((this)is)a)test))"
)


for s in s1:
    m = check_brackets(s)
    print("{}: {}".format(s, m))
```

The only statements that should match are the first three.

True

False

True

This code works just fine. The push operation and the pop operation of the structure both attract o(1), The data structure is used for the implementation of a number of different functionalities in the real world. For example, the forward and back buttons in a web browser, redo and undo features in word processing programs, and so on, are all forms of stack.

Chapter 9: Queues

Queues are another type of special list. This is not much different from a standard queue, one that you could be part of in the real world. Anyone who has stood in a queue at a fast food place or at an airport, or anywhere, they know how queues work.

Queues are a very basic and important concept to understand because many of the Python data structures are built on one.

A queue works like this – the first person to join will be seen to first if everything is equal. This is where FIFO comes in – First In, First Out. In any queue, the person or item at the front is served first and the only time that a person or an item leaves the queue is when they have been served, at the front. Strictly, it is considered illegal to join a queue at the front. A queue participant must join at the very end; it doesn't matter what length the queue is, joining at the end is the only accepted and legal way to join a queue.

As humans, the queues that we join do not, in any way, conform to these rules. There may be people who decide to drop out of the queue or have someone standing in their place while they do something else. We cannot model the dynamics of a real queue but being able to abstract a queue and its behavior is what helps us solve multiple computing challenges.

We'll be looking at several queue implementations, but they will all be based on the same concept of FIFO. The operation that adds an element will be called enqueue and the operation that removes an element will be called dequeue. Whenever an element is enqueued, the size or length of that queue increases by one and when one is removed, the size is decreased by one. As a way of demonstrating those two important operations, the details below shows what happens when elements are added and removed from a queue:

Queue Op	Size	Contents	Results
Queue()	0	[]	creation of queue object
Enqueue "Simon"	1	['simon']	Simon added to the queue
Enqueue "Billy"	2	['simon', 'billy']	Billy added to the queue
Size()	2	['simon', 'billy']	Number of queue items returned
Dequeue()	1	['simon']	Billy dequeued and returned
Dequeue()	0	[]	Simon dequeued and returned

List-Based Queues

To put all that we have talked about into a code, we'll use the list class in Python to implement a simple queue. We will encapsulate all the queue operations inside the class called ListQueue:

```
class ListQueue:

    def __init__(self):

        self.items = []

        self.size = 0
```

The initialization method, __init__ is where we set the instance variable for items to []. This means when the queue is created, it is empty. The queue size has been set to zero and enqueue and dequeue are the two interesting methods we will look at now.

Enqueue Operation

Enqueue() takes the insert method from the list class and inserts data or items at the front of the queue:

```
    def enqueue(self, data):

        self.items.insert(0, data)

        self.size += 1
```

Note that insertions are implemented at the end of the queue. The first position of any array or list is index 0, but using a Python list to implement a queue in our code, index 0 of the array is the only place where we can insert a new element. Insert() moves the existing element up a position and then puts the new data at index 0 in the space that has been created.

To ensure that our queue reflects this new element, we increase the size by one:

self.size += 1

Dequeue Operation

We use the dequeue() operation to take items out of the queue. This will capture the point at which the first customer to join the queue is served:

def dequeue(self):

data = self.items.pop()

self.size -= 1

return data

The List class in Python has a pop() method which does the following:

- Removes the final item from the list
- Returns the item removed back to the code or the user responsible for calling it.

When the last list item is popped, it is saved in the variable called data and, the data is returned in the final line of the method.

Stack-Based Queue

A different queue implementation is a pair of stacks. Again, we use the list class to simulate the stack:

class Queue:

def __init__(self):

self.inbound_stack = []

self.outbound_stack = []

The queue class sets the instance variables to empty lists when initialization happens. These two stacks will help with the implementation of the queue and, in this case, our stacks are just lists that we can call pop() and push() on.

Elements that have been added to the queue are stored in inbound_stack and this is all that can happen on this stack, nothing else.

Enqueue Operation

We use enqueue() to add an element to the queue:

def enqueue(self, data):

self.inbound_stack.append(data)

This is a simple method that will receive only the data that is required to be appended to the queue. The data then gets passed to inbound_stack in the queue class, to the append() method. That append() method also mimics the push() operation, which puts the elements to the top. Enqueuing data on the inbound_stack is done like this:

queue = Queue()

queue.enqueue(5)

queue.enqueue(6)

queue.enqueue(7)

print(queue.inbound_stack)

Dequeue Operation

Dequeue() is slightly more complex than enqueue(). When an element is added to the queue it goes straight to the inbound_stack and instead of taking elements from that stack, we go to the outbound_stack and an element can only be deleted through that outbound_stack():

def dequeue(self):

  if not self.outbound_stack:

    while self.inbound_stack:

      self.outbound_stack.append(self.inbound_stack.pop())

    return self.outbound_stack.pop()

First, the if statement will check to see if there is anything in outbound_stack. If there is something in it, the element at the start of the queue is removed like this:

return self.outbound_stack.pop()

If outbound_stack is empty, all the inbound_stack elements are moved over to outbound_stack and then the front element gets popped:

while self.inbound_stack:

  self.outbound_stack.append(self.inbound_stack.pop())

And the code will continue to be executed. The while loop will go on for as long as the inbound_stack contains elements. The self.inbound_stack.pop() statement will take the newest element added to inbound_stack and pop the data to the method call self.outbound_stack.append().

To start with, the inbound_stack had the elements of 5, 6, and 7 and after the while loop is executed the final line of dequeue() will return a result of 5 after the outbound_stack pop operation.

return self.outbound_stack.pop()

The outbound_stack now has just two elements in it 6, and 7.

When the next dequeue operation gets called, the while loop doesn't execute because outbound_stack does not contain any elements; this causes failure of the outer if statement. The pop()operation will be called immediately so that the element waiting for the longest in the queue is returned.

Below is a typical code used for running this kind of queue implementation:

queue = Queue()

queue.enqueue(5)

queue.enqueue(6)

queue.enqueue(7)

print(queue.inbound_stack)

queue.dequeue()

print(queue.inbound_stack)

print(queue.outbound_stack)

queue.dequeue()

print(queue.outbound_stack)

This code adds some elements into the queue and then prints all the elements contained in the queue. We call the dequeue() method and then we see a change to the element numbers when the queue gets printed again.

Node-Based Queues

It provides a great understanding of queues when Python lists are used for implementation. It is possible to implement our own data structure by making use of what we learned about pointer structures.

We can use doubly linked lists to implement queues and the deletion and insertion operations will both have a time complexity of O(1). The node class definition remains exactly the same as that as Node when we looked at the doubly linked lists and we can use this list as a queue, provided it follows the rules of FIFO for data-access.

The Queue Class

The queue class looks much like the doubly linked list class:

```
class Queue:

  def __init__(self):

    self.head = None

    self.tail = None

    self.count = 0
```

As soon as a queue class instance is created, the self.head and self.tail pointers will be set to None and the instance variable called count is maintained and set to 0 so the nodes in Queue can be counted.

Enqueue Operation

Again, we add the elements to the Queue object using enqueue(); in this case the elements are the nodes:

```
  def enqueue(self, data):

    new_node = Node(data, None, None)

    if self.head is None:

      self.head = new_node

      self.tail = self.head

    else:

      new_node.prev = self.tail

      self.tail.next = new_node

      self.tail = new_node


    self.count += 1
```

We already explained this code in doubly linked lists for the append operation – it is the same code. A node is created for the data that has been passed to the enqueue method and it is appended to the end of the queue; it will point self.head and self.tail to the new node only if we have an empty queue. And self.count +=1 increases the total element count.

Dequeue Operation

The dequeue() method is the other method to make a doubly linked list act as a queue; it is the method used to remove the first node in the queue. Removing the first element that is pointed to by self.head requires an if statement:

```
def dequeue(self):

    current = self.head

    if self.count == 1:

        self.count -= 1

        self.head = None

        self.tail = None

    elif self.count > 1:

        self.head = self.head.next

        self.head.prev = None

        self.count -= 1
```

Initialization of current is done by pointing it to self.head. If self.count is set as 1 there is a single node in the list and in the entire queue. To remove that node we set the variables of self.head and self.tail to None. If there are several nodes the head pointer will be moved to point at the next node of self.head.

Once the if statement has been run, the method will return the node that head pointed to. We decrement self.count by one in whichever way the execution path for the if statement flows.

Using these methods, we now have a queue that is heavily based on a doubly linked list.

In the next chapter, we will look at trees including major operations and the spheres in which the data structure is applied.

Chapter 10: Trees

Trees are a type of hierarchical data structure. When we looked at the lists, the stacks and queues, the items followed one another, but in a tree, we have a parent-child relationship between the items. To visualize a tree, imagine a real tree, growing in the ground. Now turn it upside down so the roots are at the top. Trees are drawn from the top down, so you would start with the root node at the top. The root node is from where all other nodes descend.

Trees can be used for all manner of things - searches and parsing expressions for starters. Some document types may be represented by trees too, like HTML and XLM. In this section, we will be looking at tree definitions and terms, binary trees, binary search trees, and tree traversal.

Tree Traversal

Here are some of the terms that surround trees:

- **Node** - a structure that holds data.
- **Root Node** – the node that all other nodes descend from.
- **Sub-Tree** – a tree that has nodes descending from the root node of another tree.
- **Degree** – how many sub-trees are from a node. A tree with one node has a 0 degree while a tree with two nodes would have a degree of 2.
- **Leaf Node** – a 0-degree node.
- **Edge** – the connection between a pair of nodes. On occasion, an edge may connect one node to itself, creating what looks like a loop.
- **Parent** – a node that has connecting nodes in the same tree.
- **Child** – a node connected to the parent node.
- **Sibling** – all the nodes that are connected to the same parent.
- **Level** – the number of connections that come from the root node to a given node.
- **Height** – how many levels are in the tree.
- **Depth** – how many edges there are from the root to the given node.

Tree Nodes

As in the other data structures that we have come across, a tree is constructed of nodes, but the difference is these nodes must each contain information relevant to the parent-child relationship. We'll start by using Python to build a binary tree node class:

class Node:

  def __init__(self, data):

    self.data = data

    self.right_child = None

    self.left_child = None

Nodes are containers that hold data and reference other nodes. Because this is a binary tree, the references go to the right and left children. Let's create some nodes and test the class:

n1 = Node("root node")

n2 = Node("left child node")

n3 = Node("right child node")

n4 = Node("left grandchild node")

The next step is connecting the nodes to one another. The root node is n1 and the children are n2 and n3. Then n4 is connected to n2 as the left child so that when the left sub-tree is traversed, we get some iterations:

n1.left_child = n2

n1.right_child = n3

n2.left_child = n4

Now the structure of the tree is set, and we can traverse the left sub-tree, print the mode, and move down to the next node (left). This continues until the left sub-tree has been traversed.

current = n1

while current:

   print(current.data)

   current = current.left_child

This needs a lot of client code work because the tree structure needs to be manually built.

Binary Trees

Binary trees consist of nodes that each have no more than two children. It is a common type of tree and it is what we will use to construct a Python binary search tree (BST) implementation. Each child is either the right or the left of the parent node and because the parent is also a node, each of the nodes refers to a left and right node even if they are not in existence.

There are no rules how elements are arranged in regular binary trees; it just needs to satisfy the condition that there are no more than two children per parent node.

Binary Search Trees (BST)

A BST is a special binary tree, one that is, in structural terms, a binary tree. In functional terms, nodes are stored in a way that the tree can be efficiently searched. BSTs do have a structure. For a node that has a value, all nodes from the left sub-tree are equal to or less than the value of the node. Right sub-tree nodes are greater than the value of the parent node.

Implementing BST

Let's start implementing a BST that holds a reference to the BST root node:

class Tree:

   def __init__(self):

     self.root_node = None

That simple piece of code maintains the tree's state so let's look at the fundamental operations.

BST Operations

To have a BST that is useful, there are two operations needed – insert and remove. Both operations must abide by the rule that they maintain the principle that provides the BST structure. Before we look at those two operations, there are some other operations that will help to understand them better.

Finding Min and Max Nodes

The BST structure makes it very easy to find the min and max nodes. To find the min, we traverse from the tree root and whenever we get to a sub-tree, we go to the left node. To find the max, we do the opposite and go the right node of each sub-tree. This also applies to find the min and max of a sub-tree. The method to return the min node is:

   def find_min(self):

     current = self.root_node

     while current.left_child:

       current = current.left_child

     return current

The while loop will carry on to obtain the left node until the final left node points at None. It really is very simple; to return the max node, current_left_child would be replaced with current_right_child. To find the min or max of a BST, it takes O(h) – h = the tree height.

Inserting Nodes

The insert operation is important as it is what allows data to be added as nodes. In our first implementation, we added the nodes manually but now we are going to give the tree the job of storing its own data. To make it possible to search, nodes need to be stored in certain ways. For each node, the left child will have data that is less than the node value while the right child's data will be greater than the parent.

We will create another BST, this time one of integers, beginning with the data 5. We need to create a node whose data attribute is set to 5. Then, we add another node with a value of 3 which will be compared with the root node. Because 5 is more than 3, it will be placed into the left sub-tree of the node 5.

This trees fully satisfies the BST rule of all left sub-tree nodes being less than the parent node.

Adding another node with a value of 7 requires starting from the root node of 5 and comparing the values. As 7 is greater than 5, the new node will go to the right of the root.

What would happen if the node we wanted to add was equal in value to a node that already exists? We would add it on the left and keep that rule maintained through the structure.

If a node has a child in the place where the new node is to be placed, we must traverse down the tree and attach it elsewhere.

Now we will add a further node with a value of 1 and, starting at the top again, we compare 5 and 1. As 1 is lower than 5, we look at the left node for 5, which has a value of 3. The comparison reveals that 1 is less than 3 and so we move to the level below and left of 3. There isn't a node, so we can create one with 1 as a value and then associate it with the left node of node 3.

So far, we have considered only the nodes that have numbers or integers as values. For the numbers, we have clearly defined ideas of lesser or greater than. A string comparison would be alphabetical so that wouldn't cause any issues either, but if you had custom data types that you wanted to store in a BST, you would need to ensure that the class had support for ordering.

Let's create the function that allows us to add nodes to the BST in the form of data; it starts with the declaration:

def insert(self, data):

We already know that the data must be encapsulated inside the node so that we can hide the node class from our client code or user who only needs to concentrate on the tree.

node = Node(data)

The first thing to check for is whether there is a root node; if not, since a tree must have a root node, the new node will become that root:

if self.root_node is None:

self.root_node = node

else:

As we traverse down the tree, we must track the node we are currently working on along with the parent node and we always use the variable called current to do this:

current = self.root_node

parent = None

while True:

parent = current

Now we perform the comparison. We need to see if the data in our new node is less than that of the current node before checking to see if the current node has got a left child. If not, the new node is inserted there or, if it does, we keep moving:

if node.data < current.data:

> *current = current.left_child*
>
> *if current is None:*
>
> > *parent.left_child = node*
> >
> > *return*

Lastly, we look for the case for greater than or equal to. If there is no right child with the current node, the new node is inserted there; otherwise, we need to keep moving and looking for another point:

> *else:*
>
> > *current = current.right_child*
> >
> > *if current is None:*
> >
> > > *parent.right_child = node*
> > >
> > > *return*

Inserting nodes into BSTs will take O(h) – h = tree height.

Deleting Nodes

Removal of nodes is another very important operation and there are three possible scenarios that we need to take into account when we do it. The node for deletion may not have any children, it may have one child, or it may have two. No children is definitely the easiest to deal with; all we do is detach the node from the parent.

If we want to remove a node that has a single child, the parent must point to the child of the node for removal. It is important to preserve the parent-child relationship which is why we need to take note of the way in which the two are connected. The child node for the parent node that was deleted will be stored and then the parent node of the deleted one is connected to the stored child node.

Things get more complicated when there are two children connected to the parent node. We can't, for example, replace the node with the 9 value with that of 6 or 13 so we need to find the next largest descendent; in our case, this would be 12. To get to 12, we go to the right side of 9 and then we go left to the node at the outermost left. 12 is known as the "in-order successor" of 9 and step two is representative of the moves needed to find the max node in the sub-tree.

So, 9 is replaced with 12 and 12 is removed. By doing this, we are left with an earlier form of removal; 12 doesn't have any children so the first rule of removal will apply.

The node class has no parent reference and that means we need a helper method to find the node and return it with its parent. This is much the same as the search() method:

```
def get_node_with_parent(self, data):

    parent = None

    current = self.root_node

    if current is None:

        return (parent, None)

    while True:

        if current.data == data:

            return (parent, current)

        elif current.data > data:

            parent = current

            current = current.left_child

        else:

            parent = current
```

```
        current = current.right_child


    return (parent, current)
```

The difference is, before the current variable can be updated in the loop, the parent is stored using parent=current. The removal of the node starts with the code below:

```
def remove(self, data):

    parent, node = self.get_node_with_parent(data)


    if parent is None and node is None:

        return False


    # Get children count

    children_count = 0


    if node.left_child and node.right_child:

        children_count = 2

    elif (node.left_child is None) and (node.right_child is None):

        children_count = 0

    else:

        children_count = 1
```

The parent is passed to parent and the node we found is passed to node, using parent, node = self.get_node_with_parent.data. As always, we need to know how many children there are in the node for deletion and that is why we use the if statement.

After we do this, we must start handling the conditions that govern the deletion of a node. The first bit of the if statement handles the situation where there are no children:

if children_count == 0:

   if parent:

     if parent.right_child is node:

      parent.right_child = None

    else:

      parent.left_child = None

  else:

    self.root_node = None

When the BST has just one node, we can use if.parent.

Where the node for deletion has a single child, the elif bit of the statement will do this:

elif children_count == 1:

  next_node = None

  if node.left_child:

    next_node = node.left_child

  else:

    next_node = node.right_child

```
    if parent:

        if parent.left_child is node:

            parent.left_child = next_node

        else:

            parent.right_child = next_node

    else:

        self.root_node = next_node
```

We use next_node to track the position of the single node that the node for removal points to; we can then make the connection between parent.left_child or parent.right_child to the next_node.

The last thing we do is handle a condition when the node for deletion has two children:

```
    ...
    else:

        parent_of_leftmost_node = node

        leftmost_node = node.right_child

        while leftmost_node.left_child:

            parent_of_leftmost_node = leftmost_node

            leftmost_node = leftmost_node.left_child


        node.data = leftmost_node.data
```

We move over to the right-hand node using leftmost_node = node.right_child to find the 'in order successor'. So long as a left node exists, leftmost_node.left_child is always going to return True and the while loop will continue running. When we reach the leftmost node, it will either have a right child or it will be a leaf node, which means there are no children.

The node that is to be removed is updated with the in-order successor value using node.data = leftmost_node.data:

if parent_of_leftmost_node.left_child == leftmost_node:

parent_of_leftmost_node.left_child = leftmost_node.right_child

else:

parent_of_leftmost_node.right_child = leftmost_node.right_child

This statement lets us attach the leftmost node parent to any child node. What is on the right of the = remains unchanged – this is because the in-order successor is only able to have a right child.

The remove() operation will take O(h) – height = tree height.

Searching a Tree

Because the insert method will organize the data specifically, we use the same kind of procedure to find data. In the following implementation, if the data is found, we will return it; if not, None will be returned:

def search(self, data):

Our search must start at the root node:

current = self.root_node

while True:

If we passed a leaf node, the tree will not have the data and None is returned to the user:

if current is None:

return None

If we found the data, it will be returned:

```
elif current.data is data:

    return data
```

Going by the rules of data storage in the BST, if the data we want to find is less than the current node, we traverse the left of the tree:

```
elif current.data > data:

    current = current.left_child
```

We have one option left; if the data is more than that in the current node, we traverse the right of the tree:

```
else:

    current = current.right_child
```

We can now write the code to test the BST. The tree is created, a few numbers inserted and then we run a search for numbers within the range. Those that exist will be printed:

```
tree = Tree()

tree.insert(5)

tree.insert(2)

tree.insert(7)

tree.insert(9)

tree.insert(1)


for i in range(1, 10):

    found = tree.search(i)
```

print("{}: {}".format(i, found))

We can traverse the nodes in a tree in one of two ways – breadth-first or depth-first. These traversal modes are for all trees in general, not just BSTs.

Depth-First Traversal

In this mode, an edge or branch is followed to its very limit before it recoils and continues transversal upwards. We will make use of a recursive approach for this traversal.

Depth-first traversal takes three separate forms:

- In-Order
- Pre-Order
- Post-Order

We'll look at all three in turn.

In-Order Traversal with Infix Notation

Most people are used to using this form of arithmetic expression because this is how the schools teach us. We insert an operator (infix notation) in between the operands, for example, 5 + 9. Where needed, we can create more complex expressions using parentheses, for example, (5 + 9) * (8 − 4).

In this traversal mode, the left sub-tree would be visited first, then the parent, and then the right sub-tree. The recursive function that we use for returning in-order node listings is like this:

def inorder(self, root_node):

  current = root_node

  if current is None:

   return

  self.inorder(current.left_child)

  print(current.data)

```
self.inorder(current.right_child)
```

To visit the node, we print it and then we make two recursive calls using current.left_child and current.right_child.

Pre-Order Traversal with Prefix Notation

We commonly refer to prefix notation as Polish notation; the operator is placed before the operands, for example, + 5 9. Because there is none of the ambiguity surrounding the precedence, we don't need to use any parentheses - * + 5 9 – 8 4.

Traversing a tree in pre-order mode involves visiting the node, the left sub-tree, then the parent and the right sub-tree, in that particular order.

The recursive function used in this type of traversal would look like this:

```
def preorder(self, root_node):

    current = root_node

    if current is None:

        return

    print(current.data)

    self.preorder(current.left_child)

    self.preorder(current.right_child)
```

Pay special attention to what order the recursive call is made in.

Post-Order Traversal with Postfix Notation

Postfix notation, better known as Reverse Polish Notation, will put the operands first and then the operator, for example, 5 9 +. As we saw with Polish notation, operator precedence is not in any doubt, so we can dispense with the parentheses, for example, 5 9 + 8 4 - *.

The order of traversal is left sub-tree, right sub-tree and then the node.

The method for the post-order traversal is:

def postorder(self, root_node):

  current = root_node

  if current is None:

   return

  self.postorder(current.left_child)

  self.postorder(current.right_child)

  print(current.data)

Breadth-First Traversal

Breadth-first traversal begins at the root and goes to the node from one tree level to the other. Let's say that the level 1 node is 4; we can visit this by printing the value. Then we go to all the nodes on the next level, in this case, 2 and 8. Lastly, on level three, we go to the nodes called 1, 3, 5, and 10. The output would be 4, 2, 8, 1, 3, 5, 10.

We use a queue data structure to do this type of traversal. We first push the root node into a queue. The node that is at the start of the queue is dequeued and printed or stored. The left then right nodes get added in that order and, because we do not have an empty queue, we continue with the process.

If we do a dry run of this algorithm, root node 4 gets enqueued then dequeued and then accessed. As 2 and 8 are the left and the right nodes, they are enqueued; 2 is dequeued so it can be accessed. The left and right nodes of 2, which are 1 and 3, then get enqueued. The first node in the queue is 8 which will be dequeued and accessed, followed by the enqueueing of the left node and right nodes. This process will carry on until the queue has been emptied.

The algorithm is:

```
from collections import deque

class Tree:

    def breadth_first_traversal(self):

        list_of_nodes = []

        traversal_queue = deque([self.root_node])
```

The root node is enqueued and a list of the visited nodes kept stored in list_of_nodes. The queue is maintained using the dequeue class:

```
        while len(traversal_queue) > 0:

            node = traversal_queue.popleft()

            list_of_nodes.append(node.data)


            if node.left_child:

                traversal_queue.append(node.left_child)


            if node.right_child:

                traversal_queue.append(node.right_child)

        return list_of_nodes
```

If there are more elements in traversal_queue than zero, the loop body will be executed. The first node in the queue is popped off and is then appended to the list_of_nodes. The first of the if statements enqueue the left child of the node should that left node exist. The next if statement repeats that for the right child and the last statement will return the list_of_nodes.

Parsing Reverse Polish Expressions

The next tree we will build is one written in postfix notation and we will calculate the result. The implementation will be kept simple; we are going to grow this tree by using a number of smaller trees, so we only need to implement the tree node:

class TreeNode:

   def __init__(self, data=None):

     self.data = data

     self.right = None

     self.left = None

We will use a stack to build our tree and it will be clear why shortly. For now, we will create a relevant arithmetic expression and set the stack up:

*expr = "4 5 + 5 3 - *".split()*

stack = Stack()

Because Python has sensible defaults, the split() method will split, by default on whitespace. The result will be that expr ends up as a list that has values of 4, 5, +, 5, 3, -, *.

Each of the elements in expr will be one of two things – an operand or an operator. If it is an operand, it is embedded in a tree node and pushed to the stack. If it is an operator, it is embedded in a tree node and then the two operands that go with it are popped to the left and right children of the node.

The code to build this tree is:

for term in expr:

   if term in "+-/":*

     node = TreeNode(term)

```
        node.right = stack.pop()

        node.left = stack.pop()

    else:

        node = TreeNode(int(term))

    stack.push(node)
```

The conversion is performed from string to int where operands are concerned. In the end, there should be just one element in the stack and that is what holds the entire tree.

Now, we might want to evaluate this expression, so we use this function to help us:

```
def calc(node):

    if node.data is "+":

        return calc(node.left) + calc(node.right)

    elif node.data is "-":

        return calc(node.left) - calc(node.right)

    elif node.data is "*":

        return calc(node.left) * calc(node.right)

    elif node.data is "/":

        return calc(node.left) / calc(node.right)

    else:

        return node.data
```

This is a simple function. A node is passed in; if it has an operand, the value of it is returned. If it has an operator, the operation represented by that operator is performed on the children of the node. However, one or both of those children may also contain an operator or operand so we need to call the function called calc() recursively on the child nodes. Keep in mind that all the children of all of the nodes are also nodes.

Now, the root node is popped off and passed to calc() and the calculation result is:

root = stack.pop()

result = calc(root)

print(result)

We should get a result of 18 = (4 + 5) * (5 − 3).

Balancing a Tree

We said earlier that, provided all the nodes get inserted in a sequential order, the tree acts like a list with each node having one child. Normally, we want the tree height as small as possible, so we make sure each row is filled. We call this 'balancing'.

There are several types of self-balancing tree, like AA trees, red-black trees, and scapegoat trees and each of these balances the tree every time an operation is performed to modify the tree, operations like delete and insert.

Then there are some external algorithms that also balance trees and the benefit of using these is that we don't need to balance every time we do an operation; instead, the balancing is left until it really needs to be done.

Heaps

It's time to introduce a type of data structure called a heap. This is a tree specialization in which all the nodes are in a specific order. Heaps are divided in two – min and max. In the min heap, the parent nodes must be the same as or less than both children and the root node will hold the lowest value. By contrast, in a max heap, the parent nodes are the same as or greater than the children, so the root node holds the greatest value.

Next, we move on to graphs and other algorithms.

Chapter 11: Graphs and Other Algorithms

Graphs are a concept that descends from a branch of math called graph theory and they are used to solve all sorts of computing problems. A graph has less structure than the other data structures we looked at and traversal is somewhat more unconventional.

By the time this section is done you will:

- Understand what a graph is
- Understand the different types of graph and their constituents
- Know how to represent and traverse a graph
- Understand priority queues and how to implement them
- Be able to determine what the ith smallest element is in a list

<u>Graphs</u>

A graph is nothing more than a set of vertices and the edges that form the connections between those vertices. More formally, graphs G are ordered pairs of sets of vertices V and a set of edges E. The formal notation is G = (V, E). The following are some graph definitions:

- **Vertex or Node** – a point in a graph normally represented by a dot.
- **Edge** – the connection between a pair of vertices.
- **Loop** – when a node edge is an incident on itself, it forms a loop.
- **Degree of a Vertex** – the number of vertices incident on a specific vertex.
- **Adjacency** – the connection between nodes and their neighbors.
- **Path** – vertices sequence where an edge connects each adjacent pair.

Direct and Undirected Graphs

Classification of graphs is based on whether they are directed or undirected. The undirected graph edges are represented as lines between nodes. We are not given any extra information regarding the relationship between those nodes; all we know is that they are connected.

With a directed graph, as well as connecting the nodes, the edges also provide orientation which means the edges are drawn as lines with arrows that point to the direction in which the edges connect the nodes.

Weighted Graphs

Weighted graphs provide the edges with a bit more information; this may be a numerical value that has a meaning. For example, let's say that we want to go from A to D. There are several ways to do it; we could go straight there, we can pass through B, C or both. The information associated with each of the edges tells us how long the journey will take to the next node. The journey AD could require us to walk or ride a bicycle; B and C may be indicative of train stations; when we get to B, we would need to change trains to go on to C. Lastly, CD might indicate a short walk between the two points.

In the example we use, AD and ABCD are two separate paths and a path is nothing more than a sequence of edges that must be passed through between the nodes. We could say that going AD takes 40 minutes while going ABCD takes just 25 minutes. If time is your only concern, then the second path is your best bet, even having to change trains.

The sheer fact that these edges may be directed, along with the extra information they hold is quite interesting. In the data structures we looked at earlier, the lines that were drawn between the nodes were nothing more than connectors; even when arrows were used for pointing to a node, we could easily represent that in our node class using parent OR child, or next OR previous. With a graph, it is sensible to see both the nodes and the edges as objects; like a node and edge have the additional information needed to follow a path.

Graph Representation

We can interpret a graph in two fundamental forms – an adjacency matrix and an adjacency list. We'll start with the list.

Adjacency List

We can present a graph using a simple list; the list indices are representative of the vertices or nodes of the graph. At every index, we store the vertex's adjacent nodes. However, lists can be restrictive because we have no way of using the vertex labels directly. A dictionary is far more suitable, and we could use these statements to represent a graph:

graph = dict()

graph['A'] = ['B', 'C']

graph['B'] = ['E','A']

graph['C'] = ['A', 'B', 'E','F']

graph['E'] = ['B', 'C']

graph['F'] = ['C']

Now we can see that vertex A has two adjacent vertices, B and C while F only has one neighbor, C.

Adjacency Matrix

The adjacency matrix is another way of representing a graph. Matrices are 2D arrays and the idea is for the cells to be represented with either a 0 or a 1, depending on whether an edge connects two vertices. To create the adjacency matrix, we use a sorted list containing graph keys:

matrix_elements = sorted(graph.keys())

cols = rows = len(matrix_elements)

The matrix dimensions are provided by the length of the keys and those dimensions are stored in cols and rows; the values in these are equal:

adjacency_matrix = [[0 for x in range(rows)] for y in range(cols)]

edges_list = []

Next, an array of cols by rows is set up, filled with zeros. The variable called edges_list stores the tuples that make up the graph edges. An example of this would be the edge between A and B – this would be stored as (A, B).

A nested for loop is used for filling the multidimensional array:

for key in matrix_elements:

  for neighbor in graph[key]:

    edges_list.append((key,neighbor))

We use graph[key] to obtain the neighbors of a given vertex and this key together with neighbor is used for creating the tuple that edges_list stores. The iteration will output the following:

```
>>> [('A', 'B'), ('A', 'C'), ('B', 'E'), ('B', 'A'), ('C', 'A'),
    ('C', 'B'), ('C', 'E'), ('C', 'F'), ('E', 'B'), ('E', 'C'),
    ('F', 'C')]
```

What we need to do now is complete the multidimensional array and we do this with a 1 marking an edge using this code line:

adjacency_matrix[index_of_first_vertex][index_of_second_vertex] = 1:

for edge in edges_list:

  index_of_first_vertex = matrix_elements.index(edge[0])

  index_of_second_vertex = matrix_elements.index(edge[1])

  adjacency_matrix[index_of_first_vertex][index_of_second_vertex] = 1

The rows and cols in the array called matrix_elements run from A to E, indices 0 to 5. The tuples list is iterated through using a for loop and the index() method used for obtaining the corresponding index where the edge will be stored.

The adjacency matrix will look like this:

```
>>>
[0, 1, 1, 0, 0]
[1, 0, 0, 1, 0]
[1, 1, 0, 1, 1]
```

[0, 1, 1, 0, 0]

[0, 0, 1, 0, 0]

The 0 at col 1, row 1 represents the fact that there is no edge in between A and A, whereas the 1 at col 2, row 3 indicates that C and B do have an edge between them.

Traversing Graphs

Because a graph doesn't really have an ordered structure, traversal is a little more involved. Normally, traversal requires us to track the vertices or the nodes we already visited as well as those which haven't been visited. One strategy which is common is to follow a path to a dead end, back up, and go back until another path is found. It is also possible to move from one node to another iteratively as a way of traversing some or all the graph. We'll be looking at two graph traversal algorithms – breadth-first and depth-first.

Breadth-First

The breadth-first algorithm begins at one node, choosing it as the root, and then going to the neighboring nodes; it then moves to the neighbors on the next graph level and so on. An example of an adjacency list for a graph would be:

graph = dict()

graph['A'] = ['B', 'G', 'D']

graph['B'] = ['A', 'F', 'E']

graph['C'] = ['F', 'H']

graph['D'] = ['F', 'A']

graph['E'] = ['B', 'G']

graph['F'] = ['B', 'D', 'C']

graph['G'] = ['A', 'E']

graph['H'] = ['C']

To use breadth-first traversal, we use a queue. A list is created for storing the nodes that are visited throughout the traversal. We will begin, as an example, from the node called A.

A is added to the queue and to the list of nodes visited. A while loop would then be used to start graph traversal. In that loop, A is dequeued. The adjacent nodes of B, G, and D, as yet unvisited, are sorted into alphabetical order and added to the queue, in the order of B, D, G. They also are put in the list of visited nodes. The while loop iterates once more because we do not have an empty queue and that means we are not finished with the traversal.

B gets dequeued; it has three adjacent nodes – A, F, E. We already visited A, so only E and F are added to the queue in alphabetical order. E and F are also added to the visited nodes list. At this point, the queue holds D, G, E, F, while the visited node list holds A, B, D, G, E, F.

D is the next to be added to the queue, but it can be dequeued straightaway because we already visited all the adjacent nodes. G is also enqueued and then dequeued for the same reason. F is the only node left in the queue.

F is dequeued and we can see that of all the nodes adjacent to F, only C remains unvisited. C is enqueued; it has two nodes adjacent to it – F, H. We already visited F so we enqueue H and add it to the list of the nodes visited.

Lastly, the while loop will iterate leading to H being dequeued. C is the only adjacent node and that has been visited; the queue is empty, the while loop breaks.

The Python code for the breadth-first search algorithm is:

```
from collections import deque


def breadth_first_search(graph, root):
    visited_vertices = list()
    graph_queue = deque([root])
```

```
    visited_vertices.append(root)

    node = root


    while len(graph_queue) > 0:

        node = graph_queue.popleft()

        adj_nodes = graph[node]


        remaining_elements = set(adj_nodes).difference(set(visited_vertices))

        if len(remaining_elements) > 0:

            for elem in sorted(remaining_elements):

                visited_vertices.append(elem)

                graph_queue.append(elem)


    return visited_vertices
```

If we used the Worst-Case Scenario, each of the nodes would be traversed and the time complexity would be O(|V| + |E|) − V = vertices and E = Edges.

Depth-First

As the name indicates, the depth-first algorithm traverses a given path by depth before it traverses the breadth. Because of this, the child nodes are seen before the sibling nodes. This algorithm works well on finite graphs and a stack is required to maintain the algorithm state:

```
def depth_first_search(graph, root):

    visited_vertices = list()
```

```
graph_stack = list()


graph_stack.append(root)

node = root
```

The depth-first algorithm starts by creating a list to which all the visited nodes are stored. To help with traversal, we use graph_stack and, for the sake of continuity, our stack is a normal Python list. The root node is passed along with the adjacency matrix and graph.root is passed to the stack. The first node that is on our stack is held in node=root.

```
def depth_first_search(graph, root):

    visited_vertices = list()

    graph_stack = list()


    graph_stack.append(root)

    node = root

    while len(graph_stack) > 0:


        if node not in visited_vertices:

            visited_vertices.append(node)


        adj_nodes = graph[node]



        if set(adj_nodes).issubset(set(visited_vertices)):
```

```
        graph_stack.pop()
    if len(graph_stack) > 0:
        node = graph_stack[-1]
        continue
    else:
        remaining_elements = set(adj_nodes).difference(set(visited_vertices))



    first_adj_node = sorted(remaining_elements)[0]
    graph_stack.append(first_adj_node)
    node = first_adj_node
return visited_vertices
```

The while loop body is executed so long as the stack isn't empty. If node is not included in the visited nodes list, we add it in. To collect all the nodes adjacent to node, we use adj_nodes=graph[node]; if they have all been visited, that node is popped from the stack and node is set to graph_stack[-1] – this is the first node of the stack. The continue statement goes back to the start of the test condition in the while loop.

If some of the adjacent nodes have not been visited, we need to get them and we do this by comparing adj_nodes and visited_vertices with:

remaining_elements=set(adj_nodes).difference(set(visited_vertices)) statement to find the difference. The first item that appears in sorted(remaining_elements) is assigned to first_adj_nodes and is pushed to the stack; the top of the stack then is pointed to the node.

When the while loop is in existence, visited_vertices is returned.

An example of an adjacency list of a graph would be as follows:

graph = dict()

graph['A'] = ['B', 'S']

graph['B'] = ['A']

graph['S'] = ['A','G','C']

graph['D'] = ['C']

graph['G'] = ['S','F','H']

graph['H'] = ['G','E']

graph['E'] = ['C','H']

graph['F'] = ['C','G']

graph['C'] = ['D','S','E','F']

The beginning node is A which is pushed to the stack and then added to the list called visited_vertices. Doing this marks the node as visited. A Python list is used to implement graph_stack. The stack has one element, A, whose adjacent nodes are examined – these are B and S. To test whether they have been visited or not, the if statement is used:

if set(adj_nodes).issubset(set(visited_vertices)):

  graph_stack.pop()

  if len(graph_stack) > 0:

    node = graph_stack[-1]

  continue

The top of the stack is popped off if all the nodes have been visited, but if graph_stack isn't empty, the node at the top of the stack is assigned to node and the while loop starts another iteration. If all of the nodes present in adj_nodes are a subset of visited_vertices, then set(adj_nodes).issubset(set(visited_vertices)) evaluates True. If we see a failure of the if statement, there are still some nodes that are to be visited and we can get a list of those nodes by using:

remaining_elements=set(adj_nodes).difference(set(visited_vertices)).

The list of nodes would be accessed in alphabetical order:

first_adj_node = sorted(remaining_elements)[0]

graph_stack.append(first_adj_node)

node = first_adj_node

The remaining_elements is sorted, and the first node is returned to adj_node. The returned node is appended to graph_stack, thus pushing it onto the stack and is assigned to node to prepare it for access.

When the while loop iterates again, the node is added to the visited nodes list and the only adjacent node has already been visited. The node is popped off the stack leaving the adjacent node on the stack. This is returned and examined to see if all adjacent nodes have been visited; if it has one that hasn't been visited, this is pushed to the stack and we start over.

Depth-first algorithm searches tend to be used in applications to find connected components, solving maze problems, finding graph bridges and so on.

More Useful Graph Methods

Mostly, a path is wanted that is between a pair of nodes, but sometimes, all the paths between them may be wanted to be discovered. One method that is useful would be to find the shortest path and with an unweighted graph, that path would be the one with the least amount of edges between the nodes. With a weighted graph, we might need to calculate the total weight passing through the whole set of edges.

Another situation may require finding either the shortest or the longest path. The customer waiting times are 4, 30, 2 and 1 so the average waiting time is (4+34+36+37)/4, resulting in 27.75. However, let's say that the order of service is changed so that those waiting the least amount of time are served first; that gives us a new average waiting time. To calculate it, we now do this (1+3+7+37)/4 and this gives a new waiting time of 12, which is much better. There is clearly some merit in serving those who have waited the least amount of time first. The method of using priority to choose the next item or perhaps some other criterion is on which priority queues are based.

Heaps are data structures used to satisfy the heap property; this property states that parent and child nodes require a certain relationship and the property needs to apply through the entire heap. With a min heap, that relationship is the parent must always be less than or the same as the child, so the root node must be the lowest. In a max heap, it's the opposite; the parent is higher than or the same as the child and, as such, the root node is the largest.

The heap is a type of binary tree, but we are going to use a list to represent the tree. We can do this because a complete binary tree may be stored in a heap. A complete binary tree is a tree in which each row of the tree must be entirely filled before the next tree can be started.

We are going to make things easier; the first item in our list at index 0 is going to be left empty. Then the tree nodes will be placed into the list from left to right, top to bottom. We'll start by looking at an implementation of a min heap; it won't be too hard to reverse the logic to get a max heap:

class Heap:

def __init__(self):

self.heap = [0]

self.size = 0

The heap list is initialized with a zero, which represents the first element. A variable is created to hold the heap size; this isn't normally necessary because we can easily determine a list size, but we would need to keep reducing it by one, so it is easier to use a separate variable.

Inserting

It is a very simple job to insert an item; the new element is added to the end of the list and the heap is incremented by the size of one. However, after each element has been inserted, the new element may need to be floated up. To do this, we need a helper method named float. This is how it is meant to work. We want to insert a value into our heap. When the new element has been slotted in it is compared with its parent. We divide the index value of the new element by its actual value to give us the index of the parent. The element at that index is higher in value than the new element so they are swapped. The new element moves up a level and this will continue until we get to the top of the heap. The following shows an implementation of this:

def float(self, k):

We continue to loop until we get to the root node; this allows us to keep floating the element upwards until it gets as high as it needs to be. Because integer division is used, once we drop below 2, the loop breaks out:

while k // 2 > 0:

Next, parent and child are compared and, if the parent is greater than the child, the two values are swapped:

if self.heap[k] < self.heap[k//2]:

self.heap[k], self.heap[k//2] = self.heap[k//2], self.heap[k]

Lastly, we move up the tree:

k //= 2

Using this method, we can ensure that the elements are properly ordered; all that's left to do is call it from the insert method:

def insert(self, item):

self.heap.append(item)

self.size += 1

self.float(self.size)

The final line in the insert method is calling the float() method so the heap can be reorganized as needed.

POP

As with insert, the pop() method is simple. The root node is removed and the heap size is decremented by one. However, when the root has been popped off, a new root node is required. We'll make this simple; the final item in our list is made into the root – we move it to the start. However, that means the lowest value may not now be the root, so we need to do the opposite of float and allow the root to sink as needed.

Let's see how this works. When the root node is popped off, we have a rootless heap. We can't have this; if we move a child up, the whole tree will need to be rebalanced somehow, so we'll do something very different instead. We will take the final element of the list and move it up to take the position of the root node.

In the very likely event that this is not the lowest value in the heap, we need to sink it and first we need to work out where to sink it. The two children are compared to ensure that the one with the lowest element floats up as the root sinks.

For argument's sake, we'll say that the child on the right has the lowest value so we now compare the new root with this value. The node jumps down and we must now compare it with the lower of the children. We only have one child here so there aren't any issues and there is no need to swap. If there is just one row then that's it, all done. We can now implement the sink() method, but before we do, we must work out to which child the parent node is to be compared. We can do that like this:

def minindex(self, k):

If we wind up going past the end of the list, the index of the left child is returned:

*if k * 2 + 1 > self.size:*

*return k * 2*

Otherwise, the index of the lesser child is returned:

*elif self.heap[k*2] < self.heap[k*2+1]:*

    *return k * 2*

else:

    *return k * 2 + 1*

Now the sink() function can be created:

def sink(self, k):

Like we did before, we use a while loop so that the element can be sunk as low as needed:

*while k * 2 <= self.size:*

Next, we need to determine which child to compare against – left or right. This is where minindex() function comes in:

mi = self.minindex(k)

As with float(), the parent and child are compared to see where the swap needs to happen:

if self.heap[k] > self.heap[mi]:

    self.heap[k], self.heap[mi] = self.heap[mi], self.heap[k]

And we also need to ensure that we don't get stuck in the loop, so we move down the tree:

k = mi

The last thing to do is implement pop(). This is easy because the sink() method does most of the hard work:

def pop(self):

```
item = self.heap[1]

self.heap[1] = self.heap[self.size]

self.size -= 1

self.heap.pop()

self.sink(1)

return item
```

Testing the Heap

Next, we need a piece of code that will test our heap. We create the heap and we insert some data into it:

```
h = Heap()
for i in (4, 8, 7, 2, 9, 10, 5, 1, 3, 6):
    h.insert(i)
```

The heap list can be printed so we can see the order the elements are in. If this were redrawn in a tree structure, it would be evident that it meets all the properties needed for a heap:

```
print(h.heap)
```

Now we pop the items off individually. The items will be sorted from low to high. Notice after each of the pops, the heap list will change. As we go through this, draw this using pen and paper, as a tree after each of the pops to gain a better understanding of the way sink() works:

```
for i in range(10):
    n = h.pop()
    print(n)
    print(h.heap)
```

Once our min heap works as it should and you have a good understanding of the way it works, try to reverse the logic and implement a max heap.

For the last part of this section, we will concentrate more on algorithms, as this will lead us to Part 2, Machine Learning.

Chapter 12: Sorting Algorithms

When data is collected, it needs to be sorted and, for that, we have a selection of sorting algorithms:

- Bubble
- Insertion
- Selection
- Quick
- Heap

We will consider the asymptotic behavior of these algorithms as we work with them. Some can be developed easily but may not perform very well, while others that require a bit more work to develop may perform impressively. We'll start at the top and work our way down the list.

Bubble Sort

Bubble sorting is a relatively simple idea; with a list that is unordered, the adjacent elements are compared, and with each comparison, they are placed in order of magnitude – just two elements at a time. The entire algorithm relies on a swap procedure.

We will start with a list that has just two elements – 5 at index 0, and 2 at index 1. To sort this, the two elements are swapped so 2 is now at index 0 and 5 is at index 1. To swap them, a temporary storage area is required.

Implementing the bubble sort algorithm begins with swap(). Element 5 is copied to temp, a temporary storage location. Element 2 then is moved so it occupies index 0 and 5 is then removed from temp and placed at index 1. The result is the elements have been swapped and the list is now sorted in order.

The code below swaps the elements in unordered_list[j] with unordered_list[j+1] if they are in the wrong order:

temp = unordered_list[j]

unordered_list[j] = unordered_list[j+1]

unordered_list[j+1] = temp

Now we know how to swap an array with two elements, it isn't too difficult to do this on an entire list. We'll use the swap operation to sort a double-nested loop. The inner loop is:

for j in range(iteration_number):

  if unordered_list[j] > unordered_list[j+1]:

    temp = unordered_list[j]

    unordered_list[j] = unordered_list[j+1]

    unordered_list[j+1] = temp

When we use the bubble sort algorithm it is important to know how many swaps are needed. For example, with an array of [3, 2, 1], no more than two swaps are needed, equal to the list length minus 1 – iteration_number=len(unordered_list)-1. We need to subtract 1 because it will tell us the greatest number of iterations that will need to run. If we swap the adjacent elements twice, we get the largest number occupying the last index. To ensure that we don't get any unnecessary swaps for elements that are already ordered correctly, we use the if statement. The inner for loop will only allow adjacent elements to be swapped twice in the list we are using.

However, when the for loop runs for the first time, it doesn't entirely sort the list. How many times do we need to swap for this to happen? That depends on how big the list is and to make the swapping process happen as it should, we use an outer loop. To sort our list, we need 4 comparisons so the inner and the outer loops must run len(unordered_list)-1 times to sort all the elements:

iteration_number = len(unordered_list)-1

for i in range(iteration_number):

  for j in range(iteration_number):

    if unordered_list[j] > unordered_list[j+1]:

temp = unordered_list[j]

unordered_list[j] = unordered_list[j+1]

unordered_list[j+1] = temp

We use this principle regardless of how many elements are in a list.

Bubble sort is not the most efficient of algorithms, showing a time complexity of O(n2) and it shouldn't be used on large lists. For small lists, it is fine.

Insertion Sort

We can use the principle of swapping elements for sorting to implement the next algorithm, insertion sort. With this algorithm, we start by assuming that part of the list is sorted while the remainder isn't. We can move through the part that isn't sorted choosing one element at a time. That element is used to go through the sorted part of the list and place it in the correct position so that the sorted part stays in a sorted order. To make it simpler:

Index　　　**Element**

Index	Element
0	5
1	1
2	100
3	2
4	10

The algorithm begins with a for loop that goes between index 1 and index 4. We are beginning at 1 because we have assumed that the sub-array at 0 has already been executed.

At the start of the loop execution we have:

for index in range(1, len(unsorted_list)):

  search_index = index

  insert_value = unsorted_list[index]

When the for loop starts an iteration, the unsorted_list[index] element is stored in the variable called insert_value. Later, when the right position has been found in the sorted part we store insert_value at that location:

for index in range(1, len(unsorted_list)):

   search_index = index

   insert_value = unsorted_list[index]

   while search_index > 0 and unsorted_list[search_index-1] >

      insert_value :

      unsorted_list[search_index] = unsorted_list[search_index-1]

      search_index -= 1

   unsorted_list[search_index] = insert_value

We use search_index to give the while loop information on where to find the element to insert into the list in the sorted part. The while loop will traverse through the list backward and it is guided by a pair of conditions. The first one is that if search_index=0, there are a greater number of elements in the sorted part of the list. Second, to make the while loop run unsorted_list[search_index-1] needs to be greater than insert_value. The unsorted_list array will do one of two things:

1. It will point to the element that comes just ahead of unsorted_list[search_index] before the first execution of the while loop
2. It will point to one of the elements just before unsorted_list[search_index-1] after the first execution of the while loop.

In our example, because 5>1, the while loop is executed. In the while loop body, the element from unsorted_index[search_index-1] stored at unsorted_list[search_index] and search_index -=1 moves the traversal of the list backward until it has a value of 0.

We now have a list of 5, 5, 100, 2, 10.

Once the while loop has exited, we can now use the last position of search_index, in our case it is 0, to help us know where insert_value needs to be inserted.

When the for loop does its second iteration, search_index has 2 as its value; this is the index of the third element array. Now we can begin to compare left, toward the 0 index; 100 is compared to 5; because 100>5, the while loop is not executed; 100 replaces itself because the variable of search_index wasn't decremented and that means unsorted_list[search_index]=insert_value has no effect whatsoever.

When search_index points to index 3, 2 is compared with 100 and 100 is moved to where 2 was stored; 2 then is compared with 5, which is moved to where 100 was originally stored. Now the while loop breaks and 2 is stored at index 1. The array is partially sorted holding the values [1, 2, 5, 100, 10].

For the list to be sorted entirely, the last step will happen one more time.

This algorithm is one of the more stable because it doesn't make any changes to the relative order of those elements with equal keys. It also doesn't require any more memory than what the list consumes because the swapping of values is done in place.

The worst-case value is $O(n^2)$ while best case value is $O(n)$.

Selection Sort

Selection sort is another popular algorithm; it is one of the simplest to understand but it isn't efficient, having asymptotic values for both best and worst-case of $O(n^2)$. Selection sort starts by locating the smallest element in the given array and then interchanges it with data from another array index, for example, index [0]. That operation is repeated but this time the smallest element in the remains of the list is interchanged with index [1] data. Let's look at our list with index numbers:

[Number 5 22 65 10]

[Index 0 1 2 3]

Beginning at index 0, we look through the list for the smallest item between index1 and the last index with a value in it. When that element is found, it is swapped with the value at index 0 and this is repeated until the list is in a sorted order.

The process of searching for the list's smallest element is incremental. Elements 2 and 5 are compared and 2 is chosen as the smaller; the elements are swapped. Afterward, our array looks like:

[Number 2 5 65 10]

Remaining at index 0, 2 is compared with 6 and because 65 is the bigger number, they are not swapped; 2 is then compared with 10 and again, there is no swap. Once we have compared all the elements we know the smallest element is at index 0.

We start a new comparison, this time beginning at index 1 and the entire process is repeated. The following code is used to implement the selection sort algorithm. The function argument is a list of items, unsorted, that we want to be sorted into ascending order:

```python
def selection_sort(unsorted_list):


    size_of_list = len(unsorted_list)


    for i in range(size_of_list):
        for j in range(i+1, size_of_list):


            if unsorted_list[j] < unsorted_list[i]:
                temp = unsorted_list[i]
```

$$unsorted\_list[i] = unsorted\_list[j]$$

$$unsorted\_list[j] = temp$$

An outer for loop starts the process iterating through the list called size_of_list. It will do several iterations and because that list is passed to the range() method, the result is a sequence of 0 to size_of_list-1.

The inner loop will then iterate through the list, making any swaps needed whenever it encounters an element whose value is below that to which the element unsorted_list[i] points. Note that the inner loop starts from i+1 and goes up to size_of_list-1. The inner loop begins searching for the smallest element at i+1 using the j index.

Quick Sort

This algorithm comes under the class of algorithms called Divide and Conquer. The problems are chopped down into smaller problems (divide) that are easier to solve (conquer). In our case, the unsorted array we have would be broken down into smaller sub-arrays, each of which has been partly sorted, until each element is in its correct position, and resulting in the list becoming sorted.

List Partitioning

Before our list can be divided, it must be partitioned. This is the fundamental heart of this algorithm. Partitioning the array requires selecting a pivot and all the array elements will be compared with that pivot. When the partitioning process has ended, all the elements less than the pivot will be on the left side of it and those larger will be on the right of the pivot.

Selecting the Pivot

To keep things simple, we will use the first array element as our pivot. A selection like this will show a degradation of performance particularly when the list is already sorted. And it doesn't make things any better if we randomly select the last or the middle array element either. Later, we will look at a much better way of doing this but, for now, we'll stay with the first element.

Before we look at the code, we'll have a quick look through using an algorithm to sort the list. You need to understand partitioning, so we'll look at that first.

The following is a list of integers. We will partition this list using the function that is below it:

[43, 3, 20, 89, 4, 77]

def partition(unsorted_array, first_index, last_index):

    pivot = unsorted_array[first_index]

    pivot_index = first_index

    index_of_last_element = last_index

    less_than_pivot_index = index_of_last_element

    greater_than_pivot_index = first_index + 1
    ...

The parameters of the function are the list that needs partitioning; the first and last indexes. The pivot value is stored in the variable called pivot and the related index is in pivot_index. Note that we do not use unsorted_array[0] because when we call that unsorted parameter with part of an array, index 0 may not point to the very first index. The index of the element next to the pivot, first_index+1, is marking where the last element is, and this is where the search starts for the array element that is bigger than the pivot – greater_than_pivot_index = first_index+1

The last list element is marked by less_than_pivot_index = index_of_last_element and this is where the search for the element with a lower value than the pivot begins.

    while True:

while unsorted_array[greater_than_pivot_index] < pivot and

   greater_than_pivot_index < last_index:

   greater_than_pivot_index += 1

while unsorted_array[less_than_pivot_index] > pivot and

   less_than_pivot_index >= first_index:

   less_than_pivot_index -= 1

The first of the inner loops moves to the right by one index until it arrives at index 2. This is because the value of index 2 is more than 43. Now, the first while loop will break out and will not continue. At each of the while loop test conditions, greater_than_pivot_index+=3 will only be evaluated if the test condition in the while loop is True. The search for the element that is larger than the pivot will now move to the next element to the right.

The second of the inner while loops will move to the left, one index at a time, until it gets to index 5 which has a value of 20, lower than 43. Now, neither of the while loops can be executed anymore.

  if greater_than_pivot_index < less_than_pivot_index:

    temp = unsorted_array[greater_than_pivot_index]

    unsorted_array[greater_than_pivot_index] = unsorted_array[less_than_pivot_index]

    unsorted_array[less_than_pivot_index] = temp

  else:

    break

It should be clear that greater_than_pivot_index < less_than_pivot_index and, because of that, the if statement body will swap the elements at those indexes.

The infinite loop is broken by the else condition whenever greater_than_pivot_index is more than less_than_pivot_index. What this means is that the two have crossed each other.

The break statement executes when less_than_pivot_index = 3 and greater_than_pivot_index = 4.

When we come out of the while loop, the element at unsorted_array[less_than_pivot_index] is interchanged with the element at less_than_pivot_index which is then returned as the pivot index.

unsorted_array[pivot_index]=unsorted_array[less_than_pivot_index]

unsorted_array[less_than_pivot_index]=pivot

return less_than_pivot_index

To recap – when we called the quick sort function the first time, it was partitioned around the index 0 element. After the partition function was returned, we had an array of [4, 3, 20, 43, 89, 77]. It is clear the elements on the right of 43 are greater while those on the left are smaller – the partitioning has finished.

Using 43 with an index 3 as the split point, the two sub-arrays of [4, 3,20] and [89, 77] are sorted recursively using the same process as above.

The main quick sort function has a body of:

```
def quick_sort(unsorted_array, first, last):
    if last - first <= 0:
        return
    else:
        partition_point = partition(unsorted_array, first, last)
        quick_sort(unsorted_array, first, partition_point-1)
        quick_sort(unsorted_array, partition_point+1, last)
```

The quick sort function is quite easy and has no more than half a dozen code lines. The partition function does the heavy work. When we call the partition method, the partition point will be returned, and this is the point where all the elements to the left of the pivot in unsorted_array are lower than the pivot and those on the right are greater.

When the unsorted_array state is printed right after the partition, we can see how that partition happens:

Output:
[43, 3, 20, 89, 4, 77]
[4, 3, 20, 43, 89, 77]
[3, 4, 20, 43, 89, 77]
[3, 4, 20, 43, 77, 89]
[3, 4, 20, 43, 77, 89]

Going back a step, the first sub-array following the first partition needs to be sorted. When greater_than_pivot_index is at index 2 and index 1 is where less_than_pivot_index is, the sub-array of [4, 3, 20] will stop partitioning. Now the markers have crossed over. At this stage, greater_than_pivot_index is more than less_than_pivot_index so the while loop will stop. Pivot 4 is changed with 3 and the partition point is returned as index 1.

The worst-case complexity of the quick sort algorithm is O(n²) but it is very efficient for sorting large arrays.

Heap Sort

Earlier, we looked at implementing a binary heap structure. In that implementation, we ensured that the order of the heap property was maintained after the removal or addition of an element by using the sink() and helper() methods. We can also use this data structure to implement another algorithm called heap sort. Let's start by using the following to create a simple heap:

h = Heap()

unsorted_list = [4, 8, 7, 2, 9, 10, 5, 1, 3, 6]

for i in unsorted_list:

   h.insert(i)

print("Unsorted list: {}".format(unsorted_list))

The heap, h, has been created and the elements from unsorted_list have been inserted into it. After each insert method call, the order of the heap property is restored by the float method, called afterward. Once the loop has terminated, element 4 will be at the top of the heap.

We have 10 elements in the heap; if the pop() method is called 10 times on h, the heap object and the popped elements are stored, it will result in a sorted list. After each pop() the heap will be adjusted to maintain the order property.

Below is the heap_sort method:

```
class Heap:
    ...
    def heap_sort(self):
        sorted_list = []
        for node in range(self.size):
            n = self.pop()
            sorted_list.append(n)


        return sorted_list
```

The pop method called self_size is called several times by the for loop and sorted_list will have the sorted list of elements once the loop has terminated. The insert() method is called n times and, with the float() method it will have a worst-case runtime of o(n log n), the same as the pop() method.

Next, we will be looking at design and classification of algorithms.

Chapter 13: Algorithm Design and Classification

We've looked at some algorithms, now it's time to go back a step and look at the design and classification of algorithms. As you get more experienced with Python programming you will start to see certain patterns much easier. And, as with any skilled trade, you need some principles and techniques to guide you. Where algorithms are concerned, there are plenty of techniques and principles in design and if you want to go on to harder problems, you need to understand these techniques and principles and gain a working knowledge of them.

We'll be looking at how algorithms are classified and some of the other techniques for design. The aim here is to give you an idea of how wide the algorithm expanse is, not to make you into a professional algorithm designer.

Classification of Algorithms

There are several algorithm classification schemes based on what the algorithm is to achieve. We have looked at a few algorithms and one question asked is whether they all share the same form. If they do, how are they similar and what characteristics do they share as the basis. If they don't share the same form, can they be sorted into groups of classes? We will look at both issues in the coming section.

Classification by Implementation

When a series of processes or steps are translated into an algorithm that works, there are several forms that it can take:

Recursion

Recursive algorithms call themselves until a specified condition has been met. Some problems can be expressed much easier through the implementation of their solution via recursion. Other types of recursive algorithms include:

- Single recursion
- Multiple recursion
- Indirect recursion

- Anonymous recursion
- Generative recursion

By contrast, iterative algorithms use a repetitive construct to come up with a solution. This might be nothing more than a basic while loop or some other type of loop. We also tend to think of iterative solutions more than we do recursive implementations.

Logical

One way of implementing an algorithm is to express it as a controlled logical deduction. The logical component of the algorithm contains the axioms that the computation will need while the control component determines how the deduction is applied. The expression for this is algorithm = logic + control and this is the basis of this programming paradigm. The algorithm meaning is determined by the logical component while the control component affects only the algorithm efficiency. This efficiency can be improved without any modification to the logic just by making improvements to the control components.

Serial or Parallel

On most computers, the model of RAM will assume that the instructions are given one at a time for the computation. Serial algorithms also go by the name of sequential and they tend to be executed in sequence. Execution will go from the start to the finish with no other executions.

To process multiple instructions simultaneously, we require a different technique or model. The parallel algorithm can do multiple operations at once. The PRAM model, for example, uses multiple processors sharing a global memory. These processors can do several logical and arithmetic operations at the same time or in parallel and this is what allows several instructions to be executed at the same time.

Parallel or distributed algorithms will divide the problem into smaller subproblems among all the processors for the collection of results. You can effectively parallelize some of the sorting algorithms and some iterative algorithms can be generally parallelized.

Deterministic vs Nondeterministic

A deterministic algorithm produces an identical output every time it runs with an identical input. Some problems are far too complex in the way their solutions are designed that it can be a bit challenging to express that solution deterministically. The nondeterministic algorithm can change the execution order or change one or more of the internal subprocesses and this results in a change to the end result whenever the algorithm runs. For example, if an algorithm uses the probabilistic value, the outputs will be different for each successive execution, and dependent on a random number that is generated and its value.

Classification by Complexity

Determining algorithm complexity means trying to determine the amount of memory or space and time used during the entire computation or execution.

Complexity Curves

Consider that we have a problem that is of magnitude n. To work out the time complexity, it is denoted with $T(n)$. The value may come under any of the following:

- $O(1)$
- $O(\log n)$
- $O(n)$
- $O(n \log (n))$
- $O(n^2)$
- $O(n^3)$
- $O(2^n)$

Depending on how many steps the algorithm performs, the time complexity may be affected, or it may not. $O(n)$ will capture the algorithm's growth rate.

Let's take a more practical example. How do we get to the conclusion that the quick sort algorithm works faster than the bubble sort algorithm? Or perhaps more generally, how can we measure algorithm efficiency against one another? The way to do that is to look at the Big 0 of multiple algorithms to see what their efficiencies are. This is how we get the growth rate or measure of time and this is what charts the way the algorithm behaves as n grows. Taking the runtime list, sorting it from best to worse is given as:

- $O(1)$
- $O(\log n)$
- $O(n)$
- $O(n \log n)$
- $O(n^2)$
- $O(n^3)$
- $O(2^n)$

Classification by Design

We are going to look now at the algorithm categories based on the way various algorithms are designed to solve problems. Any problem could have any number of different solutions. When we analyze the solution algorithms we can see that some of them will implement specific patterns or techniques and it is these that we will talk about briefly now.

Divide and Conquer

This is a recap because we have already talked about divide and conquer problem-solving. We know that the problems are broken down into smaller ones and all the solutions are combined in a way that the overall solution is the one that matches the original problem.

Recursion tends to be used mostly for dividing the problem and some of the algorithms that make use of the technique include binary search, quick sort, and merge-sort.

Dynamic Programming

This is like the previous technique. In divide and conquer, the subproblems must be all be solved before the result may be used on larger problems, but in dynamic programming, the solution is not computed to a subproblem already encountered; instead remembering techniques are used so that the computation is not repeated.

Greedy Algorithms

For some problems, it is not easy to determine the best solution. So, to make up for this, we turn to greedy algorithms, an approach that selects the nearest solution from a group of options that is closest to getting a solution.

The guiding rule for a greedy algorithm is that the solution selected is the one that will yield the highest benefit and carry on doing that in the hopes that the perfect solution may be reached. The technique has a goal of finding the "global optimal final solution" and it does this by making a series of choices that are locally optimal. These choices appear to lead toward the solution, but many of the choices are suboptimal, which means a bad asymptotic time complexity.

Complexity Classes

The problems that algorithms attempt to solve all fall inside a difficulty range in which the solution is found. We're going to look at 4 complexity classes:

- N
- NP
- NP-Complete
- NP-Hard Problems

P vs NP

The speedy advent of the computer system has hastened the speed at which some tasks are performed. Generally, a computer is good at perfecting calculations and any problem that may be divided into a set of computations. However, this isn't always true because there are some problem classes that take far too long to make even a decent guess, let alone solve the problem.

As far as computer science is concerned, the problem classes that a computer may solve in polynomial time using a sequence of logical steps are called P-Types – P means polynomial. These are quite easy to find solutions.

However, there is also another problem class that is hard to find a solution. We use the term "hard problem" to describe the increase in difficulty of a problem when attempting to find a solution. However, there is a good point – although these problems do have a high difficulty growth rate, it is perfectly possible to work out whether a given solution will solve that problem within polynomial time. These are known as NP-Type problems with NP meaning nondeterministic polynomial time.

We can use the Traveling Salesman problem to demonstrate the NP-Type of problem. The statement says: given n cities in this country, find the shortest route that goes between them all providing a cost-effective solution. When there are few cities, it doesn't take long to solve the problem; however, when the number of cities goes to 3 digits, it can take an awfully long time.

Many computer systems use RSA encryption algorithms and the strength and security come from it being based on a problem of integer factoring and that is an NP-Type problem.

It isn't easy to find the prime factors of any prime number made up of multiple digits. When you multiply two large prime numbers, you can only have a large non-prime number with a pair of large prime factors. Many algorithms take their strength from the factorization of that number.

P-Type problems are all subsets of the NP-Type problems and this means that, if a problem is solvable within polynomial time, it is also verifiable in polynomial time. But does P=NP? This question looks into whether a problem that is verifiable in polynomial time is solvable in polynomial time. More specifically, if they are equal it means that any problem that is solvable by attempting several solutions is solvable without having to attempt ALL possible solutions and this creates a shortcut proof. When discovered, that proof will have some serious consequences for the fields of mathematics, game theory, and cryptography, among many others.

NP-Hard/NP-Complete

A problem is classified as NP-Hard if all other NP problems are reducible or mapped to polynomial time. The problem is classified as NP-Complete if it is primarily NP-Hard and can also be in NP class.

Implementations, Tools, and Applications

While you can learn the theory of an algorithm, you will never truly understand it unless your use real-life applications. So, we are going to look at some of the algorithms and data structures that play a part in shaping the world in which we live.

One of the biggest benefits of the current time is the sheer amount of data – phone numbers, email addresses, image documents, text documents, all of these contain vast amounts of data. In this data, we can find some valuable information that gives the data a more important status, but getting this information out of the raw data requires the use of processes, data structures, and algorithms that are specialized.

We think of machine learning here because it makes use of many algorithms that will analyze the chances of certain variables and predict them. Using a numerical basis to analyze data still leaves a lot of information in the raw data. Visually presenting the data helps us to understand the data and gain a few insights. We will be looking in-depth at machine learning in the next part of this book, but we will look briefly at it now.

Tools

To go any further with machine learning, as you will learn later, you need several packages to preprocess the date and visually represent it. In brief, you will need the following packages installed in a virtual environment like pip:

% pip install numpy
% pip install scikit-learn
% pip install matplotlib
% pip install pandas
% pip install textblob

You may need to install other modules specific to your platform for these packages as well so be sure to install all relevant dependencies:

- **NumPy** – a library that contains functions for operating on matrices and n-dimensional arrays
- **Scikit-learn** – an advanced machine learning module that has several algorithms for regression, classification, and clustering, among others
- **Matplotlib** – a plotting library that uses NumPy to plot charts
- **Panda** – a library for dealing with data analysis and manipulation

Data Preprocessing

Real-world data collection is full of huge challenges and the raw data is overrun with issues. Because of this, we need to come up with ways of sanitizing data so it can be further used.

Why do we need to process the raw data? Simply because of the risk of human error. Data-entry offers huge chances for human error in data collection and even the technical and technological methods are not left out. Inaccurate device reading, bad gadgetry, and even environmental factors play a part in introducing errors in data.

You may also find that the data has become inconsistent with other records that have been collected and collated over time. Duplication of entries and records that are not complete dictate that we must treat data in such a way that we pull out the jewels hidden in the data, as well as getting past heaps of data that just isn't relevant.

Cleaning the data means that we can remove the irrelevant data which is called noise. If data is found to be incomplete, more sensible estimates can be used to replace it. And where we have inconsistent data, we must detect it and correct it.

Let's look at how NumPy and Pandas can be used for preprocessing data.

Missing Data

Data collection is awfully time-consuming and tedious and because of this, we shouldn't discard data too easily once we have collected it. There may be attributes or fields missing from a dataset, but it is still useful. We can use any one of multiple methods for filling in the missing data and one of these is to manually supply the data, use the mean dataset value, or use a global constant. Which one we choose will be based on the sensitivity and the context for which the data is being used.

Have a look at this data:

import numpy as np

import pandas

data = pandas.DataFrame([

   [4., 45., 984.],

   [np.NAN, np.NAN, 5.],

   [94., 23., 55.],

])

The data elements of data[1][0] and data[2][1] have np.NAN values, which tells us they do not have a value. If we don't want the np.NAN values in a dataset, we can set them to a constant figure. So let's do that; we'll set them to 0.1:

print(data.fillna(0.1))

The state of the data now becomes:

```
   0    1     2
0  4.0  45.0  984.0
1  0.1  0.1   5.0
2  94.0 23.0  55.0
```

If we wanted to apply mean values, we would do this:

print(data.fillna(data.mean()))

Each column's mean value is calculated and then inserted in the parts where the np.NAN values are:

```
   0    1     2
0  4.0  45.0  984.0
1  49.0 34.0  5.0
2  94.0 23.0  55.0
```

For column 0, we obtained the mean value through (4 + 94)/2 and the result of 49.0 is stored in data[1][0]. We do something similar for the other columns.

Feature Scaling

In a data frame, the columns are the features while the rows are observations or records. Have a look at this data matrix; we are referencing the data in subsections so do note it carefully:

```
[[ 58.   1.  43.]
 [ 10. 200.  65.]
 [ 20.  75.   7.]]
```

Feature 1 contains the data values of 58, 10, 20 and its values are clearly between 10 and 58. In feature 2, that date is between 1 and 200. If we gave this data to a machine learning algorithm we would get inconsistent results so we should scale our data into a specific range so the results are consistent.

Looking closely, we can see that each column is based around mean values that are different, so we need to align these features around mean values that are similar. A benefit of this is to give the learning parts of the machine learning a boost and we have a module called scikit that contains many scaling algorithms for us to use.

Min-Max Scalar

This form of data normalization takes the means and the standard deviations and boxes the data into one range between given min and max values. Mostly, the range will be 0 to 1, which is the default, but there are other ranges:

scaled_values = preprocessing.MinMaxScaler(feature_range=(0,1))

results = scaled_values.fit(data).transform(data)

print(results)

We can create a MinMaxScaler instance with a range of [0, 1] and then we pass it to the variable called scaled_values. We call the fit function to do the calculations to change the dataset internally. The transform function will do the operation on the dataset and the value is returned to results:

```
[[ 1.         0.         0.62068966]
 [ 0.         1.         1.        ]
 [ 0.20833333 0.3718593  0.        ]]
```

As we can see, the data has all been normalized and is now between the range 0 and 1; we can now apply this to the machine learning algorithm.

Standard Scalar

In the initial dataset, the features have mean values of 29.3, 92 and 38 respectively. To make them all have zero means and a unit variance, we use the standard scalar algorithm:

stand_scalar = preprocessing.StandardScaler().fit(data)

results = stand_scalar.transform(data)

print(results)

Note that we pass data to the fit method of the object that was returned from the instantiation of the class called StandardScaler. The transform method will act on all the data element and the output is returned to results:

```
[[ 1.38637564 -1.10805456  0.19519899]
 [-0.93499753  1.31505377  1.11542277]
 [-0.45137812 -0.2069992  -1.31062176]]
```

On examination of those results, we can see that the features are now distributed evenly.

Binarizing the Data

If we wanted to binarize a specified feature set, we need to use a threshold. If any of the values in a specified dataset is more than the threshold, 1 will replace that value. If it is less, it is replaced like this:

results = preprocessing.Binarizer(50.0).fit(data).transform(data)

print(results)

We create a Binarizer instance using the argument of 50.0. This is the threshold that is used in the algorithm:

```
[[ 1.  0.  0.]
 [ 0.  1.  1.]
 [ 0.  1.  0.]]
```

All the data values less than 50 have 0 and the opposite is also true; greater than will have 1 in their stead.

Machine Learning

Machine learning is classed as a "subfield of artificial intelligence". We already know that the creation of a machine that really can think is highly unlikely, but we can give a machine the models and the data by which it can learn to make a good judgment. Machine learning is focused on the creation of autonomous systems that can make decisions with very little or no intervention by a human hand.

To teach the machine what to do, the data must come from the real world. For example, if we wanted to work out which emails are spam and which are not, we would need to give the machine several examples of each. Once we have this data, we run it through the algorithms that make use of statistics and probability to find structures and patterns. Done properly, the algorithm alone will learn the ability to analyze and correctly categorize the emails and this is just one example of what a 'trained' machine can do. And that leads us neatly to the end of this part and on to Part 2 – Machine Learning.

Chapter 14: Machine Learning with Python

Thanks is given to tutorialspoint.com for the code in this section.

Python is a high-level but easy-to-use computer programming language and these days it is the language used the most for data science and for the design of algorithms for machine learning. This section is an overview of machine learning and the use of the required libraries – NumPy, SciPy, Pandas, and Matplotlib - in developing algorithms for solving real-world problems.

This will also be a practical tutorial so make sure you have everything installed that you need. The theory about machine learning is one thing, but the only real way to learn it is to get your hands dirty. We will show you how to set the required packages up and then we will delve into the most important concepts of machine learning, such as data analysis, preprocessing, extracting features, data visualization, regressing classification, and clustering along with performance evaluation.

We will be learning several projects that will teach you some of the machine learning functionalities and techniques, such as classification of news topics, detection of spam in emails, predicting, online ad clickthrough and more. First, a look at the history of machine learning.

A Brief History

We have reached a time when the lines between science fiction and science fact are becoming more and more blurred. We still have a long way to go but every day draws us ever closer to what is known widely as artificial intelligence.

Machine learning is one of the subsets of artificial intelligence in which algorithms are used to help computers learn autonomously from supplied information and datasets. A computer does not need to be programmed; instead, it can be taught to change and to improve those algorithms for the best result, all by itself.

These days, those machine learning algorithms are what enable computers and humans to communicate, autonomous cars, and much more. In time, machine learning will have a huge impact on most industries and this is just one reason why all management teams should learn at least the fundamentals of machine learning, what it's all about, and what it can do. Below is a brief timeline of events and the most important milestones in the history of machine learning:

- **1950** – Alan Turing comes up with the Turing Test to see if a computer can pass a test to fool a human into believing that the computer is also human.
- **1952** – The very first program was written for computer learning by Arthur Samuel. It was a game of Checkers – the IBM computer it was written on learned to get better every time it played by studying the moves that led to a winning game and then using those moves in its own games.
- **1957** – The very first neural network was designed for computers by Frank Rosenblatt. This was the perception, designed to simulate the human brain thought processes.
- **1967** – The algorithm called 'nearest neighbor' was written. This allowed the computer to begin using the basic recognition of patterns, allowing for shortest routes to be planned.
- **1979** – The 'Stanford Cart' was invented by Stanford University students, a cart that could get around obstacles by itself.
- **1981** – The Explanation-Based Learning concept was introduced by Gerald Dejong. The concept demonstrates a computer analyzing training data and then creating a rule by which it learns to discard data that it isn't important.
- **1985** – NetTalk is invented by Terry Sejnowski, a program that learns word pronunciation the way a baby learns.
- **1990s** – Machine learning work moves to a data-driven approach rather than knowledge-driven and scientists start to create programs for the analysis of large data amounts by computers and allows them to learn from the results.
- **1997** – Deep Blue from IBM beats the world chess champion at his own game.
- **2006** – The term, 'Deep Learning' is coined by Geoffrey Hinton. This term explains and covers new types of algorithms that allow a computer to see and distinguish between text and objects in videos and images.

- **2010** – Microsoft Kinect is released with the ability to track human features (20 of them) at a fast rate of 30 times per second so that humans can use gestures and movements as methods of interaction with the computer.
- **2011** – Watson by IBM beats human players at the game of Jeopardy.
- **2011** – We saw the development of Google Brain; it has a deep neural network that allows it to learn how to discover new objects and categorize them in a way similar to a cat.
- **2012** – A machine learning algorithm is developed by Google X Lab to browse through YouTube videos autonomously, identifying all videos with cats in them.
- **2014** – A software algorithm called DeepFace is developed by Facebook to look at photos and recognize/verify individuals in the same way as a human being does.
- **2015** – Amazon comes up with its own platform for machine learning.
- **2015** – The Distributed Machine Learning Toolkit is created by Microsoft to enable machine learning problems to be efficiently distributed across several computers at once.
- **2015** – An open letter is signed by more than 3000 AI and Robotics researchers warning of the dangers of autonomous weaponry that choose targets and engage with them with no human assistance. The letter is endorsed by Steve Wozniak, Elon Musk, Stephen Hawking and others.
- **2016** – Google's AI algorithm plays a professional Go player and beats them. This is the most complex board game in the world, much harder than Chess. The algorithm is called AlphaGo, developed by DeepMind (Google) and it won five out of five games in the competition.

So, is there any proof that we are getting ever closer to artificial intelligence? There are scientists that believe computers can never think the way humans do and that it is entirely wrong to compare algorithms and computational analysis to the way the human mind thinks. That said, the ability of a computer to see, to understand, and to interact with the real world is becoming more and more real, and the more data we produce, the more the abilities of computers will grow in processing that data, analyzing it, and learning from it.

Chapter 15: The Concepts of Machine Learning

Now we will look at the machine learning with Python concepts. With machine learning, we program the systems so that they learn by experience and they improve. By learning, we mean the recognition of input data, understanding it, and making informed decisions based on it. What is difficult to comprehend are all the possible decisions based on all the possible inputs and, to create solutions, we develop algorithms. These algorithms take specific data and build knowledge from that and from past experiences. They do this through the application of the principles of probability, statistical science, logic, reinforcement learning, mathematical optimization, and control theory.

Applications of Machine Learning Algorithms

Machine learning algorithms are used in many different applications, such as:

- Data mining

- Expert systems

- Forecasting such as stock market trends, weather

- Games

- Language processing

- Pattern recognition

- Robotics

- Vision processing

Steps Involved in Machine Learning

A machine learning project will involve these steps:

- Definition of a Problem

- Preparation of the Data

- Evaluation of the Algorithms

- Improving the Results

- Presentation of the Results

The very best way to understand machine learning is to follow a Python project from start to finish and cover the most important steps:

- Load the data

- Summarize the data

- Evaluate the algorithms

- Make predictions

This will produce a method that is replicable, which means it can be used on multiple datasets. Extra data can be added to improve the results even further.

Setting Up the Environment

Although we covered installing Python earlier, we need to look into how to install the required packages and libraries.

Installation

Installing Python can be done in two ways – the method we looked at earlier was installing directly from the Python website, or you can install a Python distribution called Anaconda. With the first method, once you have installed Python, use the following commands to install the packages:

$pip install numpy

$pip install matplotlib

$pip install pandas

$pip install seaborn

The second method, using Anaconda includes Jupyter Notebook already built-in – this is an interactive environment for Python – and it also includes the packages that you need already built-in. We download Anaconda from Continuum Analytics – it will take up to 20 minutes to do as Anaconda contains Python, the packages, a built-in code editor, and other files.

Now you can open Anaconda Navigator and go into Spyder IDE or Jupyter. Once you are in, type the following commands to import the packages:

import numpy

import matplotlib

Next, check to see if the installation has been successful by typing this command at the command line:

$ python

Python 3.6.3 |Anaconda custom (32-bit)| (default, 'system data and time')

[GCC 7.2.0] on (operating system)

The required libraries can be imported, and their versions printed:

>>>import numpy

>>>print numpy.__version__

x.xx.xx(version number)

>>> import matplotlib

>>> print (matplotlib.__version__)

x.x.x(version)

>> import pandas

>>> print (pandas.__version__)

x.xx.x(version)

>>> import seaborn

>>> print (seaborn.__version__)

x.x.x(version number)

Types of Learning

Machine learning is a type of automated learning that has little to no intervention by humans. The purpose is to explore data and to construct algorithms that are able to learn from old data and make predictions on new data. The input data is training data, and this is what represents the experience; the output is the expertise, normally a separate algorithm that performs some kind of task. Input data can be in many formats – text, numerical, visual, audio, or multimedia. The output that corresponds to the input can be a float (floating point number), an integer or an image of some description.

The Learning Concepts

Machine learning is the process of taking experience and turning it into knowledge or expertise. We can classify learning into three broad categories, each based on the learning data nature and the interaction between the environment and the learner:

- Supervised Learning

- Unsupervised Learning

- Semi-supervised Learning

In the same way, machine algorithms can also be categorized in four ways:

- Supervised learning algorithm

- Unsupervised learning algorithm

- Semi-supervised learning algorithm

- Reinforcement learning algorithm

Supervised and unsupervised are the two most common ones and they are the ones we will discuss now.

Supervised Learning

Supervised learning is the commonly used method for real-world applications, like speech or facial recognition, sales forecasts and more. We can classify supervised learning as two distinct types – regression and classification.

- Regression trains on data and predicts responses that are of a continuous value   type, like the prediction of real-estate prices.

- Classification tries to find the right class label, for example, analysis of positive or negative sentiment, the distinction between male and female, between malignant and benign tumors, unsecured or secured loans, and so on.

With supervised learning, all the data is complete with a description, a label, the targets or the output desired; the goal of it is to find the generalized rule that will map the inputs to the outputs. We call this kind of data labeled data and the rule that has been learned is then used to label the new data with outputs that are unknown.

Supervised learning is building a model that is based on data samples with labels. For example, if we wanted a system that estimated house or land prices based on certain features, we would need to create the database with the features in it and then label it. The algorithm needs to be taught what features correspond to which prices and, based on the data it gets, it learns how to make the price calculation using the input features values.

With supervised learning, we are dealing with a computer system that takes available training data and learns a function from it. The algorithm analyzes the data producing a function that can then be used for new examples. Types of supervised learning algorithms include neural networks, logistic regression, Naïve Bayes, and support vector machines while common supervised learning examples include labeling web pages as per the content they have, voice recognition, facial recognition, and learning to classify an email as spam or not spam.

Unsupervised Learning

We use unsupervised learning to detect oddities, to put customers with like behaviors together in groups for sales campaigns, detect outliers like defective equipment or fraud, and so on. It is the complete opposite of the supervised learning and none of the data is labeled.

When the training data have no labels and no descriptions, and just a few indications, it is down to the coder or down to the algorithm to work out what the structure is to the underlying data. The algorithm needs to find the patterns hidden in the data or work out how the data should be described. We call this data unlabeled.

Let's assume that we have several data points and we want them classified into a number of groups. At this stage, we probably don't know what the classification criterion is, so the unsupervised algorithm will attempt to classify the data into a given number of groups using the optimum way.

These are incredibly powerful algorithms for the analysis of data and for finding any trends or patterns in that data. They are used mostly for clustering similar inputs into groups in a logical way. Some of the common unsupervised algorithms include hierarchical clustering, random forests, and K-Means among others.

Semi-supervised Learning

If we have a dataset with some labeled and some unlabeled data, we call it semi-supervised learning. This algorithm uses the unlabeled data to train on and the labeled data to test on. It tends to be used where it is too expensive in computational terms to get a dataset that is fully labeled while labeling a smaller subset is a good deal more practical. For example, we sometimes need experts who are highly skilled to label some images, perhaps remote sensing images, and a lot of field experiments to find oil in a specific place; the acquisition of unlabeled data is quite easy by comparison.

Reinforcement Learning

With reinforcement learning, the data will provide feedback so that the system can adjust itself dynamically to achieve a specific objective. The system will evaluate its own performance based on that feedback and it will react accordingly. Some of the best-known uses for reinforcement learning are AlphaGo, which we mentioned earlier and the self-drive cars.

The Purpose of Machine Learning

We know that machine learning is a subset of Artificial Intelligence (AI) because the ability to take experience and turn into expertise or to see a pattern in a bunch of complex data is human or animal-level intelligence. As a science field, machine learning shares a number of concepts with disciplines, such as information theory, statistics, optimization, and game theory. Its objective as an IT subfield is to program a machine so that it can learn.

However, it must be realized that machine learning is not just about building a duplication of human or animal intelligent behavior; machine learning can also be used for the detection of patterns that are way beyond the scope of both animal and human perception.

Preprocessing, Analysis, and Visualization of Data

The real world is full of raw data that is not in a fit state for a machine learning algorithm to process. It must be preprocessed before being fed into the algorithms and so we will look at how this is done, the techniques used in preprocessing with Python.

Data Preprocessing

This is going to be a practical section; open any file with an extension of.py in your text editor and add this code to the file:

```
import numpy as np
```

```
from sklearn import preprocessing
```

We have imported two packages so now we need to create a little sample data and add the following line to the file:

```
input_data = np.array([[3, -1.5, 3, -6.4], [0, 3, -1.3, 4.1], [1, 2.3, -2.9, -4.3]])
```

Now we can do some operations on the data:

Techniques for Preprocessing

There are a number of techniques that we can use for preprocessing data:

Mean Removal

Mean removal takes the mean out of each feature, centering it on zero. Mean removal is helpful in removing the bias out of the features. This code may be used:

```
data_standardized = preprocessing.scale(input_data)
```

```
print("\nMean = ", data_standardized.mean(axis = 0))
```

```
print("Std deviation = ", data_standardized.std(axis = 0))
```

On your terminal, run this command:

$ *python (name of file).py*

You should see an output like this:

Mean = [5.55111512e-17 -3.70074342e-17 0.00000000e+00 -1.85037171e-17]

Std deviation = [1. 1. 1. 1.]

Note that mean is pretty much zero while the standard deviation = 1.

Scaling

All the features in the data point have a value and that can range between randomized values. Because of that, we should scale those values so that specified rules are matched. You can use this code:

data_scaler = preprocessing.MinMaxScaler(feature_range = (0, 1))

data_scaled = data_scaler.fit_transform(input_data)

print("\nMin max scaled data = ", data_scaled)

If you run this code you should see something like this:

Min-max scaled data = [[1. 0. 1. 0.]

[0. 1. 0.27118644 1.]

[0.33333333 0.84444444 0. 0.2]

]

All values have now been scaled so they fall in the given range.

Normalization

Normalization is about adjusting the feature vector values so they can be measures on a common scale. In our example, we adjust those values to sum up to 1. Add this code to your new.py file:

data_normalized = preprocessing.normalize(input_data, norm = 'l1')

print("\nL1 normalized data = ", data_normalized)

Run the code and you should see:

L1 normalized data = [[0.21582734 -0.10791367 0.21582734 -0.46043165]

[0. 0.35714286 -0.1547619 0.48809524]

[0.0952381 0.21904762 -0.27619048 -0.40952381]

]

We use normalization for ensuring that boosting of the data points cannot happen – this is possible because of their features.

Binarization

Binarization is used for the conversion of a numerical feature vector so it becomes a Boolean vector. This code is for binarization:

*data_binarized =
preprocessing.Binarizer(threshold=1.4).transform(input_data)*

print("\nBinarized data =", data_binarized)

Running the code should give you this:

Binarized data = [[1. 0. 1. 0.]

[0. 1. 0. 1.]

[0. 1. 0. 0.]

]

Binarization is very useful when we have some knowledge about the data upfront.

One-Hot Encoding

You may find that your numerical values are few and far between and scattered and it may also be that these values do not need to be stored. In this situation, the one-hot encoding technique is useful. Let's say that we have k distinct values; one-hot encoding transforms the vector into a k-dimensional vector – one of the values is a 1 and all the others are 0.

This code can be used for one-hot encoding:

encoder = preprocessing.OneHotEncoder()

encoder.fit([[0, 2, 1, 12],

[1, 3, 5, 3],

[2, 3, 2, 12],

[1, 2, 4, 3]

])

encoded_vector = encoder.transform([[2, 3, 5, 3]]).toarray()

print("\nEncoded vector =", encoded_vector)

Running the code should give you something along these lines:

Encoded vector = [[0. 0. 1. 0. 1. 0. 0. 0. 1. 1. 0.]]

Using that example, we will look at the third feature in every one of the feature vectors. The values we are interested in are 1, 5, 2, 4. These are four entirely separate values, giving the one-hot encoded vector a length of 4. Now let's say that we want the value of 5 encoded; the vector will be [0, 1, 0, 0]. We can only have one value 1 and as the second element has that value, it indicates that 5 is the value as per our string of four values.

Label Encoding

With supervised learning, we tend to see a range of different labels and these labels may be words or numbers. If they are the latter, the algorithm can use them directly. However, mostly these labels must be readable, so they tend to be words.

Label encoding is about changing those word labels so they are numbers that the algorithm can understand and perform operations on them. Let's look into how label encoding is done.

Make a new file in Python and input the following to import our preprocessing package:

from sklearn import preprocessing

label_encoder = preprocessing.LabelEncoder()

input_classes = ['opel', 'suzuki', 'opel', 'bmw', 'suzuki', 'mercedes']

label_encoder.fit(input_classes)

print("\nClass mapping:")

for i, item in enumerate(label_encoder.classes_): print(item, '-->', i)

Run the code:

Class mapping:

mercedes --> 0

suzuki --> 1

opel --> 2

bmw --> 3

As you can see in the output, the words in the file have changed to numbers with 0-indexing. Now, whenever we have a set of labels that we need to deal with, we can do the following to transform them:

labels = ['bmw', 'suzuki', 'opel']

label_encoder.fit(labels)

encoded_labels = label_encoder.transform(labels)

print("\nLabels =", labels)

print("Encoded labels =", list(encoded_labels))

Run the code:

Labels = ['bmw', 'suzuki', 'opel']

Encoded labels = [3, 1, 2]

This is far more efficient than maintaining the mapping manually between the words and the numbers. If you want to doublecheck the mapping, transform the numbers back to words like this:

encoded_labels = [3, 2, 0, 2, 1]

decoded_labels = label_encoder.inverse_transform(encoded_labels)

print("\nEncoded labels =", encoded_labels)

print("Decoded labels =", list(decoded_labels))

Run the code:

Encoded labels = [3, 2, 0, 2, 1]

Decoded labels = ['bmw', 'opel', 'mercedes', 'opel', 'suzuki']

You can see from the output that the mapping has been perfectly preserved.

Data Analysis

In this section, we will look at data analysis using Python.

Loading the Dataset

The dataset can be directly loaded from the UCI Machine Learning Repository. We are going to use pandas to do this and to explore the data using both data visualization and descriptive statistics. Look at this code and note that we have given specific names for each of the columns when the data is loaded. We are loading the pima_indians.csv from the repository:

import pandas

data = 'pima_indians.csv'

names = ['Pregnancies', 'Glucose', 'BloodPressure', 'SkinThickness', 'Insulin', 'Outcome']

dataset = pandas.read_csv(data, names = names)

When this code is run, the dataset will load, and the data can be analyzed.

Summarizing our Dataset

We can summarize the data as follows:

- We can check the dataset dimensions.

- We can list all the data.

- We can see a statistical summary of every attribute.

- We can break the data down by the class variables.

Dataset Dimensions

The command below can be used for checking the number of rows (instances) and columns (attributes) in the data with the property of shape:

print(dataset.shape)

In the code, using the imported pima_indians.csv, we have 769 rows and 6 columns:

(769, 6)

Listing All the Data

We can see all the data summarized:

print(dataset.head(20))

The command above will print the specified number of data rows, in our example, 20:

No.	Pregnancies	Glucose	BloodPressure	Skin Thickness	Insulin	Outcome
1	6	148	72	35	0	1
2	1	85	66	29	0	0
3	8	183	64	0	0	1
4	1	89	66	23	94	0
5	0	137	40	35	168	1
6	5	116	74	0	0	0
7	3	78	50	32	88	1
8	10	115	0	0	0	0
9	2	197	70	45	543	1
10	8	125	96	0	0	1
11	4	110	92	0	0	0
12	10	168	74	0	0	1
13	10	139	80	0	0	0
14	1	189	60	23	846	1
15	5	166	72	19	175	1
16	7	100	0	0	0	1
17	0	118	84	47	230	1
18	7	107	74	0	0	1
19	1	103	30	38	83	0

Viewing Statistical Summary

The statistical summary of every attribute will include four attributes – count, unique, top, freq – and the can be seen with this command:

print(dataset.describe())

You should see an output of this:

	Pregnancies	Glucose	Blood Pressure	Skin Thickness	Insulin	Outcome
count	769	769	769	769	769	769
unique	18	137	48	52	187	3
top	1	100	70	0	0	0
freq	135	17	57	227	374	500

Breaking the Data Down Via Class Variable

We can also examine how many rows belong to each of the different outcomes as absolute count with this command:

print(dataset.groupby('Outcome').size())

The outcome will be:

Outcome

0   500

1   268

Outcome   1

dtype: int64

Data Visualization

We can use two plot types to visualize our data:

- Univariate for understanding each of the attributes

- Multivariate for understanding the relationship between the attributes

Univariate Plots

A univariate plot is a plot of an individual variable. Let's assume that all the input variables are of a numeric type. We want to create a 'box and whisker' plot of each one. The code below is importing the infamous iris dataset:

import pandas

import matplotlib.pyplot as plt

data = 'iris_df.csv'

names = ['sepal-length', 'sepal-width', 'petal-length', 'petal-width', 'class']

dataset = pandas.read_csv(data, names=names)

dataset.plot(kind='box', subplots=True, layout=(2,2), sharex=False, sharey=False)

plt.show()

Box and Whisker Plots

The code below can be used for creating a histogram for each of the input variables; this will give us some idea of their distribution:

#histograms

dataset.hist()

plt().show()

Looking at the output, it is clear that a couple of the variables are of a Gaussian distribution. These plots are helpful to give us a clue of the algorithms that can be used in the program we are working on:

Multivariate Plots

A multivariate plot is useful to see the way the variables interact:

Scatter Plot Matrix

The scatterplot shows every attribute pair. These are very useful to see where there may be a structured relationship between the input variables:

from pandas.plotting import scatter_matrix

scatter_matrix(dataset)

plt.show()

In the output we would see a diagonal group of some of the attribute pairs and this is indicative of a high-level of correlation and a relationship that is predictable.

Training and Test Data

These are two of the most important of all the machine learning concepts and we'll be looking at both test and training data in this section.

Training Data

What the algorithm observes in the training data is what it uses to learn. Under supervised learning, every observation is made up of an output variable and at least one input variable.

Test Data

Test data is an observation set that is used to evaluate model performance using a set of given metrics. One important thing is that none of the training set observations are included in the test data set. If there is any training data it won't be easy to determine if the algorithm has just memorized the training set or has learned generalization.

If a program can generalize well it can perform tasks very effectively with new data. By contrast, if a program memorizes the data through the learning of a model that is complex it may be able to predict the training set response variable values with accuracy but it won't be able to predict any response variable values for new data examples. The term applied to memorization of the data is "overfitting" and when a program memorizes the observations won't do a very good job at its task because it may end up memorizing structures or relations that are nothing more than noise or pure coincidence. One of the biggest problems faced by machine learning algorithms is trying to balance generalization (underfitting) and memorization (overfitting). In some cases, to cut the risk of overfitting, regularization is applied to the model.

There is another observation set called the "hold-out" or "validation" set that may be required on occasion. This observation set is used for tuning hyperparameters, which are a type of variable that controls the way the algorithm learns the model. The test set is still used to evaluate the model, providing a performance estimation for the real-world but the validation set performance shouldn't be used for real-world performance because the model is tuned only to the validation data. Commonly, a supervised observation set is split into three – test, training, and validation. There are no specific requirements for the partition sizes; it will depend on what data is available and how much there is of it. The most common partition sizes are at least 50% of data to training, 25% to test and the rest to validation.

Some of the training sets may have no more than a couple of hundred observations while others may have several million, even billions; the reasons behind these massive training sets are reduced storage costs, smartphones packed with different sensors, more options for network connections, and a change in attitude toward data and user privacy.

That said, every machine learning algorithm will follow one axiom – GIGO. This stands of Garbage in, Garbage Out. An example: Two students have an examination due. One studies from a large book that is somewhat confusing with a lot of errors while the second studies the same subject in a short book that is very well-written. Who will score higher? Neither. They will both score approximately the same. Likewise, an algorithm that has been trained on a dataset that is large with a lot of noise, data that hasn't been labeled correctly, or that is irrelevant will perform no better than the algorithm that is trained on the smaller dataset that better represents real-world problems.

Most of the supervised training sets are either prepared by a semi-automated process or manually. In some domains, the cost of creating large supervised datasets is too high, but thankfully, Scikit-learn contains a number of built-in datasets, which leaves you free to experiment with different models.

In the development phases, especially when there is little training data, we use "cross-validation" for the purpose of training and validating algorithms on the data. With cross-validation, we partition the training set and then train the algorithm using all partitions except for one. That final partition is used to test the algorithm. We then rotate all the partitions multiple times, training and evaluating the algorithm on all data in turn.

Let's consider that our dataset has been partitioned into five equal-sized subsets. Those subsets are given labels of A, B, C, D, and E. To start with, partitions B to E are used for training and A for testing. On the next go around, we use partitions A, C, D, E for training and B for testing. The partitions are rotated for each partition until the algorithm has been trained and tested on every partition. With cross-validation, we obtain better accuracy in the performance estimate than we do when we use a single partition for testing.

Variance and Bias Performance Measures

There are quite a few metrics that may be used to effectively measure how a model learns task performance. Where supervised learning is concerned, there are many different performance metrics for prediction error measurements. There are two things that could cause prediction error in a model – variance and bias. Let's say that we have far too many data training sets. Each is unique but each represents the population equally. If you have a high-bias model, the errors for any given input will be similar no matter which training set is used because the model's assumptions are biased about the relationship the training data demonstrates over the proper relationship. By contrast, a high-variance model produces errors that are different for a given input depending entirely on the training set used. High-bias models are not flexible but high-variance models can be over-flexible to the point where even the noise in a training set is modeled. In other words, a high-variance model may overfit the data while high-bias models may underfit.

In an ideal scenario, a model would have low-variance and low-bias but any efforts made to reduce one inevitably results in the other one increasing. The terms for this is the "bias-variance trade-off". With unsupervised learning, there is no error signal that can be measured. Instead, the performance metrics are used to measure some of the data structure attributes but most of the performance measures can only be used to work out specific task types.

The performance measures used to evaluate the machine learning systems should be representative of the costs of real-word errors. This may look trivial but the next example will demonstrate using a performance measure that is generally right for a given task but is not right for the specific application of that task.

Accuracy, Precision, Recall

Think about a classification task; the machine learning system is observing different tumors and its goal is to predict whether they are malignant or benign. One of the obvious measures of the program performance is accuracy, i.e. correctly classified instances as a fraction. However, while the accuracy is a performance measurement, what it doesn't do is distinguish between the benign tumors incorrectly classified as malignant and vice versa, the malignant tumors wrongly classified as benign. There may be similar or identical costs incurred on all the error types in some applications, but with this specific task, failure to correctly identify the tumors that are malignant is a far worse error than incorrectly classifying a benign tumor as being malignant.

The possible predictions can be measured in a way that provides us with different perspectives of the classifier's performance. When a tumor is correctly classified as malignant, we have a "true-positive" prediction, but when a benign tumor is classified as malignant we have a "false-positive" prediction. By the same token, an incorrect classification of a benign tumor is a "false-negative" and a correct classification of a benign tumor is a "true-negative". All four of those outcomes can be used to calculate a number of performance measures, such as precision, accuracy, recall and more.

We use this formula to calculate accuracy:

$$ACC = (TP + TN)/(TP + TN + FP + FN)$$

In this formula:

- TP = how many true positives there are
- TN = how many true negatives there are
- FP = how many false positives there are
- FN = how many false negatives there are

For precision, we are calculating the fraction of correctly classified malignant tumors and we use the following formula:

$$PREC = TP/(TP + FP)$$

For recall, we calculate the fraction of identified malignant tumors and, for that, we use this formula:

$$R = TP/(TP + FN)$$

In our example, precision is being used as a way to measure the fraction of correctly predicted malignant tumors while recall is used to measure the fraction of detected malignant tumors. Both these measures together may show that a classifier with great accuracy may not detect many of the tumors that are malignant. A classifier that never predicts a malignant tumor would show a high accuracy level if the vast majority of the tumors are benign. Another classifier with low-accuracy and high-recall would probably be better for the problem because it can and will detect the bulk of the tumors that are malignant.

Before we move on, let's look briefly at the machine learning techniques.

Classification

This technique uses known, existing data to determine how new data will be classified into categories that are already in existence. When the system classifies a set of data it will do the following:

- A learning algorithm is used to prepare a brand-new data model
- That model is tested
- Later, it will be used for examining new data and determining what its class should be.

Classification is also sometimes termed as categorization and, in a classification task, the model learns to look at the dependent input and output variables and predict a discrete value for each one using the independent variables. Put simply, the program needs to predict the class that is the most probable label, class, or category for new data. It is a supervised learning form and is widely used by email providers to classify email as spam or not spam.

Naïve Bayes Classifier

One of the more common classification techniques is the Naïve Bayes Classifier, a very simple technique for the construction of classifiers. It is not a single training algorithm; it is a group and it is used to construct models that will classify instance in problems using the data available to it.

One of the more important features of this classifier is that it only needs a little data to estimate what the necessary parameters are for the classification.

Regression

With regression, the program will predict values for response variables or continuous output using the explanatory variables or the input.

Recommendation

One of the more popular methods is called recommendation; this will make use of user information to provide us with close recommendations. This is a method that tends to be used by Amazon and Google to show users a list of recommended items or websites based on their previous choices. This is done by a recommender engine that works behind the scenes for this purpose to capture the behavior of users. This is also how Facebook sends you recommendations and suggestions for friends.

Clustering

A cluster is a group of observations that are related and one of the most common of the unsupervised learning tasks is to look through training data to find the clusters. Clustering may also be defined as a process of taking a given collection and ordering the items inside it based on features that are similar.

We often use the clustering technique to explore datasets. For example, if the dataset were a set of book reviews, clustering would look for groups of negative and positive reviews. However, it does not have the capacity to label those clusters only that, through one or more clusters, the groups are similar in some way.

There are two main types of clustering – flat and hierarchical. Flat clustering will create flat cluster sets that do not have a clear structure but can relate clusters to one another. Hierarchical clustering, on the other hand, will create cluster hierarchies which are then given an output that provides even more information than the flat clustering. You do not need to specify how many clusters there are before but it is a less efficient method than flat clustering is.

Clustering Algorithms

Clustering algorithms are required for any given date to be clustered and there are two commonly used clustering algorithms – canopy and K-Means. Canopy is unsupervised and it is a pre-clustering algorithm that is generally used as a K-Means or Hierarchical preprocessing step. We use it for speeding up the clustering operations done on the big datasets where the size may dictate that it isn't possible to use any other algorithm.

K-Means is also important; the K is representing how many divisions there will be in the clustering data, for example, if k=3 in the algorithm then the data is divided by that algorithm into three clusters. A vector in space is used to represent each of the objects and, to start with, the algorithm will randomly choose the k points and treat them as centers – all the objects closest to a given center will be clustered. Vector files are required as the k-means input so we need to create them before we can use the k-means algorithm.

Machine Learning Algorithms

These are the most common machine learning algorithms, all of which can be used on any real-world problem:

- Decision Tree

- Dimensionality Reduction Algorithms

- Gradient Boosting algorithms such as XGBoost, GBM, Catboost, and LightGBM

- K-Means

- KNN

- Linear Regression
- Logistic Regression

- Naïve Bayes

- Random Forest

- SVM

We will now look at each one in more detail.

Linear Regression

We use linear regression algorithms for the estimation of real-world values that are based on one or more continuous variables. Those values could be house prices, sales calls, the total number of sales, and so on. Linear regression is used to create a relationship between both independent and dependent variables and it does this by finding the best line and fitting it. We call this line the "regression line" and the linear equation that represents it is Y= a *X + b. The breakdown of this equation is:

- Y is the 'dependent' variable
- a is the slope
- X is the 'independent' variable
- b is the intercept

We take the distance between the regression lines and the data points, square the result and minimize the sum to derive a and b.

Perhaps the best way to understand linear regression is to look at an example. Let's say we have a class of students and we arrange them in ascending order of their weight. We can visualize the students and use a combination of an analysis of build and height (parameters); we arrange them in order as per these parameters by determining that both build and height directly correlate to weight through a relationship that looks much like the equation from earlier.

Linear Regression Types

There are two main types of linear regression – simple and multiple. The characteristic of a simple linear regression is a single variable that is independent while linear multiple regression has at least one, usually more of these independent variables. When we are looking for the best fit line we can fit curvilinear or polynomial regression.

The following code works:

import matplotlib.pyplot as plt

plt.scatter(X, Y)

*yfit = [a + b * xi for xi in X]*

plt.plot(X, yfit)

How to Build a Linear Regressor

Regression is the estimation of the relationship that exists between the input data and the output data, which is continuously valued. The data tends to be in the format of real numbers; we want to try to estimate what underlying function controls the input to output mapping.

The following is an example of the input to output mapping:

1 --> 2

4 --> 8

5.2 --> 10.4

9.3 --> 18.6

As a way of estimating what the relationship is between the inputs and the outputs, we can look at the pattern. We can see, quite easily in this case, that the output is equal to twice the value of the input; in this scenario, $f(x) = 2x$ would be the transformation.

With linear regression, we estimate what the function is by a linear combination of all the input values. The example above has a single instance each of an input and output variable. The goal of this algorithm is the extraction of the correct model that creates a relationship between the input and output variables. The aim is to take the real output and the output that was predicted, determine the differences between them, sum the result, and minimize it using a linear function. We call this the "ordinary least squares" method. You could, possibly correctly, assume that a curvy line would fit better but this isn't allowed in linear regression. One of the benefits of linear regression is its lack of complexity and, while you may find non-linear regression models that are far more accurate, they will also be a lot slower. With linear regressions, the algorithm attempts to find an approximation of the input data points with a straight, not curvy, line.

We'll now look at how to use Python for building a linear regression model.

We'll start by assuming that we have a data file. It has a name of data_singlevar.txt. In this file are lines separated by commas; the input value is the first element, and the corresponding output value is the second element. We will use the following as our input argument:

Assuming that we have the best fit line for the set of data points, it is:

y = a + b * x

In this:

- b = (sum(xi * yi) - n * xbar * ybar) / sum((xi - xbar)^2)

- a = ybar - b * xbar

We can use this code:

 # sample points

X = [0, 6, 11, 14, 22]

Y = [1, 7, 12, 15, 21]

 # solve for a and b

def best_fit(X, Y):

  xbar = sum(X)/len(X)

  ybar = sum(Y)/len(Y)

  n = len(X) # or len(Y)

  numer = sum([xi*yi for xi,yi in zip(X, Y)]) - n * xbar * ybar

  denum = sum([xi**2 for xi in X]) - n * xbar**2

```
    b = numer / denum

    a = ybar - b * xbar


    print('best fit line:\ny = {:.2f} + {:.2f}x'.format(a, b))


    return a, b


# solution
a, b = best_fit(X, Y)
#best fit line:
#y = 0.80 + 0.92x


# plot points and fit line
import matplotlib.pyplot as plt
plt.scatter(X, Y)
yfit = [a + b * xi for xi in X]
plt.plot(X, yfit)
plt.show()
```

best fit line:

y = 1.48 + 0.92x

Coefficients, variance score and the residual squares sum can be calculated with this program:

```
import matplotlib.pyplot as plt

import numpy as np

from sklearn import datasets, linear_model

from sklearn.metrics import mean_squared_error, r2_score

# Load the diabetes dataset

diabetes = datasets.load_diabetes()

# Use only one feature

diabetes_X = diabetes.data[:, np.newaxis, 2]

# Split the data into training/testing sets

diabetes_X_train = diabetes_X[:-30]

diabetes_X_test = diabetes_X[-30:]


# Split the targets into training/testing sets

diabetes_y_train = diabetes.target[:-30]

diabetes_y_test = diabetes.target[-30:]

# Create linear regression object

regr = linear_model.LinearRegression()

# Train the model using the training sets

regr.fit(diabetes_X_train, diabetes_y_train)
```

```
# Make predictions using the testing set

diabetes_y_pred = regr.predict(diabetes_X_test)

# The coefficients

print('Coefficients: \n', regr.coef_)


# The mean squared error

print("Mean squared error: %.2f"

    % mean_squared_error(diabetes_y_test, diabetes_y_pred))

# Explained variance score: 1 is perfect prediction

print('Variance score: %.2f' % r2_score(diabetes_y_test, diabetes_y_pred))


# Plot outputs

plt.scatter(diabetes_X_test, diabetes_y_test, color = 'black')

plt.plot(diabetes_X_test, diabetes_y_pred, color = 'blue', linewidth = 3)

plt.xticks(())

plt.yticks(())

plt.show()
```

And, when that code is run, the result is an output along these lines:

Automatically created module for IPython interactive environment

('Coefficients: \n', array([941.43097333]))

Mean squared error: 3035.06

Variance score: 0.41

Logistic Regression

This technique has been "borrowed" from the field of statistics and is the commonly used method for the binary classification tasks, i.e. those tasks that have two class values. Logistic regression is not, as you might think, a regression algorithm; rather it is one of the classification algorithms and it is used to estimate discrete values based on the specified independent variable set. The algorithm is used to predict the probability that an event will occur, and this is done by taking a logit function and fitting data to it, hence the alternative name of "logit regression". Because it is used for binary tasks and because it predicts probabilities, the output values will always be between 0 and 1.

Understanding logistic regression is best done with an example. Let's assume that we have a puzzle that needs solving and it has just two possible outcomes – it has a solution, or it doesn't. Now let's assume that we have several puzzles that we can use to test a student to see what are his or her best subjects. If that student were given, for example, a trigonometry puzzle to solve, there could be an 80% chance of them solving it, but with a geography puzzle, there may only be 20% chance. Logistic regression helps here. As with mathematics, we use a linear combination of the variables (predictor) to express the outcome's log odds:

odds = p/ (1-p) = probability of event occurrence / probability of not event occurrence

$\ln(\text{odds}) = \ln(p/(1-p))$; ln is the logarithm to the base 'e'.

$\text{logit}(p) = \ln(p/(1-p)) = b_0 + b_1 X_1 + b_2 X_2 + b_3 X_3 \ldots + b_k X_k$

As p contains the probability that the interest characteristic is present, it will pick the parameters that will improve the likelihood that the sample values are observed rather than those that reduce the squared errors sum, as happens with ordinary regression.

These points are useful to learn for logistic regression:

- Logistic regression is like ordinary regression in that it has the objective of finding the values of those coefficients that are used to weight each of the input variables.
- Logistic regression is not like linear regression in that the output prediction is located using a logistic function, which is non-linear.
- The logistic function is sometimes called the "s-function" because it looks like a large S and it can change any given value to the 0 to 1 range. This means that we can give the logistic function's output a rule that says it must assign a value of 0 and 1 and then predict the class values.
- A logistic regression model learns in such a way that its predictions can be used as probabilities for specified data instances that belong to one of two classes – 0 or 1. This is helpful for tasks where more reasoning is required for a prediction to be made.
- As with linear regression, the logistic regression works much better when output variable attributes that are unrelated are removed along with any similar attributes.

With the next code, you can see how a plot is developed for logistic regression using a synthetic dataset that has been classified into 0 or 1 values, making use of logistic curve:

import numpy as np

import matplotlib.pyplot as plt

from sklearn import linear_model

 # This is the test set, it's a straight line with some Gaussian noise

xmin, xmax = -10, 10

n_samples = 100

np.random.seed(0)

```
X = np.random.normal(size = n_samples)

y = (X > 0).astype(np.float)

X[X > 0] *= 4

X +=.3 * np.random.normal(size = n_samples)

X = X[:, np.newaxis]


# run the classifier

clf = linear_model.LogisticRegression(C=1e5)

clf.fit(X, y)


# and plot the result

plt.figure(1, figsize = (4, 3))

plt.clf()

plt.scatter(X.ravel(), y, color='black', zorder=20)

X_test = np.linspace(-10, 10, 300)

def model(x): return 1 / (1 + np.exp(-x))

loss = model(X_test * clf.coef_ + clf.intercept_).ravel()

plt.plot(X_test, loss, color='blue', linewidth=3)

ols = linear_model.LinearRegression()

ols.fit(X, y)

plt.plot(X_test, ols.coef_ * X_test + ols.intercept_, linewidth=1)
```

```
plt.axhline(.5, color='.5')

plt.ylabel('y')

plt.xlabel('X')

plt.xticks(range(-10, 10))

plt.yticks([0, 0.5, 1])

plt.ylim(-.25, 1.25)

plt.xlim(-4, 10)

plt.legend(('Logistic Regression Model', 'Linear Regression Model'),

loc="lower right", fontsize='small')

plt.show()
```

Decision Tree Algorithm

A decision tree is a supervised learning algorithm that is commonly used in classification problems. It will work for two variable types – continuous dependent and discrete. This algorithm divides the population into at least two sets, based on the attributes that are the most significant, so that the sets are as distinct as they can be.

Decision trees are common in machine learning and they cover regression and classification. With decision analysis, the decision tree will represent both the decision and the decision-making explicitly and visually, using a decision model that looks something like a tree.

Decision trees are upside down trees, with the branches below and the root at the very top. The tree will divide into branches or edges depending on a given condition or internal node; where a branch end does not divide anymore, it is called the decision or leaf.

An example would be the passengers on the Titanic. We have a dataset that contains all the passengers and we want to predict whether a given passenger survives the disaster or not. We could use three attributes or features from the dataset – the age, the sex and the sibsp (number of children or spouse) and the decision tree will use those features to predict whether they died or not.

Some examples will show that the population is divided into groups and classified using several attributes to determine "whether they do this or not". Several techniques are used to divide the population including entropy, Chi-square, Information Gain, and Gini, to name a few. One of the best ways to understand a decision tree and the way it works is to play a game called Jezzball. This is a classic Microsoft game whereby you are in a room where the walls move; your goal is to create new walls to clear the maximum area without the balls. Each time the room is divided by a new wall, you are, in effect, creating two separate populations in the same area. Decision trees work in much the same way; the population is divided into groups that are as different as they possibly can be.

As a final example, have a look at this code and the output:

```
#Starting implementation

import pandas as pd

import matplotlib.pyplot as plt

import numpy as np

import seaborn as sns

# matplotlib inline

from sklearn import tree

df = pd.read_csv("iris_df.csv")

df.columns = ["X1", "X2", "X3","X4", "Y"]

df.head()
```

#implementation

from sklearn.cross_validation import train_test_split

decision = tree.DecisionTreeClassifier(criterion="gini")

X = df.values[:, 0:4]

Y = df.values[:, 4]

trainX, testX, trainY, testY = train_test_split(X, Y, test_size = 0.3)

decision.fit(trainX, trainY)

print("Accuracy: \n", decision.score(testX, testY))

#Visualization

from sklearn.externals.six import StringIO

from IPython.display import Image

import pydotplus as pydot

dot_data = StringIO()

tree.export_graphviz(decision, out_file=dot_data)

graph = pydot.graph_from_dot_data(dot_data.getvalue())

Image(graph.create_png())

The output is:

Accuracy:

0.955555555556

Support Vector Machines

A support vector machine is often coined as an SVM and it is one of the best-known of the supervised algorithms for classification; the SVM is used to separate different data categories. The SVM is classified through optimization of the line so that in each of the data groups the closest point is the furthest away from the other groups. By default, the vector is linear and is visualized as such. However, it can also be non-linear provided the type of the kernel is changed so it is no longer Gaussian, or linear.

SVM is a method of classification where each of the data items is plotted as a point in n-dimensional space – n= the number of features – and the value from each of the features is also the value of a specific coordinate. For example, let's say that we have two features for an individual – hair length and height. Both variables should both be plotted in 2D space first; each of the points will have a pair of coordinates which are called Support Vectors.

A line is found that will divide the data into two groups of data, each classified differently, and it is this line that determines that the distance from each group's closest point is also the furthest away. This line is called the "black line" because the closest points are the furthest from that line. The line is the classifier, and depending on the where and how the test data is divided either side of the line, the new data can then be classified:

from sklearn import svm

df = pd.read_csv('iris_df.csv')

df.columns = ['X4', 'X3', 'X1', 'X2', 'Y']

df = df.drop(['X4', 'X3'], 1)

df.head()

from sklearn.cross_validation import train_test_split

support = svm.SVC()

```
X = df.values[:, 0:2]

Y = df.values[:, 2]

trainX, testX, trainY, testY = train_test_split( X, Y, test_size = 0.3)

sns.set_context('notebook', font_scale=1.1)

sns.set_style('ticks')

sns.lmplot('X1','X2', scatter=True, fit_reg=False, data=df, hue='Y')

plt.ylabel('X2')

plt.xlabel('X1')
```

If you were to execute this code, you would get an output of:

Text(0.5,27.256,'X1')

Naïve Bayes Algorithm

The Naïve Bayes algorithm has its basis in the Bayes theorem, assuming that we have independent predictor variables. Simply put, the Naïve Bayes classifier will make the assumption that, although a specific feature may be present in a class, it is not related in any way to any of the other features that are present.

An example would be a fruit; if it is round, colored orange, and has a diameter of around 3 inches, it is classified as an orange. Even if those three features depended either on one another or on other features, the Naïve Bayes classifier sees that all the characteristics contribute independently of one another to the probability of the fruit being an orange.

It is very easy to create a Naïve Bayesian model and it is of huge usefulness where large datasets are concerned. Aside from being one of the simplest, the Naïve Bayes algorithm has been shown to vastly outperform some of the most advanced methods of classification.

The Bayes theorem provides a method to calculate the posterior probability, which is P(c|x) from P(c), P(x) and P(x|c). The equation is P(c/x) = P(x/c)P(c)/P(x). Breaking the equation down:

- P(c|x) is the target attribute's posterior probability
- P(c) is the class's prior probability

- P(x|c) is the likelihood – the probability of the given class's predictor

- P(x) is the predictor's prior probability

The following example will explain this better:

Let's assume that we have a training dataset called weather; the target variable that corresponds to it is called Play. We want to classify whether a player can or can't play based on the weather conditions. To do this, we need to follow these steps:

1. The dataset needs to be converted into a frequency table.

2. A Likelihood table needs to be created – to do this, find the probabilities of Playing – 0.64 and Overcast = 0.29.

3. A Naïve Bayesian may now be used to calculate what each class's posterior probability is and the prediction outcome will be the class that has the highest posterior probability.

The problem is this – if the weather is sunny, will the players play?

To solve that problem, we use the method we talked of earlier, so it would look like this:

P(Yes | Sunny) = P(Sunny | Yes) * P(Yes) / P (Sunny)

In our example, P (Sunny |Yes) = 3/9 = 0.33, P(Sunny) = 5/14 = 0.36, P(Yes) = 9/14 = 0.64

So, P (Yes | Sunny) = 0.33 * 0.64 / 0.36 = 0.60, because this has the highest probability.

The Naïve Bayes algorithm makes use of a similar method to predict probabilities of classes that are based on different attributes. We tend to use this algorithm more for text classification and where we have a task that has several classes.

You can see one example of an implementation of Naïve Bayes below:

```
import csv

import random

import math


def loadCsv(filename):
    lines = csv.reader(open(filename, "rb"))
    dataset = list(lines)
    for i in range(len(dataset)):
        dataset[i] = [float(x) for x in dataset[i]]
    return dataset


def splitDataset(dataset, splitRatio):
    trainSize = int(len(dataset) * splitRatio)
    trainSet = []
    copy = list(dataset)
    while len(trainSet) < trainSize:
        index = random.randrange(len(copy))
```

```python
        trainSet.append(copy.pop(index))
    return [trainSet, copy]


def separateByClass(dataset):
    separated = {}
    for i in range(len(dataset)):
        vector = dataset[i]
        if (vector[-1] not in separated):
            separated[vector[-1]] = []
        separated[vector[-1]].append(vector)
    return separated


def mean(numbers):
    return sum(numbers)/float(len(numbers))


def stdev(numbers):
    avg = mean(numbers)
    variance = sum([pow(x-avg,2) for x in numbers])/float(len(numbers)-1)
    return math.sqrt(variance)


def summarize(dataset):
```

```python
    summaries = [(mean(attribute), stdev(attribute)) for attribute in
zip(*dataset)]


def summarizeByClass(dataset):

  separated = separateByClass(dataset)

  summaries = {}

  for classValue, instances in separated.iteritems():

    summaries[classValue] = summarize(instances)

  return summaries


def calculateProbability(x, mean, stdev):

  exponent = math.exp(-(math.pow(x-mean,2)/(2*math.pow(stdev,2))))

  return (1 / (math.sqrt(2*math.pi) * stdev)) * exponent


def calculateClassProbabilities(summaries, inputVector):

  probabilities = {}

  for classValue, classSummaries in summaries.iteritems():

    probabilities[classValue] = 1

    for i in range(len(classSummaries)):

      mean, stdev = classSummaries[i]

      x = inputVector[i]
```

```
      probabilities[classValue] *= calculateProbability(x, mean,stdev)
  return probabilities


def predict(summaries, inputVector):
  probabilities = calculateClassProbabilities(summaries, inputVector)
  bestLabel, bestProb = None, -1
  for classValue, probability in probabilities.iteritems():
    if bestLabel is None or probability > bestProb:
      bestProb = probability
      bestLabel = classValue
  return bestLabel


def getPredictions(summaries, testSet):
  predictions = []
  for i in range(len(testSet)):
    result = predict(summaries, testSet[i])
    predictions.append(result)
  return predictions
def getAccuracy(testSet, predictions):
  correct = 0
  for i in range(len(testSet)):
```

```
    if testSet[i][-1] == predictions[i]:

        correct += 1

    return (correct/float(len(testSet))) * 100.0


def main():

    filename = 'pima-indians-diabetes.data.csv'

    splitRatio = 0.67

    dataset = loadCsv(filename)

    trainingSet, testSet = splitDataset(dataset, splitRatio)

    print('Split {0} rows into train = {1} and test = {2}
rows').format(len(dataset), len(trainingSet), len(testSet))

    # prepare model

    summaries = summarizeByClass(trainingSet)

    # test model

    predictions = getPredictions(summaries, testSet)

    accuracy = getAccuracy(testSet, predictions)

    print('Accuracy: {0}%').format(accuracy)
main()
```

Running this long code provides this output:

Split 1372 rows into train = 919 and test = 453 rows

Accuracy: 83.6644591611%

K-Nearest Neighbors

K-Nearest Neighbors, usually shorted to KNN, is one of the supervised classification algorithms. It is one of the simpler ones used for storing all the available cases and then for classifying the new cases using a K-nearest majority vote. The class is assigned the case that is commonest among KNN and this is measured using a distance function.

Distance functions fall into 4 categories – Minkowski, Euclidean, Hamming, and Manhattan. Hamming is used for variables that are categorical and the others are for functions that are continuous. So, if K = 1, the case will be assigned to the class of the nearest neighbor. Sometimes it can be a challenge to choose K will you are carrying out KNN modeling.

KNN examines the different centroids and will use a function, normally Euclidean, to compare the distance. Those results are then analyzed, and each point is assigned to the group – this is to ensure it is optimally placed with all its nearest points.

KNN can be used for regression and for classification problems but it tends to be more used in the latter; KNN is also easy to map to real-life. Before you select KNN, note the following:

- In computational terms, KNN is expensive
- You should normalize variables otherwise the higher-range variables may bias it
- Before you choose KNN, work on the pre-processing stage first, like removing noise, etc.

The following piece of code will show you how KNN works:

#Importing Libraries

from sklearn.neighbors import KNeighborsClassifier

```python
#Assumed you have, X (predictor) and Y (target) for training data set and
x_test(predictor) of test_dataset

# Create KNeighbors classifier object model

KNeighborsClassifier(n_neighbors=6) # default value for n_neighbors is 5

# Train the model using the training sets and check score

model.fit(X, y)

#Predict Output

predicted= model.predict(x_test)

from sklearn.neighbors import KNeighborsClassifier

df = pd.read_csv('iris_df.csv')

df.columns = ['X1', 'X2', 'X3', 'X4', 'Y']

df = df.drop(['X4', 'X3'], 1)

df.head()

sns.set_context('notebook', font_scale=1.1)

sns.set_style('ticks')

sns.lmplot('X1','X2', scatter=True, fit_reg=False, data=df, hue='Y')

plt.ylabel('X2')

plt.xlabel('X1')

from sklearn.cross_validation import train_test_split

neighbors = KNeighborsClassifier(n_neighbors=5)

X = df.values[:, 0:2]
```

Y = df.values[:, 2]

trainX, testX, trainY, testY = train_test_split(X, Y, test_size = 0.3)

neighbors.fit(trainX, trainY)

print('Accuracy: \n', neighbors.score(testX, testY))

pred = neighbors.predict(testX)

The output from this code is:

('Accuracy: \n', 0.75555555555555554)

K-Means

K-Means is an unsupervised algorithm used to deal with clustering problems. The K-Means procedure is a very simple way of classifying a provided data set through a specific number of k-clusters. The data points within a cluster are homogenous, and to peer groups, they are heterogenous.

How K-Means Forms a Cluster

K-Means follows the steps below to form a cluster:

1. It first chooses centroids – a k number of points for each of the clusters.
2. Each of the data points will form a cluster with the centroids nearest to it – k-clusters.
3. K-Means will then locate the centroid of each of the clusters. It bases this on members of existing clusters. We have got new centroids.

Because our centroids are new, steps 2 and 3 must be repeated to find the closest distance from the centroids for each of the data points. An association must be made with new k-clusters and the process must be repeated until there is convergence, i.e. the centroids no longer change.

Determining the Value of K

Each cluster in K-Means has a centroid. The sum of the square of the difference between the data points and the centroid in the cluster is equal to the sum of the cluster's square value. When the sums of all the square values for all the clusters are added together, we get the total within the sum of the square value for the clustering solution.

As the cluster number rises, the value will continue to decrease; however, if you plot that result, you will see a sharp decrease in the sum of the squared distance up to a given k-value and then it will decrease more slowly after. This is how we find the optimum cluster number.

Look at this code:

```
import numpy as np

import matplotlib.pyplot as plt

from matplotlib import style

style.use("ggplot")

from sklearn.cluster import KMeans

x = [1, 5, 1.5, 8, 1, 9]

y = [2, 8, 1.8, 8, 0.6, 11]


plt.scatter(x,y)

plt.show()

X = np.array([ [1, 2],

        [5, 8],

        [1.5, 1.8],
```

```python
              [8, 8],

              [1, 0.6],

              [9, 11]])

kmeans = KMeans(n_clusters=2)

kmeans.fit(X)

centroids = kmeans.cluster_centers_

labels = kmeans.labels_

print(centroids)

print(labels)

colors = ["g.","r.","c.","y."]


for i in range(len(X)):

    print("coordinate:",X[i], "label:", labels[i])

    plt.plot(X[i][0], X[i][1], colors[labels[i]], markersize = 10)

plt.scatter(centroids[:, 0],centroids[:, 1], marker = "x", s=150, linewidths = 5,
zorder = 10)

plt.show()
```

Running this code provides the following output:

[[1.16666667 1.46666667] [7.33333333 9.]]

[0 1 0 1 0 1]

('coordinate:', array([1., 2.]), 'label:', 0)

('coordinate:', array([5., 8.]), 'label:', 1)

('coordinate:', array([1.5, 1.8]), 'label:', 0)

('coordinate:', array([8., 8.]), 'label:', 1)

('coordinate:', array([1., 0.6]), 'label:', 0)

('coordinate:', array([9., 11.]), 'label:', 1)

Try this code to help you understand better:

```
from sklearn.cluster import KMeans

df = pd.read_csv('iris_df.csv')

df.columns = ['X1', 'X2', 'X3', 'X4', 'Y']

df = df.drop(['X4', 'X3'], 1)

df.head()

from sklearn.cross_validation import train_test_split

kmeans = KMeans(n_clusters = 3)

X = df.values[:, 0:2]

kmeans.fit(X)

df['Pred'] = kmeans.predict(X)

df.head()

sns.set_context('notebook', font_scale = 1.1)

sns.set_style('ticks')

sns.lmplot('X1','X2', scatter = True, fit_reg = False, data = df, hue = 'Pred')
```

And the output of this is:

<seaborn.axisgrid.FacetGrid at 0x107ad6a0>

Random Forest

Random Forest is one of the more popular of the supervised ensemble algorithms. By "ensemble", we mean that it uses a group of "weak" learners and getting them to work together to form a predictor that is stronger. In the Random Forest, the weak learners are decision trees that are randomly implemented and brought together to form the forest.

Look at this code:

from sklearn.ensemble import RandomForestClassifier

df = pd.read_csv('iris_df.csv')

df.columns = ['X1', 'X2', 'X3', 'X4', 'Y']

df.head()

from sklearn.cross_validation import train_test_split

forest = RandomForestClassifier()

X = df.values[:, 0:4]

Y = df.values[:, 4]

trainX, testX, trainY, testY = train_test_split(X, Y, test_size = 0.3)

forest.fit(trainX, trainY)

print('Accuracy: \n', forest.score(testX, testY))

pred = forest.predict(testX)

The output is:

('Accuracy: \n', 1.0)

Ensemble methods have the goal to combine predictions from multiple base estimators that have been built using a specified learning algorithm and the idea is to improve generalization over one estimator.

Inside the module called sklearn.ensemble, there are 2 averaging algorithms that have their basis in random decision trees – the method called Extra-Trees and the algorithm called RandomForest. Both are classified as 'perturb and combine' techniques designed specifically for trees. What this means is that a diverse classifier set is created by pushing randomness into the construction of the classifier. The ensemble prediction is the average prediction of all the individual classifiers.

Each forest classifier must be fitted with 2 arrays:

- A dense or a sparse array X of size [n_samples, n_features]

- A Y of size array [n_samples]

These arrays hold the class labels, or target values, for all the training samples, as in the next code:

from sklearn.ensemble import RandomForestClassifier

X = [[0, 0], [1, 1]]

Y = [0, 1]

clf = RandomForestClassifier(n_estimators = 10)

clf = clf.fit(X, Y)

Like a decision tree, forests will extend to problems that are multi-output, for example, Y is an array of size [n_samples, n_outputs]. In scikit-learn, classifiers are combined through an average of probabilistic prediction, rather than each of the classifiers voting for one class.

Random Forest is a trademark that describes a decision tree ensemble. Each collection of these decision trees is called a "forest", and for a new object to be classified on attributes, each of the trees will provide a classification and the tree will 'vote' for that class. The forest will choose the classification that earns the most votes.

Each of the trees in the forest is planted and then grown like this:

- If there are N number of cases contained in the training set, a random sample of N cases will be taking but replaced. This sample will become the training set required for the tree to grow.

- If the tree has M number of input variables, m<<M number will be specified in such a way that, at each tree node, random m variables are selected from M and the node is split based on the best split of m. The m value will remain constant throughout the growth of the forest.

- Each of the trees will be grown as large as possible and no pruning will happen.

Dimensionality Reduction Algorithm

Another of the commonly used unsupervised learning tasks is dimensionality reduction. Some problems can have hundreds of thousands, even up to millions of explanatory or input variables and these are computationally expensive. Not only that, if some of those variables are full of noise or bear no relevance to the underlying relationship, the generalization ability of the program could be diminished significantly.

We use dimensionality reduction to find those input variables that will cause the biggest changes in the response or output variable. We can also use dimensionality reduction for visualization of the data. Regression problems can be easily visualized, such as those that predict property prices from the size and plot the property size on the x-axis with the price plotted on the y-axis of the graph. In much the same way, we can easily visualize the same problem of price regression when we add in another explanatory variable. We could, for example, plot how many rooms are in the property on the z-axis. However, when we have a problem that has thousands of these input variables, it isn't possible to visualize it.

With dimensionality reduction, we can reduce impossibly large sets of these explanatory variables to more manageable sets of input variables that will hold on to the most information they possibly can.

The one-dimensionality algorithm that is very useful for data analysis is PCA. With this, we can reduce how many computations are needed in a model when we have thousands of input variables, all different. Because PCA is unsupervised, the user will still be required to analyze all the results and ensure that around 95% of the behavior from the original dataset is maintained.

This can be better understood by the following code:

```
from sklearn import decomposition

df = pd.read_csv('iris_df.csv')

df.columns = ['X1', 'X2', 'X3', 'X4', 'Y']

df.head()

from sklearn import decomposition

pca = decomposition.PCA()

fa = decomposition.FactorAnalysis()

X = df.values[:, 0:4]

Y = df.values[:, 4]

train, test = train_test_split(X,test_size = 0.3)

train_reduced = pca.fit_transform(train)

test_reduced = pca.transform(test)

print(pca.n_components_)
```

This code will output the following:

In the last decade, we have seen an aggressive rise in the capture of data at all possible points and levels. Not only are we seeing research organizations, governmental agencies and corporations producing new sources of data, they are also capturing extremely detailed data at multiple stages and points.

For example, we see e-commerce businesses capturing more and more customer data, such as browsing preferences, demographics, purchase history, dislikes, likes, and more as a way of giving more personalized attention to their customers. The available data may have many thousands of different features and it is challenging to try reducing that data while keeping most of the information. This is where dimensionality reduction can really help.

Boosting Algorithms

Boosting algorithms are a family of algorithms that are able to change a weak learner into a strong one. We can understand this better by looking at the problem of identifying spam emails. The first step is identifying whether an email is spam by using this criterion:

- An email contains just one advertising image – this is spam
- An email has only got links – this is spam
- The body of the email consists of a sentence similar to "you have a won a cash prize of $xxx" – this is spam
- An email is from an official domain that you are a member of and you know it to be real – this is not spam
- The email comes from a source that you know, such as a friend or family member – this is not spam

What we have done here is define a number of rules that initially classify an email as being spam or not spam. However, each individual rule is not strong enough to classify the emails and, as such, the rules are weak learners.

To change a weak learner to a strong one, the predictions from each of the weak learners are combined through methods such as:

- Using an average or weighted average
- Consider a prediction that has a much higher vote than the others

For example, let's say that we have 7 of these weak learners defined. Of these, 5 have been voted as spam and 2 are not spam. By default, an email is considered as spam because the highest vote is for 'spam'.

How It Works

Boosting algorithms will combine a weak or a base learner to form one strong rule. We are going to look at how weak rules may be identified by boosting.

To find weak rules, the ML or base-learning algorithms are applied with different distributions. Every time one of these base-learning algorithms is applied, we have a brand-new weak prediction rule. Iteration processes are used by this multiple times and, after several iterations, the boosting algorithm will combine all the weak rules into one strong one.

These steps should be followed to find the correct distribution for each of the rounds:

1. The base learner will take every distribution and assign each one with an equal weight.
2. If the initial base-learning algorithm causes a prediction error, a higher weight is paid to those observations that have a prediction error.

Step 2 needs to be iterated repeatedly until we reach the limit of the base-learning algorithm or we attain higher accuracy, whichever comes first. Lastly, the outputs from the weak learners are combined and a strong learner is produced and this will, in time, improve the model's predictive powers. Boosting algorithms focus more on the examples that have not been classified properly or because of weak rules, they have a much higher level of errors.

Boosting Algorithm Types

There are three main boosting algorithms:

- XGBoost
- Gradient Tree Boosting
- Adaptive Boosting – AdaBoost

We are going to discuss in more detail the two most common ones, Gradient and AdaBoost.

AdaBoost

AdaBoost will use different weighted data for fitting sequences of weak learners. The first thing it does is predict the original set of data and provide each observation with an equal weight. If the first learner produces wrong predictions, higher weights are applied to the incorrectly predicted observations. Because this is an iterative process, the learners will continue to be added until a given limit either in the accuracy or in the model number is reached.

With AdaBoost, decision stamps are used most of the time but the base learner can be any type of machine learning algorithm provided it will accept weights on the data in the training set. AdaBoost can be used for regression and classification and the following Python code may be used:

#for classification

from sklearn.ensemble import AdaBoostClassifier

#for regression

from sklearn.ensemble import AdaBoostRegressor

from sklearn.tree import DecisionTreeClassifier

dt = DecisionTreeClassifier()

clf = AdaBoostClassifier(n_estimators=100, base_estimator=dt,learning_rate=1)

#The base estimator is a decision tree but you can use any machine learning learner provided it will take sample weights.

clf.fit(x_train,y_train)

Tuning Parameters

The parameters for optimal algorithm performance can be tuned and the key parameters to be tuned are:

- **n_estimators** – Used for controlling how many weak learners are used.

- **learning_rate** – Used for controlling what contribution is made by the weak learners when they are combined at the end. There will be a trade-off between n_estimators and learning_rate.

- **base_estimators** – These are used to help in specifying the different machine learning algorithms.

The base learner parameters can be tuned to optimize their performance as well.

Gradient Boosting

With gradient boosting, a lot of models are sequentially trained. Each new one will minimize the loss function of the entire system using gradient descent: y = ax + b + e (e indicates the error term). The learning method will fit the new models consecutively to provide a response variable estimate that is far more accurate.

The idea is to construct some new base learners which can then be correlated optimally with the loss function negative gradient, relevant to the entire ensemble. The sklearn library in Python has Gradient Tree Boosting (GBRT) a boosting generalization to loss functions that are arbitrarily differentiable. We can use GBRT for classification and regression and the following code may be used:

#for classification

from sklearn.ensemble import GradientBoostingClassifier

#for regression

from sklearn.ensemble import GradientBoostingRegressor

clf = GradientBoostingClassifier(n_estimators = 100, learning_rate = 1.0, max_depth = 1)

clf.fit(X_train, y_train)

The terms we used here are:

- **n_estimators** – To control the weak learner numbers.

- **learning_rate** – To control what contribution the weak learners make to the final combination; again, there is a trade-off between n_estimators and learning_rate.

- **max_depth** – The maximum depth to which the individual estimators (regression) will go and this will limit how many nodes are in a tree. This parameter is tuned to get the best performance; the best value will depend on what interaction there is between the input variables.

You can also tune the loss function for a much better performance.

Applications for Python Machine Learning

Machine learning and Artificial Intelligence are everywhere we go. There's a good chance that you already use them in your day-to-day life and are not even aware of it. With machine learning, devices, software, and computers all perform using cognition that is very much like that of the human brain.

Some of the more common applications of machine learning that have proved successful include programs for detecting and decoding handwriting, voice, facial and speech recognition programs, programs for detecting spam email, weather forecasts, stock predictions, and more. We'll look at some of these in more detail to finish this section of the book.

Virtual Personal Assistants

Most of us use these now – Google Now, Siri, and Alexa are just 3 examples of VPAs, used to help us search out information when we ask them to by voice. All you need to do is activate the assistant and ask it a question. To answer, the assistant application will look for the correct information, look at previous queries you may have made and will also look at other sources to get the right answer. You can also use a virtual personal assistant to do things like set an alarm or to set reminders.

Analysis and Prediction of Traffic Congestion

Something many of us use is GPS navigation and these monitor your location, your velocity and then use them to build a current traffic map, to help prevent traffic congestion. This kind of machine learning is helpful to estimate areas where congestion is common based on earlier records.

Automated Video Surveillance

Most video surveillance is AI-powered, using machine learning technology to detect crimes and prevent them before they happen. These systems will track suspicious behavior and notify human attendants by alert giving them the chance to help prevent crime and accidents.

Social Media

Perhaps the most well-known use of machine learning is social media like Facebook. It constantly monitors your search patterns, your friends, interests, where you work or live, and so on, to provide you with a list of recommendations for friends. Twitter does the same, as do many of the other social media sites.

Face Recognition

When you upload an image of you and a friend, sites like Facebook will recognize that friend immediately. Facial recognition is also used in many security technologies and the core technology behind the Computer Vision techniques of extracting information from videos and images is machine learning.

Filtering Email Spam and Malware

Machine learning is used a great deal to detect spam and malware. The databases that hold the relevant information are constantly being updated for more efficient detection.

Customer Support Online

Many websites offer customer support in the form of an online chat where you chat with a computer in most cases. These are called chatbots and they will extract information from your query and from the website to get the right answer for you. As time goes by, the chatbots will learn a better understanding of your queries and will become more efficient to provide the best answer. All of this is made possible using machine learning algorithms.

Refining Search ENGINE Results

Most search engines will make use of machine learning to provide better results for users. Whenever a search request is made, the algorithms will watch the responses from the searchers. Depending on these results, those algorithms will work to improve the results.

Recommendations for Products

When you make a purchase online or you search for a specific product, you will often receive emails offering similar products or adverts about the product you searched for or your purchases. Based on your previous online behavior, the online company will send you recommendations for other products.

Online Fraud Detection

Lastly, machine learning is used to track financial fraud online. PayPal uses machine learning to stop money laundering for example; they use a toolkit that will help them to compare transactions in the millions making distinctions between illegal and legal transactions between parties.

That concludes machine learning with Python. It is by no means an exhaustive discussion because the subject is simply too large and too complex to discuss in such a short space, but I hope I have been able to give you an overview. Next, we look at Python and Django.

Chapter 16: Python and Django

An Introduction to Django

When the internet first came about, every web page would be written by hand and updates to websites would have meant editing the HTML by redoing each page individually. It didn't take long to realize that this kind of approach was never going to work. To fix this, hackers at the National Center for Supercomputing Applications (NCSA) allowed external programs to spawn from the server and these could generate the HTML dynamically. Thus, Common Gateway Interface (CGI) was born, and it changed the face of the internet forever.

However, CGI wasn't without its problems, mostly in the need for repetitive coding. So PHP was designed to fix those problems, fast becoming the most used tool for website creation. But again, PHP had its problems – bad code, insecure, and more. This is why new web frameworks were developed, the ones we use today. These new frameworks have brought about an increase in ambition with web developers being expected to do much more as each day passes and that's where Django steps into the picture.

A Brief History of Django

Django came to life in 2003 when Simon Williamson and Adrian Holovaty, web programmers for the Lawrence Journal-World newspaper, started using Python to build applications. Because the nature of news websites means they needed to be built and updated fast, Adrian and Simon built a web development framework that saved time allowing them to build applications that could be maintained under hard deadlines.

In 2005, the team opted to release their framework to the public as an open-source framework naming it after Django Reinhardt, a jazz guitarist. Because it was first built to service news sites, Django has a number of features that make it ideal for so-called "content sites", like Craigslist and Amazon, websites that offer dynamic information driven by databases, as well as being effective to build other types of website.

It's also important to note that, because Django rose from real-world code, it has a focus on real-world problems, those faced by the developers when they developed the framework and those being faced now; that is what makes Django dynamic, constantly updated to be improved. The idea of Django is to save developers time, ensure maintainable applications can be built, and to perform effectively even when heavily loaded.

Django allows developers to build websites that are deep and dynamic in a very short time. It takes the hard work out of developing leaving users to focus on the fun and taking away the repetitive parts of the job. Because of this, Django can provide high-level abstractions of the most common patterns in web development, shortcuts for programming jobs done frequently, and very clear conventions on solving problems. While providing all this, Django does its best not to get in the way leaving you to do as much work outside the framework scope as you want. Django is about making web development fun and easy. Over the course of this section, we will look at the basics of installing and using the framework.

Installing Django

To get going with Django, you need to know how to install it and you need to understand the Model-View-Controller (MVC) design pattern. The latter is very important for those who are new to computer programming or who have previously used a programming language that doesn't make a clear separation between the logic and the data behind the website to the way it is shown on screen.

The philosophy behind Django is called 'loose coupling' and this is also the philosophy that underlies MVC. We'll go into more detail about this later because an understanding of MVC means a better understanding of Django. First though, let's install some software.

There are three steps to doing this:

- Install Python – you should already have this
- Install a PVE – Python Virtual Environment
- Install Django

These installation instructions are aimed at Windows users; for Mac and Linux users it is best to go directly to the Django website for full installation instructions. Windows users should also consider using Visual Studio Code Editor. Microsoft provides this free of charge as a way of providing support to both Python and Django programmers.

Creating Your Project Directory

Before we get started, we need a project directory. This can be saved anywhere on your desktop or laptop although you should really create it within your user directory – this will avoid any issues with permissions later. For now, we'll use the My Documents folder.

1. Create a new folder in My Documents and call it mysite_project
2. Open a command window on your computer (Press the Windows and X buttons on your keyboard and choose Command Window or PowerShell, depending on which version of Windows you are running).
3. We need to create a virtual environment so, at the command prompt, type in the following command (don't forget to replace *your name* with the name of your user directory:

C:\Users*your name*\OneDrive\Documents\mysite_project> virtualenv env_mysite

You should see something like this:

Using base prefix 'c:\\users*your name*\\appdata\\local\\programs\\python\\python36-32'

New python executable in C:\Users*your name*\OneDrive\Documents\mysite_project\env_mysite\Scripts\python.exe

Installing setuptools, pip, wheel...done.

4. Once that is done open the project directory in Windows Explorer to see what has been created. You should see a folder named \env_mysite – open this folder and the following should be in it:

\Include

\Lib

\Scripts

pip-selfcheck.json

Inside \Lib, virtualenv has created a separate installation of Python allowing you to work on the project without any effect on the rest of your computer software.

5. The next step is to activate the virtual environment before you use it. Go back to the command window and type the following at the prompt:

env_mysite\scripts\activate

The activate script from the \scripts folder will run and you should see this at the command prompt:

(env_mysite) C:\Users*your name*\OneDrive\Documents\mysite_project>

6. Next, we must install Django. To do this, go to your command prompt once more and type:

pip install django==2.0

This tells pip to install Django and you should see the following output:

(env_mysite) C:\Users*your name*\OneDrive\Documents\mysite_project> pip install django==2.0

Collecting django==2.0

Using cached Django-2.0-py2.py3-none-any.whl

Collecting pytz (from django==1.11)

Using cached pytz-2018.2-py2.py3-none-any.whl

Installing collected packages: pytz, django

Successfully installed django-2.0 pytz-2018.2

At the time of writing, v2.0 is the latest Django version; if it has moved on by the time you read this, make sure you install the latest version. Now you can test to see if the installation worked; at the virtual environment command prompt, type python and press enter. If the installation worked, the Django module can be imported, and you will see this:

(env_mysite) C:\Users*your name*\OneDrive\Documents\mysite_project> python

Python 3.6.1 (v3.6.1:69c0db5, Aug 14 2018, 17:54:52) [MSC v.1900 32 bit (Intel)] on win32

Type "help", "copyright", "credits" or "license" for more information.

>>> import django

>>> django.get_version()

'2.0'

>>>

Starting Your New Project

Now that everything is installed, we can create a new project – this is just a collection of the settings needed for a new instance of Django. If you have never used Django before, you will need to do a little bit of setting up first. Some code needs to be auto-generated to establish your project and this code has the settings needed for the Django instance – Django options, database configurations, and the settings specific to the application. You should still be using your virtual environment for this and you should be in the mysite_project directory.

Go to the command line in your virtual environment and type:

django-admin startproject mysite

This will create a directory called mysite inside the project directory and will also provide the files needed for a very basic Django website that is fully functioning.

Note

Do NOT name any projects the same as any of the built-in Django or Python components. For example, do not use the name Django as it will cause conflict with Django and do not use the name 'test' as it will cause conflict with a package built-in to Python.

Let's see what startproject did:

mysite/

manage.py

mysite/

__init__.py

settings.py

urls.py

wsgi.py

These are the files that were created by startproject. Here's what each one does:

- **mysite/** - outer - this is the root directory and is nothing more than a project container. Can be renamed as anything.

- **manage.py** – command line utility for interaction with the Django project
- **mysite/** - inner – Python package for the project and is the name used for importing anything in the project.
- **mysite/ __init__.py** – empty file informing Python that the directory should be seen as a Python package.
- **mysite/settings.py** – settings and configuration for the project
- **mysite/urls.py** – URL declarations for the project, a table of contents if you like
- **mysite/wsgi.py** – entry-point for web servers that are WSGI-compatible to serve the Django project

Setting Up the Database

By default, there are several applications in Django already and some of these will use at least one, usually more, database table. Because of this, we must create the tables in a database before they can be used. To do this, we go into the mysite folder that we just created by typing cd mysite at the command prompt and then type this command:

python manage.py migrate

This command will create an SQLite database and the required tables as per the settings file that the startproject command created. If everything goes as it should, you will see something like this:

(env_mysite) C:\Users*your name*\OneDrive\Documents\mysite_project\mysite>python manage.py migrate

Operations to perform:

Apply all migrations: admin, auth, contenttypes, sessions

Running migrations:

Applying contenttypes.0001_initial... OK

Applying auth.0001_initial... OK

Applying admin.0001_initial... OK

Normally, this would not be something that a beginner should attempt, but Django makes life very easy by installing SQLite and configuring it for you.

Development Server

Now we should make sure that the project works so if needed, go to the outer mysite directory at the command prompt and then run these commands:

python manage.py runserver

You should see the following output:

Performing system checks...

System check identified no issues (0 silenced).

August 14, 2018 - 16:48:29

Django version 1.11, using settings 'mysite.settings'

Starting development server at http://127.0.0.1:8000/

Quit the server with CTRL-BREAK.

What we have done is started the development server for Django. This is a lightweight server that has been written in Python. It was included in Django to allow for rapid development without the need to configure production servers until you need them.

Do NOT use this server in a production environment as it is purely for development. Now that it is up and running, open your web browser and go to http://127.0.0.1:8000 and you will be taken to a page that says, "Welcome to Django".

You will find that the server will reload the Python code automatically as required for each request. There is no need to restart for any changes to the code to take effect but some things, such as adding files, will require a manual restart.

That is it for installation, time to look at MVC.

MVC – Model-View-Controller Design Pattern

This concept is almost as old as the hills but since the development of the internet, it has grown significantly since it is the best way of designing applications based on client-server. Pick any good web framework and you'll find it has been built using this concept and it is one that you will find very easy to understand:

- **M (Model)** – data model or representation. This is not the data, merely an interface to it and it will let you pull the data out of the database without needing to know the intricacies of that database. The model will provide you with an abstraction layer, so it can be used with more than one database.
- **V (View)** – this is what you see, the model presentation layer. On a computer, the view is what is displayed in a browser for web applications as the user interface in a desktop application. You will also get an interface used for collection of user input.
- **C (Controller)** – this will control the way the information flows between the first two components – M and V. Logic programmed into it is used to determine what information should come from the database through the model and what gets passed on to the view. It will also take the user information from view and will implement business logic, by modifying the data via the model, changing the view or doing both.

It starts getting a bit difficult because there are some very different interpretations about what goes on at each layer, but you don't need to worry about this. All you need to understand at this stage is how the MVC design pattern is implemented by Django and how closely it follows that pattern. However, despite this, Django does insert its own logic into the implementation.

The framework handles the 'C' part of MVC and a lot of the exciting stuff in Django takes place in the models, templates, and views – for this reason, you will often see Django called an MTV pattern and, in this:

- **M** is Model – this is the data-access layer and it holds everything relating to the data – how it is accessed, validated, the behaviors the data has and any relationships that exist between data.
- **T** is Template – this is the presentation layer and it holds all decisions related to presentation, such as how information is displayed on web pages or some other document.
- **V** is View – this is the business logic layer and it holds the logic that is responsible for accessing the model and deferring to the right template. It is something like a bridge that joins the models and the templates.

You now have Django and everything else you need installed, your development server is up and running so it's time to start looking into Django. We will start with Django views and the basics of using Django to serve a web page.

Views and URL-Confs

In this part, you will begin to learn how to create web pages in Django, in particular, dynamic web pages. We will start with the Hello World, the example that all programming languages use as their first one. What we want to do is create a web page that says "Hello World" on it. If you were not using a framework, all you would do is type the text "Hello World" in a text file, save it as hello.html, and then upload it into a web server directory. What you provide are two key pieces of information – the contents of the web page and the URL.

Your First View

With Django, you still provide that same information but differently – you use a View function for the webpage contents and a URLconf to specify the URL. Let's get down to business and write the view function.

Go to the inner mysite directory that you created earlier and, inside it, create a new file named views.py – this is where your views will be stored. Ensure that the file is saved in the inner mysite directory – it mustn't go in the directory that has manage.py in it because it won't work.

In that file, type in the following code – this is the whole view function for "Hello World", including the import statements:

from django.http import HttpResponse

def hello(request):

  return HttpResponse("Hello world")

It's quite an easy piece of code. We started by importing the class called HttpResponse from the module called django.http. This class is going to be used later in the code. Next, a function is defined, called hello. This is our view function and, like all view functions, it will take one or more parameters – in Django, these are called requests. This request is an object and in it is all the information pertaining to the web request that triggered off the view. It is an instance of a class called django.HttpRequest.

We're not going to do anything with this request, but regardless of that, it has to be the first view parameter. Note that it doesn't matter what the view name is. Django doesn't require a specific naming convention to recognize it; we've called it hello purely because it indicates what the view is about.

The function does nothing more than finding an HttpResponse object that was instantiated with the "Hello World" text and return it. Later we'll look at how Django finds the function, but for now, all you need to understand is that a view is nothing more than a function with an initial parameter of HttpRequest that returns an HttpResponse instance. A Python function must do both to be considered a Django view.

Your First URLconf

If you were to run python manage.py runserver at this stage, you would still be faced with the message "Welcome to Django". You won't see "Hello World" anywhere on the page and this is because we haven't yet told mysiteproject that there is a hello view. What we need to do is explicitly tell Django that this view is to be activated at a specific URL. To do this, we need to use a URLconf.

What is a URLconf? Think of it as being a contents table for your website. It is nothing more than a mapping between the URLs and the relevant view functions. It is the way in which we tell Django that we want a specific code called for a specific URL. In the last section, django-admin startproject was executed, a URLconf was automatically created, a file called urls.py. The default URLconf looks like this:

from django.conf.urls import url

from django.contrib import admin

urlpatterns = [

   url(r'^admin/', admin.site.urls),

]

In line 1, we are importing two functions. These come from django.conf.urls and include, which lets you add a Python import path that leads to a second URLconf module and url, which makes use of a regular expression to match the pattern of the URL to a Django module.

Next, we call admin, a function in the module called django.contrib. The include function will call this so that the URLs for the admin site can be loaded. Last, urlpatterns is simply a list of the instances of url().

The important thing here is urlpatterns, a variable that Django wants to see in the module called URLconf. It is responsible for defining the mapping from the URL to the handling code. Adding a URL and a view to URLconf is a simple matter of adding a mapping from a URL pattern to a view function.

This is how we pull in our hello view:

```
from django.conf.urls import url

from django.contrib import admin


from mysite.views import hello


urlpatterns = [

    url(r'^admin/', admin.site.urls),

    url(r'^hello/$', hello),

]
```

Note that there are two changes:

First, the hello view was imported from the module, mysite/views.py. in the import syntax for Python, this reads as mysite.views. Secondly, url(r'^hello/$', hello), was added to urlpatterns. We call this line a URLpattern and the url() function is telling Django how the URL you configure should be handled. The initial argument is the pattern-matcher string while the second is view function needed for the pattern.

Note the 'r' at the start of the regular expression. This tells Python that it is dealing with a raw string, i.e. backslashes should not be interpreted by the contents. In a normal string, a backslash is used to escape a special character, for example, \n – a string of one character with a newline. When it is turned into a raw string, the backslash escape is not applied so r'\n' will become a string of two characters, with a newline and a literal backslash. Best practice with Django regular expressions is to use raw strings to avoid the collision that occurs between regular expression backslashes and the way that Python uses the backslash.

What we just did was told Django that the hello view function should handle any requests to the /hello/ URL. As it might not be obvious, we'll just take a bit of time to discuss this syntax. We want the /hello/ URL matched but the pattern doesn't look quite as it should and here's why:

Django takes the slash away from the start of all incoming URLs before URLpattern is checked. What this means it that URLpattern will not have that first slash in /hello/. Although this doesn't look intuitive, it does make things much simpler, especially when URL-confs are included inside other URLconfs.

Second, there is a caret and a dollar sign in the pattern. Both are characters that have special meanings in regular expressions. The caret is denoting that the pattern must match the beginning of the string and the dollar sign is denoting that the pattern must match the end. In short, if we had specified ∧hello/ and not used a dollar sign, any of the URLs that begin with /hello/ would match while using hello/$, without the caret would cause a match with any URL that ended with hello/. The only way to make sure an exact match is found is to use both ∧ and $.

One other thing of note: the hello view function has been passed as an object without the function being called. This is one of the best things about Python; a function is a first-class object that means they can be passed around the same way as any variable.

Open your Python virtual environment and run python manage.py runserver and this will detect any changes to your code automatically and will reload it as required. This means there is no need to restart the server when you make a change. Because the server is running at http://127.0.0.1:8000/, open your browser and then open http://127.0.0.1:8000/hello/ - you should now see Hello World on the webpage.

Regular Expressions

Often termed as a regex, a regular expression is a neat way to specify a pattern within the text. In practice, you will likely only use a small selection of the regex symbols, the most common of which are shown below:

. (dot)

Match with any single character

\d

Match with any single digit

[A-Z]

Match with any of the characters between uppercase A and Z

[a-z]

Match with any of the characters between lowercase a and z

[A-Za-z]

Match with any of the characters between a and z but case-sensitive

+

Match at least one of the last expression. i.e. \d+ will match at least one digit

[^/]+

Match at least one character up to but not including the forward slash

?

Match Zero or one of the last expression. i.e. \d? will match at least zero digits

*

Match Zero or more of the last expression. i.e. \d* will match at least zero digits

{1,3}

Match one to three of the last expression. i.e. \d{1, 3} will match up to three digits

Django Request Processing

Before we move on, let's see how requests are processed by Django. What is Django doing to show you the Hello World message when you visit the URL? It all begins with the file called Settings. When python manage.py runserver is run, the script will search in the inner mysite directory for a file with the name of settings.py. This file has the configuration for the project and each one is in uppercase i.e. DATABASES, TEMPLATES, etc.

ROOT_URLCONF.ROOT_URLCONF is the most important because it is telling Django the name of the Python module required as the URLconf. Think back to when settings.py and urls.py were create by django-admin startproject; settings.py contained a setting for ROOT_URLCONF that pointed to urls.py. Open settings.py and you should see this:

ROOT_URLCONF = 'mysite.urls'

This directly corresponds to a file named mysite/urls.py and, when a request is received for a specific URL, Django will load the URLconf to which ROOT_URLCONF points. It will then go through each URLpattern in the URLconf to find a match to the requested URL. When a match is found, the view function for the pattern is called and the first parameter passed to it is an

HttpRequest object. And, as you know, view functions must return HttpResponses. Once this is done, Django will convert that object into a web response containing the webpage content.

Dynamic Content – Second View

Now we'll look at the second view, dynamic content. The view for Hello World was helpful in showing how Django works but it isn't a dynamic webpage. Why? Because the content never changes. Whenever you go to /hello/ the same thing will be displayed.

For the second view, we'll create a webpage that shows the current time and date, a little more dynamic. This is quite simple because no databases are needed and no user input – it is the output from the internal clock in the server.

This view must do two things – determine the date and time and return that value in an HttpResponse. Python already has a datetime module for calculation of dates so look at this demo using the interactive interpreter in Python:

C:\Users*your name*>python

Python 3.6.1 (v3.6.1:69c0db5, Aug 14, 2018, 17:54:52) [MSC v.1900 32 bit (Intel)] on win32

Type "help", "copyright", "credits" or "license" for more information.

>>> *import datetime*

>>> *now = datetime.datetime.now()*

>>> *now*

datetime.datetime(2017, 5, 20, 14, 32, 25, 412665)

>>> *print (now)*

2017-05-20 14:32:25.412665

```
>>>
```

That is easy enough and Django didn't get involved at all; it is nothing more than Python code. For a Django view that shows the updated time and date, we need the datetime.datetime.now() statement hooked into the view and an HttpResponse returned. The updated views.py will look like this:

from django.http import HttpResponse

import datetime

def hello(request):

  return HttpResponse("Hello world")

def current_datetime(request):

  now = datetime.datetime.now()

  html = "<html><body>It is now %s.</body></html>" % now

  return HttpResponse(html)

What we have done is added an import datetime at the top so the dates can be calculated. The function called current.datetime will determine the date and time and store the datetime.datetime object as a local variable.

In line 2, we use the built-in format-string capability from Python to construct the HTML response. % inside the string is a placeholder and % at the end is saying that the % in the preceding string should be replaced with the current value of the variable called now. That variable is nothing more than a datetime.datetime object; it isn't a string but the use of the % converts it into a string representation and the result of this is an HTML string.

Lastly, an HttpResponse object is returned by view and this contains the response. After this has been added to views.py, the URLpattern is added, informing Django of the URL that should handle the view; like this:

from django.conf.urls import url

from django.contrib import admin

from mysite.views import hello, current_datetime

urlpatterns = [

   url(r'^admin/', admin.site.urls),

   url(r'^hello/$', hello),

   url(r'^time/$', current_datetime),

]

Again, two changes have been made. First, the function called current.datetime has been imported at the start and second, most important, a URLpattern that maps URL/time/ to the new view has been added.

Loose Coupling and URLconfs

Now would be a good time to look at one of the underlying philosophies of both URLconfs and Django – loose coupling. In basic terms, loose coupling is a developmental approach that supports the interchangeability of pieces. If we loosely couple two bits of code, a change made to one piece will not affect the other or, if it does, it will be minor.

The URLconfs in Django is a good example; in a web application built with Django, the URL definitions and their view functions are loosely coupled. This means that the URL decision for a function and the function implementation are in two different places.

For example: the current_datetime view we are using. If we need to make a change to the URL, i.e. from /time/ to /current-time/, we would change URLconf and the view would not be affected. In the same way, if we needed to make a change to the view function, perhaps change the logic, the URL would not be affected.

In the following example, the current_datetime is at two different URLs:

urlpatterns = [

    url(r'^admin/', admin.site.urls),

    url(r'^hello/$', hello),

    url(r'^time/$', current_datetime),

    url(r'^another-time-page/$', current_datetime),

]

Dynamic URLs – Third View

Back to our current_datetime view, the page contents are dynamic, but the URL called /time/ is static. Most of the time, the URL will have parameters that have a direct influence on the page output. What we want to do is create another view that shows the current date and the time but offset by several hours. Our goal is to make our site in a way that page/time/plus 1/ will show us the date and time an hour ahead, page /time/ plus 2/ is two hours ahead and so on.

A beginner would likely write new view functions for each of the offsets and this would give us a URLconf that looks like this:

urlpatterns = [

  url(r'^time/$', current_datetime),

```
url(r'^time/plus/1/$', one_hour_ahead),

url(r'^time/plus/2/$', two_hours_ahead),

url(r'^time/plus/3/$', three_hours_ahead),
]
```

The flaws here should be evident. Not only would we be creating view functions that are redundant, we also have an application that has been limited to just the hour ranges that have been defined. What we want to do is allow the application to handle any offset and the key to this is using wildcard URLpatterns. We know that a URLpattern is just a regular expression, so we can use one of the expression symbols we mentioned earlier, and that is d+ and this matches at least one digit:

```
urlpatterns = [

    #...

    url(r'^time/plus/\d+/$', hours_ahead),

    #...
]
```

The new pattern will match any URL that starts /time/ plus/. We will set a limit of 99 hours; to do this, we allow only one or two-digit numbers to be matched. The regex syntax for that is \d{1, 2}:

```
url(r'^time/plus/\d{1,2}/$', hours_ahead),
```

Now that we've designated a wildcard for the URL, we need a way of passing that wildcard data to the view function so that we can use a single view function for any arbitrary hour offset. We do this by placing parentheses around the data in the URLpattern that we want to save. In the case of our example, we want to save whatever number was entered in the URL, so let's put parentheses around the \d{1,2},
like this:

url(r'^time/plus/(\d{1,2})/$', hours_ahead),

If you're familiar with regular expressions, you'll be right at home here; we're using parentheses to *capture* data from the matched text. The final URLconf including our previous two views, looks like this:

from django.conf.urls import include, url

from django.contrib import admin

from mysite.views import hello, current_datetime, hours_ahead

urlpatterns = [

   url(r'^admin/', admin.site.urls),

   url(r'^hello/$', hello),

   url(r'^time/$', current_datetime),

   url(r'^time/plus/(\d{1,2})/$', hours_ahead),

]

You could, if you already have experience at programming, decide to use a query string parameter along the lines of /time/plus?hours=3 and the hours parameter will designate the hours in the query string that comes after '?'. This is possible, but Django likes its URLs to be smooth and beautiful.

A better way is to use the URL of /time/plus/3/ and is a good deal cleaner and infinitely more readable. Nice clean URLs are a good characteristic of a good web application and Django makes it much easier to use good URLs.

We can now write our view called hours_ahead. It is much like current_datetime but it has an additional argument and that is the number of offset hours:

```
from django.http import Http404, HttpResponse

import datetime


def hours_ahead(request, offset):

    try:

        offset = int(offset)

    except ValueError:

        raise Http404()

    dt = datetime.datetime.now() + datetime.timedelta(hours=offset)

    html = "<html><body>In %s hour(s), it will be  %s.</body></html>" %
(offset, dt)

    return HttpResponse(html)
```

In the hours_ahead view function, we have two parameters:

- request – this is an HttpRequest object
- offset – this is the string that the parentheses inside URLpattern captures.

The variable has been named as offset, but you can name it what you want so long as it stays within the conventions of naming Python identifiers. The name is irrelevant; what is important is that, after request, this is the second argument.

In the function, the very first thing to do is call, on offset, int(). This will change the Unicode value to an integer. If you were to call this on a value that may not be converted, you will get a ValueError. You might be wondering how this could happen given that our regular expression will only capture digits, and as a result, the offset can only ever be a string of digits. In theory, it can't happen but there is always the chance that the view function may be called another way. Therefore, make it part of your best practice to check for ValueErrors and only implement a view function in such a way that no assumptions are made about the parameters – loose coupling!

The next line is where the current date and time are calculated, and the right number of hours added. We saw the datetime.datetime.now() function in current_datetimeview but the concept with the new one is that date and time arithmetic can be performed with an object called datetime.timedelta, with a datetime.datetime object added to it. The result is then stored in the dt variable. We can also see why int() was called on offset – datetime.timedelta requires that an integer is used for the hours parameter.

Next, the HTML output of the view function is constructed using the format-string capability from Python with a pair of values. Note that there is a pair of % symbols.

Lastly, the HTML HttpResponse is returned.

Now you can start your Django development server again and go to:

http://127.0.0.1:8000/time/plus/3/ to see if it works. Also try:

 http://127.0.0.1:8000/time/plus/17/ and http://127.0.0.1:8000/time/plus/72/.

Last, go to http://127.0.0.1:8000/time/plus/100/ to make sure that the URLconf pattern will only take numbers of one or two digits – you should see a "Page Not Found" error.

Up to now, our view functions have been written into the Python code using hard-code HTML. In reality, this doesn't happen. Django has a very powerful yet simple template engine that lets you keep the page design separate from the code so let's look at that now.

Django Templates

Although we used hardcoding to show you views in practice, it isn't really a good idea because, if you need to make a change to your page design, you need to change the code. It would be incredibly convenient if we could change the design without changing the code and we can do that by using the template system in Django.

Django templates are text strings used to keep presentation and data separate. Templates will define placeholders, along with basic logic for regulating presentation. What you must understand is that a Django template is NOT Python code embedded in HTML.

Let's look at a very simple example. This template has a description of an HTML page that is used for thanking someone when they place an order:

<html>

<head>

  <title>Ordering notice</title>

</head>

<body>

  <h1>Ordering notice</h1>

  <p>Dear {{ person_name }},</p>

  <p>Thank you for placing an order with {{ company }}. It will ship on {{ s

hip_date|date:"F j, Y" }}.</p>

  <p>Here are the items you've ordered:</p>

  <ul>

    {% for item in item_list %}

<li>{{ item }}</li>{% endfor %}

</ul>

{% if ordered_warranty %}

<p>Your warranty information is included in the packaging.</p>

{% else %}

<p>

You didn't order a warranty, so when things go wrong, you are on your own.

</p>

{% endif %}

*<p>Sincerely,
{{ company }}</p>*

</body>

</html>

This is HTML with template tags and variables. If a text is inside a pair of braces (), it is a variable. If text is inside curly braces with % signs, {%}, it is a template tag which is used for telling the system what it should do.

In this example, we have a for tag and an if tag. For tags work like Python for statements providing the ability to loop through each sequence item while the if tag works like an if statement. In our case, it checks to see if a given value will evaluate True. If yes, the template shows everything between a set of specified brackets; if not, different information is shown.

We also have a filter, an easy way to change a variable's format. In this template, in {{ ship_date|date:"F j, Y" }}, we pass the variable called ship_date to the date filter and provide that the filter with the argument of "F, j, Y". the dates are formatted as specified by the arguments and the pipe filter, |, is used to attach filters.

Every Django template can access a number of built-in filters and tags and we'll be talking briefly about some of these.

Using the Template System

We can configure any Django project with one or more templates and Django has a backend for its own templates called the Django Template Language (DTL). Before we move on, we'll look into DTL just to see how it works. First, we'll look at the easiest way to use the template system inside Python code and that is to provide a string as the raw template code to create the template object.

First, the object render() method is called using specified variables. This is called context. A rendered template is returned as a string and all variables and tags are evaluated as per this context. If we used the custom Python shell in Django of python manage.py shell, it would look like this:

>>> *from django import template*

>>> *t = template.Template('My name is {{ name }}.')*

>>> *c = template.Context({'name': 'Paul'})*

>>> *print (t.render(c))*

My name is Paul.

>>> *c = template.Context({'name': 'Michael'})*

>>> *print (t.render(c))*

My name is Michael.

Creating Template Objects

Direct instantiation is the best way to create a template object. The class called Template is in the module called django.template and one argument is taken by the constructor. That argument is the raw code. Open python manage.py shell from your mysite project directory and input the following:

>>> from django.template import Template

>>> t = Template('My name is {{ name }}.')

>>> print (t)

You should see this:

<django.template.base.Template object at 0x030396B0>

Ignore the number at the end; it will change every time and is nothing more than Python's way of identifying the template object.

When the object is created, the template system will compile the raw code so it is an optimized form ready to be rendered. If there are any syntax errors in the code, you will get a TemplateSyntaxError exception:

>>> from django.template import Template

>>> t = Template('{% notatag %}')

Traceback (most recent call last):

File "", line 1, in?

...

django.template.exceptions.TemplateSyntaxError: Invalid block tag on line 1: 'notatag'.

Did you forget to register or load this tag?

"block tag" is referring to {% notatag %}. Both "block tag" and "template tag" are the same and the error could have been raised for any one of these reasons:

- The tags are invalid
- Valid tags have invalid arguments

- The filters are invalid
- Valid filters have invalid arguments
- The template syntax is invalid
- Tags are left unclosed

Template Rendering

Data can be passed to a template object by providing it with a context, and this is nothing more than a set of variable names and the values that go with them. These are used to populate the variables of the template and a way of evaluating the tags. The context class is used to represent a context and this is found in the module called django.template. The constructor will take a single optional argument, a dictionary that maps the variable names to their values. The render() method is called with a context that tells it to fill up the template:

>>> from Django.template import Context, Template

>>> t = Template('My name is {{ name }}.')

>>> c = Context({'name': 'Stephen'})

>>> t.render(c)

'My name is Stephen.'

Dictionaries and Contexts

Python dictionaries are a map between keys and values of variables. Contexts are similar but have more functionality. A variable name must start with an uppercase or lowercase letter and may have letters, dots, underscores, and digits. They are also case-sensitive. Look at this example of the compilation and rendering of a template:

>>> from django.template import Template, Context

>>> raw_template = """<p>Dear {{ person_name }},</p>

...

```
... <p> Thank you for placing an order with {{ company }}. It will

... ship on {{ ship_date|date:"F j, Y" }}.</p>

...

... {% if ordered_warranty %}

... <p>Your warranty information is included in the packaging.</p>

... {% else %}

... <p> You didn't order a warranty, so when things go wrong, you are on your
own.</p>

... {% endif %}

...

... <p>Sincerely,<br />{{ company }}</p>"""

>>> t = Template(raw_template)

>>> import datetime

>>> c = Context({'person_name': 'Billy Bunter',

...     'company': 'Outdoor Equipment',

...     'ship_date': datetime.date(2017, 7, 2),

...     'ordered_warranty': False})

>>> t.render(c)

"<p>Dear Billy Bunter,</p>\n\n<p>Thank you for placing an order with
Outdoor Equipment. It\

will \nship on July 2,2017.</p>\n\n\n<p>You didn't order a warranty, so
when\
```

things go wrong\nyou're on your own.</p>\n\n\n<p>Sincerely,<br\

/>Outdoor Equipment</p>"

First, the Template and the Context classes are imported from the django.template module. The raw text is saved into the raw_template variable. Note the use of triple quotes for the string – this is because it goes over several lines.

We pass raw_template to the class constructor for Template to create an object, t. The datetime module is imported from the standard library in Python – it will be needed for the next statement.

A Context object, c, is then created and the constructor will take a dictionary which will map the names of the variables to the values.

Lastly, the render() method is called on the template object and passed to context. The rendered template is returned.

That is the basics of the template system in Django – write your template string, create the template object, create the Context, call render().

Multiple Contexts on One Template

It is perfectly possible to render several contexts through one template object like this:

>>> *from django.template import Template, Context*

>>> *t = Template('Hello, {{ name }}')*

>>> *print (t.render(Context({'name': 'John'})))*

Hello, John

>>> *print (t.render(Context({'name': 'Julie'})))*

Hello, Julie

```
>>> print (t.render(Context({'name': 'Pat'})))
```

Hello, Pat

Looking Up Context Variables

So far, we have only passed the contexts simple variables, strings and one example of datetime.date. However, the Django template system can easily handle data structures that are more complex, like dictionaries, lists, and custom objects. The key is in the dot character and this can be used for accessing attributes, keys, methods or object indices. We can see how this works better with some examples. First, accessing dictionary values by key:

```
>>> from django.template import Template, Context

>>> person = {'name': 'Sally', 'age': '43'}

>>> t = Template('{{ person.name }} is {{ person.age }} years old.')

>>> c = Context({'person': person})

>>> t.render(c)
```

'Sally is 43 years old.'

In the same way, a dot lets you gain access to object attributes. The datetime.date object has three attributes – year, month, day. Here's how to access them:

```
>>> from django.template import Template, Context

>>> import datetime

>>> d = datetime.date(2018, 8, 14)

>>> d.year
```

2018

```
>>> d.month
```

8

>>> *d.day*

14

>>> *t = Template('The month is {{ date.month }} and the year is {{ date.year }}.')*

>>> *c = Context({'date': d})*

>>> *t.render(c)*

'The month is 8 and the year is 2018.'

We can also use a dot to refer to an object method. For example, each string in Python contains the upper() and isdigit() methods and these can be called like this:

>>> *from django.template import Template, Context*

>>> *t = Template('{{ var }} -- {{ var.upper }} -- {{ var.isdigit }}')*

>>> *t.render(Context({'var': 'hello'}))*

'hello -- HELLO -- False'

>>> *t.render(Context({'var': '123'}))*

'123 -- 123 -- True'

Lastly, accessing list indices:

>>> *from django.template import Template, Context*

>>> *t = Template('Item 2 is {{ items.2 }}.')*

>>> *c = Context({'items': ['apples', 'bananas', 'carrots']})*

>>> *t.render(c)*

'Item 2 is carrots.'

Note – negative indices cause a TemplateSyntaxError.

Python List Indices

If you are new to programming, it is worth keeping in mind that all Python lists have zero-based indices. What this means is that the index starts at 0, item 2 is at index 1, item 3 is at index 2 and so on.

We can summarize a dot lookup in this way – when the Django template system comes across a dot in the name of the variable, it will attempt the lookups in this order:

- Dictionary
- Attribute
- Method call
- List Index

The system will go through the lookups and will make use of the first one it comes across that works. We call this "short-circuit" logic. All dot lookups may be nested and there is no real limit on how many levels deep this nesting can go. For example, the next code makes use of {{ person.name.upper }} – this is a dictionary lookup of (person['name'] followed by a method call of (upper()):

>>> *from django.template import Template, Context*

>>> *person = {'name': 'Sally', 'age': '43'}*

>>> *t = Template('{{ person.name.upper }} is {{ person.age }} years old.')*

>>> *c = Context({'person': person})*

>>> *t.render(c)*

'SALLY is 43 years old.'

Method Call Behavior

A method call is a little bit more complex in behavior than all the other types of lookup so you need to keep some things in mind:

During the method lookup, if an exception is raised by the method, that exception is propagated. The only exception is if an attribute of silent_variable_failure is attached to the exception and this has a value of True. If this attribute is attached, the variable is rendered as a value of the string_if_valid config option of the engine and this is by default, an empty string. Look at this example:

```
>>> t = Template("My name is {{ person.first_name }}.")

>>> class PersonClass3:

...     def first_name(self):

...         raise AssertionError("foo")

>>> p = PersonClass3()

>>> t.render(Context({"person": p}))

Traceback (most recent call last):

...

AssertionError: foo


>>> class SilentAssertionError(Exception):

...     silent_variable_failure = True

>>> class PersonClass4:

...     def first_name(self):
```

...   raise SilentAssertionError

>>> p = PersonClass4()

>>> t.render(Context({"person": p}))

'My name is.'

Method calls only work if there are no required arguments to the method. If there aren't any, the system moves on to the next type of lookup. By its design, Django will limit, intentionally, how much logic processing is made available in the template, so it isn't possible to pass an argument to any method call that has been accessed from within a template. Data must be calculated in a view and passed for display to the template.

Some methods will have side-effects and it would not be good practice to let the template system have access to them, not to mention it being a potential security risk. Let's say that you have an object called BankAccount and it has a method called delete(). If a template were to have, for example, {{ account.delete }}, in which account is an object of BankAccount, when the template has been rendered, the object is deleted. To stop this from happening, the function attribute of alters_data should be set on the method:

def delete(self):

   # Delete the account

   delete.alters_data = True

If any method has been marked like this, it will not be executed by the template system. Carrying on from the example, if {{ account.delete }} is included in a template, and alters_date=True is set on the delete() method, that delete() method won't get executed when template rendering happens; instead the variable is replaced by the engine with string_if_valid.

Note. The delete() and save() methods that are generated dynamically on the Django model objects will automatically have alters_data=true set.

Invalid Variable Handling

In general, if a variable is not in existence, the string_if_valid config option value of the engine is inserted by the template system – by default, this is an empty string. An example is:

>>> from django.template import Template, Context

>>> t = Template('Your name is {{ name }}.')

>>> t.render(Context())

'Your name is.'

>>> t.render(Context({'var': 'hello'}))

'Your name is.'

>>> t.render(Context({'NAME': 'hello'}))

'Your name is.'

>>> t.render(Context({'Name': 'hello'}))

'Your name is.'

This is far better behavior than it is to raise an exception because it is designed to be more resilient where human error is concerned. In our case, every lookup failed because the names of the variables were named wrong or has the wrong case. In the real world, it is not acceptable for websites to be inaccessible because of nothing more than a syntax error in the template.

Template Tags and Filters

We already mentioned that templates come with built-in filters and tags. We're going to look the more common ones in this section.

Tags

if/else

The tag, {% if %} will carry out variable evaluation and the variable evaluates True, i.e. it is in existence, it is not empty, it does not have a value that is a false Boolean, and everything that falls between {% if%} and {% endif %} will be displayed. An example of this is:

{% if today_is_weekend %}

   <p>Welcome to the weekend!</p>

{% endif %}

A tag of {% else %} is optional:

{% if today_is_weekend %}

   <p>Welcome to the weekend!</p>

{% else %}

   <p>Get back to work.</p>

{% endif %}

Every {% if %} must be closed with {% endif %}; if it isn't, a TemplateSyntaxError is thrown by Django.

The if tags are also able to take at least one {% elif %} clause:

{% if athlete_list %}

   <p>Number of athletes: {{ athlete_list|length }}</p>

{% elif athlete_in_locker_room_list %}

   <p>Athletes should be out of the locker room soon!</p>

```
{% elif...

...

{% else %}

    <p>No athletes.</p>

{% endif %}
```

The {% if %}tag will take 'and', 'or' or 'not' for the purpose of testing several variables or even for the negation of a specified variable. For example:

```
{% if athlete_list and coach_list %}

    <p>Both athletes and coaches are available.</p>

{% endif %}
```

```
{% if not athlete_list %}

    <p>There are no athletes.</p>

{% endif %}
```

```
{% if athlete_list or coach_list %}

    <p>There are some athletes or some coaches.</p>

{% endif %}
```

```
{% if not athlete_list or coach_list %}

    <p>There are no athletes or there are some coaches.</p>
```

{% endif %}

{% if athlete_list and not coach_list %}

   <p>There are some athletes and absolutely no coaches.</p>

{% endif %}

It is perfectly allowable to use both 'and' clauses and 'or' clauses in the same tag; just remember that 'and' is higher in precedence than 'or'. For example:

{% if athlete_list and coach_list or cheerleader_list %}

Would be interpreted as:

if (athlete_list and coach_list) or cheerleader_list

It is also worth noting that using parentheses in an 'if' tag is not valid syntax. If parentheses are required to indicate what the preference is, nested if tags should be used. You will also find that there is no support for using parentheses for the control of operation order. Again, if you think that you need the parentheses, think about performing the logic external to the template and then pass the result as a dedicated variable, or you could just use nested tags.

You can use the same logical operator several times but combining different operators is not allowed. This is a valid example:

{% if athlete_list or coach_list or parent_list or teacher_list %}

{% if %} will also take in / not in to test whether specified values are or are not inside the given container; is / is not can also be used to test whether two separate entities are, in fact, the same object. For example:

{% if "bc" in "abcdef" %}

This will appear because "bc" is a substring of the string "abcdef"

{% endif %}

{% if user not in users %}

If there is a list called users, this appears if list is not a list element:

{% endif %}

{% if somevar is True %}

This will only appear if somevar evaluates True

{% endif %}

{% if somevar is not None %}

This will only appear if somevar is not None

{% endif %}

for

You can use the {% for %} to loop over the items in a sequence. As we see in the syntax of the for statement in Python, for X in Y and Y is the sequence to be looped over, while X is the variable name used for a specified loop cycle. For every loop, the template system renders anything that shows up between {% for %} and {% endfor%}. For example, the following code could be used for displaying a list of the athletes, given a variable called athlete_list:

<ul>

   {% for athlete in athlete_list %}

  <li>{{ athlete.name }}</li>

{% endfor %}

</ul>

If you want to loop back over the list in reverse order, the tag would need to be 'reversed', like this:

{% for athlete in athlete_list reversed %}

...

{% endfor %}

{% for %} tags can also be nested:

{% for athlete in athlete_list %}

<h1>{{ athlete.name }}</h1>

<ul>

  {% for sport in athlete.sports_played %}

  <li>{{ sport }}</li>

  {% endfor %}

</ul>

{% endfor %}

If you have a list of lists that you need to loop over, the values of each sublist can be unpacked into separate variables. For example, if you have a list of (x, y) coordinates or points in the context, the following code could be used for outputting the list of points:

{% for x, y in points %}

  <p>There is a point at {{ x }},{{ y }}</p>

{% endfor %}

You will also find this useful if you have a dictionary and you need to access the items in it. For example, if you have dictionary data in the context, you could use the following to display the dictionary keys and values:

{% for key, value in data.items %}

   {{ key }}: {{ value }}

{% endfor %}

One of the most common patterns is to look at the list size before it is looped over and if the list is empty, outputting special text:

{% if athlete_list %}

   {% for athlete in athlete_list %}

     <p>{{ athlete.name }}</p>

   {% endfor %}

{% else %}

   <p>There are no athletes. Only computer programmers.</p>

{% endif %}

Because this is such a common pattern, the for tag provides support for an optional *{% empty %}* clause; this clause will allow you to define what the output should be in the event of an empty list. The next example is the equivalent of the last one:

{% for athlete in athlete_list %}

   <p>{{ athlete.name }}</p>

{% empty %}

<p>There are no athletes. Only computer programmers.</p>

{% endfor %}

Breaking out of a loop before it is finished is not supported. If you want to do this, the variable being looped over must be changed so that it only has the values that are to be looped over. In a similar way, there is not a built-in support to continue statements that tell the loop processor to go to the loop front straightaway.

With every {% for %} loop, you automatically gain access to forloop, which is a template variable. This has some attributes that provide information about the loop progress. We always set the forloop.counter to an integer that is representative of how many times a loop has been entered into. It is one-indexed so, when the loop is gone through the first time, forloop.counter is set to 1. Look at this example:

{% for item in todo_list %}

  <p>{{ forloop.counter }}: {{ item }}</p>

{%endfor %}

The forloop.counter() is much like forloopcounter with one exception – it is zero-indexed rather than one-indexed and has a value of 0 on the first loop. We always set forloop.revcounter as an integer that represents how many items are left in the loop. When the loop is gone through the first time, forloop.revcounter is set to the number of the items in the sequence being looped over. On the last loop, it is set as 1.

The forloop.revcountero is similar to forloop.revcounter with the exception that it is a zero-index. On the first lop, it is set as the number of the sequence elements minus 1, and on the last loop, it is set as 0.

The forloop.first is a Boolean value. It is set as True on the first loop and this is very convenient where special-casing is concerned:

{% for object in objects %}

```
{% if forloop.first %}

    <li class="first">

{% else %}

    <li>

{% endif %}

{{ object }}</li>
```

{% endfor %}

The forloop.last is another Boolean value that has been set as True if the loop is the last one. This is commonly used to place a pipe character in between a links list:

{% for link in links %}

    {{ link }}{% if not forloop.last %} | {% endif %}

{% endfor %}

The output of this might look something like:

Link1 | Link2 | Link3 | Link4

This is also used for inserting commas in between words in lists:

<p>Favorite places:</p>

{% for p in places %}

    {{ p }}{% if not forloop.last %}, {% endif %}

{% endfor %}

The forloop.parentloop is referencing the parent loop's forloop object where you have nested loops. An example:

```
{% for country in countries %}

  <table>

    {% for city in country.city_list %}

    <tr>

      <td>Country #{{ forloop.parentloop.counter }}</td>

      <td>City #{{ forloop.counter }}</td>

      <td>{{ city }}</td>

    </tr>

    {% endfor %}

  </table>

  {% endfor %}
```

Comments

As it in in Python or in HTML, DTL allows comments and these are designated using {# #}:

{# This would be a comment #}

The comment is ignored by the interpreter and won't be output on template rendering. However, you cannot use this syntax if you have a comment that goes over several lines; this is for single line comments only. This limitation provides improvement to the performance of template parsing.

In the next template, the output that is rendered looks identical to the template – the comment tag isn't parsed as a comment:

This is a {# this is not

a comment #}

test.

Where multi-line comments are required, you need to use the template tag of {% comment %}, in this way:

{% comment %}

This is now a

multi-line comment.

{% endcomment %}

Comment tags can optionally have notes that explain why a specific piece of code may have been commented out:

{% comment "This is an optional note" %}

...

{% endcomment %}

You cannot nest comment tags.

Filters

A template filter is nothing more than an easy way to change variable values before they are displayed. They make use of the pipe character in this way:

{{ name|lower }}

This shows the name variable value after it goes through the lower filter – this changes the text to lowercase. We can chain filters, i.e., we can use them together in such a way that the output of the first filter is applied to the second and so on. The following example converts the first list element to uppercase:

{{ my_list|first|upper }}

Some filters can take an argument, and this will follow a colon and must be inside a set of double quotes. An example:

{{ bio|truncatewords:"20" }}

This shows the first 20 words of the variable called bio.

Now we look at some of the more important filters:

- **addslashes** – puts a backslash in front of another backslash, double quote or single quote, and is useful for when you want to escape a string.
- **date** – this formats dates or datetime objects as per a given format-string in the parameter.
- **length** – will return the value length. In the case of a list, this would be the number of list elements, and for a string, it would return the number of string characters.

Templates in Views

We learned how to use the template system, now it's time to use that to create a view.

Earlier, we used the view called current_datetime, found in mysite.views. It looks like this:

from django.http import HttpResponse

import datetime

def current_datetime(request):

  now = datetime.datetime.now()

  html = "<html><body>It is now %s</body></html>" % now

  return HttpResponse(html)

We're going to change this, so it uses the template system in Django. You might think that the way to do that would be like this:

```
from django.template import Template, Context

from django.http import HttpResponse

import datetime


def current_datetime(request):

    now = datetime.datetime.now()

    t = Template("<html><body>It is now {{ current_date }}.</body></html>")

    html = t.render(Context({'current_date': now}))

    return HttpResponse(html)
```

Yes, that would make use of the template system, but it doesn't go anywhere near solving the problems we discussed. The template is still in Python code, so we cannot have true data and presentation separation. We can fix that by placing our template into a new file and that is where the view will load from. The first thing you should do is save the template on your filesystem and then read the contents of it using the file-opening functionality built-in to Python. That would look something like this, assuming, of course, that we used the path file\users\djangouser\templates\mytemplate.html:

```
from django.template import Template, Context

from django.http import HttpResponse

import datetime
```

```
def current_datetime(request):


    now = datetime.datetime.now()

    # Simple way of using templates from the filesystem.

    # This is BAD because it doesn't account for missing files!

    fp = open('\\users\\djangouser\\templates\\mytemplate.html')

    t = Template(fp.read())

    fp.close()


    html = t.render(Context({'current_date': now}))

    return HttpResponse(html)
```

This isn't a very nice approach though and here's why:

- It doesn't deal with the missing file case. If mytemplate.html cannot be read or doesn't exist, open() call will throw up an IOError exception.
- Your template location is hardcoded. If you did this for all the view functions, all you would achieve would be template location duplication, not to mention sore hands from that typing!
- There is a load of boilerplate code; really, you don't need to be writing continuous open(), fp.read() and fp.close() calls every time you want to load a template.

Solving these problems requires the use of template loading and directories.

Template Loading

In Django, there is a very powerful and convenient API that loads the templates from the filesystem. This to get rid of the redundancy in the templates and the loading calls. To use the API, you need to let the framework know where your templates are being stored. You should store your templates in the settings file – settings.py, which was discussed earlier when ROOT_URLCONF was introduced. So, open settings.py and look for the TEMPLATES setting. This is nothing more than a configuration list, one configuration for each engine:

```
TEMPLATES = [

    {

        'BACKEND': 'django.template.backends.django.DjangoTemplates',

        'DIRS': [],

        'APP_DIRS': True,

        'OPTIONS': {

            #... some options here...

        },

    },

]
```

A dotted Python path, BACKEND leads to the template engine class and this implements the backend API for the Django templates. The backends built-in are:

django.template.backends.django.DjangoTemplates, and

 django.template.backends.jinja2.Jinja2.

Most engines will load a template from a file and, because of this, each engine's top-level configuration has three settings that are common:

- DIRS – this defines the directory list where the engine searches for template source files and this is done in search order.

- APP_DIRS – this indicates if the engine should be looking inside the installed applications for the templates. By convention, is APP_DIR is set as True, DjangoTemplates will search for \templatessubdirectory inside each INSTALLED_APPS. This way, even if DIRS is empty, the template engine can still find the application templates.
- OPTIONS – this is where the settings specific to the backend are stored.

Template Directories

By default, DIRS is just an empty list. You need to let the mechanism to load templates in Django know where to find the templates, so choose a directory for your templates and then add it to DIRS, in this way:

'DIRS': [

   '/home/html/templates/site',

   '/home/html/templates/default',

  ],

There are a couple of things you need to be aware of:

Unless your program is going to be simple,with no applications, it is better to leave DIRS empty. APP_DIRS is configured to True by the settings file; instead, set up a subdirectory called "Templates" in your own Django application.

If you wanted a master template set at the project root, for example, mysite\templates, you would need to set DIRS like this:

 'DIRS': [os.path.join(BASE_DIR, 'templates')],

You do not need to name your templates directory as "Templates". Django doesn't restrict any of the names you use but it makes things just a little easier for you if you can stick to a naming convention. If you want a directory other than the default one selected, you will need to specify that directory, but ensure that both the directory and the templates saved in it can be read by the user account that the web server is running.

If you are using Windows, you need to make sure the letter that indicates the drive is specified along with forward and to backslashes, like this:

'DIRS':

[

'C:/www/django/templates',

]

We haven't created any Django app yet, so we'll see how template loading works using a very easy configuration. The first thing to do is set DIRS to this path, as per the above example:

[os.path.join(BASE_DIR,'templates')]

Check your settings file; it should look something like this:

TEMPLATES = [

    {

        'BACKEND': 'django.template.backends.django.DjangoTemplates',

        'DIRS': [os.path.join(BASE_DIR,'templates')],

        'APP_DIRS': True,

        'OPTIONS': {

            #...

Now that DIRS has been set, you need to create a directory for your templates and this is done in the root \mysite folder. When you have done that, you should see something like the following as your folder structure:

\mysite_project

  \mysite

    \mysite

    \templates

    manage.py

Next, you need to change your view code so that the Django functionality to load templates is used; this eliminates the need to hard-code the paths. Going back to the current_datetime view you've been working on, you can change it like this:

#mysite\mysite\views.py

from django.template.loader import get_template

from django.http import HttpResponse

import datetime

def current_datetime(request):

  now = datetime.datetime.now()

  t = get_template('current_datetime.html')

  html = t.render({'current_date': now})

  return HttpResponse(html)

In general, a Django template-loader will be used and not the template API we used previously. For this current example, we are going to use the function called django.template.loader.get_template() instead of going to the filesystem to manually load the template. The function called get_template) will take the name of a template as the argument; it will then work out where the template is on the filesystem, open it, and will return a Template object that has been compiled.

Note that there is a difference between the render() method we are using here and the one we used previously. Until now, we have called django.template.Template.render and this needs a context object passed to it. The one we are using now, get_template(), will return a Django template that is backend-dependent. This comes from django.template.backends.base.Template; here, the render() method can only take a dictionary object and not a Context.

The template we are using in this example is called current_datetime.html but don't make the mistake of thinking that the.html extension is anything special. Your templates can have an extension so long as it makes sense for the application you are building; you can even leave off the extensions altogether if you want.

To find out where the template is on the filesystem, get_template, look at these in order:

- If you are using the DTL and APP_DIRS has been set to True then get_template will look in the current application for a /templates directory.
- If the template can't be found in the current application, get_template() will take the template name that you have passed and combine it with the template directories in DIRS and it will go through each in order until the required template is found. For example, if you set the first DIRS entry to /home/django/mysite/templates, then the get_template() call will look for a template called /home/django/mysite/templates/current_datetime.html
- If a template can't be found with the provided name, a TemplateDoesNotExist exception is raised.

If you want to know what one of these template exceptions looks like, go to your Django project directory and run python manage.py runserver. From your browser, open the website that is being used to activate the current_datetime view – in our case, this is http://127.0.0.1:8000/time. Assuming that you have your DEBUG mode set as True and you don't have a template called current_datetime.html, you will see an error page showing the TemplateDoesNotExist error.

This is quite like the error page we looked at earlier but this one has an extra bit of information for debugging purposes – a section for "Template-loader postmortem". This tells us the templates that Django attempted to load and why each of them failed. For example, it could be that the file didn't exist. This is valuable information for when you want to debug loading errors with the templates.

To fix the problem we have with a missing template, we need to use the following code to create a current_datetime.html file:

 # \mysite_project\mysite\templates\current_datetime.html


```
<html>

  <body>

    It is now {{ current_date }}

  </body>

</html>
```

It is now {{ current_date }}.

Save this to your \mysite\templates directory and then refresh your web page. The page should now show up as fully rendered.

Shortcut - render()

We have looked at loading the templates, filling Contexts, and returning HttpResponse objects using the results from the rendered templates. Next, we looked at using get_template() rather than going down the route of hard-coding each template and its path. The thing is, the developers of Django had already seen that this was going to be one of the most common uses, so they created a shortcut that would do everything with just one code line. That shortcut is render() and it resides in the module called django.shortcuts.

You will use render() most of the time, instead of loading each template and then manually creating the Context and the HttpResponse objects. However, you should learn the entire process and remember it because it will be handy when you have non-standard uses to fulfill.

Using render(), this is what our current_datetime example now looks like:

from django.shortcuts import render

import datetime


```
def current_datetime(request):

    now = datetime.datetime.now()

    return render(request, 'current_datetime.html', {'current_date': now})
```

Now doesn't that look neater! Let's look at what changed.

There is now no need for HttpResponse, Template, get_template() or Context to be imported. Instead, django.shortcuts.render is what is imported and we retain the import datetime.

Inside the function called current_datetime, now still needs to be calculated but the call to render() takes care of loading the templates, creating the context, rendering the templates, and creating HttpResponse. And, as render() will still return an HttpResponse object, that value can be returned in the view.

The request is render() and is the first argument, while the second argument is the name of the template that is to be used. If there is a third argument, it would be the dictionary that is to be used for Context creation in the template. If there is no third argument, an empty dictionary is used instead.

Template Tags – Include

Now we know how the loading mechanism works for templates, we can look at a template tag, built-in that will take full advantage of that mechanism. That tag is called {% include %}.

This tag will let you add the contents from another template and the tag's argument must be the name of that additional template. That name may be a variable or it may be a quoted hard-coded string – it can be in single quotes or double so long as the opening and closing quotes match.

If you are ever using the same code in more than one template, you should always consider using the {% include %} tag to get rid of the duplicate content. The next two examples have the contents of the template called nav.html. They are both the same; one shows single quotes, the other double quotes.

Duplicated content:

{% include 'nav.html' %}

{% include "nav.html" %}

This example has the nav.html contents:

{% include 'includes/nav.html' %}

This has the contents of the template named in the variable of template_name:

{% include template_name %}

{% include %} supports relative paths:

{% include './nav.html' %}

{% include '../nav_base.html' %}

As it was in get_template(), the template file name is determined in one of two ways:

- If APPS_DIR is set to True, the path is added to the current Django application, in the directory called \templates.
- The DIRS template directory is added to the specified template name. All the templates get evaluated using the context of the including template.

The following is an example of these templates:

 # mypage.html

<html>

<body>

  {% include "includes/nav.html" %}

  <h1>{{ title }}</h1>

</body>

</html>

 # includes/nav.html

  You are in: {{ current_section }}

If mypage.html is rendered with a context that contains current_section, the variable is made available inside the "included" template.

If a template with the specified name is not found in the {$ include} tag, Django will then do one of these things:

- Provided DEBUG is set as True, the TemplateDoesNotExist error will be thrown

- Provided DEBUG is set as False, the tag will silently fail and nothing will be shown.

Included templates do not share a state; each is a rendering process in its own right, and independent from the others. A block is evaluated before it will be included, and this means that, if a template has blocks that come from another template, it will have blocks that have been evaluated already and have been rendered, rather than blocks that could potentially be overridden by a template that has extending abilities.

Template Inheritance

So far, the templates we used have been minute snippets of HTML but, out in the real world you will be creating whole pages of HTML with Django's template system. This leads to a problem common in web development – how do we reduce redundancy and duplication of common areas on pages across a website, perhaps like navigation across the entire site?

One of the classic ways to solve a problem like this is to make use of server-side includes. These are directives that may be embedded in the HTML pages including one page in another and Django has support for that, using the {% include %} tag we discussed earlier.

However, there is a better way of doing this in Django and that is to use a very nice strategy known as Template Inheritance. What this is, in basic terms, is a strategy that provides you with the ability to build a kind of skeleton template as the base. This base has all the common bits of the website and it will define blocks that can be overridden by child templates. As an example, we'll create a template that is somewhat more complete for the current_datetime view and we do this by editing the html file we created earlier:

<!DOCTYPE HTML PUBLIC "-//W3C//DTD HTML 4.01//EN">

<html lang="en">

```
<head>

   <title>The current time</title>

</head>

<body>

   <h1>My helpful timestamp site</h1>

   <p>It is now {{ current_date }}.</p>

   <hr>

   <p>Thanks for visiting my site.</p>

</body>

</html>
```

All that looks OK but what would happen if we wanted a template created for another view, let's say for the hours_ahead view that we created a while before? If we wanted, once again, to create a full HTML template that is fully valid, we can do this:

```
<!DOCTYPE HTML PUBLIC "-//W3C//DTD HTML 4.01//EN">

<html lang="en">

<head>

   <title>Future time</title>

</head>

<body>

   <h1>My helpful timestamp site</h1>

   <p>
```

In {{ hour_offset }} hour(s), it will be {{ next_time }}.

</p>

<hr>

<p>Thanks for visiting my site.</p>

</body>

</html>

It's clear that a great deal of HTML has just been duplicated! What would happen if we had a typical website, one that had a couple of style sheets, a navigation bar, a bit of JavaScript? What would happen is we would be placing a lot of HTML in each of the templates of HTML that is redundant.

Using server-side include will factor the common parts of the templates out and put them into individual template snippets. These then get added to each of the templates. For example, you put the top part of the template into a file that you name header.html:

<!DOCTYPE HTML PUBLIC "-//W3C//DTD HTML 4.01//EN">

<html lang="en">

<head>

And the bottom part of the template in a file named footer.html:

<hr>

<p>Thanks for visiting my site.</p>

</body>

</html>

Using this kind of strategy, it's easy to deal with footers and headers; it is not so easy for the rest of the page. In our example, we have a title on both pages but it's quite a long title and it won't go into header.html – the title is different on each page. If <h1> were included in the header, the title would need to be included and that would eliminate our ability to do per page customization.

With the inheritance system in Django, we can fix these problems easily. Think of it as being a version of the server-side include from the inside out. Rather than defining the common snippets, we define those that are a bit different.

First, the base template is defined. This is the page skeleton that will be filled in later by the child templates. Look at this skeleton template as the example we are currently using:

```
<!DOCTYPE HTML PUBLIC "-//W3C//DTD HTML 4.01//EN">

<html lang="en">

<head>

    <title>{% block title %}{% endblock %}</title>

</head>

<body>

    <h1>My helpful timestamp site</h1>

    {% block content %}{% endblock %}


    {% block footer %}

    <hr>

    <p>Thanks for visiting my site.</p>

    {% endblock %}

</body>
```

</html>

We will name this template base.html; it defines a very simple skeleton document in HTML and we can use this for every page on our website. The child templates will add to, override, or leave the block contents alone. Now, we save this template as base.html in our template directory.

The template tag we use here is one you haven't been introduced to yet – {% block %. This tag will inform the template engine that the specified parts of the template may be overridden by a child template.

Now that we have our new base template, we can make some changes to the current_datetime.html template we are already using:

{% extends "base.html" %}

{% block title %}The current time{% endblock %}

{% block content %}

   <p>It is now {{ current_date }}.</p>

{% endblock %}

Let's also make a new template for hours_ahead, the view we created earlier. Change hours_ahead so it will make use of the template system rather than hard-code HTML. It should look like this:

{% extends "base.html" %}

{% block title %}Future time{% endblock %}

{% block content %}

<p>

   In {{ hour_offset }} hour(s), it will be {{ next_time }}.

</p>

{% endblock %}

This is much nicer. Each of the templates has just the code that is unique to it and there is no need for any redundancy. If we need to make a change that is site-wide, all we do is change the base.html template and every other template will reflect those changes.

So, here's how this all works. When the current_datetime.html template is loaded, the {% extends %} tag gets seen by the template engine as a child template. Immediately, the engine will load base.html, which is the parent template. The template engine will now notice that there are three of the { block %} tags inside base.html and it replaces them with the child template contents. A title was defined in {$ block title %} and this will be used alongside the {% block content %}.

Note: the footer block is not defined by the child block; the parent template value is used by the template system instead. It is worth noting that, where there is a {% block %} tag inside a parent template, the content in it will always be used as something to fall back on.

The template context is not affected by inheritance. So, any of the templates that are inside the inheritance tree will be able to gain access to each of the template variables from within Context. There is no limit to how much inheritance we can use and one of the most common of using it is by the three-level approach described below:

1. A base.html template is created to hold the fundamental feel and look of the website. This is the parts of the site that really don't change much, if at all.
2. Next, a base_SECTION.html template is created for each of the sections on the website. These templates will extend the base.html template and will all include styles and design that are specific to the template.
3. Last, an individual template is created for each page type, like a Gallery page, Forum page, etc. These will extend the templates for each related section.

Taking this route means that code reuse is maximized and adding items to shared parts of the website is much easier.

Read and learn the following guidelines for template inheritance:

- If {% extends %} is used inside a template, it must be the first tag; if it isn't, the inheritance will not work.
- The more of the {% block %} tags used in a base template, the better it is. Remember that a child template is not required to define all the parent blocks; this means that reasonable defaults may be filled in for some blocks and only those needed for the child templates may be defined. More hooks are always better than too few.
- If you are duplicating your code in multiple templates, you should consider using a {% block %} t house than code in a parent template.
- Use {% block super %} to get the block content out of the parent template. This variable is "magic" and it provides us with the parent template's rendered text. This is incredibly useful if we want the parent block contents added to and not overridden.
- You cannot define several {% block %} tags that have identical names inside the same template. This is because block tags work both ways, which means they don't just give us something to fill, it also tells us what content to use in filling the parent hole. If two of the block tags had similar or the same names in one template, the parent would not know from which of the blocks to take the content.
- The name of the template that is passed to {% extends %} uses the same method as get_template() does for loading purposes. That is to say, the name is appended to the DIRS setting – the Django app's \templates folder.
- Most of the time, a string is used as the {% extends %} argument, but it can be a variable as well – you won't always know what name the parent template has until its runtime.

Now that we know how the template system works, we can move on. Most of the websites we see today are driven by databases which means relational databases are used to store the website contents. This means that we get a much cleaner data/logic separation. Next, we are going to look at what Django provides us with for database interaction.

Django Models

Earlier, we explained how to use Django to build a dynamic website – the views and the URLconfs. Views, as you know, are responsible for doing some logic and returning responses and, in one example we used, the logic we did was to calculate what the current time and date were.

In a web app of today, this logic will often require database interaction, and in the background, this means connecting to a database server, getting some information out of it, and then showing that information on a webpage. The website might also give users a way to populate the database for themselves.

Many of the more complex sites provide some combination of both; Amazon, for example, is one of the best examples of a website driven by a database. Each of the product pages on Amazon is nothing more than a query to the website's database of products, formatted in HTML; when a customer posts a review, it will go straight into the database that holds the customer reviews.

Django is a great tool to create these websites that are database-driven because it has everything you need to use Python to perform a database query. In this chapter, we are going to look at this functionality a bit closer. To use the Django database layer, you don't need to have much knowledge of SQL or relational databases, but it does help. That is beyond this book's scope, but you should continue to read because everything will be kept as simple as possible.

Dumbing Down Database Queries in Views

Earlier, we talked about a 'dumb' way of producing an output in a view – simply hardcode your text into the view. Now we are going to look at a 'dumb' way of getting the data out of a database that is in a view. It really is quite simple – an SQL query is executed, using any library from Python, and then we take the results and we do something with them. On our view, we are connecting to a MySQL database using the MySQLdb library. We get some records out of it and then we put into a display template to be displayed as the contents of a webpage.

```python
from django.shortcuts import render

import MySQLdb


def book_list(request):

    db = MySQLdb.connect(user='me', db='mydb', passwd='secret', host='localhost')

    cursor = db.cursor()

    cursor.execute('SELECT name FROM books ORDER BY name')

    names = [row[0] for row in cursor.fetchall()]

    db.close()

    return render(request, 'book_list.html', {'names': names})
```

This does work but you should have immediately spotted what the problems are:

- First, the connection parameters to the database have been hardcoded. In an ideal world, the Django configuration would be used to store these.
- Second, there is a lot of boilerplate code here; the connection is created, a cursor is created, a statement is executed, and the connection is closed. Really, what we want to do is specify that results that we are after.
- This code is tying us into using MySQL. If we wanted to change later to PostgreSQL, it would mean having to write a lot of the code again. Ideally, we would be using an abstracted database server; this way, changes to the server could be done in one place.

Of course, there is a solution to all of this and it's the Django database layer.

The Configuration of the Database

Keeping all that in mind, we'll start to look at this database layer. First of all, we'll look at the configuration that was put into settings.py when the application as created:

```
DATABASES = {

    'default': {

        'ENGINE': 'django.db.backends.sqlite3',

        'NAME': os.path.join(BASE_DIR, 'db.sqlite3'),

    }

}
```

This is quite simple; ENGINE is determining the database engine that will be used. In our case, we will leave it as the django.db.backends.sqlite3 default. NAME is informing Django what name your database goes under.

Because we have used SQLite, a filesystem path was created by startproject leading to the database file.

That's all we need to do for the setup.

Our First App

Now we know the connection works, we can start creating an app in Django. This is just some code that includes views and models, all living in one package. We will review the terminology used because this is where some new users tend to get stuck. Earlier, we created a project but how does a project differ from an app? The answer to that lies in configuration versus code.

Projects are instances of a set of specified Django apps and their configurations. Technically, all we require from a project is that it gives us a settings file. This should define the information that relates to the database connection, the apps installed, the DIRS, and more.

Apps are sets of the functionality that usually includes the views and the models, all in one package. Django has a number of built-in apps and one thing about apps that is key is that they are portable and can be reused across several projects.

As far as rules go for fitting our Django code in, there are few to worry about. If it's just a simple website that we are building we can get away with one app while a complex website that has multiple parts all unrelated may need to be split into different apps; this will allow us to reuse each one in the future, as and where it is needed.

Really, we don't even need to create any apps. We've already seen that we can create a views.py file, add a few view functions, and then point URLconf to the functions. However, there is one thing to be aware of; if we use the database layer in Django, we must create Django apps. Models can only live in apps. So to write the models, we must first create the app.

Inside mysite project directory, let's start creating a books app by typing this command:

python manage.py startapp books

We won't get any output from this but we will get a new directory in the mysite directory; it's called books and we can see what the contents should be by looking at the tree below:

\mysite_project

  \books

    \migrations

    __init__.py

    admin.py

    apps.py

    models.py

tests.py

views.py

\mysite

\templates

manage.py

All the views and the models that we need for the app are in these files. For example, open views.py and models.py in our text editor. We will see that both have nothing in them bar comments and, in models.py, an import. This is our blank piece of paper, ready for our new Django app.

Defining the Django Models

A model is a description of the data that is represented by the code in our database. It is basically the layout of the data, the SQL CREATE TABLE, but in Python, not SQL and it has more in it than just definitions of database columns.

Models are used by Django to execute behind-the-scenes SQL code, turning it into Python data structures that represent the database table rows. Models are also used as a way of representing concepts that SQL may not be able to handle because they are high-level. You might, if you have some familiarity with databases, be wondering why we would bother to use Python for defining data models when we have SQL. Well, there are several reasons why Django works as it does:

- Introspection is not perfect, and it needs overhead. So that Django can provide data-access APIs that are convenient, it must know what the database layout is, and this is done in one of two ways. First, we could use Python to describe the data explicitly and, second, the database could be introspected at runtime in order to determine the data models. Introspection puts in a layer of overhead that is not acceptable and may not be accurate; because of this it was determined by the Django developers that the best option was the first.

- Python is more fun and, if you can keep everything within Python, it cuts down on how often your brain needs to switch contexts. Productivity is much higher if you stay in one programming environment for as long as you can whereas flicking between languages can be disruptive.
- If you can store your data models as code then it is much easier for models to be kept under version control and changes can be better tracked that are made to the data layout.
- SQL limits what level of metadata can be kept regarding a data layout. Most of the database systems have no special data type for URL or email representation, for example, whereas a Django model does. High-level data types offer one main advantage – more productivity and code that can be reused.
- SQL is not consistent across all database platforms. If a web application is being distributed, it is better to use a Python module that defines the layout of the data than it is to use a lot of separate SQL CREATE TABLE statements.

There is a drawback; there is every possibility that the Python code can lose sync with the database contents. When the Django model is changed in any way, the exact same changes must be made in the database, so they remain consistent.

Our First Model

We'll use the layout of the book, author and publisher for this, simply because the relationship between all three is well-known. We will follow these assumptions:

- Every author has a first and last name and also an email address.
- Every book has a title and it has a publication date. There may also be a many-to-many relationship, i.e. more than one author and a one-to-many relationship, i.e. one publisher.
- Every publisher has a name and an address, a country, and their own website

The very first step we take in the Django database layout is expressing it in Python. Open the models.py file and input the following:

```python
from django.db import models


class Publisher(models.Model):
    name = models.CharField(max_length=30)
    address = models.CharField(max_length=50)
    city = models.CharField(max_length=60)
    state_province = models.CharField(max_length=30)
    country = models.CharField(max_length=50)
    website = models.URLField()


class Author(models.Model):
    first_name = models.CharField(max_length=30)
    last_name = models.CharField(max_length=40)
    email = models.EmailField()


class Book(models.Model):
    title = models.CharField(max_length=100)
    authors = models.ManyToManyField(Author)
    publisher = models.ForeignKey(Publisher)
    publication_date = models.DateField()
```

Let's look at the code. Notice that a Python class represents each of the models and that class is a django.db.models.Model subclass. Models is the parent class, and this has everything needed to ensure the objects can interact with a database leaving the models responsible only for the definition of their fields, using neat syntax.

This really is all we need to write to have data-access. Each of the models will correspond to one database table with each model attribute corresponding to a column in the table. The name of the attribute corresponds to the name of the column and the field type will correspond to the column type. For example, the model called Publisher is the equivalent of this table, assuming the syntax of the PostgreSQL CREATE TABLE:

```
CREATE TABLE "books_publisher" (

    "id" serial NOT NULL PRIMARY KEY,

    "name" varchar(30) NOT NULL,

    "address" varchar(50) NOT NULL,

    "city" varchar(60) NOT NULL,

    "state_province" varchar(30) NOT NULL,

    "country" varchar(50) NOT NULL,

    "website" varchar(200) NOT NULL

);
```

Django is able to automatically generate the CREATE TABLE statement. There is one exception to the rule of one class to one database and that is the many-to-many relationships. In the example that we are using, Book has a field called Authors and this is a ManyToManyField which designates a book as having one or more authors, but the database table called Book does not have a column called Authors. Instead, another table is created by Django and this one is a many-to-many joint table. This takes care of the books to authors mapping.

Lastly, we did not explicitly define primary keys for any model. Unless you tell Django otherwise, it will give each model a primary key field of an auto-incremental integer. This field is called id and each model in Django must have a primary key for "single column".

Installing Our Model

The code is written and now we need to come up with the database tables. To do this, we first need to activate our models in the project. We add our books app to settings file in the installed apps list. The settings.py file can be edited again and then we can look for the setting for INSTALLED_APPS. This informs Django of the apps that are activated for any given project and it will look like this by default:

INSTALLED_APPS = [

'django.contrib.admin',

'django.contrib.auth',

'django.contrib.contenttypes',

'django.contrib.sessions',

'django.contrib.messages',

'django.contrib.staticfiles',

]

For the "books" app to be registered, the following should be added to INSTALLED_APPS – books.apps.BooksConfig – the settings file should now look like this:

INSTALLED_APPS = [

'books.apps.BooksConfig',

'django.contrib.admin',

'django.contrib.auth',

'django.contrib.contenttypes',

'django.contrib.sessions',

'django.contrib.messages',

'django.contrib.staticfiles',

]

A full Python path represents every app inside INSTALLED_APPS. This is a dotted path of packages that end in the app package. In our case, the path leads to the BooksConfig class created by Django in apps.py.

The Django app has now been activated so we can get on with creating the database table. First, the models need to be validated and we do that with this code:

python manage.py check

This will run the system check framework in Django and this is a series of static checks used to validate every project in Django. If everything is OK, a message will appear saying 'System check identified no issues (0 silenced). If you don't see that message, you need to check that the model code was typed incorrectly.

If you have valid models, the following code can be run to let Django know that a few changes have been made to the models – in our case, we have a new one:

python manage.py makemigrations books

The output should look a bit like this:

Migrations for 'books':

 0001_initial.py:

  - Create model Author

- Create model Book

- Create model Publisher

- Add field publisher to book

A migration is how Django stores any changes made to the models and, by extension, the database schema; they are just files. In our example, if we look in our books app inside the folder called \migrations, there should be a file named 0001_inital.py. With the migrate command, the newest migration file is used to automatically update the schema. First, though, we need to see what SQL gets run by the migration. The command of sqlmigrate will return the SQL of each migration name:

python manage.py sqlmigrate books 0001

Now you should see something like this:

BEGIN;

CREATE TABLE "books_author" (

   "id" integer NOT NULL PRIMARY KEY AUTOINCREMENT,

   "first_name" varchar(30) NOT NULL,

   "last_name" varchar(40) NOT NULL,

   "email" varchar(254) NOT NULL

);

CREATE TABLE "books_book" (

   "id" integer NOT NULL PRIMARY KEY AUTOINCREMENT,

   "title" varchar(100) NOT NULL,

```
    "publication_date" date NOT NULL

);

CREATE TABLE "books_book_authors" (

    "id" integer NOT NULL PRIMARY KEY AUTOINCREMENT,

    "book_id" integer NOT NULL REFERENCES "books_book" ("id"),

    "author_id" integer NOT NULL REFERENCES "books_author" ("id"),

    UNIQUE ("book_id", "author_id")

);

CREATE TABLE "books_publisher" (

    "id" integer NOT NULL PRIMARY KEY AUTOINCREMENT,

    "name" varchar(30) NOT NULL,

    "address" varchar(50) NOT NULL,

    "city" varchar(60) NOT NULL,

    "state_province" varchar(30) NOT NULL,

    "country" varchar(50) NOT NULL,

    "website" varchar(200) NOT NULL

);

CREATE TABLE "books_book__new" (

    "id" integer NOT NULL PRIMARY KEY AUTOINCREMENT,

    "title" varchar(100) NOT NULL,

    "publication_date" date NOT NULL,
```

```
    "publisher_id" integer NOT NULL REFERENCES

    "books_publisher" ("id")

);


INSERT INTO "books_book__new" ("id", "publisher_id", "title",

"publication_date") SELECT "id", NULL, "title", "publication_date" FROM

"books_book";


DROP TABLE "books_book";


ALTER TABLE "books_book__new" RENAME TO "books_book";


CREATE INDEX "books_book_2604cbea" ON "books_book" ("publisher_id");


COMMIT;
```

Note

We get our table names by putting the app name, which is books, together with the model name in lowercase.

For each table, Django automatically adds primary keys, and these are called idfields. '_id' is appended by Django to the name given to the foreign key field.

A REFERENCES statement is used to make the key relationship explicit.

Each CREATE TABLE statement is specifically made for the database. Field types that are specific to the database like serial in Postgre SQL, auto_increment in MySQL or SQLite's integer primary key, are automatically handled, as is the double or single quoting that happens with the names of the columns.

The command, sqlmigrate, doesn't create a table, nor does it interact with the database; what it does is print the output so that we see what is executed by SQL Django if requested. This SQL could be copied and pasted to the database client but there is a better way of doing this – using the migrate command:

python manage.py migrate

Run the above command and you should see an output like this:

Operations to perform:

Apply all migrations: admin, auth, books, contenttypes, sessions

Running migrations:

Applying books.0001_initial... OK

Should we end up with a load more migrations, this will be because the initial migrations weren't run earlier. When we migrate for the first time, Django creates every system table needed by Django for the apps that are built-in.

Basic Data-Access

Django provides us with a Python API for working with our models and we can try this out – go to your virtual environment and run python manage.py shell; input the following:

>>> from books.models import Publisher

>>> p1 = Publisher(name='Apress', address='2855 Telegraph Avenue',

...   city='Berkeley', state_province='CA', country='U.S.A.',

```
...     website='http://www.apress.com/')
>>> p1.save()
>>> p2 = Publisher(name="O'Reilly", address='10 Fawcett St.',
...     city='Cambridge', state_province='MA', country='U.S.A.',
...     website='http://www.oreilly.com/')
>>> p2.save()
>>> publisher_list = Publisher.objects.all()
>>> publisher_list
```

<QuerySet [<Publisher: Publisher object>, <Publisher: Publisher object>]>

This actually does quite a lot:

First, the model class called Publisher is imported. This allows us to interact with the publisher's database table.

Next, a Publisher object is created; this is done through instantiation providing each field with values.

The object is saved into the database by calling the save() method of the object. In the background, an SQL INSERT statement is being executed by Django.

We use the Publisher.objects attribute to get the publishers out of the database and we use Publisher.objects.all() to get a list from the database of the Publisher objects. Again, Django is working behind the scenes, executing an SQL SELECT statement.

In case this example didn't make it clear: when we use the Django model API to create an object, Django won't save that object not the database until the save() method has been called:

```
p1 = Publisher(...)
```

 # Right now, p1 has not been saved to the database.

p1.save()

 # It has now.

If we wanted to take just one step to create and save an object in the database, we would need to use the method called objects.create(). The following example uses the above example but with the new method:

>>> p1 = Publisher.objects.create(name='Apress',

...   address='2855 Telegraph Avenue',

...   city='Berkeley', state_province='CA', country='U.S.A.',

...   website='http://www.apress.com/')

>>> p2 = Publisher.objects.create(name="O'Reilly",

...   address='10 Fawcett St.', city='Cambridge',

...   state_province='MA', country='U.S.A.',

...   website='http://www.oreilly.com/')

>>> publisher_list = Publisher.objects.all()

>>> publisher_list

<QuerySet [<Publisher: Publisher object>, <Publisher: Publisher object>]>

Model String Representations

When the publisher list was printed, the output we got was not very helpful and made it very hard to distinguish the Publisher objects from one another. It should have looked like this:

<QuerySet [<Publisher: Publisher object>, <Publisher: Publisher object>]>

This is easily solved: all we do is add another method to the Publisher class – the __str__() method. All __str__() methods let Python know how to show an object representation in a format readable by the human eye. If you add a __str__) method to our three models, we can see how this works:

```python
from django.db import models


class Publisher(models.Model):
    name = models.CharField(max_length=30)
    address = models.CharField(max_length=50)
    city = models.CharField(max_length=60)
    state_province = models.CharField(max_length=30)
    country = models.CharField(max_length=50)
    website = models.URLField()

    def __str__(self):
        return self.name


class Author(models.Model):
    first_name = models.CharField(max_length=30)
    last_name = models.CharField(max_length=40)
    email = models.EmailField()
```

```python
    def __str__(self):

        return u'%s %s' % (self.first_name, self.last_name)


class Book(models.Model):

    title = models.CharField(max_length=100)

    authors = models.ManyToManyField(Author)

    publisher = models.ForeignKey(Publisher)

    publication_date = models.DateField()


    def __str__(self):

        return self.title
```

The __str__() method does whatever is necessary to return a readable object representation:

- The __str__() methods added to Book and Publisher return the title and the name of each object
- The __str__() method added to Author is a little more involved. It will add the first_name field to the last_name field with a space between the two.

__str__() methods have just one requirement – that a string object is returned. If a string object is not returned and we get an integer instead, and a TypeError is raised by Python.

When we add a __str__() method, for the changes to happen, we need to come out of the Python shell and go back into it through python manage.py shell. Now this is a much better output:

> >> *from books.models import Publisher*

> >> *publisher_list = Publisher.objects.all()*

> >> *publisher_list*

<QuerySet [<Publisher: Apress>, <Publisher: O'Reilly>]>

For the sake of convenience when we use the interactive interpreter, we ensure a __str__() method is defined for all models. This is also helpful to Django because it uses the __str__() output in multiple laces when it has objects to be displayed.

Lastly, using __str__() is also one of the best ways to give a model new behaviors. Django models don't only define the layout of the database table for an object; they also define the functionalities that the object does, one of which is __str__().

Inserting Data and Updating It

We do this by inserting a database row which requires us to use keyword arguments to create a model instance, like this:

> >> *p = Publisher(name='GNW Independent Publishing',*

...   *address='123 Some Street',*

...   *city='Hamilton',*

...   *state_province='NSW',*

...   *country='AUSTRALIA',*

...   *website='http://djangobook.com/')*

This instantiation method does not do anything to anything to the database; until save() is called, the record will not be saved:

> >> *p.save()*

This is translated roughly into the following for SQL:

INSERT INTO books_publisher

  (name, address, city, state_province, country, website)

VALUES

  ('GNW Independent Publishing', '123 Some Street', 'Hamilton', 'NSW',

   'Australia', 'http://djangobook.com/');

The Publisher model is using a primary key id that auto-increments so the first save() call will do an additional thing – it will work out what the primary key value is for the record and, on the instance, is set to idattribute:

>>> p.id

3   # this will depend on what your data is

Any further save() calls will save that record and will not create a new one, i.e. an SQL UPDATE statement is performed rather than INSERT:

>>> p.name = 'GNW Independent Publishing'

>>> p.save()

This translates roughly into the following for SQL:

UPDATE books_publisher SET

  name = 'GNW Independent Publishing',

  address='123 Some Street',

  city='Hamilton',

  state_province='NSW',

  country='AUSTRALIA',

website='http://djangobook.com/')

WHERE id = 3;

All fields are updated, not just those we made changes to. Depending on what the application is, we could end up with a race condition. Later we look at how to update several objects in a single statement to execute the following query which is a little different:

UPDATE books_publisher SET

   name = 'GNW Independent Publishing'

WHERE id=3;

Selecting the Objects

While it is important to know how to create a database record and update it, there is a good chance that most of the web apps that you will be building will likely query objects that already exist rather than creating new objects. We know how to get all the records in any specified model:

>>> Publisher.objects.all()

<QuerySet [<Publisher: Apress>, <Publisher: O'Reilly>, <Publisher: GNW Independent Publishing>]>

In SQL this would be:

SELECT id, name, address, city, state_province, country, website

FROM books_publisher;

Note that SELECT * is not used by Django when data is being looked up. Rather, all the fields are explicitly listed. This is in the design – there are circumstances where SELECT * is quite a lot slower and, if you read and understood the Zen of Python at the start of the book, you will have picked up that field listing follows one specific principle – "Explicit is better than implicit".

Let's break down the Publisher.objects.all() line:

First is the Publisher model. Whenever we have data we want to look up, we need the model that relates to that data.

Second is the objects attribute, known as a manager. A manager is used to look after the table-level data operations including the most important one, data lookup. Every model has an objects manager given to it automatically and these are used when we need to look up any model instance.

Last we use the all() method, an objects manager method that will, in a QuerySet, return every row in a database. A QuerySet is an object used to represent a given set of database rows.

Pretty much any database lookup will follow this pattern – methods are called on the manager that goes with the model we are querying.

Filtering the Data

It isn't very often that everything in a database will be selected at once; mostly, just a subset of the data will be wanted. There is a method in the Django API called filter() that lets filter which data is wanted:

>>> Publisher.objects.filter(name='Apress')

<QuerySet [<Publisher: Apress>]>

The filter() method will take keyword arguments that are subsequently translated into the right SQL WHERE clauses. The above example would look like this:

SELECT id, name, address, city, state_province, country, website

FROM books_publisher

WHERE name = 'Apress';

The filter() method can take several arguments at once, helping to narrow the requirements down even more:

>>> *Publisher.objects.filter(country="U.S.A.",*

state_province="CA")

<QuerySet [<Publisher: Apress>]>

Again these arguments are translated, this time in SQL AND clauses so the above example would look like this:

SELECT id, name, address, city, state_province, country, website

FROM books_publisher

WHERE country = 'U.S.A.'

AND state_province = 'CA';

By default, the SQL = operator is used by the lookups for exact matches:

>>> *Publisher.objects.filter(name__contains="press")*

<QuerySet [<Publisher: Apress>]>

In between name and contains, we have a double underscore, and this is used in both Django and Python to indicate a bit of magic. In this case, the __contain bit of this code is translated to an SQL LIKE statement, like this:

SELECT id, name, address, city, state_province, country, website

FROM books_publisher

WHERE name LIKE '%press%';

Other lookup types include icontains, which translates to LIKE (Case-insensitive), startswith, endswith, and range, which translates to SQL BETWEEN.

Retrieving a Single Object

All the filter() examples we used above returned the same – a QuerySet, which may be treated as a list. However, sometimes it might be better to retrieve just one object rather than a QuerySet and that is what we use the get() method for:

>>> Publisher.objects.get(name="Apress")

<Publisher: Apress>

Instead of getting a QuerySet, only one object is returned and, as such, a query that results in several objects will end up with an exception being raised:

>>> Publisher.objects.get(country="U.S.A.")

Traceback (most recent call last):

...

books.models.MultipleObjectsReturned: get() returned more than one Publisher - it returned 2!

And, if the query doesn't return any objects at all, that will also raise an exception:

>>> Publisher.objects.get(name="Penguin")

Traceback (most recent call last):

...

books.models.DoesNotExist: Publisher matching query does not exist.

The exception called DoesNotExist is an attribute of the class belonging to the model – Publisher.DoesNotExist. The following needs to be done in your applications to catch those exceptions:

try:

  p = Publisher.objects.get(name='Apress')

except Publisher.DoesNotExist:

   print ("Apress isn't in the database yet.")

else:

   print ("Apress is in the database.")

Ordering the Data

As you get to grips with the examples we used so far, you might start to notice that the objects are returned in what seems to be a random order. No, you are not seeing things. Up to now, the database has not been told how the results should be ordered so the data is given back in an order that the database chooses. When you build your applications, you will most likely want your results ordered using a specific value, say, numerically or alphabetically. We do this using the method called order_by():

>>> Publisher.objects.order_by("name")

<QuerySet [<Publisher: Apress>, <Publisher: GNW Independent Publishing>, <Publisher: O'Reilly>]>

This looks much like the all() example we used earlier but now SQL has a specific order:

SELECT id, name, address, city, state_province, country, website

FROM books_publisher

ORDER BY name;

You can use whatever field you want to order by:

>>> Publisher.objects.order_by("address")

<QuerySet [<Publisher: O'Reilly>, <Publisher: GNW Independent Publishing>, <Publisher: Apress>]>

>>> *Publisher.objects.order_by("state_province")*

<QuerySet [<Publisher: Apress>, <Publisher: O'Reilly>, <Publisher: GNW Independent Publishing>]>

If you want to order using multiple fields, multiple arguments are required:

>>> *Publisher.objects.order_by("state_province", "address")*

<QuerySet [<Publisher: Apress>, <Publisher: O'Reilly>, <Publisher: GNW Independent Publishing>]>

And you can also do reverse ordering by adding a minus character (-) to the start of the field name:

>>> *Publisher.objects.order_by("-name")*

<QuerySet [<Publisher: O'Reilly>, <Publisher: GNW Independent Publishing>, <Publisher: Apress>]>

All that said, while the flexibility is great, it can get quite repetitive to keep using order_by(). Mostly, you are going to have a specific field that you want used for ordering and, in cases like this, Django allows you to specify default ordering within the model:

class Publisher(models.Model):

  name = models.CharField(max_length=30)

  address = models.CharField(max_length=50)

  city = models.CharField(max_length=60)

  state_province = models.CharField(max_length=30)

  country = models.CharField(max_length=50)

  website = models.URLField()

```
def __str__(self):

    return self.name


class Meta:

    ordering = ['name']
```

We've looked at a new concept called the Meta class. This class is embedded in the definition of the Publisher class and it can be used on whatever model you want to specify any options that are specific to the model. There are several Meta options, but we are only interested in the ordering option here. When we use it, we are telling Django that, unless order_by() specifies an explicit order, the name field is used to order the Publisher objects by whenever the database API is used to retrieve them.

Chaining Your Lookups

We looked at filtering and ordering data but, on many occasions, you will want to do both. This entails chaining the lookups, like this:

>>> Publisher.objects.filter(country="U.S.A.").order_by("-name")

<QuerySet [<Publisher: O'Reilly>, <Publisher: Apress>]>

The SQL translation is to SQL WHERE and SQL ORDER BY:

SELECT id, name, address, city, state_province, country, website

FROM books_publisher

WHERE country = 'U.S.A'

ORDER BY name DESC;

Slicing the Data

What if you only wanted to look up a set number of the database rows? You could have a database that is full of publishers, thousands of them, but you only want to display the first one. Django allows for QuerySets to be treated as lists and this means you can use the standard syntax in Python for list slicing:

>>> *Publisher.objects.order_by('name')[0]*

<Publisher: Apress>

This is translated to something like:

SELECT id, name, address, city, state_province, country, website

FROM books_publisher

ORDER BY name

LIMIT 1;

In much the same way, a specified subset of the data can be retrieved with the standard syntax for range-slicing in Python:

>>> *Publisher.objects.order_by('name')[0:2]*

Two objects are returned which translate to something like:

SELECT id, name, address, city, state_province, country, website

FROM books_publisher

ORDER BY name

OFFSET 0 LIMIT 2;

Note – there is no support for negative slicing:

>>> *Publisher.objects.order_by('name')[-1]*

Traceback (most recent call last):

...

AssertionError: Negative indexing is not supported.

We can get around this quite easily; all we do is make a change to the order_by statement:

>>> *Publisher.objects.order_by('-name')[0]*

Updating Several Objects in a Single Statement

Earlier, we discussed the save() method to update the columns in a database row. Depending on what the application does, we might only want some of the columns updated. For example, let's assume that we want the Apress Publisher to change from the name Apress to Apress publishing. If we used save(), it would look like this:

>>> *p = Publisher.objects.get(name='Apress')*

>>> *p.name = 'Apress Publishing'*

>>> *p.save()*

A rough translation of that would be:

SELECT id, name, address, city, state_province, country, website

FROM books_publisher

WHERE name = 'Apress';

UPDATE books_publisher SET

   name = 'Apress Publishing',

   address = '2855 Telegraph Ave.',

city = 'Berkeley',

state_province = 'CA',

country = 'U.S.A.',

website = 'http://www.apress.com'

WHERE id = 1;

In this example, we are assuming that the publisher id of Apress is 1. The save() method sets the values for all columns, not just that of the name column. If our environment causes the other database columns to change because of another process, the smart thing to do is to only change the column we need to change. We use the update() method for this on the QuerySet objects:

>>> Publisher.objects.filter(id=1).update(name='Apress Publishing')

The SQL translation here is much more efficient and has no chance of race conditions:

UPDATE books_publisher

SET name = 'Apress Publishing'

WHERE id = 1;

This method will work on all QuerySets and this gives us the means to edit bulk records. Let's say that we want to changer U.S.A. to USA in each record in Publisher:

>>> Publisher.objects.all().update(country='USA')

3

The return value of the update() method is an integer that represents the number of records changed. In our example, it was 3.

Deleting an Object

If we want an object deleted from the database, we call the delete() method for that object:

```
>>> p = Publisher.objects.get(name="O'Reilly")

>>> p.delete()

(1, {'books.Publisher': 1})

>>> Publisher.objects.all()

<QuerySet [<Publisher: Apress>, <Publisher: GNW Independent Publishing>]>
```

Note Django's return value when an object is deleted. First, the total number of affected records is listed – in our case, it's one). Then a dictionary lists the models that are affected, and the number of records deleted out of each table.

Objects can be bulk deleted too. Simply take the result of a QuerySet and call delete() on it. This is much like the update() method from before:

```
>>> Publisher.objects.filter(country='USA').delete()

(1, {'books.Publisher': 1})

>>> Publisher.objects.all().delete()

(1, {'books.Publisher': 1})

>>> Publisher.objects.all()

<QuerySet []>
```

Be very careful when you delete data. Django has a failsafe in place to stop you accidentally deleting the entire contents of a table – explicit use of all() if you want everything deleted. The following example would NOT work:

```
>>> Publisher.objects.delete()
```

Traceback (most recent call last):

 File "", line 1, in

AttributeError: 'Manager' object has no attribute 'delete'

But, if you use the all() method, it will work:

>>> *Publisher.objects.all().delete()*

If we only want a subset of the data deleted, all() does not need to be used:

>>> *Publisher.objects.filter(country='USA').delete()*

We should now be able to write a basic application that is based on a database. When we have defined the models, the database must be populated with data. We could have some legacy data, or we might be relying on our website users to supply the data for us – we'll need a form for that. Sometimes we might need to manually input data, and, for this, it would be very helpful if we had an interface that we could use for the entry and management of the data. That leads us to the admin interface in Django.

Django Admin Site

Most of today's websites have an admin interface as an integral part of their infrastructure. The admin interface is web-based and can only be used by a trusted admin of the website. It is where site content is added, edited, and deleted. Think of a WordPress blog, for example; the interface where the content is added is the admin interface. If you built a website for a client, the admin interface is the way in which they update their website, and so on.

Admin interfaces do have one problem though – they are incredibly boring to build. Web development is meant to be fun and wasting time on boring jobs simply isn't fun. You need to display forms, handle them, authenticate site users, validate all input, and more. Not only is it boring work, but it is also very repetitive.

So, what does Django do? It does everything for us. Admin interfaces are solved problems in Django, so we are going to take a look at the Django admin site, how it works and what we can do with it.

How to Use the Django Admin Site

Earlier you ran django-admin startproject mysite and when you did that the default admin site was created by Django and configured. All that is left for you to do is create the superuser (admin user) and then you can gain access to your admin site.

Open the virtual environment for your project and run this command:

(env_mysite) C:\...\mysite_project\mysite> python manage.py createsuperuser

Type in the username you want to use and hit the Enter key – in our case, we are using admin as the username:

Username: admin

Next, type in the email address you want to use:

Email address: admin@example.com

Lastly, you will be asked to put your password in, and then re-enter it to confirm. You will need a secure password, even for the purpose of testing.

Django will run a test on your password strength; if it is too simple or too common you won't be able to use it. This is somewhat irritating when you are testing but you can be safe in the knowledge that Django will not let you use a weak or stupid password to break through the security that it crafts very carefully.

Password: **********

Password (again): *********

Superuser created successfully.

Start the Development Server

The latest version of Django activates the admin site by default so the next step is to run the development server and have a look around. We start the server like this:

(env_mysite) C:\...\mysite_project\mysite> python manage.py runserver

Next, go to your web browser and type in your local domain – you want the admin section so you would type something like http://127.0.0.1:8000/admin/. The login screen should open. Translation is activated by default so you may see the screen in your language, although this is dependent on what your browser settings are and whether Django can translate your particular language.

Enter the Admin Site

Log in using the superuser account you just created. The admin index page will load and there should be two types of content that you can edit – Users and Groups. These come from django.contrib.auth, which is Django's authentication framework. The Django admin site has been designed with non-technical users in mind, so it should be relatively easy to use. However, the following is a walk-through of the basics.

Each data type within the admin site has two things – a change list and a form for editing. The change list is where you can see all the database objects while the editing form is where you add records, change them or delete them. To bring up the users change list page, go to the "Users" row and click on "Change".

The page will show you all the database users; if you are following our example, you should only see a single user for now but when you add more, the options for sort, filter, and search will become far more useful.

To get the options for filtering, look to the right side of the page; for sort, click on any column header, and the search facility is at the top giving you the option to use the username as a search filter. Click on the name of the user you created earlier, and the edit form will load. Here, you change the user's attributes, such as name and permissions. Note you will not see the password – raw passwords are not stored by Django, so you can never retrieve one – instead, you must change it.

One more thing you need to note is that fields that have different types are given different widgets. For example, the fields for data and time are given controls for a calendar, while a Boolean field will be given checkboxes, and character fields are given simple fields for inputting text.

To delete records, simply click on the Delete button on the edit form for the record – the button is at the bottom left of the page. From there, you go to a confirmation page which, where necessary, will also show you a list of the record's dependent objects which will also be deleted. For example, deleting a publisher would mean any books related to that publisher would be also deleted.

To add a record, go to the relevant column on the home page and click on Add. You will be given an empty edit page; just fill it in with the relevant details. Input validation is handled by the admin interface; if you were to leave a required field empty or input a date in an invalid format, you get an error when you attempt to save the record.

When you want to edit an object, you see a History link in the window; whenever you make any change through the interface, it is logged and you can click on the History link to see this log.

How it Works

So how does it all work behind the scenes?

It's really quite easy; at server startup when Django loads, the admin.autodiscover() function is run. This will iterate over INSTALLED_APPS looking for the admin.py file in each of your installed apps. If it finds it, the code in the file is executed and this will happen for every app the file is found in.

The admin site displays the edit/change interface for any model that has been registered explicitly with admin.site.register(_ in the admin.py file of the app. The django.contrib.auth app has an admin.py file of its own and this is why you can see Users and Groups.

Other than that, the admin site is a Django application. It has models, it has templates and views, and it has URLpatterns. It can be added into your own application; simply hook it into URLconf in the same way your views are hooked. The templates can be inspected, as can the URLpatterns, and the views by going into django/contrib/admin in your Django codebase. Don't change anything though, you could cause a lot of problems.

Adding Models to The Django Admin Site

There is one very important thing we have not looked at yet, and that is adding models to the admin site. We want to do this so that we can use this interface to add objects, change, or delete objects in our database tables. We'll continue with the example we have been using all through this section. In mysite_project\mysite\books, look in startapp – there should now be an admin.py file. If there isn't, just make one and input this code:

from django.contrib import admin

from.models import Publisher, Author, Book

admin.site.register(Publisher)

admin.site.register(Author)

admin.site.register(Book)

This is telling Django that an interface is required for each of the models. You can now go back to the admin home page by going to http://127.0.0.1:8000/admin/ - there should be a section for Books that has links in it for Authors, Publishers, and Book. If you don't see the changes; stop the server and restart it.

What you have now is an admin interface that is functional for each of the models.

Now take a bit of time out to play around with it; add some records, change them, delete them, and see how it all works.

One thing to mention is the way the Django admin site handles many-to-many relationships and foreign keys. Both can be seen in the model called Book. Just to remind you, this is the book model:

class Book(models.Model):

  title = models.CharField(max_length=100)

  authors = models.ManyToManyField(Author)

  publisher = models.ForeignKey(Publisher)

  publication_date = models.DateField()

  def __str__(self):

   return self.title

On the Add Book page, which you will find at http://127.0.0.1:8000/admin/books/book/add/, you will see a select box this represents the ForeignKey (the publisher); a multiple-select box is used to represent the ManyToMany field (the authors). Both the fields have a green plus icon beside them allowing you to easily add records that are related.

Click the plus next to Publisher, for example, and a window will load allowing a publisher to be added. Once the new publisher has been created, the form for Add Book is updated with the details.

Making a Field Optional

After you've been getting to know the site for a while, you will notice that there is one glaring limitation – every field on the edit form must be completed. Most of the time you are likely to want some of the fields to be optional. Let's assume that we want the email field for the Author model to an optional one, i.e. a blank string can be allowed. In reality, you may not have this information for every author so, to specify this field as an optional one, we need to edit the model. Go to mysite/books/models.py, open the Author model and, for the email field, add blank=True:

class Author(models.Model):

  first_name = models.CharField(max_length=30)

  last_name = models.CharField(max_length=40)

  email = models.EmailField(blank=True)

What we've done here is told Django that we will allow a blank value for the email addresses; by default, every field is set as blank=False, meaning that we can't have any blank values.

Something quite interesting is going on – up to this point, leaving the __str__() method aside, all the models have been used as database table definitions, in essence, a Python expression of the SQL CREATE TABLE statement. By putting blank=true, we are now moving our model away from just a simple table definition.

The model class is beginning to get a little richer in terms of the information, what the Author objects are, and what they are able to do. A VARCHAR column represents the email field in our database, but the email field is also, as far as contexts like the admin site go, an optional field.

Now, once you have completed the above code, reload the edit form for "Add Author" and you will see that the email field label is no longer in bold, which tells you it is no longer a requirement. Authors can now be added to the database without the need to provide an email address for each one.

Making the Date and Numeric Fields Optional

One of the more common mistakes that relate to blank=true surrounds the numeric and date fields. SQL has its own unique way to specify a blank value and that is by using a value known as NULL. This may be used to mean "invalid" or "unknown" or anything else that may be specific to the application. The NULL value in SQL is not the same as an empty string in the same way that the NONE object in Python is not the same as an empty string.

What all this means is that a character field may have both an empty string value and a NULL value. this can cause no end of confusion and to help avoid this, the CREATE TABLE statements that are generated automatically in Django add to each of the column definitions an explicit NOT NULL. The example below shows the statement generated for the Author model:

CREATE TABLE "books_author" (

　　"id" serial NOT NULL PRIMARY KEY,

　　"first_name" varchar(30) NOT NULL,

　　"last_name" varchar(40) NOT NULL,

　　"email" varchar(75) NOT NULL

);

Most of the time, this kind of behavior will be the best thing for your application and will save you from headaches surrounding inconsistent data, not to mention working very well with everything else in Django. That includes the admin site which uses an empty string rather than the NULL value when a field is left blank.

However, there is an exception as far as the column types that don't consider an empty string to be valid – this includes numbers, times and dates. If you were to try putting an empty string into an integer or date column, you will more than likely get an error, depending on the database – PostgreSQL will definitely throw up an exception while MySQL may or may not.

In our case, the only way we can specify empty values is to use NULL. With a Django model, NULL is specified by doing something similar to what we did earlier, this time giving a field a value of null=True. That was all rather a long way of saying that when you want blank values to be accepted in date or numeric fields, you must use blank=true as well as null=True.

Let's edit the Book model so that publication_date will accept a blank value. The new code should look like this:

class Book(models.Model):

  title = models.CharField(max_length=100)

  authors = models.ManyToManyField(Author)

  publisher = models.ForeignKey(Publisher)

  publication_date = models.DateField(blank=True, null=True)

Adding blank=True is quite a bit easier than it is to add null=True simply because the latter will change the database semantics. What it does is change the CREATE TABLE statement so that NOT NULL is removed from publication_date. A database update is needed to complete this.

For several reasons, Django will not make database schema changes automatic – it is down to you to execute python manage.py migrate when a change is made. Going back to our admin site, the edit form for "Add Book" should now allow the publication date field to stay blank.

Customizing the Field Labels

On each of the edit forms on the admin site, it is the name of the model field that generates the field labels and the algorithm is one of the simplest – Django takes the underscores away and inserts spaces in their place and then makes the character a capital letter, i.e. the publication_date field in the Book model has a label of "Publication date".

That said, a field name won't always lead to a nice label for the corresponding admin field which will mean you may need to do some customization on occasion. To do this, you need to specify verbose_name in the right field. For example, to change the Author.emailfield so it reads "e-mail", we would do this:

```
class Author(models.Model):

    first_name = models.CharField(max_length=30)

    last_name = models.CharField(max_length=40)

    email = models.EmailField(blank=True, verbose_name ='e-mail')
```

When you have done this, the server must be reloaded, and the new label can be seen on the edit form for Author. Do NOT make the first letter of verbose_name a capital unless it is one that should always be a capital. Django will put capital letters where and when needed and the exact value for verbose_name will be used somewhere else where capitalization is not required.

Custom ModelAdmin Classes

So far, we have only made model-level changes – null=True, blank=True, and verbose_name. None of these are admin-level – they are all a basic part of our model and may be used by admin but are not admin-specific.

Going past those, the admin site has quite a few options that allow you to customize the way the admin site operates for any given model. You can find these options inside the ModelAdmin classes, each containing the configuration for the given model in a given instance of the admin site.

Customizing the Change Lists and Forms

Let's look into customizing admin by specifying which fields are to be shown on the Author model change list. By default, the __str__() result is shown on the change list for each of the objects. Earlier, the __str__() method was defined for Author objects so it showed both the first and last names together:

```
class Author(models.Model):

    first_name = models.CharField(max_length=30)

    last_name = models.CharField(max_length=40)

    email = models.EmailField(blank=True, verbose_name ='e-mail')
```

```
def __str__(self):

    return u'%s %s' % (self.first_name, self.last_name)
```

The result of this is that the Author object change list will now show both the first and last names together.

This, however can be improved by putting a few extra fields on our change list display. For example, what if we add the email addresses for each author to the display? Plus, it would be quite nice if we could sort by both first and last name.

We can do this by giving our Author model a ModelAdmin class, the key to admin customization. One of the fundamental uses is to specify which fields are to be shown on the change list and we do all of this by editing admin.py:

```
from django.contrib import admin

from.models import Publisher, Author, Book


class AuthorAdmin(admin.ModelAdmin):

    list_display = ('first_name', 'last_name', 'email')


admin.site.register(Publisher)

admin.site.register(Author, AuthorAdmin)

admin.site.register(Book)
```

What we did is create the AuthorAdmin class put django.contrib.admin.ModelAdmin as a subclass and is home to a custom configuration for a given admin model. All we did was specify a single customization, which was list_display. This has been set in order that a field named tuple will show on the change list. Obviously, the field names must already exist within the model.

Next, we changed admin.site.register() so that AuthorAdmin is after Author. This function will take a second argument, optional, of a ModelAdmin subclass. If a second argument hasn't been specified, the default options for admin are used by Django.

Once that is done, we can reload the page and should now see three columns titles First Name, Last Name, E-Mail Address. Each column can also be sorted – just click the header on the column you want to be sorted.

Next, we want a search bar added so we give AuthorAdmin a search_fields, like this:

class AuthorAdmin(admin.ModelAdmin):

　list_display = ('first_name', 'last_name', 'email')

　search_fields = ('first_name', 'last_name')

Reload the page and a search bar will be at the top. What we did was tell the change list for admin that we want a search bar that we can use to search both the first_name and the last_name fields. This is not case-sensitive, and both fields will be searched. If you wanted to search for a string of "bar", you would find the results would be an author that has the last name of Hobarson and one with the first name of Barney.

Now we want some date filters added to the change list for Book model:

from django.contrib import admin

from.models import Publisher, Author, Book

class AuthorAdmin(admin.ModelAdmin):

　list_display = ('first_name', 'last_name', 'email')

```
    search_fields = ('first_name', 'last_name')



class BookAdmin(admin.ModelAdmin):

    list_display = ('title', 'publisher', 'publication_date')

    list_filter = ('publication_date',)
```

```
admin.site.register(Publisher)

admin.site.register(Author, AuthorAdmin)

admin.site.register(Book, BookAdmin)
```

This is a different option set that we are dealing with, so a new ModelAdminClass has been created called BookAdmin. First, a list_display was defined so the change list looks better. Second, a list_filter was used and set the tuple of fields that will be used for creating filters on the right-hand side of the change list. As far as date fields are concerned, shortcuts are provided by Django, so the list can be filtered by four options:

- Today
- Past 7 days
- This month
- This year

We can also use list_filter on other types of field, not only DateField and the filters will appear if there are two or more values. We can also use the date filters by using the admin option of date_hierarchy, in this way:

```
class BookAdmin(admin.ModelAdmin):

    list_display = ('title', 'publisher','publication_date')
```

```
list_filter = ('publication_date',)

date_hierarchy = 'publication_date'
```

Once all this is done, we now have a change list that shows a navigation bar for dates; the drop-down starts with all the years that are available, then the months and then the days.

Be aware that date_hierarchy does not take tuples, only strings because the hierarchy is made from a single date field. Lastly, the default order is changed so that, on the change list, the books are ordered in descending order by date of publication.

The default setting is for the change list to order all the objects as per the ordering of their model in the Meta class, but we didn't specify this, so we have undefined ordering:

```
class BookAdmin(admin.ModelAdmin):

    list_display = ('title', 'publisher','publication_date')

    list_filter = ('publication_date',)

    date_hierarchy = 'publication_date'

    ordering = ('-publication_date',)
```

The above ordering option will work the exact same way as the Meta ordering with the exception that only the first field name is used. If we want the order to be in descending order, we pass a tuple of field names or a list and put a minus sign on the relevant field.

Reload the page and you will see all your changes. The header for Publication date now displays an arrow that tells you the way the records have been sorted.

Although we only covered a few of the list option changes, these are the main ones and will give you the tools needed to produce an incredibly powerful interface that is for data editing in just a line or two of simple code.

Customizing the Edit Forms

In the same way that we can customize the change list, we can also customize the edit form. First, let's change the order of the fields. The default order will correspond to how they are in the model but that can be changed by going to the ModelAdmin subclass and using the fields option, like this:

class BookAdmin(admin.ModelAdmin):

   list_display = ('title', 'publisher', 'publication_date')

   list_filter = ('publication_date',)

   date_hierarchy = 'publication_date'

   ordering = ('-publication_date',)

   fields = ('title', 'authors', 'publisher', 'publication_date')

Once you have done this, the Books edit form will now use the new order for the fields. It looks better to have the author name follow the title of the book, but the order of the files will depend entirely on data-entry workflow. Every form is going to be different.

Something else that we can do with the fields option is make it impossible to edit some fields. All you do is leave out the relevant fields. We could consider doing this if we only trust the admin users to edit specific parts of the data or if external processes change some fields.

In the book database, for example, the publication_date field could be hidden so it can't be edited:

class BookAdmin(admin.ModelAdmin):

   list_display = ('title', 'publisher','publication_date')

   list_filter = ('publication_date',)

   date_hierarchy = 'publication_date'

ordering = ('-publication_date',)

fields = ('title', 'authors', 'publisher')

The result is that the books edit form no longer lets us specify the date of publication. In some cases, this would be quite useful; perhaps an editor doesn't want their authors pushing publication dates back, a hypothetical example. When the incomplete form is used to add new books, publication_date is set as None by Django, so it is important to ensure that null=True has been added to the field.

One more customization to the edit form that is quite common relates to the many-to-many fields. Multiple-select boxes are used to represent each of the ManyToMany fields but these boxes are not easy to use. If we need multiple items selected, the CTRL or CMD key must be held down on the keyboard first.

Although the text is added to explain this, when we have lots of options to choose from it all gets a bit awkward to use. The solution provided by the admin site is called filter_horizontal so let's put this into BookAdmin to see what happens>

class BookAdmin(admin.ModelAdmin):

  list_display = ('title', 'publisher','publication_date')

  list_filter = ('publication_date',)

  date_hierarchy = 'publication_date'

  ordering = ('-publication_date',)

  filter_horizontal = ('authors',)

Reload the form and the section for Authors now has a nice JS interface that allows for dynamic searching of the options and the ability to move an author from the Available Authors section to Chosen Authors – this works the other way too.

It is recommended that filter_horizontal be used for ManyToMany fields that contain 10 or more items. It is a good deal easier than a multiple-select box and, if we wanted to use filter_horizontal in multiple fields, we just ensure that the tuple contains each of the field names.

Support for filter_vertical is also there in the ModelAdmin class and this works the same way as filter_horizontal but with the boxes being stacked vertically. Which one we choose is down to personal requirements.

Neither of these options works on ForeignKey fields, only on ManyToMany. The select boxes are used by default for ForeignKey field but we won't always want every object to show up in the drop-down menu. Let's assume that our book database now contains thousands of different publishers; our form for "Add Books" is going to take quite a while to load because each publisher is displayed in the select box. There is a way to solve this and that is to use the raw_id_fields option:

class BookAdmin(admin.ModelAdmin):

   list_display = ('title', 'publisher','publication_date')

   list_filter = ('publication_date',)

   date_hierarchy = 'publication_date'

   ordering = ('-publication_date',)

   filter_horizontal = ('authors',)

   raw_id_fields = ('publisher',)

This should be set to a tuple of the ForeignKey field names which will be shown in admin in a text input box and not a select box. In this box goes the publisher's database ID and, because we humans tend not to memorize these IDs, we also get a handy magnifying glass that will bring up a window where we can choose the correct publisher.

Users, Groups and Permissions

Because you are a superuser, you get the tools to create objects, edit them and delete them. The site admin for Django uses a system of permissions that allow you to provide certain users access to the parts of the interface that they require and no more. These accounts are supposed to be generic so that they can be used elsewhere but, for our purposes, they'll be seen as admin user accounts.

Users and permissions may be edited in the same way as any other object is in the admin interface. A user object has a standard field – username, password, real name, and email but they also have another set of fields that allow you to define what that user can do.

First, we have three Boolean flags:

- **Active Flag** – this controls if the user is active or not; if set to off and the user attempts to log in, they will be denied access;
- **Staff Flag** – this control if the user is actually considered staff and is able to log in. The same system is used for public access sites, so this flag is intended to differentiate between public and admin users;
- **Superuser Flag** – this provides the user with total access, so they can add, delete or create an item within the interface. If set, all the regular permissions, or the lack thereof are ignored.

A normal admin use, i.e. an admin user who is not a superuser, is given access via a set of permissions assigned to them. Each of the objects that may be edited in the admin interface has three of these permissions: create, edit, and delete.

When a user is assigned permission, the user can only do what the permission allows. When a user is first created, no permissions are set so they must be provided; as an example, a user may be given permission to add a publisher or edit an existing one but not to delete any.

Permissions must be defined on a per-model basis, not per-object; the latter is very complicated and not within the scope of this book.

Note - more of a warning really. When you provide a user with the permission to edit users, they can also make changes to their permissions – it wouldn't take much for them to change themselves into a superuser! Lastly, users can be assigned to groups which provide the same permissions to a group of users.

So far, we have created some models and configured our interface to edit data. Now it is time to move on to the real part of web development – creating and processing forms.

Django Forms

HTML forms are a fundamental part of any interactive website. The search box for Google, the submission forms for a blog comment, right up to the incredibly complex interfaces for data-entry – everything is an HTML form. In this section we will look at how Django may be used to access user data submitted on a form, how to validate that data, and use it. We'll also look at Form object and HttpRequest objects.

Retrieving Data from Request Object

We talked briefly about HttpRequest object earlier, when we looked at the view functions but now we'll go into them in more detail. Remember that every view function will take, as its first parameter, a HttpRequest object, as we saw in the hello() view function:

from django.http import HttpResponse

def hello(request):

  return HttpResponse("Hello world")

An HttpRequest object has several methods and attributes that you should get to know so you know what can be done with them. These attributes may be used to gain information on the current request, for example the browser used for loading the Django-powered webpage, at the same time as the view function execution.

URL Information

Every HttpRequest object also contains some information about the URL that is currently being requested. Below is the different HttpRequest methods, their attributes, and an example:

request.path

entire path, without the domain but with the "/hello/" leading slash

request.get_host()

host or domain "127.0.0.1:8000"

request.get_full_path()

path and query string, if available "/hello/?print=true"

request.is_secure()

if HTTPS used for request, evaluates True; True or False, if otherwise, evaluates False

Rather than hard-coding an URL into your views, use the above attributes; the code will be far more flexible and reusable. A simple example is:

 # BAD!

```
def current_url_view_bad(request):

   return HttpResponse("Welcome to the page at /current/")
```

```
# GOOD

def current_url_view_good(request):

   return HttpResponse("Welcome to the page at %s"

% request.path)
```

Other Request Information

A Python dictionary called request.META is where the HTTP headers available for the specified request are found and that includes the IP address of the user, and the user-agent, usually the web browser name, and operating version. The list will depend entirely on what headers were sent by the user and those that are set by your web server. Some of the more common keys in the dictionary are:

- HTTP_REFERER – The referring URL, if there is one. Note that REFERER is misspelled – this is not a mistake on my behalf!
- HTTP_USER_AGENT – The user-agent string from the user's browser, if there is one.
- REMOTE_ADDR – Client's IP address, for example, 12.345.67.89. If there is more than one address, each will be separated by a comma.

If the user attempted to access a key that didn't exist, a KeyError exception would be thrown. This is because of request.META is nothing more than a basic dictionary. HTTP headers come via a user's browser and that means they are considered external data. Because of this they are not to be trusted and your application should be designed to fail if a header does not exist or is empty. To handle undefined keys, use get() or a try/except clause:

```python
# BAD!

def ua_display_bad(request):

    ua = request.META['HTTP_USER_AGENT']  # Might raise KeyError!

    return HttpResponse("Your browser is %s" % ua)


# GOOD (VERSION 1)

def ua_display_good1(request):

    try:

        ua = request.META['HTTP_USER_AGENT']

    except KeyError:

        ua = 'unknown'

    return HttpResponse("Your browser is %s" % ua)


# GOOD (VERSION 2)

def ua_display_good2(request):

    ua = request.META.get('HTTP_USER_AGENT', 'unknown')

    return HttpResponse("Your browser is %s" % ua)
```

Try to write a view that will show all of the data in request.META so that it can be seen and understood. That view might look like this:

```python
def display_meta(request):

    values = request.META
```

html = []

for k in sorted(values):

  html.append('<tr><td>%s</td><td>%s</td></tr>' % (k, values[k]))

return HttpResponse('<table>%s</table>' % '\n'.join(html))

Another excellent way of seeing what a request object contains is to look at the error pages thrown up by Django when the system is crashed. These pages contain quite a bit of useful information including the HTTP headers and any other request object.

Information Regarding Submitted Data

Aside from the metadata, an HttpRequest object has another two attributes that each have user-submitted information in them. Those attributes are: request.GET and request.POST. Both are dictionary-like, and provide access to the POST and GET data. POST data usually comes from an HTML form and the GET data comes from a form or from the page URL query string.

Being described as dictionary-like means that, although they are not dictionaries, they act like a standard Python dictionary. They both contain the methods get(), values(), and keys() within request.GET to iterate over the keys. The reason there is a distinction is that these two both have methods that can't be found in normal dictionaries.

Django Form-Handling – a Simple Example

Carrying on with our examples of books, we'll now create a view that will allow a user to search through the book database using titles. In general, development of a form is in two parts – the interface (HTML) and the backend code that will process the data. The first bit is easy; we set up a view that will show a search-form. We already have views.py in our \books folder so we'll open it and add a new view:

 # \books\views.py

```
from django.shortcuts import render


def search_form(request):

    return render(request, 'books/search_form.html')
```

Next, the template needs to be created, but before that, we are going to need some new folders. The APP_DIRS in settings should be set to True; if it isn't, we'll change it now. This will force Django to look for a \templates folder in all our apps.

In our books app folder, we'll make a new \template folder and then, inside that, we'll create another called books. The structure should look like books\templates\books. This new books folder is very important in terms of name spacing our existing templates. Django looks for a match in all our apps so having a namespace will ensure that the correct template is used if we have two of the same name.

The following is a search_form.HTML file; we'll create it and then save it in the new folder:

```
# mysite_project\mysite\books\templates\books\search_form.html


<html>

<head>

  <title>Search</title>

</head>

<body>
```

```
<form action="/search/" method="get">

    <input type="text" name="q">

    <input type="submit" value="Search">

</form>

</body>

</html>
```

Next a URLconf must be created so that the new view can be found. In the books folder, we'll make a new urls.py file (this is not created by startapp) and then add this pattern to the new file:

 # mysite\books\urls.py

from django.conf.urls import url

from books import views

urlpatterns = [

   url(r'^search-form/$', views.search_form),

]

When Django makes a search for URL pattern, it only looks in the mysite\urls.py file. If we want it to search elsewhere we need to add the specific URL patterns so we'll make a change to urlpatterns:

 # mysite\urls.py

```python
from django.conf.urls import include, url
```

```python
urlpatterns = [

#...

    url(r'^', include('books.urls')),

]
```

The new pattern should go at the end of the existing urlpatterns list and the reason for this is that r'^'regex will send everything to the books.url file and we need to make sure there are no other matching patterns; then Django can look in books\urls.py for the match. We'll go to http://127.0.0.1:8000/search-form/ to see our new search interface.

If we submit that form; we should get a 404 error because the form is pointing to a path that has not been implemented. We can solve that with another view function:

```python
# books/urls.py
```

```python
urlpatterns = [

    url(r'^search-form/$', views.search_form),

    url(r'^search/$', views.search),

]
```

```python
# books/views.py
```

```
from django.http import HttpResponse

#...


def search(request):

    if 'q' in request.GET:

        message = 'You searched for: %r' % request.GET['q']

    else:

        message = 'You submitted an empty form.'

    return HttpResponse(message)
```

All this will do is show the search term that was input, allowing us to ensure that Django gets the data in the proper way and so that we have an idea of the way the search terms flow throughout our system. A basic way of describing this is:

- A variable called q is defined by the HTML <form>. When submitted, q's value goes via the GET method to URL/search/
- The Django view responsible for handling URL/search/ will be able to access the value of q in request.GET

One thing of note is the explicit checking to ensure that q is in request.GET – as mentioned earlier, never put trust in anything submitted by a user. If this check was not included and an empty form was submitted, we would get a KeyError:

```
# BAD!

def bad_search(request):

    # The following line will raise KeyError if 'q' hasn't been submitted!
```

message = 'You searched for: %r' % request.GET['q']

return HttpResponse(message)

Query String Parameters

GET data is processed in a query string so that means request. GET can be used to access variables in query strings. You already know how to access the parameters in the query strings inside your views. POST data works in much the same way; you just use request.POST instead. So, what is the difference between the two?

GET should be used when form submission is nothing more than a request to 'get' some data. POST should be used when form submission will have an effect of some kind, i.e. sending an email, changing some data, or anything that goes beyond the display of the data. In our example, we used GET because our query is not making any changes to any of the data on the server.

Now we know that request.GET has been properly passed in, we can hook the search query into the database in views.py:

from django.http import HttpResponse

from django.shortcuts import render

from books.models import Book

def search(request):

  if 'q' in request.GET and request.GET['q']:

   q = request.GET['q']

   books = Book.objects.filter(title__icontains=q)

   return render(request, 'books/search_results.html',

{'books': books, 'query': q})

    else:

       return HttpResponse('Please submit a search term.')

A note or two or what we've done:

We checked that q existed in request.GET and we also checked that the value of request.Get['q'] is non-empty before it can be passed into the database query.

We are querying the book table using Book.objects,filter(title_icontains=q) to look for any book that has a title with the provided submission. icontains is a type of lookup that we can translate this statement as something along the lines of "get any books with a title containing q, not case-sensitive".

This is one of the easiest ways of searching for a book, but if we are searching on a large production database, icontains is not the best type of query to use as it isn't fast. A list of the book objects, called books, is passed to the template and, so the search-form works, we need to create a file called search_results.html:

 # \books\templates\books\search_results.html

<html>

  <head>

  <title>Book Search</title>

  </head>

  <body>

    <p>You searched for: {{ query }}</p>

    {% if books %}

```
<p>Found {{ books|length }} book{{ books|pluralize }}.</p>

<ul>

  {% for book in books %}

  <li>{{ book.title }}</li>

  {% endfor %}

</ul>

{% else %}

  <p>No books matched your search criteria.</p>

{% endif %}

</body>

</html>
```

Note that we use a pluralized template filter; an 's' is outputted where required based on how many books were found.

When we run the development server now and go to http://127.0.0.1:8000/search-from, we should get a useful result.

Improving Our Example

We looked at a simple example of form-handling, now we need to look at some of the problems and how we can fix them. First, the way our search() view handles empty queries is not very good; all it does is display a message that asks the user to submit a search term. This means the user has to hit their browser's back button. This is not professional and if we were ever to do something like that, we can be sure that we wouldn't have any Django privileges left!

The easiest thing to do is display the form again with an error – this would let us try *again straightaway and the best way of doing that is to render the template once more:*

from django.shortcuts import render

from django.http import HttpResponse

from books.models import Book

def search_form(request):

  return render(request, 'books/search_form.html')

def search(request):

  error = False

  if 'q' in request.GET:

    q = request.GET['q']

    if not q:

      error = True

    else:

      books = Book.objects.filter(title__icontains=q)

      return render(request, 'books/search_results.html', {'books': books, 'query': q})

  return render(request, 'books/search_form.html', {'error': error})

We've made some improvements to our search() method so that the search_form.html template can be rendered once more should the query be empty. Because an error message needs to be displayed in the template, a template variable needs to be passed. Now, search_form.html can be edited so it checks for an error variable:

```html
<html>
<head>
    <title>Search</title>
</head>
<body>
    {% if error %}
        <p style="color: red;">Please submit a search term.</p>
    {% endif %}
    <form action="/search/" method="get">
        <input type="text" name="q">
        <input type="submit" value="Search">
    </form>
</body>
</html>
```

The template of search_form() that was in the original view can still be used because it doesn't pass the template an error and that means that the error message won't display.

Now that we have made the change, we have a better application, but it raises a question – do we really need a dedicated search_form()? As it is now, putting in a request to URL/search with no GET parameters, we will see an empty form that has an error on it. The search_form () view can be removed together with the URLpattern associated with it so long as search() is changed so the error message is hidden when a user goes to /search/ without using any GET parameters:

```
def search(request):

    error = False

    if 'q' in request.GET:

        q = request.GET['q']

        if not q:

            error = True

        else:

            books = Book.objects.filter(title__icontains=q)

            return render(request, 'books/search_results.html', {'books': books, 'query': q})

    return render(request, 'books/search_form.html', {'error': error})
```

In our newly updated view, when a user goes to/search/ without any GET parameters, they will be confronted with a search-form and no error message. If the form is submitted with an empty q value, the search-form is accompanied by the error message. Lastly, if a non-empty value is provided for q when the form is submitted, the search results will show up.

There is one final change that can be made to get rid of some of the redundancy. Now the two views have been rolled into one, together with the URLs, and we have /search/ handling the search_form and results displays, we don't need a URL hard-coded in the HTML form inside search_form.html:

```
<form action="/search/" method="get">
```

It can be changed to this:

<form action="" method="get">

action="" stands for "Submit the form to the same URL as the current page", and with this change, we will not need to remember that the action has to be changed as the search() view is hooked to another URL.

Django Form Validation

Right now, we still have quite a simple search example, especially where data validation is concerned. All we are doing is making sure we don't have an empty search query. Most HTML forms will have some kind of validation that is a little more complex than doing this. We've all been faced with error messages when we try to input data on a web form, such as:

"Please enter a valid phone number. 888 is not a valid area code"

"Please enter a valid email address. Xxx.com is not a valid provider"

And so on.

Let's make a change to our search() view to make it validate whether our search terms is equal to or less than 20 characters. How would we do that? Well, the easiest way to do it is to embed our logic in the view:

def search(request):

  error = False

  if 'q' in request.GET:

    q = request.GET['q']

    if not q:

      error = True

    elif len(q) > 20:

```python
            error = True
        else:
            books = Book.objects.filter(title__icontains=q)
            return render(request, 'search_results.html', {'books': books, 'query': q})
    return render(request, 'search_form.html', {'error': error})
```

If we were to try submitting a query that was more than 20 characters now, we wouldn't be able to; instead, we would get an error message. At this stage, that message simply reads, "Please submit a search term". This needs to be changed:

```html
<html>
<head>
  <title>Search</title>
</head>
<body>
  {% if error %}
    <p style="color: red;">
      Please submit a search term 20 characters or shorter.
    </p>
  {% endif %}

  <form action="/search/" method="get">
    <input type="text" name="q">
```

```html
    <input type="submit" value="Search">

  </form>

</body>

</html>
```

This isn't very pretty! We have an error message that could be quite confusing because it comes up for anything including an empty submission. Why would we need to know about characters in an empty form? Error messages must always be specific, and they should never confuse the user. Our problem lies in the fact that we are only using a Boolean value for our error; what we should be using is a list containing various error strings. We could fix that like this:

```python
def search(request):

  errors = []

  if 'q' in request.GET:

    q = request.GET['q']

    if not q:

      errors.append('Enter a search term.')

    elif len(q) > 20:

      errors.append('Please enter at most 20 characters.')

    else:

      books = Book.objects.filter(title__icontains=q)

      return render(request, 'search_results.html', {'books': books, 'query': q})

  return render(request, 'search_form.html', {'errors': errors})
```

Now we just need to make a small change to our search_form.html template to show that an errors list is being passed and not a Boolean value.

```html
<html>

<head>

  <title>Search</title>

</head>

<body>

  {% if errors %}

    <ul>

      {% for error in errors %}

      <li>{{ error }}</li>

      {% endfor %}

    </ul>

  {% endif %}

  <form action="/search/" method="get">

    <input type="text" name="q">

    <input type="submit" value="Search">

  </form>

</body>

</html>
```

Making Contact Forms

We've iterated over our book form a few times now and we've made it a bit nicer than it was, but it is still really simple. It's just one field called 'q'. As forms become more and more complex, the above step must be repeated over and over for each of the form fields we are using, and this does nothing more than introduce a lot of unnecessary stuff and it increases the margin for human error. Luckily, Django is on our side and we have a high-level library built-in that will handle all the tasks related to forms and validation.

Our First Form Class

Django has a built-in form library called django.forms. This will handle many of the problems we have talked about so far so let's get straight into it and edit out contact form app using this framework. The main way of using it is to define a Form class for each of the HTML<forms> we have. At the moment, we have just one form, so we will only have one class. Convention dictates that we should keep our Form classes in a file called forms.py so we'll start by creating this in mysite\views.py with the following code:

 # mysite_project\mysite\mysite\forms.py

from django import forms

class ContactForm(forms.Form):

  subject = forms.CharField()

  email = forms.EmailField(required=False)

  message = forms.CharField()

This is quite an intuitive code and it is much like the model syntax in Django. Each form field is represented by a Field class, the type of which will depend on the field. We are using EmailField and CharField as the Form class attributes.

These are required fields, by default so we have specified require=False to make the email field optional.

Over to our interactive interpreter and see what we can do with this class. First, it will display as HTML:

(env_mysite) C:\Users\...\mysite> python manage.py shell

>>> from mysite.forms import ContactForm

>>> f = ContactForm()

>>> print(f)

<tr><th><label for="id_subject">Subject:</label></th><td><input type="text" name="subject" required id="id_subject" /></td></tr>

<tr><th><label for="id_email">Email:</label></th><td><input type="email" name="email" id="id_email" /></td></tr>

<tr><th><label for="id_message">Message:</label></th><td><input type="text" name="message" required id="id_message" /></td></tr>

A label is added to each of the fields by Django and the <label> tags to make them more accessible. What we want is for the default behavior to be as optimal as it possibly can be. The output is, by default, an HTML <table> but there are some other outputs built-in:

>>> print(f.as_ul())

<li><label for="id_subject">Subject:</label> <input type="text" name="subject" required id="id_subject" /></li>

<li><label for="id_email">Email:</label> <input type="email" name="email" id="id_email" /></li>

```
<li><label for="id_message">Message:</label> <input type="text"
name="message" required id="id_message" /></li>
```

>>> *print(f.as_p())*

```
<p><label for="id_subject">Subject:</label> <input type="text"
name="subject" required id="id_subject" /></p>

<p><label for="id_email">Email:</label> <input type="email" name="email"
id="id_email" /></p>

<p><label for="id_message">Message:</label> <input type="text"
name="message" required id="id_message" /></p>
```

Note that we have not included the opening or closing <table>, <form> or <url>
tags in the output; this allows us to add extra rows or any customizations we
want. The HTML can also be displayed for specific fields:

>>> *print(f['subject'])*

```
<input type="text" name="subject" required id="id_subject" />
```

>>> *print f['message']*

```
<input type="text" name="message" required id="id_message" />
```

Form objects can also validate data; to do this, we create a Form object and then
pass a dictionary of data to it. This dictionary will map the field names to the
data:

>>> *f = ContactForm({'subject': 'Hello', 'email': 'Paul@example.com',
'message': 'Nice site!'})*

When data has been associated with a Form instance, a 'bound' form has been
created:

>>> *f.is_bound*

True

To find out if data is valid you can call is_valid() on a bound form. In our example, a valid value was passed for each field so the whole Form is valid:

>>> f.is_valid()

True

If the email field is not passed, it will still be valid because required=False has been specified for the field:

>>> f = ContactForm({'subject': 'Hello', 'message': 'Nice site!'})

>>> f.is_valid()

True

But if the message or the subject is omitted, the Form won't be valid anymore:

>>> f = ContactForm({'subject': 'Hello'})

>>> f.is_valid()

False

>>> f = ContactForm({'subject': 'Hello', 'message': ''})

>>> f.is_valid()

False

You can go right down to retrieve messages that are specific to certain fields:

>>> f = ContactForm({'subject': 'Hello', 'message': ''})

>>> f['message'].errors

['This field is required.']

>>> *f['subject'].errors*

[]

>>> *f['email'].errors*

[]

Each of the bound Form instances will have an errors attribute; this will provide a dictionary that maps the field names to lists of error messages:

>>> *f = ContactForm({'subject': 'Hello', 'message': ''})*

>>> *f.errors*

{'message'`: ['This field is required.']}

Lastly, with a Form instance that has valid data, there is a cleaned_data attribute. This attribute is a dictionary containing the submitted data after it has been cleaned. The forms framework in Django will validate the data and then convert the values to the correct types in Python to clean it:

>>> *f = ContactForm({'subject': 'Hello', 'email': 'Paul@example.com',* *'message': 'Nice site!'})*

>>> *f.is_valid()*

True

>>> *f.cleaned_data*

{'subject': 'Hello', 'email': 'Paul@example.com', 'message': 'Nice site!'}

Our example form will only take strings that have been cleaned up into string objects but, should we use a DateField or an IntegerField, the framework will still make sure that cleaned_data makes use of the correct datetime.data objects or integers for the relevant fields.

Tying Forms to Views

Our contact form isn't good at the moment because our users cannot see it. We need to make an update to mysite\views.py:

```
# mysite_project\mysite\mysite\views.py


from django.http import Http404, HttpResponse, HttpResponseRedirect

from django.shortcuts import render

import datetime

from mysite.forms import ContactForm

from django.core.mail import send_mail, get_connection


#...


def contact(request):

    if request.method == 'POST':

        form = ContactForm(request.POST)

        if form.is_valid():

            cd = form.cleaned_data

            con = get_connection('django.core.mail.backends.console.EmailBackend')

            send_mail(
```

```
            cd['subject'],

            cd['message'],

            cd.get('email', 'noreply@example.com'),

            ['siteowner@example.com'],

            connection=con

        )

        return HttpResponseRedirect('/contact/thanks/')
    else:

        form = ContactForm()

    return render(request, 'contact_form.html', {'form': form})
```

The contact function has been added to our view to handle the form submission. With the function, we can see if POST method has been used to submit the request. If not, a blank form is displayed. We can also see if there is valid data on the form; to do this, call is_valid(). If the form does have valid data, the email is sent and the user is sent to another view - /contact/thanks/. If there is no valid data, the if block will jump to the last render() and the form goes to the browser.

There is no error handling in the view because the Form class does that for us. If there is no validation an error list is created by Django and then appended to the response.

Contact forms are not a lot of use if there is no way for the contact information to be sent to the site owner. One of the most common ways of doing this is by sending an email and Django has that ability built-in. The email functions are found in the module called django.core.mail and we imported this at the top of views.py. The send_mail() function is being used to send an email to a dummy account.

Send Emails in Development

We've used django.core.mail.get_connection() as a way to retrieve a mail connection to django.core.mail.backends.concole.EmailBackend(), which is a special backend for email. This is a useful backend in development because there is no need to set up email servers while developing applications in Django. The email output is sent by the console.EmailBackend to the console. This can be checked in the terminal window after the form is submitted.

Now, to display the contact form, we need to create a contact form and save it to mysite\templates\:

 # mysite_project\mysite\templates\contact_form.html

<html>

<head>

  <title>Contact us</title>

</head>

<body>

  <h1>Contact us</h1>

  {% if form.errors %}

    <p style="color: red;">

      Please correct the error{{ form.errors|pluralize }} below.

    </p>

  {% endif %}

```
<form action="" method="post" novalidate>

  <table>

    {{ form.as_table }}

  </table>

  {% csrf_token %}

  <input type="submit" value="Submit">

</form>

</body>

</html>
```

Because this is a POST form, it can modify our data; so we need to consider something called Cross Site Request Forgeries. Once again Django comes to the rescue and provides us with a system that protects against this. All POST forms that target an internal URL should have the template tag of {% csrf_token %}.

There is something else in the <form> tag – a novalidate attribute. When HTML5 is used in newer browsers, particularly in Chrome, the browser will validate the fields automatically. The attribute is used to tell the browser it doesn't need to do this because we need Django to do it.

Lastly, urls.py needs to be changed so our contact form is displayed at /contact/:

```
#...

from mysite.views import hello, current_datetime, hours_ahead, contact


urlpatterns = [
```

```
#...

url(r'^contact/$', contact),

url(r'^', include('books.urls')),

]
```

We run this by loading the form, submitting with no fields completed. Then we submit it with an email address that isn't valid. Lastly, we submit it with completely valid data. When the final form is submitted, a Page Not Found error, not what we would expect. But there is a reason for this; we haven't yet created a URLconf or a view to redirect a user to /contact/thanks/. That is something that we can do.

Changing the Way Fields are Rendered

When this form is locally rendered, the message field is an <input type="text"> whereas we need it to be a <textarea>. This is easily sorted by setting the widget for the field:

```
from django import forms


class ContactForm(forms.Form):

    subject = forms.CharField()

    email = forms.EmailField(required=False)

    message = forms.CharField(widget=forms.Textarea)
```

The presentation logic for each of the fields is separated into sets of widgets by the forms framework. There is a default widget for each of the field types but that can be overridden or you can use custom widgets. Basically, the Field classes are representative of validation logic while the widgets are representative of presentation logic.

Set Maximum Length

One of the more common needs for validation is to see if a field is a specific size. We can do this by improving the ContactForm so the subject is limited to 100 characters. All we do is give the CharField a max_length like this:

```
from django import forms


class ContactForm(forms.Form):

    subject = forms.CharField(max_length=100)

    email = forms.EmailField(required=False)

    message = forms.CharField(widget=forms.Textarea)
```

There is also a min_length but this is optional.

Setting the Initial Value

We can improve this even more by giving the subject field an initial value. We'll make this say, "I love your site!" and we do it by using the argument whenever a Form instance is created:

```
def contact(request):


    #...


    else:
        form = ContactForm(
            initial={'subject': 'I love your site!'}
```

)

return render(request, 'contact_form.html', {'form':form})

The subject field will now be displayed with the statement already there. Passing the initial data is not the same as passing the data that will bind the form. The main difference is with initial data the form is unbound, meaning there are no error messages.

Custom Validation Rules

Let's suppose that our feedback form has been launched and we are starting to see emails come in. There is a problem – some of the messages submitted only have a couple of words in them and this is not enough to make sense. We need a new policy for validation purposes – four or more words.

There are several ways to hook some custom data into Django for validation purposes; if we have a rule that is going to be constantly reused, we can use a custom type for the field. Usually, a custom validation tends to be a one-off thing though, and these can be tied into the Form class directly. We need our message field to have some extra validation, so the Form class is given a clean_method:

from django import forms

class ContactForm(forms.Form):

   subject = forms.CharField(max_length=100)

   email = forms.EmailField(required=False)

   message = forms.CharField(widget=forms.Textarea)

```
def clean_message(self):

    message = self.cleaned_data['message']

    num_words = len(message.split())

    if num_words < 4:

        raise forms.ValidationError("Not enough words!")

    return message
```

The form system in Django will automatically look for methods with a name starting with clean_ and ending with a field name. If a method is found, it will be called during the validation. More specifically, clean_message() is called once the default logic validation has been called. Our field data has been processed partly so we can get it from self.cleaned.data.

We also don't need to be concerned about checking to see if a value exists and is a non-empty value because the default validator will do this for us. Perhaps naively, we use a len() and split() combination to count how many words there are; if there aren't enough, a forms.ValidationError is raised. The user will see the string from this exception as one of the error list items.

One thing that is incredibly important is that the cleaned field value is explicitly returned when the method ends so that we can modify our value inside the custom validation method we created. If we don't input the return statement, we will get a value of None returned and our original value gets lost.

Specifying the Labels

By default, the auto-generated form HTML labels are created by putting spaces where the underscores are and making the first letter a capital; the email field label would be "Email". This is the algorithm used by models in Django to calculate the verbose_name field values. In the same way as we did with the models, these labels can also be customized for specified fields. To do that, we use a label like this:

```
class ContactForm(forms.Form):

    subject = forms.CharField(max_length=100)

    email = forms.EmailField(required=False, label='Your e-mail address')

    message = forms.CharField(widget=forms.Textarea)
```

Form Design Customization

Right now, the contact_form.html template displays our form using
{{form.as_table}} but we can use other methods to give us better control over
our display. There is a very quick way to customize the presentation of our
forms by using CSS. Our error lists could do with a bit of sprucing up and this is
why the error list that is automatically generated uses <ul class+"errorlist"> - so
they can be CSS-targeted. To make the errors more prominent, we'll add this
CSS into contact_form.html in the <head></head> section:

```
<style type="text/css">

    ul.errorlist {

        margin: 0;

        padding: 0;

    }
.errorlist li {

        background-color: red;

        color: white;

        display: block;

        font-size: 1.2em;

        margin: 0 0 3px;
```

```
      padding: 4px 5px;

   }

</style>
```

It is convenient for us to have the HTML generated automatically for our forms but there will be times when we want the default rendering overridden. We can use {{ form.as_table }}, among others, as shortcuts while our application is being developed but pretty much everything that goes into displaying a form may be changed, usually in the template, and we will do this.

The widget for each field may be individually rendered by going into {{ form.fieldname }} inside the template and, if there are errors associated with fields, they can be accessed in form.fieldname.errors }}. Bearing this in mind, a custom template can now be constructed for the contact form using this code:

```
<html>

<head>

   <title>Contact us</title>

</head>

<body>

   <h1>Contact us</h1>


   {% if form.errors %}

      <p style="color: red;">

         Please correct the error{{ form.errors|pluralize }} below.

      </p>

   {% endif %}
```

```html
<form action="" method="post">
  <div class="field">
    {{ form.subject.errors }}
    <label for="id_subject">Subject:</label>
    {{ form.subject }}
  </div>
  <div class="field">
    {{ form.email.errors }}
    <label for="id_email">Your e-mail address:</label>
    {{ form.email }}
  </div>
  <div class="field">
    {{ form.message.errors }}
    <label for="id_message">Message:</label>
    {{ form.message }}
  </div>
  {% csrf_token %}
  <input type="submit" value="Submit">
</form>
</body>
```

```
</html>
```

In this code, {{ form.message.errors }} is showing <ul class="errorlist"> if there are any errors and, if there aren't but the field is valid, there is a blank string. The same applies to all fields on the form.

The form.message.errors can also be treated as Boolean or it can be iterated over as a list. This is very useful when a field may have several errors associated with it. For example:

```
<div class="field{% if form.message.errors %} errors{% endif %}">

  {% if form.message.errors %}

    <ul>

    {% for error in form.message.errors %}

      <li><strong>{{ error }}</strong></li>

    {% endfor %}

    </ul>

  {% endif %}

  <label for="id_message">Message:</label>

  {{ form.message }}

</div>
```

Where validation errors are concerned, an errors class is added to the <div> and the list of errors that are associated with the field are displayed as unordered.

That is the end of this section and you have more than enough information to start building a basic Django application. In the next section we are going to move on to Python and ArcGIS.

Chapter 17: Python and ArcGIS Development

ArcGIS is a mapping and geographic system – Geographic Information System – that is used to create and use maps, to analyze data from the maps, to compile geographic data, to share the information discovered, to use maps in a variety of different applications, and manage the geographic information in databases.

The system provides users with the infrastructure needed to make the maps and the information on them available throughout the organization, across entire communities or on the internet. ArcGIS has the following software for Windows desktops:

•	ArcReader – to view and query maps that were created using another ArcGIS product

•	ArcGIS for Desktop Basic – used to be called ArcView, allows the viewing of spatial data, the creation of layered maps and basic analysis of spatial information

•	ArcGIS for Desktop Standard – used to be called ArcEditor and includes additional tools to manipulate geodatabases and shapefiles

•	ArcGIS for Desktop Advanced – used to be called ArcInfo, and includes data manipulation capabilities, analysis, and editing.

We will start by looking at how to set up an environment for ArcGIS.

Before we look into ArcGIS and how to use it, there is some information needed about Python and ArcGIS.

What You Need

Your computer will require a minimum of 2 GB RAM, be 32-bit or 64-bit configuration, Windows 7 as an absolute minimum, and Python. You will also need the latest version of ArcGIS. Python will be installed when you install ArcGIS.

Important Modules

Python modules are libraries that a script can call to add to its potential; they are built-in to Python or can be added later. Most get written in the Python language, but on occasion, they may be written using another programming language and then wrapped up in Python so they can be used in a Python script. Modules also make it possible for Python to use other programs. The modules you are going to need are:

ArcPY

This module has two purposes. First, it is a wrapper that helps you to interact with the tools in ArcGIS; ArcGIS then executes these in internal code format. Second ArcPY is a code base that allows better control of map production and geospatial analysis. ArcPY controls the ArcToolBox tools, even though they are not written in Python; it is ArcPY that allows us to use those tools.

We can also use ArcPY to control MXDs – ArcGIS Map Documents – and any object included in the MXD, such as images, legends, layers, titles, and the map view. ArcPY also contains a set of tools external to ArcToolBox, such as the incredibly powerful data cursors. These Data Analysis Cursors enable a much better interface with the GIS data.

Being able to have better geospatial analyses control helps to integrate the ArcGIS tools into a workflow that may have additional Python modules. Because Python is a glue language, ArcGIS is made more useful because there is no need to use special methods for geospatial data.

OS Module

This is in the standard Python library and is how Python gains access to the functionality in the operating system. One of the more common uses is using a method called os.path to divide file paths into directory paths or folders and base paths or files.

Another method called os.walk goes through a directory and then returns all the files found in folders, right down to the subfolders. When we carry out GIS analysis, the OS module will be continuously accessed.

SYS Module

This module is also in the standard library and it references the actual Python installation. In the sys module are several methods that will retrieve information about Python including the version number, and also about the script, as well as any parameters that have been given to it – this is done using sys.argv(). Another useful method in the sys module is sys.path used for appending the file path which means that any folder with a script may be referenced by any other script so that the functions in them can be imported to another script as needed.

XLRD and XLWT

These are used to read and write spreadsheets from Excel. They can extract the data from a legacy sheet and turn it into data that can be used for GIS analysis or when the geospatial analysis is finished they can write the results. Neither module is in the standard library but will be installed with ArcGIS and Python.

Built-in Functions

There are several of these that will be used, the main two being:

- **str** – string functions are used to convert data to string ints. The int (integer) function converts a float or string to an integer and, to avoid errors, a string that is passed to int has to be a number.
- **float** – float functions convert strings or ints into floats, and is similar to the int function.

Standard Library Modules

These modules need to be imported:

- **datetime** – used to retrieve date and time information and convert string format dates to Python dates
- **math** – used for high-level math functions that will be required from time to time, like calculation of a number's square or obtaining a Pi value
- **string** – used to manipulate strings

- **csv** – used to create files of comma-separated values and to edit them

That covers the basics, next we will start looking at configuring Python so it can be used with ArcGIS and how we use IDEs for script writing.

Configuring Python

In this part, we will be configuring Python and our computer systems so that they work to execute scripts written in Python. We will need to configure both environment and path variables so that our import statements work correctly and that a script runs when asked to. We'll look at Python folder structures and the ArcPY module in the folder structure for ArcGIS. Finally, we will look at IDEs, or Integrated Development Environments and how we use them to create and execute code.

What Are Python Scripts?

A Python script is nothing more than a text file that uses a formalized language to write commands. The file extension is.py and this is all that will allow us to tell it apart from other text files. We can use a text editor, like Notepad, to open these files.

Python scripts do not contain Python. If we don't use the Python interpreter, we cannot run the scripts and none of the commands contained in the scripts will be executed.

How Are Scripts Executed?

This is just as important to learn as it is to learn Python itself; if you take just a little time to set Python up properly, you can save yourself a great deal of time debugging and checking errors. Because Python is an interpretive language, scripts first need to be changed into bytecode and we'll be covering that later.

What is the Interpreter?

The interpreter is a program with the.exe extension which means it is executable. The Python Interpreter was written in the C language, much older than Python and used in languages that have more complex syntax. Any program that has been written in the C language, usually a text file to begin with, must first be changed to an executable file by a compiler. This program turns text commands into machine code for the creation of.exe programs. This is a laborious process, but it has the benefit of producing programs that can stand alone and do not require any dependencies to run. Conversely, Python will interpret the commands and execute them quickly, which makes it one of the best languages for scripting. However, those scripts cannot be executed until they go through the interpreter.

The Python interpreter will look at a Python script and will interpret the commands contained in it. When the script is run, the first thing that happens is the syntax is checked to ensure that it follows all the Python rules, such as indentation, and that the variables are named following convention. Provided it is a valid script, the commands will be converted to bytecode which can then be executed by a virtual machine that was written in the C language, the bytecode interpreter. This interpreter will then turn that bytecode into the right code for the machine being used. The script is then executed by the CPU. This is quite a complicated process which all takes place behind the scenes, giving Python an air of simplicity.

Where is the Python Interpreter?

This is a very important thing to learn and understand. Very often, Python will be downloaded from the official website and installed separately to ArcGIS. However, every version of ArcGIS needs a specific version of Python so when you download ArcGIS, Python is included. Your Python folder structure can be found on your C: drive unless you tell it to install elsewhere. The folder will be C:\Pythonxx (xx denoting the version of Python). In that folder is a folder named ArcGISxx.x (again, x denotes the version number and/or the operating system).

Inside this folder are more folders and python.exe along with an interpreter version called pythonw.exe which will execute scripts without terminal windows. Pythonw.exe, like python.exe, contains all the commands in Python and is usable for script execution.

Which Interpreter?

Generally, you should use pythonw.exe as the interpreter to execute your scripts as it does not bring up the terminal window. When you need to see your code outputs in a window or you want to test snippets of code, use python.exe. When you start this, you will see the interpreter console. Just under the header that tells you which version you have, you will see three chevrons (>>>) – this is the prompt where you enter your code, line by line, rather than entering an entire script. This is useful to test small amounts of code and help you understand Python syntax. ArcMap and ArcCatalog both contain a version of the interpreter called Python Window.

How Does My Computer Know Where to Find the Interpreter?

To understand this, you need admin access and a good idea of how Windows looks for programs. We need to go into the advanced system settings and change a variable to tell it where the interpreter is. Go into your computer's control panel and then into the option for Security/System. Click the option for Advanced System Settings and then on System Properties. At the bottom you will see a button that says Environment Variables – click this. At the bottom of the menu that loads, move through the window for System Variables until you see the Path variable. Click it and click Edit.

There are two components to the Path variable – the variable name or path and the value, which is several folders, each separated by a semicolon. This path is what Windows searches through to find the executables associated with a specific extension. You will add a path that has the interpreter in it – c:\Pythnxx\ArcGISxx.x – and this is added to the field for the variable value ensuring a semicolon is used to separate it. Click OK three times to exit out of the menu entirely. Now, your computer knows where that interpreter is and will search every folder listed in the path variable looking for the python executable file. You can test how your edit worked by opening a command window on your computer and typing in python. You should see the interpreter running. And you should see the header with the Python version and the three chevrons.

How to Make a Python Script Executable When Clicked On

The last thing to do to make a script run when clicked on, which will also allow them to run externally to ArcGIS, is to ensure that the files with the.py extension are properly associated with the interpreter. If this hasn't been done, the files will appear as a text file or as an unknown type.

Changing this is quite simple; choose your script and right-click it. Choose Open With and Choose Default Program. If you do not see python.exe or python.exe as a choice, go to the folder that houses them and choose one of them – the best one is pythonw.exe for script execution and python.exe to test code.

The IDE – Integrated Development Environment

In the Python interpreter is everything you need to execute or test a script. However, to write that script you need a text editor and there are two on a Windows PC – WordPad and Notepad. However, these are simplistic - they are OK for an emergency but they don't really have too much in the way of functionality to make long scripts or multiple scripts easier to write.

To correct that, the IDE has been developed. This is a series of programs and there is one for every computer language. In the IDE are functions like code assist, variable listing, and much more, to make them perfect for writing those scripts. We'll look at two of the best ones, all well-established within the different communities that surround Python:

IDLE

When you install Python, you get IDLE, an integrated IDE. To start it in Windows, find the ArcGIS folder on your computer. Inside the Python folder you will see IDLE as a choice – to start IDLE, select it. IDLE has an interactive interpreter built-in and can easily run full scripts. The GUI module built into Python is used to write IDLE so it is the same language as the one it will execute.

IDLE has another advantage over python.exe in that script outputs, including print statements, are sent straight to the interactive window in IDLE, and this doesn't disappear once the script has executed. IDLE also uses little memory.

There are disadvantages too; not much in the way of code assist, i.e. autocomplete, and not much in the way of organization in terms of logical projects. Every variable in a script cannot be located like in other IDEs and there is a limit to the number of scripts listed in the Recent Files menu – this is a bit of an obstruction when it comes to finding scripts that haven't been run for a while. IDLE isn't a bad IDE, it is ideal if there aren't any other options and it can be used to quickly test a snippet of code.

PythonWin

Python for Windows, or PythonWin, includes a number of useful modules and the IDE for using Python with Windows. Download the latest version of PythonWin and select the right version of the 32 module for your Python version. Run the.exe file and, if everything is correct, Python will be recognized in the registry by the installation GUI and it will then install itself.

In PythonWin, there is an interactive window where the user and the interpreter can interact. The user can also open scripts in PythonWin and there are some tiling commands to organize who the interpreter is and where the open scripts are displayed.

PythonWin has another advantage that IDLE doesn't have; it can show different parts of a script in the same window. If a script is too long, it is a nuisance to have to keep scrolling through it in order to edit it. In PythonWin, the top of the script can be pulled down to create another window which will show another part of the script. Another window can be opened to show all the variables and classes, which makes it far easier to go to a certain section of the script.

The PythonWin interactive window may also search through code statements that were previously entered. To do this, at the prompt (>>>), hold the CTRL key and use the arrow keys to go through each line until you find what you want.

Overall, PythonWin is a useful IDE used by most ArcGIS professionals. The only thing it can't do is organize scripts into logical projects or list the script variables.

There are lots of other IDEs for Python coding. It really is down to personal choice which to choose, the one that works best for you. You may find that you need to use different ones for different tasks so test several until you find the one or ones that you want.

Python Folder Structure

You will find much more than the interpreter in the folder structure. Inside the subfolders are several scripts, modules for C language and some digital link libraries. You won't use all the scripts all the time but every one of them works to make it possible to use Python for programming. The folder called site-packages is the most important one because that contains most of the modules that scripts will import.

Inside every one of the Python folders is another one called lib and inside the lib folder is the site-packages folder.

Using sys Module

Adding modules is done by using the sys module. It gives access to a vast number of system tools that are included in the interpreter. As we mentioned earlier, sys.path is an incredibly useful tool, one that can be modified to change where Python finds its modules without the need for administrative access.

When ArcGIS installs Python, the installer uses the functions in sys.path to add the ArcPY path which should look something like this:

C:\Program Files (x86)\ArcGIS\Desktopxx.x\arcpy.

You can test this by opening the interpreter or your IDE and inputting the following:

>>> import sys

>>> print sys.path

The output is as follows:

[", 'C:\\WINDOWS\\SYSTEM32\\python27.zip',

'C:\\Python27\\ArcGIS10.2\\Dlls', 'C:\\Python27\\ArcGIS10.2\\lib',

'C:\\Python27\\ArcGIS10.2\\lib\\plat-win',

'C:\\Python27\\ArcGIS10.2\\lib\\lib-tk',

'C:\\Python27\\ArcGIS10.2\\Lib\\site-packages\\pythonwin',

'C:\\Python27\\ArcGIS10.2', 'C:\\Python27\\ArcGIS10.2\\lib\\site-packages',

'C:\\Program Files (x86)\\ArcGIS\\Desktop10.2\\bin', 'C:\\Program Files (x86)\\ArcGIS\\Desktop10.2\\arcpy', 'C:\\Program Files

(x86)\\ArcGIS\\Desktop10.2\\ArcToolbox\\Scripts',

'C:\\Python27\\ArcGIS10.2\\lib\\site-packages\\win32',

'C:\\Python27\\ArcGIS10.2\\lib\\site-packages\\win32\\lib']

In the system path are the folders needed by ArcPY for the automation of ArcGIS. All the directories from the environment variable called PYTHONPATH, if that variable has already been created. This is not the same as the environment variable for the Windows path that we talked about earlier. Both variables work together helping Python to find the modules.

sys.path.append()

Because the function sys.path is a list, it can be appended or extended to add other file paths pointing to modules that can be imported. So that we don't need to change sys.path, we should copy the entire module into our site-packages folder. If you can't do this, there is another way; using sys.path.append():

>>> *sys.path.append("C:\\Projects\\Requests")*

>>> *sys.path*

['', 'C:\\WINDOWS\\SYSTEM32\\python27.zip',

 'C:\\Python27\\ArcGIS10.2\\Dells',

 'C:\\Python27\\ArcGIS10.2\\lib',

..'C:\\Python27\\ArcGIS10.2\\lib\\plat-win',

..'C:\\Python27\\ArcGIS10.2\\lib\\lib-tk',

..'C:\\Python27\\ArcGIS10.2\\Lib\\site-packages\\pythonwin',

..'C:\\Python27\\ArcGIS10.2',..'C:\\Python27\\ArcGIS10.2\\lib\\site-packages', 'C:\\Program

..Files (x86)\\ArcGIS\\Desktop10.2\\bin', 'C:\\Program Files

..(x86)\\ArcGIS\\Desktop10.2\\arcpy', 'C:\\Program Files

..(x86)\\ArcGIS\\Desktop10.2\\ArcToolbox\\Scripts',

..'C:\\Python27\\ArcGIS10.2\\lib\\site-packages\\win32',

..'C:\\Python27\\ArcGIS10.2\\lib\\site-packages\\win32\\lib',

..'C:\\Projects\\Requests']

When this method is used, the change is only a temporary one. If the change is to be permanent, go to System Properties and change the PYTHONPATH variable.

Once more important thing to note is if you want to import modules without making those changes or copying the module to site-packages, you must put the relevant module into the folder that contains the importing script. So long as the configuration is correct on the module, it will all work.

Programming in ArcGIS:

GIS analysts don't necessarily need to know how to program to do their jobs, but they can be sure that, if they can program in Python, they will go a lot further. That said, this isn't as easy as you might think if you have no clue where to start. Earlier we talked about what you would need to get started because GIS programming does begin with Python, even though it doesn't end there.

Python is a great language for both programming and scripting but, when it is combined with ArcGIS, Python scripting is great for task automation. For that reason, it is important to learn the basics of using Python and that includes the syntax, commands, data types, functionalities, loops and everything else that goes with it. You don't need to know Python inside out, much of it can be learned as you get to grips with ArcGIS. One more thing you should learn is how to get help files via the interpreter and how to list all the modules, functionalities and methods instead of having to keep going to the external files for help.

There are many free tutorials online to help you learn Python basics and they will all cover the same things – syntax, strings, data types, functions, etc., everything you need to learn. Python 3 is best for GIS users although the ArcGIS desktop does still use Python 2. If you already have ArcGIS desktop on your computer, Python has already been installed so you don't need to worry about getting the right version. Just go to the Windows taskbar and find the ArcGIS submenu. Click it and click on IDLE and the Python terminal will open with the command line. Here, you can write code and press Enter to execute that code.

Practice is also important. You can't just read something, do it once, and that's it; you will need to find free exercises online or in books and keep practicing them until you know what you are doing. Once you have the basics down then you can move onto Python scripting, know the difference between writing a script and running it, along with how to use the interactive interpreter. This won't really be covered in many of the free online courses, so you will need to do some searching – this is vital to learn though if you want to be a GIS analyst. Write a few scripts even if they are only simple ones and run them. Learn about commenting code – it will help you later.

You should use an Integrated Development Environment (IDE) for your scripts; this isn't complicated; it is just software, a code editor that lets you write code, run it, save it, and debug it. An IDE will color code depending on the elements, to help you pick up on errors much easier. You should also take time to look at some of the functionality built into Python, like the Math module in the standard library. Numbers are an important part of GIS and you might need to refresh what you learned at college. Python gives you the ability to work with object geometrics within a GIS so understanding what the library has to offer will be handy. You can access the online and offline Python documentation to help you with this, along with learning how to write data into new files, ensuring source paths are correctly written, the correct way to write SQL statements, about error messages, and about the 'try' and the 'except' blocks.

Python and ArcGIS

Once you have had some practice with Python, try using it in ArcGIS. One of the best ways to start is by using the Python window to learn the arcpy site package, which is a module collection that gives users access to some great features including the geoprocessing functions. ArcGIS Pro requires Python 3 and ArcMap requires Python 2. There is an interactive Help window in the Python window that will help you to write code. It allows you to specify a tool's parameter and provides for code autocompletion that can save you a great deal of time. This is one of the best ways to learn arcpy and it should really be your starting point; get some confidence with arcpy, use local GIS data to write a few standalone scripts and run them, and see what they do.

Use your best friend here – common sense. Spelling paths and filenames wrong is common and, yes, it will cause errors. Python scripts can be properly checked for errors by the IDE, but there may be those that get missed, such as incorrectly spelled names, commands, tools and paths. Another common mistake is to misuse capital letters, something to which Python is very sensitive. One way of controlling your script process is to allow it to 'print' messages, such as "print("geodatabase correctly created"). This way you can check the progress. If your script terminates error-free, go to ArcMap and run a visual of your results. If you don't see the output you expect to see, check your code again.

Again, there are plenty of tutorials and help online to get you acquainted with Python scripting and with arcpy. You can find plenty of detailed information about how it all works. Start at the bottom and work your way through the basics. Make use of the ArcGIS help section to get to know arcpy and then look for books that contain scripts, heavily annotated, and those that contain expertly created data that you can use to experiment.

Beyond Scripting

Once you have some experience, you might want to know where you should head next. Don't be too quick to start on other languages or other frameworks as a way of improving your code, such as using a list comprehension to refactor some of it. Instead, try finding new geospatial modules that can help improve your code; look at professional works, compare them, and look for code habits that you can you use.

This learning path is not going to be easy; it will take time and it will be iterative, i.e. you will be going between stages, back and forth continuously, learning something new every time. It is fun though, and it is surprising. The more you practice, you more you learn, and the easier it will get. Python is an excellent way of extending GIS with so many extra geospatial libraries at your disposal.

After you learn the basics of Python, of scripting and of ArcGIS, you can go in so many other directions. For example, you can use the ArcGIS Python API that ESRI has recently released enabling you to use Python and maps on the internet; this takes it beyond desktop use.

Why We Need GIS Automation

GIS, or Geographic Information Systems, are able to manipulate spatial datasets, as well as analyzing them. This is to solve problems of a geographic nature and GIS analysts will do all sorts of data operations to find the solution for a specific problem. Included in this are:

- Clipping
- Reprojection
- Merging
- Buffering
- Mosaicking
- Extraction of data subsets

There are many other operations of course, all of which are called geoprocessing in the ArcGIS software and tools are used to perform them.

Being successful in GIS analysis means that you need to be able to choose the right tools for the data operation. In ArcGIS, there is a toolbox metaphor for the organization of the tools suite; you choose the tools and make sure they run in the right order.

Let's say that part of your job is to choose the sites for a chain of restaurants. You could use one tool for the selection of the parcels of land on a major road; another one for parcels that are 0.25 acres or more, and so on. If you only had a small area to work with for your selection process, you would probably be better off doing the work manually.

However, assume that you need to do exactly the same kind of analyses but over multiple areas in the country. This is where automation comes in - when you need to use the same tool sequence for multiple areas. Automation brings a number of benefits to the table:

- It makes work much easier. Once a process has been automated, you won't need to do so much work to remember which tools you need or in which the order they need to be used.
- It makes work much faster. Computers can open tools and execute them in the right sequence much quicker than you can do it with a mouse.
- It provides a higher level of accuracy. Whenever a task is manually performed, there is always a margin for error. The more tasks and the more complex they are, not to mention the fatigue you will experience when you need to repeat a task over and over, will all increase the margin for error. Conversely, once you have configured an automated task, the computer will get on with the task at hand accurately and as many times as needed.

There are three ways that ArcGIS allows for automation of geoprocessing tasks. These options are all different, each requiring a different level of skill in producing an automated solution and in what each can address in the way of scenarios.

Option one involves using ModelBuilder to build a model. This program is interactive, allowing you to link a series of tools so that the output from one becomes the input to the next. ModelBuilder offers an excellent feature in that it can be used for the automation of complex workflows without needing to do any programming.

There are tasks that need more flexibility than ModelBuilder offers; for this, scripts are recommended. Scripts will generally execute a sequence of steps and you can opt to either run the tools one at a time or you can link them together. Conditional logic can be added to handle a case where the output from one operation will affect the tool that needs to be run next. Iteration can be included so that one action may be repeated over and again until a task is finished.

Scripting can be done using one of many different languages, but Python is the main one as it tends to be included with ArcGIS as standard.

The last option is to use ArcObjects to build an automation solution because it allows you to customize the interface, so it has the commands and tools needed for more focused work. These tools may be standard ArcGIS tools, or you can modify them, so they work as you need them to. We won't be touching on this option in this book; instead we will be concentrating on the scripting side and on ModelBuilder.

All the tools that Python and ModelBuilder are based on ArcObjects but, when you use Python scripting there is no requirement to learn the logic behind these tools; all you need to do is learn what the tools are and the order they need to be run to complete a specific task.

First, we will look at some of the concepts behind writing scripts and model building, starting with the ArcGIS toolbox and how they fit in with ModelBuilder. After that, we'll look at some Python basics and how the tools work in a script.

The ArcGIS Toolbox

The ArcGIS software is home to hundreds of different tools that can be used to manipulate and analyze GIS data. In the early days, ArcGIS did not have a graphical user interface (GUI) so commands were needed to access the tools.

These days, there is a sequence of toolboxes that you can point and click through via the ArcCatalog or you can go to ArcMap and use the Catalog window. You might have seen these toolboxes before, but we can take a look at them now:

Launch ArcMap

If you don't see the Catalog window, click Windows>Catalog. Pin this window, so it doesn't hide so you can see it whenever you need to.

In Catalog, go to Toolboxes and then System Toolboxes and continue to go through the ones you want to see. Notice that they have all been organized and are in toolboxes and in toolsets. You might find it faster to go to Geoprocessing>Search and look for the specific tool you want.

For the purposes of this, open Analysis Tools>Proximity and click the Buffer tool.

If you are familiar with ArcGIS tools, you might already have seen this tool. This time, I want you to pay close attention to how the user interface is constructed. In particular, you are seeing one dialog that has multiple fields. Each of the geoprocessing tools will have a requirement for inputs and outputs and you will see these indicated by a green dot. These are representative of the absolute minimum level of information needed for a tool to run. For Buffer, you need to supply a location for the input features, that is the features that are to be buffered, and you need to supply a buffer distance. Alongside that is the requirement to indicate a class location where the newly buffered features will go.

Some tools also have a set of optional parameters and these are modifiable if required. If these are not supplied, default values will be used to run the tool. As far as the Buffer tool goes, the optional parameters include:

- Side Type
- Dissolve Type
- End Type
- Dissolve Fields

Generally, the optional parameters will follow the required parameters.

Look for the Show Help button in the bottom-right corner of the Buffer tool and click it. Choose a parameter and click it to see an explanation appear in the window on the right. This is a great way of learning what parameters mean. For example, keeping the Help open, in the Buffer tool, click the input box called Side Type – it should say Full. Help will show you what the parameter means, and it will show you all the options – FULL, RIGHT, LEFT, OUTSIDE_ONLY.

If you require more help, you can go to the ArcGIS Desktop help documentation where you will find full explanations of each one, along with Python examples. To get the help pages you will need:

Open ArcGIS and click on Help>ArcGIS Desktop Help**.**

Click the tab for Contents and then click on Tools>Tool Reference. Each of the help topics has been placed in toolsets and toolboxes for your ease.

Continue to go through the table until you get to Analysis Toolbox. Click on Proximity Toolset and then on Buffer. Look through the topic; you will find plenty of information about the tool, what it does, how it should be used, and how the parameters should be supplied.

When you are happy, move on to the Code Sample section where you will find Python examples of how to run the tool automatically.

The ArcGIS Python Window

One of the best ways to introduce Python is to look at some code so we'll now run the Buffer tool in the ArcGIS Python window. In this window, you can run a series of commands without having to draw up a permanent script. What we will do this time is make some buffers of a distance of 15 miles around some cities:

Open ArcMap so you have an empty map.

Download the us_cities.shp dataset from Github and add it to the map.

Click the button for Python Window on the Standard toolbar and then drag the open window to the bottom or side of the screen – this will dock it.

Input the following code to the Python window (minus the >> prompt – that will already be there). Don't copy and paste it, type it in so you get used to doing it:

>>> import arcpy

>>> arcpy.Buffer_analysis("us_cities", "us_cities_buffered", "15 miles", "", "", "ALL")

Now zoom in and look at the buffers you just created. You don't need to have a full understanding of this at this stage but there are a few things to note:

The first line, import arcpy, informs the interpreter that you will need special functions and tools for scripting from ArcGIS. If you don't add this line of code, Python will not have any knowledge of ArcGIS, so you must remember to add this in on any code related to ArcGIS. Technically, when you are working within the ArcMap Python window, arcpy has already been imported so you won't need to do it, but you will need it in scripts written outside of this window.

The second line is what runs the tool. To run any tool in Python, all you need to do is input arcpy, followed by a dot and the name of the tool, i.e. arcpy.buffer, to run that tool. You also include an underscore and the toolbox name. This is required because there are tools that have the same names but are in different toolboxes, so you must specify which toolbox to look in.

All the parameters are separated with a comma and the entire list must be inside a set of parentheses. Again, this is a pattern that you need to get used to because it is required with all tools. We also added a few optional parameters; in places where we wanted the default values used, we left a set of empty quotes.

The big question is, how do you know what parameter structure or syntax to use? For the distance, do you input 15MILES, 15 Miles, '15Miles' or '15 Miles'? To find the answer to questions such as this you should go back to the help page we discussed earlier. All the topics in the reference section will show you command lines and structure examples. All optional parameters will be inside a set of braces, requisite parameters are not. From our example, you can see that we used '15 miles' as the distance – because a space is inserted between the words, it must be inside single quotes.

Did you spot that the Python Window offers a bit of help? It gives you several options for each parameter and we call this autocompletion. It's a helpful feature when you are a novice at running the tools and are not sure of the right way to type the parameters.

There are some notable differences between using a program like PythonWin to write your code and writing it in the Python Window. In the window, it is a simple matter to reference the map document layers using just their names; in any other program, you would need to specify the file path. As such, we could type something easy like "us_cities" rather than specifying the whole path. We could also come up with a new name for a new layer, "us_cities_buffered" and have it added by default to the map once the code was run. The lesson here is, if you use any program other than PythonWin, you need to use the full file path.

When the scripts are more complex, it is better to use an IDE and later we will look closer at the PythonWin IDE. For now, think back to when we talked about linking tools together in ModelBuilder to solve problems. Well, we can do this in Python too so, to give you a bit of grounding, we'll start off with a bit of work on the Python basics.

The Basics of Python and ArcGIS

We already know that the Python computer language is great for writing scripts to automate computer-related tasks. We also know that automation makes it easier and faster as well as far more accurate. The same applies to computer science, in particular GIS and, by learning Python, you will be a far better GIS analyst.

Because Python is what is known as a 'high-level' language, you can use it quite easily without needing to understand how a computer works. The syntax Python uses is quite simple to read, to write, and understand and you don't need much in the way of overheads to get up and running with a Python program.

We can use Python in ArcGIS for something called "coarse-grained" programming and what this means is that it is easy to use for geoprocessing tools, such as Buffer. You could, if you wanted to, use ArcObjects and some finer-grained programming but this takes time and, for the most part, is not necessary. It is far easier to call a tool using a Python script and a single code line.

There is an additional way to get help with the Python syntax, the language structure, for any individual tool:

Interactively run the tool using your input and output data and any parameters that are relevant to the tool.

Go to Geoprocessing>Results and find the tool.

Right-click it to run it.

Choose the option for Copy Python Snippet and then paste it into the Python window or PythonWin – you will be shown how the operation you ran would be coded.

How to Install PythonWin

Python comes with a built-in editor, a simple one called IDLE. However, we are going to be using PythonWin IDE. This is free and already has basic features for debugging built into it. We can get PythonWin from Source Forge but make sure you download the win32 version, and nothing else.

Once you have downloaded PythonWin, launch the file by right-clicking on it and choosing Run as Administrator.

The PythonWin wizard will start, click on Next to get the installation started. You will need to make your own PythonWin desktop shortcut as there isn't one automatically made.

Let's Explore PythonWin

Before we start, open up PythonWin; it will make it easier to follow as we work through the main bits of the program.

When you open PythonWin, the first thing that you will see is the Interactive Window with the >>> prompt. Type your code here and it will be executed and the result printed, if there is one. This window is an excellent place to begin practicing using Python and you will find it is very much the same as the ArcGIS Python window.

To start writing a script, choose File>New>Python Script. You will now see a blank page that is color-coded using the Courier font which is common in programming. You can also very easily track indentation and spacing, two important factors with Python.

On the standard toolbar, you will see many tools used to load your scripts, to run them, and save them. Two important buttons are the Undo and Redo buttons – these are a godsend to new programmers as they can get you out of trouble. The Run button is also important because it gives you the opportunity to run a script for testing purposes without having to go through Windows Explorer.

You will also see a toolbar called Debugging which allows you to find errors by checking your code one line at a time. If you can't see the toolbar, click on View>Toolbars>Debugging. This is another important toolbar and is perhaps the most important reason to use an IDE instead of another text editor.

Using ArcGIS

It is now time to move on to using ArcGIS. One of the most important parts of any GIS is the data that is representative of geographic feature location and the attributes that go with the features. This is what will take GIS way beyond simple mapping – being a GIS analyst involves adding new features and attributes, modifying existing ones, and deleting them from a GIS.

Aside from data maintenance, you will also need to understand querying data and selecting that which is important to the projects you are undertaking. You may even want to look into a dataset and query it to find specific records, perhaps those that match to particular criteria, and use only those records to calculate some stats.

It can become tiresome and time-consuming to do all these tasks, not to mention increasing the chances of errors when you do it all manually. Scripts are a much better, more efficient way of reading large data chunks, as well as being far more accurate. We already have lots of tools at our disposal to select data and manage it, all in the ArcToolbox and you can use any of these within your Python scripts. If you wanted to modify the records in a table individually, you can make use of some special objects in arcpy. These are called cursors and are used for individual record examination.

When you use scripts, you can also take advantage of a few advantages that you don't get when you enter data manually. Checks can be added into scripts to make sure that entered data conforms to a specified format. Steps can be linked together to provide a chain of selection logic; doing this in ArcMap would be incredibly time-consuming.

What we are going to look at is how to use Python to read GIS data and write it. We will begin by examining the creation of datasets and how to open them in a script. We'll move on to using cursor objects and tools for geoprocessing to read data and write it. We'll also be looking at rasters, even though these are mostly used for vector datasets.

Storing and Retrieving Data in ArcGIS

Before looking at ways to read attributes and modify them, it would serve you well to understand how ArcGIS stores the geographic datasets. This is important if you are to learn how to open a dataset in a script and, where necessary, how new datasets are created.

The Geodatabase

ESRI, the most powerful of all the mapping software on the market, has come up with a number of methods to store spatial data and one of the best ways is to use geodatabases. A geodatabase is a well-organized structure used for the storage of and definition of the relationships between two or more datasets. Which geodatabase you use will be dependent on the data you are using:

- **Personal** – these are small geodatabases, almost deprecated now, that are used for data storage on local systems. A Microsoft Access Database is used to hold the data, and provide limits on how much can be stored.
- **File** – these are one of the more recent methods for data storage on local systems. An ESRI-developed format is used to store the data and these can hold significantly more data than the personal ones can.
- **ArcSDE** – sometimes called Enterprise, these use a central server within an RDBMS (Relational Database Management System) to store the data. This could be SQL Server, PostgreSQL or Oracle, for example. These databases are very large, and they are designed to serve an enterprise with data. RDBMSs can be hard work in themselves so the ArcSDE was developed to act as the middleman, to help you configure datasets in ArcMap or ArcCatalog and read them without going anywhere near the relational database software.

If you have one vector dataset inside one of these geodatabases, it is known as a feature class. You can, if you want, organize these classes into feature datasets and your geodatabases may also be used to store raster datasets.

The Standalone Dataset

Geodatabases are vital to store and organize data long-term but, on occasion, you might want a standalone format to access the datasets from a local system. Perhaps the best standalone format for vector data is shapefile. A shapefile is made up of multiple files that all combine to store the geometrics and their attributes. Each file shares a root name but has a different extension. Each of the files can be zipped together and emailed or placed in a folder for easy downloading. In ArcMap and ArcCatalog, the shapefiles are a single file in the browsers. A quick note here – you will sometimes see a shapefile called a feature class; so when you see that term, consider that it could be referring to vector dataset that may also be used in ArcGIS.

There is another standalone dataset that is from the early ArcGIS days –
ArcInfo Coverage. In a similar way to the shapefile, this also has a number of
files that all work in combination. These are not so common now, but if you
work for an organization that has ArcInfo WorkStation and still uses it, you may
come across them.

You will often find a raster dataset stored as a standalone rather than being in a
geodatabase. A raster may be one file, or it may be several files, like the
shapefile.

Python Scripts and Paths

More often than not you will need to add dataset paths to scripts and it isn't
always easy to know the right syntax to specify the path – this is down to the
number of storage methods. How should the dataset path be specified? You
could come up against the same with shapefiles; even though they may have
better names, they do have at least three files that participate.

Perhaps the easiest and best way to find the required paths is to go to the
ArcCatalog dataset and browse through it and look in the Location toolbar for
the path.

The following example is a way that you could use the Python script to access
the feature class:

import arcpy

featureClass = "C:\\Data\\USA\\USA.gdb\\Cities"

desc = arcpy.Describe(featureClass)

spatialRef = desc.SpatialReference

print(spatialRef.Name)

Don't forget; backslashes are reserved Python characters, so you must choose
between using a forward slash - / - or a double backslash - \\ - when you write
the path. You could also use a raw string to write the path – this will allow

backslashes to be added along with other characters that have been reserved into the string, so long as you add an 'r' as a prefix to the quotation marks:

featureClass = r"C:\Data\USA\USA.gdb\Cities"

...

Workspaces

Workspaces are often used in a geoprocessing framework to denote which geodatabase or folder you are working in at the time. When a workspace is specified inside your script, there is no need to list the entire path for each individual dataset. When a tool is run, the geoprocessor will 'see' the name of the feature class and will assume that it lives in the specified workspace.

Where workspaces really come into their own is when they are used in batch processing, where one action is performed on multiple datasets within that workspace. For example, let's say that you wanted to clip every feature class in one folder to a county boundary. The proper workflow would be:

1. Definition of the workspace
2. Creation of the list of the workspace feature classes
3. Definition of the clip feature
4. Configuration of the loop that runs on each of the listed feature classes
5. The Clip tool is run in the loop.

Look at a piece of code that will clip each of the file geodatabase feature classes to the state boundary for Alabama, followed by the output, then going to another file geodatabase. Note – the lines of code that follow the import arcpy statement relate to the 5 steps listed above:

```
import arcpy


arcpy.env.workspace = "C:\\Data\\USA\\USA.gdb"

featureClassList = arcpy.ListFeatureClasses()

clipFeature = "C:\\Data\\Alabama\\Alabama.gdb\\StateBoundary"


for featureClass in featureClassList:

        arcpy.Clip_analysis(featureClass, clipFeature,
"C:\\Data\\Alabama\\Alabama.gdb\\" + featureClass)
```

In this example, the arcpy.ListFeatureClasses() method was the important part in the list creation. The method goes through a specified workspace, listing each of the contained feature classes – this is a Python list. Once this list has been created, a for loop may be configured to act on the individual items.

Note, also, that the workspace path was designated using the file geodatabase location, C:\\Data\\USA\\USA.gdb. If these were shapefiles you were working with, all you would need for the workspace is the path that leads to the containing folder.

If it were ArcSDE you were using, the path to the.sde file would be required; this file is created when you go into ArcCatalog to connect to ArcSDE and you will find the file inside the directory for your local profile. We won't be using ArcSDE for the purposes of this section, but you may come across it – remember the ArcCatalog location toolbar can be used to understand the ArcSDE dataset paths.

How to Read the Vector Attribute Data

You know now how a dataset is opened so we need to go a bit deeper and start looking at the data records. We will be looking at reading the data tables and searching them. These tables are where you will often find the feature attributes for the vectors, but sometimes, they can be standing alone.

First, we will look at writing the data to the tables, so copy the code I give you into some scripts, so you can practice. This will help you to learn what you need to do and how it all works. Practice is everything and trial and error is how you will learn.

Data Fields

Before we discuss accessing vector data, we need to take a look at how we store the data in the software. The vector features from any ArcGIS shapefile or feature class are always stored in tables, each having rows, which are the records, and columns, which are the fields.

Each field is used to store feature geometry and the information about the attributes. Each table will have two fields that cannot be deleted. One, usually with the name of Shape, is used to store the feature geometry information and included in this are the feature vertex coordinates, allowing drawing of each feature onto the screen. Geometry information is always in binary format and it would be unlikely to make any sense if you were to see it as is. However, arcpy provides objects that allow us to read geometrics and work with them.

The second field is named either FID or OBJECTID. It is an ID field for the object and it holds a unique identifier for each ArcGIS record that is used to track features. The ID is useful to avoid any confusion when you work with the data. On occasion, two or more records may share identical attributes; for example, San Francisco and Los Angeles may have the same State attribute called California but the ID field will never hold identical values for different records.

All the other fields will contain descriptive information about the feature attributes, normally stored in text or number format.

Discovering the Field Names

When a script is written, you must specify which field names you are reading or writing. You can use arcpy.ListFields() to gain access to the field names in a Python list.

```
# Reads the fields in a feature class


import arcpy


featureClass = "C:\\Data\\USA\\USA.gdb\\Cities"

fieldList = arcpy.ListFields(featureClass)

# Loop through each field in the list and print the name

for field in fieldList:

    print(field.name)
```

This code would give you a list of all the fields under the feature class called Cities; this is in a file geodatabase called USA.gdb. If you were to try running this in PythonWin, the output would be this:

```
>>> OBJECTID

Shape

UIDENT

POPCLASS

NAME

CAPITAL
```

STATEABB

COUNTRY

Note that the static fields we mentioned earlier are there – Shape, with its record geometry information, and OBJECTID, with the unique ID number for the individual records. We also have other fields, specifying NAME, STATE, CAPITAL, and more.

The fields are treated as objects by arcpy and this means that they have properties describing them. You can only read the field properties, you can change or delete them in any way using a Field object in your script. If, for some reason, you needed to change the precision and scale of any particular field, a new field would need to be added programmatically.

Reading Records

We've looked at a horizontal traversal of the table and what fields there are. Now we need to look at vertical traversal, i.e. going through the records up and down.

Cursors, contained in the arcpy module, are useful objects that make moving through each table record easier. These are not unique in ArcGIS; if you have ever used ArcObjects, you will have seen them before.

Because multiple versions of ArcGIS are still in use, we will look at the way cursors are used in both the older and newer versions of the software before we look at the changes that make cursor usage easier and require less code. For the most part, the code we use in this section will be for the newer versions with solutions for older versions too.

First, we will look at the search cursor. This cursor was designed to make data reading simple. We will begin with the early uses of this cursor that is used in the older ArcGIS versions; you will find this code a little more, shall we say, verbose, than newer versions but it does give you a great idea of how the search cursor is working. First, the workflow:

1. The search cursor is created using arcpy.SearchCursor() method, which will take multiple parameters for the specification of the dataset and, if required, the rows required for reading.
2. Next, SearchCursor.next() is called so the first row can be read.
3. We now need to take the values from the row we are on and do something with them.
4. SearchCursor.next() is called again so the first row may be read.
5. A loop is started; this will exit when we run out of rows to read.
6. Next, we take the values in the row we are on and do something with them.
7. Last, SearchCursor.next() is called to go to the following row; because a loop was created, you will go back to the last step if another row is there to read. If not the condition for the loop has not been met and it will terminate.

When you begin to look at cursors, try visualizing the attribute table showing an arrow that indicated the current row. When you create the cursor, the arrow will point to the line above the first row. When the next() method is called for the first time, that arrow will drop to the very first row and a reference to the row is returned. Whenever next() is called after this, the arrow will move down by one row until the final row is reached. At this point, calling next() will return a data type of None.

Look at this very easy example showing a search cursor reading a cities dataset and then printing each name:

 # Prints the name of each city in a feature class

import arcpy

featureClass = "C:\\Data\\USA\\USA.gdb\\Cities"

rows = arcpy.SearchCursor(featureClass)

```
row = rows.next()
```

```
while row:

    print row.NAME

    row = rows.next()
```

Note that the final five rows of this code relate to the workflow steps above. Cursors are not always easy to understand to start with, so we'll take a closer look at each line. Look at those lines again, this time commented so that you can understand what is going on:

```
# Create the search cursor

rows = arcpy.SearchCursor(featureClass)
```

```
# Call SearchCursor.next() to read the first row

row = rows.next()
```

```
# Start a loop that will exit when there are no more rows available

while row:
```

```
    # Do something with the values in the current row

    print(row.NAME)
```

```
    # Call SearchCursor.next() to move on to the next row
```

row = rows.next()

Before we move on, there are a couple of important things to understand:

The 'while row' is a loop condition and is nothing more than a Boolean method to specify if a loop should carry on or stop. If there is a row object, the statement will return true and the loop will carry on; if there is no row object, false is returned and the loop will stop.

Field values may be read as row properties. Take row.NAME, for example; this provides a value in the field called NAME. If you had a field called POPULATION, you would use row.POPULATION to get the field value.

The names you see of 'row' and 'rows' are nothing more than variable names. They are representative of the ROW and SearchCursor objects and could, in effect, be named anything you wanted.

Look at another more complex example of the row values. In this script, we are trying to find what the average population of all counties within a given dataset. To do this, we must take the total population number and divide it by how many counties there are. The code example below is going to loop through each individual record and will make a running tally of what the population is and how many records have been counted. When all the records have been read, we only need to use a single division line to see the average:

 # Finds the average population in a counties dataset

import arcpy

featureClass = "C:\\Data\\Pennsylvania\\Counties.shp"

rows = arcpy.SearchCursor(featureClass)

row = rows.next()

average = 0

totalPopulation = 0

recordsCounted = 0

 # Loop through each row and keep running total of the population

 # and records counted.

while row:

    totalPopulation += row.POP1990

    recordsCounted += 1

    row = rows.next()

average = totalPopulation / recordsCounted

print("Average population for a county is " + str(average))

This script example may be quite a bit longer than the one we first looked it, but the pattern is the same – a search cursor is created, it goes to row one, does something with it and then repeats this until all records are dealt with.

Reading Variable Values

In our last example, we used row.POP1990 to reference a record population where the name of the field is POP1990. This is one of the easier ways to obtain field values. But what if you were to get 2009 data from the POP2009 field but need to script run again? What if you have multiple scripts, all long ones, all referencing the POP field in the exact same way? What you would need to do is look through each script very carefully for the row called POP1990 and then give it a new name – row.POP2009. This will take forever and is highly prone to errors.

Scripts can be made much more versatile if you were to represent the names of the fields using variables. Variables, like populationField, can be declared as a way to reference the field name for population, be it POPULATION, POP2009, POP1990, or whatever it is called. Our interpreter will not be able to recognize row.populationField. Instead, Row.getValue() must be used and passed as a parameter to the variable.

The next script example uses a variable name as a way of obtaining each record's population. You will see that we have commented on the lines we changed from above with a comment starting ###. Note – the population Field variable has been created and we also have a method call to row.getValue(populationField) – this will get each of the record populations.

 # Finds the average population in a counties dataset

import arcpy

featureClass = "C:\\Data\\Pennsylvania\\Counties.shp"

This row below is new

populationField = "POP1990"

rows = arcpy.SearchCursor(featureClass)

row = rows.next()

```
average = 0

totalPopulation = 0

recordsCounted = 0


# Loop through each row and keep running total of the population

#  and records counted.


while row:
### This row below is new
    totalPopulation += row.getValue(populationField)

    recordsCounted += 1

    row = rows.next()


average = totalPopulation / recordsCounted

print("Average population for a county is " + str(average))
```

Updating this script would require only that populationField = "POP2009" is set near to the start of the script. This is a great deal easier and more efficient than looking for row.POP1990 manually through the entire script. However, there is more to this; you could take it to another level and let a user input any specific name for a field that they want to be added as an argument when the script is run.

Remember when we looked at arcpy.GetParameterAsText()? This lets a user supply the variable value and this technique may be used for the population field name and for the path for the feature class, making your script incredibly versatile and flexible. The code below does not have any numbers other than 0 or 1, hard-code path names nor field names, and this means that running the script could be done with any of the feature classes that contain any population field name without a need to change any code. You could, if you wanted, use similar code to look for the averages of any of the numeric fields.

 # Finds the average population in a counties dataset

import arcpy

featureClass = arcpy.GetParameterAsText(0)

populationField = arcpy.GetParameterAsText(1)

rows = arcpy.SearchCursor(featureClass)

row = rows.next()

average = 0

totalPopulation = 0

recordsCounted = 0

 # Loop through each row and keep running total of the population

 # and records counted.

while row:

   totalPopulation += row.getValue(populationField)

   recordsCounted += 1

   row = rows.next()

average = totalPopulation / recordsCounted

print("Average population for a county is " + str(average))

For Loops With Cursors

The examples we looked at so far use while loops together with the method called next() to move the cursor. It may, however, be much easier to use a for loop for iteration. This came into use with the later ArcGIS versions and the example below shows how we can modify the previous script so a for loop can be used. Note the syntax that we have used for row in rows:

 # Finds the average population in a counties dataset

import arcpy

featureClass = "C:\\Data\\Pennsylvania\\Counties.shp"

populationField = "POP1990"

rows = arcpy.SearchCursor(featureClass)

```
average = 0

totalPopulation = 0

recordsCounted = 0


# Loop through each row and keep running total of the population

#  and records counted.


for row in rows:

    totalPopulation += row.getValue(populationField)

    recordsCounted += 1


average = totalPopulation / recordsCounted

print("Average population for a county is " + str(average))
```

We didn't even need to use the next() method in this script because the for loop implies that the script is going to iterate over every individual record. The declaration of the for loop declared the row object.

This is somewhat tighter in syntax than the while loop, but it is useful to see how the method called next() works. This is more important if you are working with early ArcGIS scripts or if you are using ArcObject cursors. Eventually, with practice, you will become used to traversing tables using a for loop and you will be unlikely to want to return to the while loops.

ArcPY Data-Access Module

In later versions of ArcGIS, that code example could be used for the search cursors or you could choose another route – a data-access module supplied by arcpy. Each of the functions has the arcpy.da prefix and they provide much faster and more efficient performance, as well as being far more robust in behavior when the cursor crashes or runs into errors.

The arcpy.da module will allow for the creation of cursor objects, much like arcpy, but the creation is a little bit different. Look at the next example very closely. The scenario from the previous code has been repeated, calculating a county's average population:

```
# Finds the average population in a counties dataset


import arcpy


featureClass = "C:\\Data\\Pennsylvania\\Counties.shp"

populationField = "POP1990"


average = 0

totalPopulation = 0

recordsCounted = 0


with arcpy.da.SearchCursor(featureClass, (populationField,)) as cursor:

    for row in cursor:

        totalPopulation += row[0]
```

recordsCounted += 1

average = totalPopulation / recordsCounted

print("Average population for a county is " + str(average))

Note that the structure of this script is basically the same as the last one but there are a couple of changes that are quite important. The first thing you should have noticed is that we used a with statement to create our cursor. Explaining this with statement is rather technical but the important thing to really understand is that the statement will let the cursor come out of the database in a graceful manner, regardless of whether it was successful or whether it crashes. This is one of the biggest problems with the cursors; if they do not get exited correctly, they may place a lock on the data and hold it there.

When you use a with statement, all the code that comes after it must be indented. Once the cursor has been created in that statement, a for loop must then be initiated to go over every individual row in your table. Extra indentation will be required for this.

The with statement has also created an object called SearchCursor and has made a declaration that the name will be cursor in any later code. When you use arcpy.da to create a search cursor, each will have different parameters for initialization than the search cursors created using arcpy. The main difference though, is that when arcpy.da is used for the creation of the cursors, you must supply a field name tuple; the cursor will return this tuple. Remember: tuples are data structures in Python that are similar to lists with the exception of a set of parentheses enclosing it and that there is no way of modifying the tuple contents.

When this tuple is supplied, the cursor's work is hastened because it no longer has any need to deal with a large number of fields that are in the dataset. In our previous script example, the tuple only has one field called populationField. Even though it has only the one item, that item must be followed by a comma, so it would look like (populationField,). If there were more than one item in the tuple, there must be a comma separating each item.

We also still have row objects in arcpy.da, the same as we do in arcpy but we no longer get the row values by using the method called getValue(). Instead, we take the field name from the tuple named when the object was created and use its index position. In the previous example, only one item was submitted within the tuple, we would use the populationField index position which, in our example is 0. Remember, we begin at 0 to count in Python, so row[0] would be used to obtain the populationField value for any specified row.

Using Attribute Queries to Retrieve Records

In our previous script examples, the SearchCursor object was used to read through individual dataset records. However, you can make your search cursor work a bit more specifically and ask it to retrieve only a subset of those records with attributes complying with specified criteria. For your information, the code snippet below shows you how to use arcpy.da to build the search cursor to work on all records in a specified dataset:

with arcpy.da.SearchCursor(featureClass,(populationField,)) as cursor:

If the search cursor is only to retrieve a subset of the dataset records based on specified criteria, an SQL expression should be supplied as an argument in the constructor used to create your SearchCursor. An example would be:

with arcpy.da.SearchCursor(featureClass, (populationField,), '"POP2009" > 150000') as cursor:

In this example, the SQL expression we use is 'POP2009">150000 and this will retrieve just the subset of records with a population from 2009 and more than 150000. SQL is a Structured Query Language and it is a specific syntax that we use when we want to query a database. If you have used ArcMap before and have ever filtered data using a Definition Query, then you will have a better understanding of what an SQL query is all about. If you are not familiar with SQL or queries, go to the Desktop Help in ArcGIS and read the help topic on Building Query Expressions, a simple overview of the SQL as far as ArcGIS is concerned.

In an SQL expression, you can use any combination of different criteria to ensure that you get the exact subset of data that you want. The only limit to your query is the data that you have available. For example, you could write an SQL query that helps you to find the States whose names begin with M, were made settlements after 1800, and that have a population of more than 150 people per square mile. That's pretty specific!

The SQL expression supplied to any search cursor will not be spatial queries, only for attribute queries. There would not be a way to use an SQL query to choose the records that are within the Canadian borders or to the north of the Arkansas River, for example, unless an attribute had been added and populated earlier to specify whether a condition is True. i.e. CANADIAN = True or REGION = 'Northern'. Later, we'll cover spatial queries using the geoprocessing tool Select By Location.

Once the subset has been retrieved, iteration through the records is done using a for loop:

with arcpy.da.SearchCursor(featureClass, (populationField,), '"POP200p" > 150000') as cursor:

 for row in cursor:

  print(str(row[0]))

Using Quotation Marks

When an SQL expression is used in the constructor for the SearchCursor, that expression must be in the format of a string. Things can get a little complicated where quotation marks are concerned. In SQL, double and single quotation marks are required in specific places but, because the expression is a string, the whole thing needs to be inside quotes. So how do we do this without running into utter confusion?

With Python, strings can be enclosed in either single or double quotes. Note from our previous example that the SQL expression was inside a set of single quotes and not double ones – '"POP2009">150000'. The reason for this was because, inside the SQL statement, the field name is surrounded by double quotes, so it is better to use the single quotes for the string. This not only makes reading the code easier; if you were to use two sets of double quote marks together, the Python interpreter would get in a muddle and would think that an empty string was being created. Using double quotes for the string is not an option in this case.

Things get a little more confusing when the SQL expression needs both single quotes and double quotes. An example of this would be if you were querying string variables. Let's suppose that, in your script, a user is allowed to enter a Parcel ID and you want to use a search cursor to find it. Some of the IDs have letters in them while others do not, so each Parcel ID would need to be treated as a string. The SQL expression could look something like this – "PARCEL" = 'B3994NRF'. The expression has double quote marks at the start and single ones at the end. So which ones do we use for the whole expression?

With this example, you can't use a single quote mark style for the whole expression. Instead, the expression needs to be broken down into separate strings. Look at this next example carefully:

ID = arcpy.GetParameterAsText(0)

whereClause = '"Parcel"' + " = '" + str(ID) + "'"

with arcpy.da.SearchCursor(featureClass, (parcelField,), whereClause) as cursor:

...

Note that we have split our SQL expression, the whereClause, into smaller chunks that don't mix up the quote styles. If a chunk has double quotes, like "Parcel", then it will be surrounded with single quotes. Vice versa, if a chunk has single quotes, like =', then double quotes are used to enclose it. In this type of case, it often helps if you add a temporary print statement into the code or if you check that the where clause has been properly constructed using debugging tools. You will also find it very helpful if you can concentrate on the + sign as the separator between each independent part of the string that you construct.

Field Delimiters

In those examples, we used double quotes to surround the field name. This is the right syntax for the two types of data we will use in this part – geodatabases and shapefiles. If, in the course of your daily work, you are using personal geodatabases, you will find that there are multiple delimiters for the field name. For other data types, or to give your script flexibility to take any data type, go to the ArcGIS Desktop Help and look up SQL reference with regards to query expressions.

Using Spatial Queries to Retrieve Records

Using an SQL expression in the search cursor will only ever be useful where attribute queries are concerned. As we mentioned earlier, they can't be used for spatial queries. You could, if you wanted, run a search cursor using an SQL expression on all the counties with the name "Lincoln", but if you wanted all those counties that included or touched on the Arkansas River, you would need to take a different approach. When you want a record subset, based on spatial criteria, you need to use the Select by Location geoprocessing tool.

For this, you need to have some knowledge about the way that ArcGIS works with selections and layers. Let's say that you are looking for all the States with a boundary touching on Oklahoma. Most of the time, there won't be any need to create new feature classes for the States. All you would need to do is maintain the records for those States in the computer memory while an attribute is updated. ArcGIS uses a concept known as feature layers as a way to represent feature class record sets in memory.

A tool called Make Feature layer is used to create a feature layer made up of all or some of the records from a specified feature class. An SQL expression may be applied when Make Feature Layer is run to use attributes to reduce the feature layer records. After that, the tool called Select Layer by Location may be used with spatial criteria to reduce the records even further.

To open a search cursor for Oklahoma and all the bordering states can be done in 4 steps:

1. Make Feature Layer is used to create a layer of all the US States; we will call this layer All States.
2. Make Feature Layer is then used to create a second layer, just Oklahoma this time. To do this, an SQL expression must be applied when the feature layer is made. We'll call this layer Selection State.
3. Select Layer by Location is used to reduce the All States layer from step 1 to the States that border Oklahoma, the Selection State layer from step 2.
4. A search cursor is opened on All States; this cursor has just Oklahoma and the bordering States in it because of the selection that we apply to All States. Remember; the feature layer is nothing more than a record set in memory. You could perhaps call it All States – as soon as a selection is applied, it would no longer have all the States in it.

Look at some example code that will apply to these 4 steps:

```
# Selects all the states whose boundaries touch

#  a user-supplied state


import arcpy


# Get the US States layer, state, and state name field

usaLayer = "D:\\Data\\USA\\USA.gdb\\Boundaries"

state = "Wyoming"

nameField = "NAME"


try:

    # Make a feature layer with all the US States
```

```
arcpy.MakeFeatureLayer_management(usaLayer, "AllStatesLayer")


# Make a feature layer containing only the state of interest

arcpy.MakeFeatureLayer_management(usaLayer,

        "SelectionStateLayer",

        "" + str(nameField) + "' =' + "'" + str(state) + "'")



# Apply a selection to the US States layer

arcpy.SelectLayerByLocation_management("AllStatesLayer","BOUNDARY_T
OUCHES","SelectionStateLayer")



# Open a search cursor on the US States layer

with arcpy.da.SearchCursor("AllStatesLayer", (nameField,)) as cursor:

    for row in cursor:

        # Print the name of all the states in the selection

        print(row[0])


except:

    print(arcpy.GetMessages())
```

 # Clean up feature layers

arcpy.Delete_management("AllStatesLayer")

arcpy.Delete_management("SelectionStateLayer")

When you use SelectLayerByLocation, you have the option of several spatial operators. The example above uses the operator called "BOUNDARY_TOUCHES" but some of the other operators include "WITHIN A DISTANCE" (which could eliminate a buffering step), "INTERSECT", "CONTAINED_BY", and "CONTAIN" among others.

Did you spot that "row", the ROW object, only returns a single field, "NAME"? We use the index position from the field list to access this, and because we have just one field, the index is therefore 0. The syntax would be row[0]. When the search cursor has been opened on the specified records, any action you desire may then be performed. The code used above prints only the name of the State, but you will probably want to update the values of the attributes or summarize them. Later, we will look at how to write the values for these attributes.

Cleaning the Cursors and Feature Layers

To delete feature layers, we need to use the Delete tool. The reason for this is that a feature layer may lock and maintain that lock on the date and this would stop the data being used by any other application until your script has been executed and is finished. In theory, arcpy does a cleanup at the end of a script but it is best to delete the feature layers manually, just in case they get missed or a crash occurs. In the previous examples, we used an except block that would catch any crashes; the script would carry on and the Delete tool would be run.

A cursor may also lock data but there is no need for explicit deletion of these; the with statement will do the cleanup automatically and this is one of the main benefits of using the data-access module cursors.

Writing Data for Vector Attributes

In a similar way to use a cursor to read the data in vector attributes, we can also use them to write the data to them as well. There are two cursor types for this purpose:

- The update cursor will allow you to edit values from records that exist or deleting records.
- The insert cursor will insert a new record.

Update the Existing Records

The update cursor is used to edit the records that already exist inside a dataset and the steps to use this cursor would be:

We call arcpy.da.UpdateCursor() for the purpose of creating the update cursor. You may, if you want, pass an argument in the form of an SQL expression to the method – a good way to reduce the rows that need editing if you really don't want to edit every table row.

A for loop is used for iteration through all the rows individually

The field values are then modified for the row that needs to be updated

UpdateCursor.updateRow() is then called so the edit can be finished.

Field Value Modification

When UpdateCursor is created and used to iterate through the rows with the variable named row, the field values can be modified through assignments made using row[<field index to be changed>] = <new value>. An example would be row[1] = "Tania Williams".

There is one thing that you must note – the index inside the square brackets, [], used for determining which of the fields is to be modified, is provided with respect the fields tuple supplied at the creation of UpdateCursor. For example, if we were to use this command to create our cursor:

with arcpy.da.UpdateCursor(featureClass, ("Company name", "Owner")) as cursor:

row[0] would be referencing the Company Name field while row[1] is referencing the Owner field.

In the script example below, we are carrying out an operation to search and replace on a table of attributes. For example, let's say that your dataset is representative of local business and that includes banks. One bank has been taken over by another bank, so we need to search for all instances of the name of the old bank and replace them with the new bank name. Using this script, that task could be automatically performed:

#Simple search and replace script

import arcpy

 # Retrieve input parameters: the feature class, the field affected by

 # the search and replace, the search term, and the replace term.

fc = arcpy.GetParameterAsText(0)

affectedField = arcpy.GetParameterAsText(1)

oldValue = arcpy.GetParameterAsText(2)

newValue = arcpy.GetParameterAsText(3)

 # Create the SQL expression for the update cursor. Here this is

 # done on a separate line for readability.

queryString = "" + affectedField + "' = ' + """ + oldValue + """

 # Create the update cursor and update each row returned by the SQL expression

with arcpy.da.UpdateCursor(fc, (affectedField,), queryString) as cursor:

  for row in cursor:

    row[0] = newValue

    cursor.updateRow(row)

Note that we have a flexible script here, having all the parameters in text format. However, because of how the query string has been set up, the script can only be used on string variables. Note that we use quotes to enclose the old value, like "'" + oldValue + "'". We could have tried to handle other variable types, but this would have lengthened the example.

Again, one very important thing to understand is the tuple passed in when the update cursor is created. In our example, we have just one field affected which, for the sake of simplicity, we have called affectedField. In the tuple, it has a position of 0 on the index. As such, we use row[0] = newValue to set the value of the field. There is no requirement to clean up the cursor when the script ends because the with statement will do this.

On the final line, we have updateRow(...) and this is required to ensure that the row we modified is written back to the table of attributes. Note that we need to pass the variable row to updateRow(...) as a parameter.

Dataset Locking

We have mentioned before that ArcGIS will occasionally put a lock on a dataset so that there can be no conflict in editing between two or more users. If you have any reason to believe that a lock is causing problems with one of your datasets, perhaps by stopping you from viewing it or making you believe that all the rows in the dataset have been removed, the only way to remove the lock is to close PythonWin. You can also check to see if ArcMap or ArcCatalog are making use of that specific data in some way. This might be a possibility if you left a data edit session open, if you have the data in an open ArcCatalog Preview tab, or if the layer is within a table of contents within an MXD, or map document that is still open.

New Record Insertion

The Insert cursor is used for adding new records to a table and these are the steps you would take:

We use arcpy.da.InsertCursor() for the insert cursor creation.

InsertCursor.insertRow() is called and a new row may be added to the dataset.

Like we did with the cursor for search and update, the insert cursor can be used in conjunction with a with statement to avoid locking issues.

An insert cursor is a bit different to a search and update cursor in that an SQL expression cannot be used when the insert cursor is created. This does make a kind of sense because, with the insert cursor, all we are doing is inputting new records; it has no need to be aware of any existing records.

When we use InsertCursor.insertRow() to add a new row, the tuple of field values for the additional row must be delimited using commas. These values must be in an order that matches the order of the affected fields value supplied in the tuple when the cursor was created. For example, if you were to use the following to create your cursor:

arcpy.da.InsertCursor(featureClass, ("First name","Last name")) as cursor:

the new row would be added with the values of Simon for "First Name" and Bobbins for "Last Name" using this command:

cursor.insertRow(("Simon","Bobbins"))

The inner set of parentheses is required to convert the values to the tuple which is then passed to insertRow(). If you were, for example, to write cursor.insertRow("Simon", "Bobbins"), you would get an error.

The next script example is creating a new point in our dataset using an insert cursor; this point is then being assigned to an attribute which is a string description. We could, potentially, use this script behind an application that the public can use, perhaps one where a user would click on a web map and write a description of some kind of incident that the specified municipality needs to deal with, like a streetlight that is broken.

```
# Adds a point and an accompanying description

import arcpy

# Retrieve input parameters

inX = arcpy.GetParameterAsText(0)

inY = arcpy.GetParameterAsText(1)

inDescription = arcpy.GetParameterAsText(2)


# These parameters are hard-coded. User can't change them.

incidentsFC = "C:/Data/Yakima/Incidents.shp"

descriptionField = "DESCR"


# Make a tuple of fields to update

fieldsToUpdate = ("SHAPE@XY", descriptionField)

# Create the insert cursor

with arcpy.da.InsertCursor(incidentsFC, fieldsToUpdate) as cursor:

    # Insert the row providing a tuple of affected attributes

    cursor.insertRow(((float(inX),float(inY)), inDescription))
```

Read through this a couple of times and make sure that you understand how the following two things are being done in this code:

- The insert cursor created with a tuple of the affected fields and stored in the fieldsToUpdate variable.

- The row is inserted using insertRow() and variables that contain the new row's field values.

One thing that you should have spotted is that the "SHAPE@XY" string is being used as a way to specify our Shape field. You could, not unsurprisingly, expect this to be Shape, but with arcpy.da, we have a choice of tokens that we can use if the field needs to be specified in a particular way. For our example, we could just give the values for X and Y points with a tuple full of coordinates. The token called "SHAPE@XY" lets us do that. If you want to learn about the other tokens, check the InsertCursor help topic.

If we put it all together, we have a script in which a tuple of the affected fields is created – ("SHAPE@XY", "DESCR"). In line number 14, the descriptionField variable is used containing "DESCR", which is the second column name in element 2 of our tuple. Using a variable to store the column name allows for easy adoption of the script later, for example, where the column may be named differently. When we insert the two, the Simone order is used to provide the item values - cursor.insertRow(((float(inX), float(inY)), inDescription)). We pass a tuple as an argument to insertRow(); this tuple contains another one, (inX, inY) and this is the point coordinates for the floating point numbers for element 1 and the "DESCR" field text as element 2.

Working with Rasters

Up until now, our scripts have only been used to read vector datasets and to edit them. This mostly consists of going through record tables, reading values and then writing them to specific fields. With raster data, things are very different; we have just a series of cells and each one has a value. So, how do we use Python to access the raster data and manipulate it?

To be honest, it isn't likely that you will ever need to use your Python to go one cell at a time through a raster and that really isn't within the scope of this book. What you will do most often is use tools that have already been defined to read and manipulate the rasters. The tools have been carefully designed to do the cell by cell computation for you on a number of different raster types making your job much easier.

Most of the ArcGIS tools that you will use with a raster will be in one of two toolsets – the Data Management>Raster or the Spatial Analyst toolbox. We can use these tools to clip, reject, mosaick, and to reclassify a raster. They can also be used to calculate the slope, aspect, and hillside rasters from DEMs.

In the Spatial Analysis toolbox, there is also a set of tools that allow us to carry out map algebra on a raster. An important part of the GIS site selection is to be able to use map algebra to multiply or link rasters together. An example: you may be looking for a good location for a brand-new restaurant and 7 different criteria need to be met. If a Boolean raster could be created with 0 for unsuitable location and 1 for a suitable location, map algebra can be used to multiply the rasters and to determine which of the cells will meet all 7 criteria and be given a value of 1.

One part of map algebra that could be tricky is in the expression construction. This expression is a string which will lay out what is supposed to be done by the map algebra. In ArcGIS Desktop, there are a number of interfaces that can be used to construct an expression for a single run. What, though, would we do if we needed the analysis to be run multiple times or to be run on different types of dataset? Even using ModelBuilder, constructing an expression that is flexible into the tools for map algebra is going to be somewhat challenging. Using Python, the expression can be manipulated as much and as often as you want.

Let's consider an example. This will take the maximum and the minimum values for the elevation as parameters and, using those values, will then do some magic with map algebra. The expression will find those areas with a greater elevation than the smallest parameter and lower than the largest parameter. Any cell that will satisfy that expression will be provided with a value of 1 because they are suitable. If a cell doesn't meet the expression, it is given the value of 0 as being unsuitable.

What if we don't want to see these values of 0 all over our raster? The script below will eliminate them by running a tool called Reclassify. This has a remap table that is very simple and that states input values of 1 must stay as 1 and 0 is not included in the remap table so it will be given a new classification of NoData:

```
# This script takes a DEM, a minimum elevation,

#  and a maximum elevation. It outputs a new

#  raster showing only areas that fall between

#  the min and the max


import arcpy

from arcpy.sa import *

arcpy.env.overwriteOutput = True

arcpy.env.workspace = "C:/Data/Elevation"


# Get parameters of min and max elevations

inMin = arcpy.GetParameterAsText(0)

inMax = arcpy.GetParameterAsText(1)


arcpy.CheckOutExtension("Spatial")


# Perform the map algebra and make a temporary raster
```

```
inDem = Raster("foxlake")

tempRaster = (inDem > int(inMin)) & (inDem < int(inMax))


# Set up remap table and call Reclassify, leaving all values not 1 as NODATA

remap = RemapValue([[1,1]])

remappedRaster = Reclassify(tempRaster, "Value", remap, "NODATA")


# Save the reclassified raster to disk

remappedRaster.save("foxlake_recl")


arcpy.CheckInExtension("Spatial")
```

Make sure you go through that script example a few times until you have understood what is happening in every line and spot the following:

We have an intermediate raster – this isn't the final output – that you don't really want in there because it just clutters up the output directory. This is known as a tempRaster and, when the script is executed, you will see this in ArcGIS. When PythonWin is shut down, it will disappear.

There are < and > signs in the expression, alongside the & operator. The expression must be wrapped in parentheses so that the & operator does not get confused.

We have our input parameters using arcpy.GetParameterAsText() and, because of this, the input must be cast to an integer before any map algebra can be done. If inMin was used on its own, for example, '3000' would be seen by the software and it would be interpreted as a string. We need to use int(inMin) to do numerical comparisons; 3000 would then be seen as the number and not as the string of '3000',

We can use map algebra for several operations and math types on a raster; it isn't limited to using "less than" or "greater than". You could, if you wanted, find a raster cosine using map algebra.

If the license manager at your place of work puts a restriction on the number of users for the Spatial Analysis extension, the extension must be checked out and then checked back into the script – note the two calls in the script, arcpy.CheckOutExtension(), followed by arcpy.CheckInExtension(). You are not restricted to passing in the Spatial extension; there are others that can be used as method arguments too.

Our script isn't using arcpy to call the spatial functions. Rather, the functions are imported from arcpy.da import * directly – this is the spatial analyst module – and the functions are also called directly. Note that instead of arcpy.Reclassify(), we have directly called Reclassify().

Look in the Help topics for Remap classes to give you a better understanding of the way we created our remap table. When Reclassify is run, a remap table needs to be created describing how to reclassify old values to new values. The example we used is a very simple one; the help documentation will tell you about more complex remap tables.

GIS Analysis and Practical Python – Modules and Functions

We didn't look at functions yet and this is one of the most basic areas of Python programming that you need to know. In this section, we will look at the functions and the ways they can be used in longer Python scripts.

In a function, there will be just one bit of focused functionality inside a code piece that is reusable. The idea is that the function is written once and called wherever needed in the code. Groups of functions that are related can be placed into a module so they can then be used in multiple scripts. When they are used properly, a function will remove a lot of repetition in the code and the code will then become much more readable and shorter.

Functions are not special to Python; they can be found in many computer programming languages and each language will have its own unique way to define the function. With Python, the def statement is used for function definition and every line of the function that comes after the def statement must be indented. Here's an example of a function written to read a circle's radius and returns an approximation of the circle's area. If you remember your math from school, you will know that area = pi [3.14159..] multiplied by the radius squared [**2]:

>>> def findArea(radius):

...   area = 3.14159 * radius ** 2

...   return area

...

>>> findArea(3)

28.27431

Note that a function may take arguments or parameters, and when we call the function above, the circle radius is placed inside a set of parentheses. The function will return the circle's area – note that we have used something new here, only a return statement.

If you have a circle that has a 3-inch radius and you want the area of it, the function call could be findArea(3) with a return value of 28.27431, which would be in inches.

It isn't uncommon for returned values to be assigned to variables and then used later in the code. For example, the lines of code below could be input to the Interactive Window:

>>> aLargerCircle = findArea(4)

>>> *print(aLargerCircle)*

50.26544

For now, I want you to go to this link. This takes you to a website called pythontutor.com where we will use the visualization feature for code execution to call and execute the findArea(...) function from our example. A browser window will open and the code will be at the top-left of it. Click on the buttons that say Forward and Backward and you can go through the code while, at the same time, see what is stored in memory by Python at any one time, and is shown at the top-right.

The first time you click Forward, the function definition will be read in, followed by the creation of a function object that goes under findArea and is then is accessible globally.

Next, the call to findArea(4) is executed (line 5). A new variable is the result of this, being given the name of the only parameter in the function. That name is radius and it is assigned with a value of 4. This variable is local and can only be accessed from within the code that is inside the function body.

The execution will go straight to the code that starts in line 1 in the function definition.

For the next step, line 2 then is executed and a local variable called area created. This is assigned with the result from the computation done in line 2, taking the local variable value of 4 (the variable called radius).

Next, we go to line 3 where the return statement will set the value of the function return to the value of the area, the local variable. At this point, the value is 50.2654.

When Forward is clicked again, we go to line 5, where we called the function. Because we are going out of the function body execution, the two function local variables called area and radius are now removed. Where the function call was in line 5, we now have the return value instead; in our case, the value has been assigned to another global variable with a name of aLargerCircle. This will appear in memory.

In the last step, the value of 50.2564 that is assigned to that variable will be printed.

What is very important for you to understand is the structures for:

- Going from the function call in line 5 to the function definition code and back.

- The creation of the local variables for each parameter and all the variables that are defined in the body of the function and how they are then discarded when we get to the end of that body. All that remains from and is returned from the function execution is the return value.

- There is no requirement for a function to return a value. You might, for example, have a function with a parameter that is a text file path. That function will read line 1 and then print it to the Interactive Windows. Because all the logic for printing happens within a function, there will not be a return value.

- There is also no requirement for functions to take parameters. You might want to write a function to calculate or retrieve a static value.

Try inputting this in the Interactive Window:

```
>>> def getCurrentPresident():

...     return "Donald Trump"

...

>>> president = getCurrentPresident()

>>> print(president)
```

Donald Trump

The getCurrentPresident() function will not take any parameters supplied by the user. It has just one purpose and that is to return the current president's name – you cannot ask it to do anything but that.

Modules

When we place the logic for getCurrentPresident() into a function, what are we gaining by doing so? What was stopping us from defining a simple string of currentPresident and then setting it as =DonaldTrump? The main reason is code reusability.

Let's say we have 15 different scripts. Each works in its own way with the current President name. Eventually, that name is going to change, so this function could be placed into a module file. That file would then be referenced in each of your 15 scripts and, when a new President takes office the name changes and you won't need to open all the different scripts and modify them. Simply open the module, modify one file and all the rest will update automatically.

You should, by now, be familiar with the pattern we use for the import of the arcpy site package at the start of each script. Site-packages can be home to many modules and, in arcpy's case, these have some of the geoprocessing functions in them.

When using Python for GIS work, you will no doubt be writing functions that may be used in numerous script types. These could be used to convert coordinates between projections or to create polygons from coordinate lists. Any of these functions will fit nicely into modules so, if you ever find yourself wanting to make improvements to any of your code, use modules; make one change in the module and it will update everywhere.

Creating Modules

Creating a module requires the creation of a new script and this is done in PythonWin. The script must be saved with a.py extension but all you need in the script are some functions, not an entire script with all the logic in it. The example below shows what a module file might look like; it is just a simple one that has a single function. That function will use a coordinates list to add a points set to a features class.

 # Save this file with the extension of.py

 # The function below creates points from a list of coordinates

 # Example list: [[-113,23][-120,36][-116,-2]]

def createPoints(coordinateList, featureClass):

   # Import arcpy and create an insert cursor

   import arcpy

   with arcpy.da.InsertCursor(featureClass, ("SHAPE@",)) as rowInserter:

      # Loop through each coordinate in the list and make a point

      for coordinate in coordinateList:

        point = arcpy.Point(coordinate[0],coordinate[1])

        rowInserter.insertRow((point,))

The createPoints function could prove useful in several scripts so it fits into a module very nicely. Notice that we have point objects and insert cursors for our script to work with so arcpy is a requirement. It is also perfectly legal in Python to import a module or a site package inside another module.

You should also have noticed that we import arcpy inside the function this time, not at the start of the module like we have been doing. Performance is the reason for this; the module can be given additional functions later, functions that do not need arcpy. Really and truthfully, arcpy should only be imported when it is absolutely needed, for example if you call a function that needs it.

You will find that the arcpy site package can only be available in the scope of the function. If we were to call other functions from the module, they would not have access to arcpy. Scope is also applicable to any variable that has been created inside the function, like rowInserter for example. Scope is also subject to limits from loops in the function. The variable called point will only be valid in the for loop that is in the function and will not work anywhere else.

Using Modules

How can we use our practice module inside a script? Let's suppose that our module has been saved, by itself, with the name of practiceModule.py. The script below shows how to import that module:

 # This script is saved as add_my_points.py

 # Import the module containing a function we want to call

import practiceModule

 # Define point list and shapefile to edit

myWorldLocations = [[-123.9,47.0],[-118.2,34.1],[-112.7,40.2],[-63.2,-38.7]]

myWorldFeatureClass = "c:\\Data\\WorldPoints.shp"

 # Call the createPoints function from practiceModule

practiceModule.createPoints(myWorldLocations, myWorldFeatureClass)

This script is quite a simple one and is also easy to read. This is because we didn't need to add in all the logic normally required to create a point. Instead the function called createPoints does that for us inside the imported module.

Note, if we want a function called from within a module, the syntax to use is module.function().

Practice

Before we go on any further, it would be a good idea to get some practice in using PythonWin. You can do this by trying the functions listed below. I won't be providing the answers, just do your best with them. You can always look on the internet for help if you really are stuck:

1. Write a function that will return a square's perimeter with one side length provided.
2. Write a function that will take a parameter of a feature class path and will return a list of all the fields contained in that feature class. Have some practice at the function calls and in printing but you shouldn't try printing the list that is inside the function.
3. Write a function that will take two coordinates and will return the Euclidean distance between the two. You can supply these coordinates as parameters in the following format – (x1, y1, x2, y2). To make things a bit more challenging, you could make use of the Pythagorean formula of A**2 + B**2 = C**2 and try using negative coordinates.

The best way to practice is to place the functions in a module and then use another script to see if you can call them. Try using the debugger to go through your code and you should see that it will go between the module and the script when a function is called in the module.

Python Dictionaries

On occasion, when we are programming, we will have large data amounts that we want to be stored. This data will all belong within one variable. Earlier, we talked about lists, one way of storing the data, and so long as you have sufficient memory, you can store as much in a list as you want; using the append() method will let you store more.

There is another way, another type of data structure that lets you use one variable to store complex, large data amounts and it's called a dictionary. Lists are used to store elements in a sequence; access to those elements is dependent on their index position. With a dictionary, the elements are simple key-value pairs; the key part of the pair is used to retrieve the value par. Think of a real dictionary – you look up a meaning (the value) stored under a specific word (the key).

Dictionaries are very useful when mapping is required. In our example, we are mapping English words to their Spanish words; this shows you how to create dictionaries, although it is a very simple example:

>>> *englishToSpanishDic = { "one": "uno", "two": "dos", "three": "tres", "four": "cuatro" }*

Note the curly brackets; these are used for delimiting our dictionary in much the same way as the squared brackets do in a list. In this dictionary, we have 4, comma-separated, key-value pairs and a colon is used to separate the key and value in each pair. The key is on the left while the value is on the right.

This dictionary stored inside a variable called englishToSpanishDic may now be used to find the Spanish equivalent of an English number, for example:

>>> *print(englishToSpanishDic["two"])*

dos

If you want to retrieve a value from the dictionary, the variable name is used, followed with a pair of square brackets inside which is the key to the dictionary value. If the same notation is used on the left of our assignment operator, a new pair can be added into the dictionary.

>>> *englishToSpanishDic["five"] = "cinco"*

>>> *print(englishToSpanishDic)*

{'four': 'cuatro', 'three': 'tres', 'five': 'cinco', 'two': 'dos', 'one': 'uno'}

We added a new value to our dictionary, "cinco" and this, as you can see, is on the right-hand side of the assignment operator (=) and is stored under the key named "five". If there were already a value stored in "five", the new value would have overwritten it. Did you notice a change in the element order in our dictionary, specifically in the output? The order doesn't matter because we always use the key to access the related value in a dictionary. If we had lots of more pairs in the dictionary, we could use it as a simple translator that would replace each English word in a text with the Spanish equivalent from the dictionary. However, this would give us some strange translations!

Let's move on to something more complex with our dictionaries. This time, we will create an index of books; this index will have the page numbers where specified keywords can be found. We will begin with a completely empty dictionary and iterate, one page at a time, through a book. When we come across a word we consider should be in the index, the word and the page number is put in the dictionary.

We'll start by making a new dictionary, an empty one with the name of bookIndex. To do this, we will use the curly brackets notation, but the brackets will be empty:

>>> *bookIndex = {}*

>>> *print(bookIndex)*

{}

Now, we are going to imagine that we are working our way through a programming book and the first word we want to add is "function" and the first place it appears is on page 1. The page number is the value and it will be stored under the key within our dictionary. However, this is not the only place that this word will appear, so rather than single page numbers as the values, we will store lists that contain multiple page numbers. In our dictionary, we will add a list with a single element of 1 (the page number):

>>> *bookIndex["function"] = [1]*

>>> *print(bookIndex)*

{'function': [1]}

The next word we want to add is 'module' and we first see this word on page 2.
We use the same method to add this to the dictionary:

>>> *bookIndex["module"] = [2]*

>>> *print(bookIndex)*

{'function': [1], 'module': [2]}

We now have two of our key-value pairs in the dictionary; for each key we have
a list. At the moment, each list has just one value in it. Next, we see the word
"function" again, on page 4 this time. The code we use to add this number to our
"function" list is a little different because there is already a dictionary value in
there and we don't want that value over-written. What we do is get the page
number list we stored earlier and use the append() method to add the next
number:

>>> *pages = bookIndex["function"]*

>>> *pages.append(4)*

>>> *print(bookIndex)*

{'function': [1, 4], 'module': [2]}

>>> *print(bookIndex["function"])*

[1, 4]

Note that we didn't need to put our list back after the new number was added.
The list was stored in a variable called pages and both the dictionary and
variable reference the very same list – this means that, when we make a change
in the variable using the append() method, the same change is made in the
dictionary.

Now we have 2 numbers in our list for "function" and just 1 for "module". You
should now be able to see how we can use this process to enlarge our dictionary.

You might also be interested to know that a dictionary can be used together with a for loop. This is to iterate through our dictionary keys and we can use this code to print our dictionary:

```
>>> for k in bookIndex:  # loop through the keys of the dictionary

...    print("keyword: " + k)              # print the key

...    print("pages: " + str(bookIndex[k]))  # print the value

...

keyword: function

pages: [1, 4]

keyword: module

pages: [2]
```

When we added the second number, we made the decision that we needed to do it differently from when the first number was added. But how would this work in code? What we can do is use an if statement and the in operator to see if a value is already being stored in a dictionary key:

```
>>> keyword = "function"

>>> if keyword in bookIndex:

...    print("entry exists")

... else:

...    print("entry does not exist")

...

entry exists
```

Assuming the current word is stored in a variable called word, and the number that corresponds to it is stored in a variable called pageNo, the next code example would make its own decision on how new numbers should be added:

word = "module"

pageNo = 7

if word in bookIndex:

       # entry for word already exists, so we just add page

       pages = bookIndex[word]

       pages.append(pageNo)

else:

       # no entry for word exists, so we add a new entry

       bookIndex[word] = [pageNo]

If we could take the code to the next level, it would also look at whether the numbers list that the if block retrieves already has the new number in readiness for when a word appears twice or more on one page. Think about how this could be done – we won't be going into it here, but it will get your brain ticking over.

Using Python CSV Module to Read and Parse Text

If you really want to be effective at GIS programming, you need to learn manipulation of information that is text-based. We looked at reading data from native ArcGIS formats, like the feature classes, but more often or not, we would be collecting our GIS data in other formats, called 'raw' formats. These include CSV spreadsheets, text files containing coordinates, XML responses and so on.

When you are faced with files like this, you must know whether the GIS software you use already contains the tools that you need or a script that is able to read this data and convert it into a usable format. If you don't have that script or tool, you will have a little work to do in terms of programming to be able to read these files and work out what text you need. This is known as 'parsing'.

For example, take a web service that returns multiple XML lines listing the readings taken from a specific weather station. All you really need from the information are the weather station coordinates and the average annual temperature. To parse these lines, we need to write code that will go through each line and each tag within the XML and isolate the values that we want.

There are a few ways that we can approach parsing. Perhaps the most commonsense method is to determine whether any module exists in Python that will go through the text for you. That module would then need to convert the text into a workable object. We will be starting our journey by looking at the csv module in Python. This module will read values delimited by commas and convert those values to a list.

If there is no library or module that can do this for you, you will need to make use of the method Python provides to manipulate strings. Perhaps the commonly used method is string.split(); this will convert one long string into several small strings based on a specified delimiting character, like a comma or a space. When you need to write a parser, it isn't easy to determine every case that you might encounter. An example of this would be a value file that is separated by commas; it may also contain substrings that have naturally occurring commas, like an address or dates. In a case like this, it is nowhere near sufficient to use a delimiting comma to split a string; additional logic will be needed.

Magic numbers are another downside to parsing, especially when they are used to slice a given number of characters from a string, or to reference a specified column number from a spreadsheet, etc. If changes are made to a data structure, or we try to apply a script to data that is structured differently, we could end up making our code useless, having to 'operate' on it to fix it. If your code is read by others and numbers other than 1 (for counter incrementation) or a 0 (to start a series) appear, those others will want to know where the numbers came from and what they are referencing. With Python programming, any number that is not a 1 or a 0 is classed as a magic number and these should really be avoided wherever possible; if they can't, a comment is needed to explain what the number references.

There are so many different parsing situations that you may come across and we are going to look at the most general approach, which is going through a single module and an accompanying example.

The Python CSV Module

The CSV file, which stands for Comma-Separated-Value, is one of the more common of the formats for interchanging text data. You often find these with tabular data or with data transferring from spreadsheets. Every line in one of these files is representing a dataset row while the columns within the data are comma-separated. A CSV file will often start with a header that has a list of the names of all fields in the file.

Certain programs, like Excel, are designed to read and understand this structure and show all the values in a grid set out in rows and columns. When a CSV file is opened inside a text editor it may not look very pretty, but you should always be in the frame of mind that it is a grid. If we were in possession of a list containing the rows and a list containing the row values in the columns, we could use loops to extract the information we need, and this is where the CSV module in Python proves useful. The best way to learn the CSV module is to work through real examples. We are going to examine a situation where we can get information from a GPS track file using the CSV module.

GPS Track File – Parsing Example

In this example, we will be taking some text that is read from a GPS device. Each file line is representative of a reading from the unit as a user traveled a route. We will start by parsing the coordinates from each of the readings and will then move on to look at another example that demonstrates writing the track to a feature class of a polyline nature.

The file, gps_track.txt, looks a bit like what is shown below:

type,ident,lat,long,y_proj,x_proj,new_seg,display,color,altitude,depth,temp,time,model,filename,ltime

TRACK,ACTIVE LOG,40.78966141,-77.85948515,4627251.76270444,1779451.21349775,True,False,

255,358.228393554688,0,0,2008/06/11-14:08:30,eTrex Venture,,2008/06/11 09:08:30

TRACK,ACTIVE LOG,40.78963995,-77.85954952,4627248.40489401,1779446.18060893,False,False,

255,358.228393554688,0,0,2008/06/11-14:09:43,eTrex Venture,,2008/06/11 09:09:43

TRACK,ACTIVE LOG,40.78961849,-77.85957098,4627245.69008772,1779444.78476531,False,False,

255,357.747802734375,0,0,2008/06/11-14:09:44,eTrex Venture,,2008/06/11 09:09:44

TRACK,ACTIVE LOG,40.78953266,-77.85965681,4627234.83213242,1779439.20202706,False,False,

255,353.421875,0,0,2008/06/11-14:10:18,eTrex Venture,,2008/06/11 09:10:18

TRACK,ACTIVE LOG,40.78957558,-77.85972118,4627238.65402635,1779432.89982442,False,False,

255,356.786376953125,0,0,2008/06/11-14:11:57,eTrex Venture,,2008/06/11 09:11:57

TRACK,ACTIVE LOG,40.78968287,-77.85976410,4627249.97592111,1779427.14663093,False,False,

255,354.383178710938,0,0,2008/06/11-14:12:18,eTrex Venture,,2008/06/11 09:12:18

TRACK,ACTIVE LOG,40.78979015,-77.85961390,4627264.19055204,1779437.76243578,False,False,

255,351.499145507813,0,0,2008/06/11-14:12:50,eTrex Venture,,2008/06/11 09:12:50

etc....

The file begins with the header, telling us what the values in the readings mean. Every line thereafter is a reading and our goal is to come up with a list that has the X and Y coordinates from each of the readings. More specifically, our script must have the ability to read the file and print out text strings like this one:

[['-77.85948515', '40.78966141'], ['-77.85954952', '40.78963995'], ['-77.85957098', '40.78961849'], etc.]

The Approach

Before parsing any file, you should know exactly what you are going to do and how. It helps to split a task into smaller tasks; this is a piece of pseudocode showing our approach:

1. Open file
2. Read header
3. Loop through the header to find the lat and long index position values
4. Read the remaining lines one at a time
5. Find relevant values corresponding to lat and long
6. Write values to a Python list

Before you can do anything, the CSV module must be imported at the start of the script, exactly as you did with arcpy. There is no need for anything special to be imported, just type the following:

import csv

The script must open the file and, in Python, we have a method built-in – the open() method. The method parameters are the file path and how you want the file opened, i.e. read, write. In our example, we are using 'r' to open it in read-only mode. For write, you would use 'w':

gpsTrack = open("C:\\data\\Geog485\\gps_track.txt", "r")

There is no need for the file to have the.csv extension for the CSV module to read it; it can have the.txt suffix so long as the text is in a CSV pattern, columns separated by commas and carriage returns between the rows. When the file has been opened, a CSV reader object needs to be created like this:

csvReader = csv.reader(gpsTrack)

The CSV reader object is similar to a cursor in that the next() method may be used to move forward a line. However, a for loop can be used to iterate through the remaining lines.

Working Through the Rest of the File

We start with the header, a line that is very different from all other lines in the file. It provides the information we need about the names of the fields. Because of that, we need to look at this line somewhat differently from the others. The first thing we do is use the next() method to move the CSV reader to the start of the header:

header = csvReader.next()

This will return a list of each of the items in the header line. Remember; that header is quite a long string, so the CSV reader will chop it into a list, each containing a part that an index number will be used to reference. The delimiter is the default one, the comma. The first part of the header is "type.indent, lat, long" so header[0] has a value of 'type' while header[1] has a value of "indent".

The information we really want is the lat and long values, so we need to note where the lat and long columns are located in the file, i.e. their positions. Using the above logic, header[2] would be used for lat and header[3] would be used for long. What would happen if you had a file where the names of the fields were ordered differently? You would not be very certain that the column with an index of 2 was representing lat, for example.

Using the list.index() is the safest way of parsing; you would request the index position of a specific name for a field, in this way:

latIndex = header.index("lat")

lonIndex = header.index("long")

in our example, latIndex has 2 as a value while lonIndex has 3 but we also now have a piece of code with the flexibility to handle instances where columns are in different positions.

As far as the remaining lines in the file go, we can use a loop to read them. For our example, csvReader would be treated as an iterable list that contains the rest of the file lines. Each time the loop runs, it will take one row and turn it into a Python list containing values. The variable called latIndex is representing the index 2 value, while lonIndex represent the index 3 value. If we have a 2 we would have the latitude, a 3 would indicate longitude. When we have the new values, they can be added to a newly created list named coordList:

 # create an empty list

coordList = []

 # Loop through the lines in the file and get each coordinate

for row in csvReader:

   lat = row[latIndex]

   lon = row[lonIndex]

   coordList.append([lat,lon])

 # Print the coordinate list

print(coordList)

There are two main things to note with this code:

The list, coordList, has multiple mini lists inside one main list. Each mini list is a pair of coordinates that represent longitude (x) and latitude (y) for a single GPS reading.

The method called list.append() adds new elements to coordList. Again, we can append lists that are representing coordinate pairs using the list.append() method.

Below is the entire code for this example:

 # This script reads a GPS track in CSV format and

 # prints a list of coordinate pairs

import csv

 # Set up input and output variables for the script

gpsTrack = open("C:\\data\\Geog485\\gps_track.txt", "r")

 # Set up CSV reader and process the header

csvReader = csv.reader(gpsTrack)

header = csvReader.next()

latIndex = header.index("lat")

lonIndex = header.index("long")

```
# create an empty list

coordList = []


# Loop through the lines in the file and get each coordinate

for row in csvReader:

    lat = row[latIndex]

    lon = row[lonIndex]

    coordList.append([lat,lon])


# Print the coordinate list

print(coordList)
```

Script Applications

At this point, you may be wondering what you could possibly do with a coordinates list. Right now, we still only have raw data that cannot be properly read by a GIS. However, the fact that we have those coordinates in a Python list means that we can easily convert them to formats that can be read as feature class points or polyline vertices. We could send this list to a web service that could reverse geocode it, which means taking each point and locating the associated address. Those points could be placed onto a web map with Google Maps API or other similar programming tools. The applications really are quite endless when you get down to it.

To parse any text, you must first understand the methods for opening files and reading the text, the text structure, the modules that will work with your text, methods for manipulating strings, and so on. In the example we used earlier, a basic text file was parsed, and we extracted the information we wanted and the coordinates stored in a small GPS unit. The CSV module was used to break the readings down and locate the lat and long values. Next, we will look at how to take this information further with polygon datasets.

Geometry Writing

As information of a geographic nature is parsed from text files and other raw sources, you might be thinking about converting it into a format that your particular GIS can read. We will now be discussing how vector geometries are written to feature classes in ArcGIS. We'll use the same GPS text file, but we'll add in another step – we are going to write each of the coordinates to a shapefile of polyline format.

When we talked about insert cursors earlier, we got a bit of experience in how to write point geometry. In review, arcpy.Point() is used to create Point objects and the object is then used in the insertRow() tuple for the "SHAPE@" geometry field:

 # Create point

inPoint = arcpy.Point(-121.34, 47.1)

...

 # Create new row

cursor.insertRow((inPoint,))

Where polygon and polylines are concerned, several Point objects can be created and added to an Array object. That array is then used to make the Polygon or Polyline object. If you use Polygons you should get into the practice of making the start and end vertex the same if you can.

Take a look at the following code example. We are creating an empty array and then using Array.add() to add in 3 points. That array then is used to create the

Polyline object. The first parameter to be passed in with any polyline will be the array that has the polyline points. The second will be a spatial reference to the map coordinates – this must always be passed to make sure that your data is precise:

```
# Make a new empty array

array = arcpy.Array()
```

```
# Make some points

point1 = arcpy.Point(-121.34,47.1)

point2 = arcpy.Point(-121.29,47.32)

point3 = arcpy.Point(-121.31,47.02)
```

```
# Put the points in the array

array.add(point1)

array.add(point2)

array.add(point3)
```

```
# Make a polyline out of the now-complete array

polyline = arcpy.Polyline(array, spatialRef)
```

Normally, you wouldn't even consider the manual creation of points using coordinates that are hard-coded. In fact, you will more than likely capture the coordinates from another source or parse them from a file of some description.

Using a GPS Track to Create a Polyline

We're now going to look at how coordinates could be parsed from a text file created from GPS data, much like the one we looked at earlier. Our code is going to read all the GPS-captured points and add them into a single polyline. That polyline then is written to a polyline shapefile that already exists and is empty. That polyline is named tracklines.shp and contains a system of geographic coordinates. If you didn't have a shapefile already, you could create one using Create Feature Class in your script:

```
# This script will read a GPS track in CSV format and

#  writes geometries from the list of coordinate pairs

import csv

import arcpy


# Set up input and output variables for the script

gpsTrack = open("C:\\data\\Geog485\\gps_track.txt", "r")

polylineFC = "C:\\data\\Geog485\\tracklines.shp"

spatialRef = arcpy.Describe(polylineFC).spatialReference


# Set up CSV reader and process the header

csvReader = csv.reader(gpsTrack)

header = csvReader.next()

latIndex = header.index("lat")

lonIndex = header.index("long")
```

```
# Create an empty array object

vertexArray = arcpy.Array()


# Loop through the lines in the file and get each coordinate

for row in csvReader:

    lat = row[latIndex]

    lon = row[lonIndex]


    # Make a point from the coordinate and add it to the array

    vertex = arcpy.Point(lon,lat)

    vertexArray.add(vertex)


# Write the array to the feature class as a polyline feature

with arcpy.da.InsertCursor(polylineFC, ("SHAPE@",)) as cursor:

    polyline = arcpy.Polyline(vertexArray, spatialRef)

    cursor.insertRow((polyline,))
```

This script starts the same way as our last one. The header line is parsed to work out what the lat and long coordinates are in the readings. However, we then created an array which holds the polyline points:

```
vertexArray = arcpy.Array()
```

That is followed by a loop that will read every line one at a time; this will use the lat and long values to create the point object, and when the loop finishes, the point goes into the array.

for row in csvReader:

   lat = row[latIndex]

   lon = row[lonIndex]

   # Make a point from the coordinate and add it to the array

   vertex = arcpy.Point(lon,lat)

   vertexArray.add(vertex)

When every line is read, the loop will terminate and "SHAPE@" is used to create an insert cursor. This is the single element in the tuple that contains the affected fields. The Polyline object creation comes next and this becomes the one and only element in the tuple that is passed to insertRow():

 # Create an insert cursor

with arcpy.da.InsertCursor(polylineFC, ("SHAPE@",)) as cursor:

   # Place the array in a polyline and write it to the feature class

   polyline = arcpy.Polyline(vertexArray, spatialRef)

   cursor.insertRow((polyline,))

Remember; the cursor is going to put a lock on the dataset, so we don't create that cursor until it is really needed, in our case, when the loop is done.

A Look at Multiple Polylines

Let's assume, just for a bit of fun, that your GPS offers the option of marking start and end points for multiple routes. This isn't a practical example so just read along.

Note, in our GPS text file, we have an additional entry – new_seg:

type,ident,lat,long,y_proj,x_proj,new_seg,display,color,altitude,depth,temp,time,model,filename,ltime

This entry is actually a Boolean property and it is used to determine whether the reading will start on a new track. If we have new_seg=True, the current polyline would need to be written to the shapefile and we would need to create another one. Look at this next example and see how it is different from the last one we used – this is to handle several polylines:

```
# This script reads a GPS track in CSV format and

#  writes geometries from the list of coordinate pairs

#  Handles multiple polylines


# Function to add a polyline

def addPolyline(cursor, array, sr):

    polyline = arcpy.Polyline(array, sr)

    cursor.insertRow((polyline,))

    array.removeAll()


# Main script body

import csv
```

```python
import arcpy


# Set up input and output variables for the script
gpsTrack = open("C:\\data\\Geog485\\gps_track_multiple.txt", "r")

polylineFC = "C:\\data\\Geog485\\tracklines_sept25.shp"

spatialRef = arcpy.Describe(polylineFC).spatialReference


# Set up CSV reader and process the header
csvReader = csv.reader(gpsTrack)

header = csvReader.next()

latIndex = header.index("lat")

lonIndex = header.index("long")

newIndex = header.index("new_seg")


# Write the array to the feature class as a polyline feature
with arcpy.da.InsertCursor(polylineFC, ("SHAPE@",)) as cursor:


    # Create an empty array object
    vertexArray = arcpy.Array()


    # Loop through the lines in the file and get each coordinate
```

```python
for row in csvReader:

    isNew = row[newIndex].upper()


    # If about to start a new line, add the completed line to the
    # feature class
    if isNew == "TRUE":
        if vertexArray.count > 0:
            addPolyline(cursor, vertexArray, spatialRef)


    # Get the lat/lon values of the current GPS reading
    lat = row[latIndex]
    lon = row[lonIndex]


    # Make a point from the coordinate and add it to the array
    vertex = arcpy.Point(lon,lat)
    vertexArray.add(vertex)

# Add the final polyline to the shapefile
addPolyline(cursor, vertexArray, spatialRef)
```

What you should have spotted first of all is that we have a function in the script. This is called addPolyline and it is, as you would expect, to add a new polyline to the feature class, given these 3 parameters:

- An insert cursor already exists

- An array

- A spatial reference – remember, we said this should be standard practice to keep your data precise.

This function reduces repeat code making the script easier to read:

 # Function to add a polyline

def addPolyline(cursor, array, sr):

   polyline = arcpy.Polyline(array, sr)

   cursor.insertRow((polyline,))

   array.removeAll()

It is absolutely fine to use arcpy in this function; this is because the script that it is in already imports arcpy. However, what you want to avoid is the use of variables that haven't been defined inside the function or haven't been passed in as an argument.

We call the function 2 times – one time in the loop, which is expected, and one time at the very end to ensure the polyline is properly added into the shapefile. This is where functions come into their own, reducing the need to keep repeating code.

As you go through the code line by line, how do you work out if a new track is started or not? First, there is another value in this script that you should be looking for:

   newIndex = header.index("new_seg")

The variable called newTrackIndex will tell us the line position that the Boolean property of new_seg holds. This property is what tells if a new polyline has been started and you might have spotted that later in the code we checked that:

isNew = row[newIndex].upper()

 # If about to start a new line, add the completed line to the

 # feature class

if isNew == "TRUE":

We used the upper() method to convert the string from lower to upper case; this means there isn't any need to worry about the way 'true' is written – it could be true, TRUE, or even True. But there is still one more situation that needs to be handled – the first file line. This should be saying 'true' but the current polyline cannot be added to the file at the moment for the simple reason that there isn't one. So, another check is carried out to ensure that the array contains more than 0 points before that array is written to our shapefile:

if vertexArray.count > 0:

addPolyline(cursor, vertexArray, spatialRef)

This checks to ensure we have one or more points in the array and then we call addPolyline, passing the cursor and the array in.

We learned that geometrics can be written to the feature classes in ArcGIS through the geometry objects prebuilt into ArcGIS. It is common the create the Point objects, add them to an Array object and then use that object, together with a spatial reference, to create both Polygon and Polyline objects. An insert cursor then is used to assign the array geometry to the geometry field of the feature class, which is normally called "Shape".

You might now be asking yourself how a multi-part feature could be created, for example, the Hawaiian State which contains several islands, or how Polygon which has a 'hole' in it could be created? We need to learn some special rules for the order and nesting of Arrays and Points to create this kind of geometry. That takes us nicely to the next section.

Automation Using Scheduled Tasks and Batch Files

We have briefly talked about how beneficial it can be to use Python to automate your work. It's great to get multiple geoprocessing tools on the go in a row without having to go through the toolboxes manually. How can it be automatic when you have to open PythonWin, open a script, click the run button and so on? In the next section, we are going to take automation to the next level by looking at ways to have your scripts run automatically.

Python Scripts and Your OS

For the most part, we have used PythonWin to run our scripts, but you can run them through Windows. You might have tried, at some point, to run a script by double-clicking on a file with a.py extension. So long as Windows is aware that a.py extension is representing a script written in Python, and that the Python interpreter should be used to run that script, it will run straight away.

You may get a Windows message telling you that the operating system doesn't know what program needs to be used to open the file. Simply browse in the dialog box to the executable which will likely be found in C:\Pythonxx\ArcGISxx.x\Python.exe. Enable the option to "Always use the selected program to open this type of file" and then click OK. Windows will now know to use Python to run.py files.

When you click the.py file, you are telling Windows to run the script. Alternatively, you can use the Windows command line to give that command. All you need to do is type in the command and your wish will be done. We won't go into too much detail about the command line here. All we need to say is that you type cmd into the Windows search box to bring the window up and then type in the Python executable path, as above, followed by the path that leads to the script, as such:

C:\Pythonxx\ArcGISxx.x\Python.exe
C:\WCGIS\yourname\filename\Project1.py

If your script requires parameters, each of the arguments must be delimited using a space. The argument is the value supplied for the parameter of the script. Look at the following example; this is a command that will run one script that has two arguments. Both arguments are strings containing the pathname. Note, the single \ should be used in paths when command line arguments are provided – never use the single / or double \\ as you do with PythonWin:

C:\Pythonxx\ArcGISxx.x\Python.exe
C:\WCGIS\yourname\filename\Project2.py C:\WCGIS\yourname\filename\
C:\WCGIS\yourname\filename\CityBoundaries.shp

If execution is successful, you should only see a command prompt, and nothing else, unless your script is tasked with printing a message; in this case, the message should appear. If your script is tasked with the modification of data or files, you can check them to ensure that the script ran as it should.

The only other time you will see anything on the screen is if the script doesn't run as it should. Sometimes the messages are not helpful, other times they are more helpful than those you see in PythonWin and makes the command line good for debugging purposes.

Working with Batch Files

Why is it important to talk about the command line when we want to talk about automation? You still need to manually open that command window and type your commands in. Well, the good thing is you can also script commands. Several commands can be listed in a text file and these are called batch files. When you run the batch file, all the commands contained in it are run.

Look at the following simple batch file example. It runs the pair of scripts we just looked at. To create the file, you could copy the text from below into a new Notepad file, save it, and ensure you give it an extension of.bat. Keep in mind that we are now talking about command syntax, not Python.

@ECHO OFF

REM Runs both my project scripts

C:\Python27\ArcGIS10.3\Python.exe
C:\WCGIS\Geog485\Lesson1\Project1.py

ECHO Ran project 1

C:\Python27\ArcGIS10.3\Python.exe
C:\WCGIS\Geog485\Lesson2\Project2.py C:\WCGIS\Geog485\Lesson2
C:\WCGIS\Geog485\Lesson2\CityBoundaries.shp

ECHO Ran project 2

PAUSE

Have a look at these notes about this file, beginning from line 1:

We use @ECHO OFF to stop every file line from printing to the command line, the console or window when the file is run. This is standard, and you should get into the habit of adding this as your first line. The exception to this is if you need to see which line is being executed, perhaps if you are debugging.

Comments are added in a batch file using REM. This is the equivalent of the # in Python.

Commands are placed into a batch file using the syntax used on the command line.

ECHO will print to the console, which is useful to use when debugging, particularly when @ECHO OFF is used at the start to stop all lines printing.

PAUSE will give a prompt to "Press any key to continue". If this is not added at the end of the file, as soon as the file is executed, the console closes. Using PAUSE will allow you to see if an error message prints while the file is being run. When the file has been tested and is working as it should be, PAUSE can be removed.

In a batch file, you can have loops, variables, comments, even conditional logic. All of this is outside the scope of the book, but if you are likely to be writing multiple scripts and running them, it is worth taking the time to learn more about batch files.

Task Scheduling

We are not far off full automation here, but we still need to be able to open and run the batch file or script. Right now, we still need to use the command line, click the file, or somehow tell the OS it needs to run it. To get full automation here, we can use an OS utility like Task Scheduler in Windows.

Task Scheduler is a hidden gem in the System tools that you may have otherwise ignored. It isn't a difficult program and it lets you schedule batch files and scripts to run automatically as and when needed. This comes in very useful when you have tasks that need to run regularly enough that manual launching becomes time-consuming. What is even more useful is when the task is quite resource-tense; you can schedule it to run at the weekend or overnight.

Let's discuss a real-world situation where it is important to use Task Scheduler, or some other similar utility. Fast Web maps use map images that are already generated and are cached server-side, making it much quicker to load. Web Map admin uses ArcGIS Server will run a tool called Manage Map Server Cache Tiles to ensure the maps are made before the web map is deployed. Once the map has been deployed, the server will send the correct maps to the users as they look through the Web Map. Sound good so far?

At times, the Source data for a map is likely to change and that means the maps cached on the server-side will be out-of-date. They are only images and do not have the required ability to change as the data changes and that means the cache must be updated on a regular basis. Creating the cached maps takes time and a lot of CPU resources so Task Scheduler is used for this task. This would normally involve a script being written or maybe a batch file that will run the Manage Map Server Cache Tiles tool, along with other necessary tools, on a schedule that runs the script overnight or at a weekend when it is unlikely to have too much impact on Web map users.

Before we move on, let us have a look in Task Scheduler:

1. Open the Start menu in Windows and go to All Programs>Accessories>System Tools>Task Scheduler.
2. Click the button to Create a Basic Task – you will now go through a wizard which will help you set the task up. Don't worry about advanced options, these can be configured later.
3. Name your task something that you will remember and, if you want, add a description. Then you can click Next.
4. Choose the frequency with which the task should run. For now, choose Daily and click on Next.
5. Choose your start time and how often the task will recur and then click on Next.
6. Click Start a Program>Next.
7. Now you need to say which batch file or script is to be run. To do this, click on Browse and go to a script that you wrote; for now, choose one that has no arguments. Click on Next.
8. Review your task information and click on Finish.
9. You should now see that task in the Task Scheduler list. Highlight it and you will see the properties of the task or right-click on it and choose Properties if you need to set them.
10. Wait until your task is first scheduled to run or, if you are a little impatient, right-click and then choose Run. A console window will appear as the script runs and it will close when it has finished. If your script is a Python script and you want the console window to stay open, add something like lastline = raw_input(">") as the last line of that script. The script will stop until the Enter button is pressed. You can take this line out when you are used to the way the script runs so that open windows don't clog your screen up.

Running ArcGIS Toolbox Tools

Sometime down the line, you will be required to use a geoprocessing tool that is not familiar to you. You may never have heard of it, let alone run it from a script or GUI. Other times, you may be aware of the tool, but you may be a little rusty on using Python or you might have forgotten or not know how the parameters should be constructed.

Either way, we use the same approach. Look at these basic steps for running ArcGIS tools with Python:

1. Find the reference for the tool. As you already know, you can get the help topic for each tool by going to ArcGIS help and looking in the section for Geoprocessing tools. Open that topic, read it first, before doing anything else. Make sure you read the section entitled Usage right at the start to make sure you have the correct tool and that it is going to be used properly.
2. Look at the tool parameters. Under the Syntax section, you will see a list of the parameters accepted by the tool. Note which ones are necessary and which are optional and then determine which one will be supplied by your script.
3. When you write your script, you must create a new variable for each of the parameters being used. When you look at the syntax section, you will see a data type with each of the parameters. If you 'String' as a data type, the variable for that parameter must be a string variable.
   On occasion, you will find that the data type does not translate very well into a variable. For example, the reference for the tool may say that you need a Feature Class variable and what this is saying is that script requires a string variable that has the path leading to the feature class in it. Another example would be the tool reference saying that a 'Long' data type is required, and this means that a numerical variable must be created, rather than a string for the parameter.

   If you are in any doubt about creating the right variable for the data type, look in the Code Sample section of the tool reference. Look for the example script; it should show you the definition of a variable that you are struggling with. Use the patterns in that script and you should be just fine.

   You will find that most tools come with great script examples; others may not be so good. If you are in any doubt, run a search on the internet and you should find what you are looking for.

4. Your next step is to run that tool and you will need error handling. Your script may be run in the Interactive Window without using any try blocks or except blocks to catch simple errors. If you don't see anything useful, add the blocks in and then add print arcpy.GetMessages() into the except block.

Map Documents

We have looked at the automation of geoprocessing tools, we looked at the update of GIS data and we looked at how to read text files. What we haven't discussed yet is working with map documents. There are several things that we can do with a map document, all perfectly suitable for automation:

- We can find text in a map/maps and replace it. For example, we could replace Copyright 2017 with Copyright 2018.
- We can repair layers that are using the wrong paths to reference a data source. For example, you may have been using a computer where the map data was in the C:\folder 1whereas now it is on a computer where it is stored in D:\data\folder 1.
- We can print data frame or map series.
- We can export maps to a PDF format and we can join them together, so we have a map book.
- We can make maps available on the ArcGIS server to other users.

Map documents tend to be in binary file format and this means they cannot be read or parsed too easily with the techniques we already looked at. Up until recent times, we had to use ArcObjects to automate any task on a map document, but ArcObjects isn't ideal for beginners and it needs a programming language that isn't Python. With the later version of ArcGIS, we got a Python module that helps us to automate common map document tasks.

ArcGIS Modules – arcpy.mapping

The arcpy.mapping module can be used with map documents in a script and one very important object in it is called MapDocument. This object will tell the script the map you want to work with. To get a MapDocument, a path needs to be referenced in this way:

mxd =
arcpy.mapping.MapDocument(r"c:\data\Arkansas\UtilityNetwork.mxd")

Note that we used r in this code line and this is to tell us that we have a string literal. What this means is that, if r is included just before a string, you can make use of Python reserved characters. An alternative to using a string path would be to use a variable that contains the path. This is more useful when you want to use a loop to iterate over the map documents contained in a folder or where the path was obtained previously in the script with something like arcpy.GetParameterAsText(). Using arcpy.mapping is convenient in the ArcMap Python window because there is no need to add the path leading to MXD. Instead, you can use the CURRENT keyword to retrieve a reference to the MXD that is already open:

mxd = arcpy.mapping.MapDocument("CURRENT")

As soon as you have your map document something must be done with it. Most of the arcpy.mapping functions will take any MapDocument object as one of their parameters. Let's look at a script and see what is happening; comments have been added to help:

 # Create a MapDocument object referencing the MXD you want to update

mxd = arcpy.mapping.MapDocument(r"C:\GIS\TownCenter_2015.mxd")

 # Loop through each text element in the map document

for textElement in arcpy.mapping.ListLayoutElements(mxd,
"TEXT_ELEMENT"):

   # Check if the text element contains the out-of-date text

if textElement.text == "GIS Services Division 2015":

 # If out-of-date text is found, replace it with the new text

textElement.text = "GIS Services Division 2016"

 # Export the updated map to a PDF

arcpy.mapping.ExportToPDF(mxd, r"C:\GIS\TownCenterUpdate_2016.pdf")

 # Clean the MapDocument object by deleting it

del mxd

In line 1 the MapDocument object is used to reference C:\GIS\TownCener_2014.mxd. We then have 2 arcpy.mapping functions – ListLayoutElements with a MapDocument parameter and a TEXT_ELEMENT parameter which details the layout element type you want to be returned.

The return from this script is a Python list containing the TextElement objects that represent every one of the Map text elements. We use a for loop to look at every element to see its TextElement.text property. The TextElement.text property can be read, and it can also be written; if you wanted to add new text you would simply use the assignment operator (=) as you can see where it says textElement.text = "GIS Services Division 2016". We have used a simple ExportToPDF function which will take the MapDocument and the output path as its parameters

Learn arcpy.mapping

As with many things, the best way to learn arcpy.mapping is to use it. It is a very simple place to practice Python and is a good way to learn how the ArcMap

Python window works mainly because the results of any action can be seen immediately.

ArcGIS and Python Scripting Limitations

We've had a good look at the basics of Python programming and we have delved into Python automation of GIS functions with ArcGIS toolboxes. Scripting provides a great deal of power and you should, by now, be starting to see ways in which you can apply that outside this book. One very important thing we need to discuss is what you can't do with scripting and ArcGIS.

Within ArcGIS, Python interactive is somewhat limited to reading data, writing it, editing map document properties, and running the ArcGIS toolbox tools. While these tools may be useful for some things, they are kind of a 'black box'. This means that you put into them and you get things out of them without having any knowledge about what goes on inside; if you were even concerned about it. If you wanted a better level of control over the way your data is manipulated by ArcGIS you would need to look at using ArcObjects.

Consider ArcObjects to be the bricks and mortar of ArcGIS, a set of Lego bricks if you like. When you program with ArcObjects, you have a huge box of Lego bricks, all different sizes and shapes. By contrast, Python scripting could be thought as being more like a kit project; you have all the pieces needed to make construction easy, but you don't have the choice available that is in ArcObjects.

ArcObjects is incredibly challenging compared to Python scripting because you have so much more available to you in the way of objects and functions. Normally, a task written in a Python script would require many more code lines if it were written in ArcObjects. However, ArcObjects does give you a much greater degree of control over what goes on in the program. One small bit of functionality can be used without needing a tool or all the parameters that are attached to the tool.

Early ArcGIS Interface Customization

So far, we have done little in the way of customization with the ArcMap interface; we haven't added any toolbars, buttons, or anything else to help kick off our programs. All we have done is made a scripting tool and a toolbox. Scripting tools are very useful but sometimes we will want the functionality taken out of the toolbox and placed into a toolbar button in ArcMap. For example, you might want a button that launches a window containing labels, text boxes, and buttons that you make yourself.

With ArcGIS v10.0, you would need to use VBA (Visual Basic for Applications, C++, or one of the.NET languages to place custom programs or functionality straight into ArcMap. It might be a simple matter of putting some customized functionality into a button or you could go further and have an entire program open, one that you developed containing menus, options, forms and more. VBA, C++ and the.NET languages all have their own IDE where custom interfaces can be designed with buttons, boxes, labels and more.

New Functionality

To provide more functionality between a Python script and a user interface in ArcMap, ArcGIS v10.1 brought with it the concept of Python add-ins. These add-ins have the option of attaching Python logic to a small amount of ArcMap actions; perhaps to open a new document, zoom in on a map, click buttons on custom toolbars and so on. An example would be creating an add-in that adds a layer set automatically whenever a specific button on the toolbar is clicked.

Python add-ins provide a selection of elements for Python script front ends. These elements include menus, buttons, toolbars, boxes, file browsing, dialog boxes, and anything else you might expect to see on a user interface. You also have access to common events that you can respond to using your code. This would include a map being opened, the extent of the map changing, a change to the spatial reference, etc. In short, with add-ins, there are many more possibilities than with the earlier ArcGIS versions.

ArcGIS and Machine Learning

We talked about Machine Learning earlier in this book. ML, as it is known, refers to techniques and algorithms driven by data,that automate the processes of predicting, classifying, and clustering data. ML plays an important role in solving problems of a spatial nature, working in many different areas and applications, such as classifying images, detecting spatial patterns, including the problems of multivariate predictions.

As well as the traditional techniques for machine learning, ArcGIS contains a subset of spatial machine learning techniques. These methods, with an incorporation of geographic notations built into the computation, can help us toward a much deeper understanding. More often than not, the spatial component will take form as a density, shape, spatial distribution, contiguity, or proximity measure. Machine learning, both spatial and traditional, play a very important part in spatial problem-solving and, with ArcGIS, we get support in several ways.

ArcGIS Machine Learning Examples

Prediction

Prediction is all about estimating the unknown by using the known. With ArcGIS, there are several techniques for both interpolation and regression that can be used to perform prediction. Applications that this pertains to include home value estimation based on recent data for sales, home and related characteristics for the community, as well as the creation of a surface of air pollution-based n measurements taken from sensors.

ArcGIS Prediction Algorithms

Prediction algorithms in ArcGIS include:

- Areal Interpolation
- EBK Regression Prediction
- Empirical Bayesian Kriging
- Exploratory Regression
- Geographically Weighted Regression
- Ordinary Least Squares Regression

Classification

With classification, we have to determine the category that a specific object is to be assigned to and that is based on a set of training data. In ArcGIS, we have several classification methods at our disposal, all focused on data that is remotely sensed. With these tools we can analyze the values of pixels and configurations that are used to categorize pixels. Examples include identification of areas where the forest is being lost or the delineation of types of land use.

ArcGIS Classification Algorithms

Classification algorithms in ArcGIS include:

- Maximum Likelihood Classification
- Random Trees
- Support Vector Machine

Clustering

Clustering is focused on a group of observation that is based on similar locations or values. In ArcGIS, there is quite a choice of algorithms that will locate a cluster based on one or more locations, attributes or both. These methods can be used to analyze things like areas that have the most activity on social media following a natural disaster or using demographics and socioeconomic characteristics to analyze school districts.

ArcGIS Clustering Algorithms:

Clustering algorithms in ArcGIS include:

- Cluster and Outlier Analysis
- Density-Based Clustering
- Hot Spot Analysis
- Image Segmentation
- Multivariate Clustering
- Space Time Pattern Mining
- Spatially Constrained Multivariate Clustering

As well as all these techniques and methods, we can also use machine learning throughout the ArcGIS platform as a way of selecting defaults that are smart and data-driven for workflow automation, and for the optimization of the results. For example, PCA (Principle Component Analysis) is used by EBK

Regression Prediction to reduce dimensions to arrive at better predictions. Density-based clustering has an OPTICS method that uses machine learning to find cluster tolerances that are based on a reachability plot, and evidence accumulation is a technique used by the Spatially Constrained Multivariate Clustering algorithm to provide probabilities that are related to the results of clustering.

Integration

Machine learning is a very deep and broad field, one that is evolving all the time. ArcGIS is a platform that is both open and interoperable, allowing techniques and methods to be integrated through R-ArcGIS Bridge or the ArcGIS Python API. With this integration, ArcGIS users get the power of solving complex tasks through a combination of tools and machine learning packages, be it TensorFlow, Scikit-Learn, Microsoft AI, and so on, while gaining the benefit from spatial validation at the same time, not to mention being able to visualize the results in ArcGIS and geoenrichment.

Chapter 18: Software Development and Testing

One of the most important parts of Python that you should learn is test-driven development. This is all about creating tests that will test your code, test that it works as it should before you write the proper code. Only when you have run these tests, only when you are completely happy with the results, should you begin to write the real code that satisfies all the conditions in your tests. If you can do this, your code will have been carefully planned to give you the confidence to start refactoring later to enable you to catch errors and bugs as they arise.

Why is this so important?

Over time, software has scaled to the extent that it isn't possible for an entire team, let alone one person, to keep abreast of all the additions and changes and how those changes interact with one another and with the rest of the code. The best way, the only proven method to build software that is reliable, is automated testing. Most of the biggest developmental failures in major software can easily be tracked back to a real lack of testing.

To be fair, you can't possibly know whether your software works or not without testing it. Yes, you can test manually; you could type in some input, click a few buttons, but automated testing is the way forward. There are several different testing types, and rather than just picking one, you should use them all. For example, isolating one function from a program to test it is called unit testing while testing two or more functions together is called integration testing. With user interface testing, you are ensuring that everything is present and correct for user interaction with the software. And, if you are testing a large program, you would be considering the use of things like browser testing, database testing and load testing. The list goes on!

Testing in Python

The culture that surrounds software development in Python is very heavily into testing. Python is what we call a 'dynamically-typed' language which means, converse to static languages, testing is even more important. We'll start by looking at the Integration and the Unit tests.

Unit and Integration Tests

If this is your first time looking at testing, then welcome. You need to understand the importance of testing your code because applications that are not tested make it virtually impossible to make improvements to code and developers of these applications could end up quite paranoid, constantly wondering what will go wrong and when. If you automate the tests on your applications, you can change things safely and know whether your changes are correct or not.

By nature, a unit test is used to isolate and test small code units or single functions. This is done to make sure that the output is as you expect it to be. Many times, because external API calls will be needed or you may need to tap into a database, a unit test can be done on fake data, known as 'mocking' - we will discuss more of this later. When you test fake data, the tests can be much faster to run, but by the same token, they may not be quite so effective, not to mention be far more difficult to maintain. Because of this, for now we are not going to use mock tests; we are going to read to the database and write to it as we need to. Rest assured, you will learn about the mock tests later, just so you know what to expect.

Bear in mind that, when a test touches a database, technically it is called an "integration' test because we are not testing just one unit.

Let's Get Started

In most situations, it won't be easy to work out how and where to start with the testing so one way around this is to consider your application in terms of what it offers the end user. For example:

- An unregistered user must register and sign in before they can use the application.
- Once a user has registered with the application, they will receive a confirmation email – at this stage, they are an unconfirmed user.
- The user may log in to the application but they cannot access it – instead, they will be taken to a page that tells them they need to action the email confirmation first.

- When the user has actioned this confirmation, they will have access to the application; they can see the home page, any content on the application, modify their user details, and log out of the application.

For now, we are only going to write the tests we absolutely need to test these functions. Testing is not easy; rather than writing tests that cover everything, concentrate only on what is the most important. Added to coverage testing (more later on that) we can construct a pretty tough suite for testing purposes.

Setup

The first thing we need to do is activate the virtualenv (remember earlier in the book) and then set these environment variables:

$ export APP_SETTINGS="project.config.DevelopmentConfig"

$ export APP_MAIL_USERNAME="foo"

$ export APP_MAIL_PASSWORD="bar"

Now we can run the test suite:

$ python manage.py test

test_app_is_development (test_config.TestDevelopmentConfig)... ok

test_app_is_production (test_config.TestProductionConfig)... ok

test_app_is_testing (test_config.TestTestingConfig)... ok

Ran 3 tests in 0.003s

OK

All we are doing right now is testing our environment variables and the configuration – this should be the most straightforward part.

If we wanted to expand our test suite, we would begin with a structure that keeps everything organized in a neat order. We'll create a couple of test files, saving them in the directory called 'tests'. We'll call the files test_main.py and test_user.py and then add this code into each of the files:

import unittest

from flask.ext.login import current_user

from project.util import BaseTestCase

#

 # Tests go here

#

if __name__ == '__main__':

   unittest.main()

Part 1: The Main Blueprint

First, we go to https://github.com/realpython/flask-registration to download the necessary files for this project. We will need all the files for Handling Email Confirmation as this is what we will be testing:

https://github.com/realpython/flask-registration/tree/v1/project - click on User and download the code files there.

When we open a hypothetical folder called views.py, located in the main/project folder, and combine it with the workflow for the main user, we would see that we needed to test one thing: the main path, which is /, is requiring that a user is logged in to the application. As such, we would add this code to our test_main.py file we created earlier:

def test_main_route_requires_login(self):

    # Ensure the main route requires a logged in user.

    response = self.client.get('/', follow_redirects=True)

    self.assertTrue(response.status_code == 200)

    self.assertTemplateUsed('user/login.html')

We are making it clear that we have a response code of 200 and that the right template is in use. If we run the testing suite now, we should find that all the tests pass satisfactorily.

Part 2: User Blueprint

In this blueprint, we would find a lot more going on, so we need testing that is somewhat more intensive. What we want to do is test our views and, to do this, the test suite needs to be broken apart. First, we need to create 2 classes – these will ensure that the tests are divided logically.

Open the test_user.py file and add the following code:

class TestUserForms(BaseTestCase):

    pass

class TestUserViews(BaseTestCase):

    pass

Forms

If we have an application based on users logging in, the main concept is around the user registering. If we don't have this, the door is open to a whole heap of trouble. Everything must work exactly as it was designed. So, if we follow the workflow of the user, we would begin with the registration form and the following code should be placed into the class called TestUserForms() that we created with the last code:

```python
def test_validate_success_register_form(self):

    # Ensure correct data validates.

    form = RegisterForm(

        email='new@test.test',

        password='example', confirm='example')

    self.assertTrue(form.validate())


def test_validate_invalid_password_format(self):

    # Ensure incorrect data does not validate.

    form = RegisterForm(

        email='new@test.test',

        password='example', confirm='')

    self.assertFalse(form.validate())


def test_validate_email_already_registered(self):

    # Ensure user can't register when a duplicate email is used
```

```
form = RegisterForm(

    email='test@user.com',

    password='just_a_test_user',

    confirm='just_a_test_user'

)

self.assertFalse(form.validate())
```

What these tests do is make sure that the form will do one of two things – pass validation or fail it and this is based entirely on what data is input. Let's look at the file called forms.py in Project/user as a comparison. In the test we performed previously, we registered the same user from the method called setUpClass() from the BaseTestCase that was in util.py.

While we are about the task of form testing, why not do the login form too:

```
def test_validate_success_login_form(self):

    # Ensure correct data validates.

    form = LoginForm(email='test@user.com', password='just_a_test_user')

    self.assertTrue(form.validate())


def test_validate_invalid_email_format(self):

    # Ensure invalid email format throws error.

    form = LoginForm(email='unknown', password='example')

    self.assertFalse(form.validate())
```

Lastly, we will test our form for changing the password:

```python
def test_validate_success_change_password_form(self):
    # Ensure correct data validates.
    form = ChangePasswordForm(password='update', confirm='update')
    self.assertTrue(form.validate())


def test_validate_invalid_change_password(self):
    # Ensure passwords must match.
    form = ChangePasswordForm(password='update', confirm='unknown')
    self.assertFalse(form.validate())


def test_validate_invalid_change_password_format(self):
    # Ensure invalid email format throws error.
    form = ChangePasswordForm(password='123', confirm='123')
    self.assertFalse(form.validate())
```

Ensure the correct imports are added:

```
from project.user.forms import RegisterForm, \
    LoginForm, ChangePasswordForm
```

Now we can run the tests:

```
$ python manage.py test
```

test_app_is_development (test_config.TestDevelopmentConfig)... ok

test_app_is_production (test_config.TestProductionConfig)... ok test_app_is_testing (test_config.TestTestingConfig)... ok

test_main_route_requires_login (test_main.TestMainViews)... ok

test_validate_email_already_registered (test_user.TestUserForms)... ok

test_validate_invalid_change_password (test_user.TestUserForms)... ok

test_validate_invalid_change_password_format (test_user.TestUserForms)... ok

test_validate_invalid_email_format (test_user.TestUserForms)... ok

test_validate_invalid_password_format (test_user.TestUserForms)... ok

test_validate_success_change_password_form (test_user.TestUserForms)... ok

test_validate_success_login_form (test_user.TestUserForms)... ok

test_validate_success_register_form (test_user.TestUserForms)... ok

----

Ran 12 tests in 1.656s

For these tests, all we did was instantiated our form and then the validate function was called; this triggers the validation, and that includes any custom validation, and the return is a Boolean that tells us whether the data in our form is valid or otherwise. That's the forms done and dusted, we'll move on to testing our views.

Views

Two very important parts of application security are logging in to the application and viewing a profile, so these are things that need to be tested properly:

login:

```
def test_correct_login(self):

    # Ensure login behaves correctly with correct credentials.

    with self.client:

        response = self.client.post(

            '/login',

            data=dict(email="test@user.com", password="just_a_test_user"),

            follow_redirects=True

        )

        self.assertTrue(response.status_code == 200)

        self.assertTrue(current_user.email == "test@user.com")

        self.assertTrue(current_user.is_active())

        self.assertTrue(current_user.is_authenticated())

        self.assertTemplateUsed('main/index.html')


def test_incorrect_login(self):

    # Ensure login behaves correctly with incorrect credentials.

    with self.client:

        response = self.client.post(

            '/login',

            data=dict(email="not@correct.com", password="incorrect"),
```

```
        follow_redirects=True

    )

    self.assertTrue(response.status_code == 200)

    self.assertIn(b'Invalid email and/or password.', response.data)

    self.assertFalse(current_user.is_active())

    self.assertFalse(current_user.is_authenticated())

    self.assertTemplateUsed('user/login.html')
```

profile:

```
def test_profile_route_requires_login(self):

    # Ensure profile route requires logged in user.

    self.client.get('/profile', follow_redirects=True)

    self.assertTemplateUsed('user/login.html')
```

Add the required imports as well:

```
from project import db

from project.models import User
```

register and resend_confirmation:

Before we write any tests for either the register view or the resend_confirmation view we look at the views file. Note that we are using send_email() from the file called email.py – this will send the user a confirmation email. Now, the question is this – should we send the email, or should we use mocking to fake it? Even if it is sent, we have no guarantee that it will arrive in the fake inbox without needing to use Selenium to load a real inbox in a web browser. We'll choose mocking for now:

confirm/<token>:

```python
def test_confirm_token_route_requires_login(self):

    # Ensure confirm/<token> route requires logged in user.

    self.client.get('/confirm/blah', follow_redirects=True)

    self.assertTemplateUsed('user/login.html')
```

The same way as our last two views, the last bits of this one may well be mocked because we need a confirmation token to be generated. However, we could do this simply by going to the token.py file and using a function called generate_confirmation_token():

```python
def test_confirm_token_route_valid_token(self):

    # Ensure user can confirm account with valid token.

    with self.client:

        self.client.post('/login', data=dict(

            email='test@user.com', password='just_a_test_user'

        ), follow_redirects=True)

        token = generate_confirmation_token('test@user.com')

        response = self.client.get('/confirm/'+token, follow_redirects=True)

        self.assertIn(b'You have confirmed your account. Thanks!', response.data)

        self.assertTemplateUsed('main/index.html')

        user = User.query.filter_by(email='test@user.com').first_or_404()

        self.assertIsInstance(user.confirmed_on, datetime.datetime)

        self.assertTrue(user.confirmed)
```

```python
def test_confirm_token_route_invalid_token(self):
    # Ensure user cannot confirm account with invalid token.
    token = generate_confirmation_token('test@test1.com')
    with self.client:
        self.client.post('/login', data=dict(
            email='test@user.com', password='just_a_test_user'
        ), follow_redirects=True)
        response = self.client.get('/confirm/'+token, follow_redirects=True)
        self.assertIn(
            b'The confirmation link is invalid or has expired.',
            response.data
        )
```

Add in our imports:

```python
import datetime
from project.token import generate_confirmation_token, confirm_token
```

And then we can run the tests – we should see one of them fail:

Ran 18 tests in 4.666s

FAILED (failures=1)

Why did our test fail? That's simple - there is an error in our view:

```python
@user_blueprint.route('/confirm/<token>')
@login_required
def confirm_email(token):
    try:
        email = confirm_token(token)
    except:
        flash('The confirmation link is invalid or has expired.', 'danger')
    user = User.query.filter_by(email=email).first_or_404()
    if user.confirmed:
        flash('Account already confirmed. Please login.', 'success')
    else:
        user.confirmed = True
        user.confirmed_on = datetime.datetime.now()
        db.session.add(user)
        db.session.commit()
        flash('You have confirmed your account. Thanks!', 'success')
    return redirect(url_for('main.home'))
```

What is this error? What went wrong?

Our flash call has not made our function exit. Because of this, the function goes to the if/else statement and the user would be confirmed regardless of whether the token was valid or not. This is an excellent reason that testing is so important:

The best thing we can do is write our function again:

```
@user_blueprint.route('/confirm/<token>')

@login_required

def confirm_email(token):

    if current_user.confirmed:

        flash('Account already confirmed. Please login.', 'success')

        return redirect(url_for('main.home'))

    email = confirm_token(token)

    user = User.query.filter_by(email=current_user.email).first_or_404()

    if user.email == email:

        user.confirmed = True

        user.confirmed_on = datetime.datetime.now()

        db.session.add(user)

        db.session.commit()

        flash('You have confirmed your account. Thanks!', 'success')

    else:

        flash('The confirmation link is invalid or has expired.', 'danger')

    return redirect(url_for('main.home'))
```

Run all those tests again and everything should pass.

So, what would happen if a generated token were to expire? We would write a test:

```python
def test_confirm_token_route_expired_token(self):
    # Ensure user cannot confirm account with expired token.
    user = User(email='test@test1.com', password='test1', confirmed=False)
    db.session.add(user)
    db.session.commit()
    token = generate_confirmation_token('test@test1.com')
    self.assertFalse(confirm_token(token, -1))
```

Now re-run the tests:

```
$ python manage.py test
```

test_app_is_development (test_config.TestDevelopmentConfig)... ok

test_app_is_production (test_config.TestProductionConfig)... ok

test_app_is_testing (test_config.TestTestingConfig)... ok

test_main_route_requires_login (test_main.TestMainViews)... ok

test_validate_email_already_registered (test_user.TestUserForms)... ok

test_validate_invalid_change_password (test_user.TestUserForms)... ok

test_validate_invalid_change_password_format (test_user.TestUserForms)... ok

test_validate_invalid_email_format (test_user.TestUserForms)... ok

test_validate_invalid_password_format (test_user.TestUserForms)... ok

test_validate_success_change_password_form (test_user.TestUserForms)... ok test_validate_success_login_form (test_user.TestUserForms)... ok

test_validate_success_register_form (test_user.TestUserForms)... ok

test_confirm_token_route_expired_token (test_user.TestUserViews)... ok

test_confirm_token_route_invalid_token (test_user.TestUserViews)... ok

test_confirm_token_route_requires_login (test_user.TestUserViews)... ok

test_confirm_token_route_valid_token (test_user.TestUserViews)... ok

test_correct_login (test_user.TestUserViews)... ok

test_incorrect_login (test_user.TestUserViews)... ok

test_profile_route_requires_login (test_user.TestUserViews)... ok

----

Ran 19 tests in 5.306s

OK

Behavior-Driven Development

Behavior-driven development is what lets us determine how our app behaves and it lets us drive the feature development. It does this by allowing us to add in new tests and to make those tests pass. By being very clear in our description of how our app will behave in multiple situations, we can have the peace of mind that the end product will do exactly what it was developed to do. By following the concepts of BDD, we can build our application up, one piece at a time, while maintaining a living document of the system; this is maintained naturally as the tests continue to pass. By the time this section is complete, you will:

- Have the ability to use the Flask framework to come up with a REST application
- Use the Lettuce library for writing acceptance/behavior tests
- Explain how your tests will be structured, using the syntax for Given, When, Then, And
- Execute your tests and debug them

What You Need

Before you begin, obviously you will need Python on your computer, but you will also need to find and download Lettuce library, Flask Framework, and Nosetests.

Your Project Structure

You are going to develop a RESTful application that will be able to handle the storage of user data as well as being able to retrieve it. To begin with, you will need a directory structure for your filesystem project. You will also need some empty files which will be added later down the line:

```
├── test
│   ├── features
│   │   ├── __init__.py
│   │   ├── steps.py
│   │   └── user.feature
└── app
    ├── __init__.py
    ├── application.py
    └── views.py
```

These files can be described as:

- __init__.py: marks the directory as a package in Python.

- steps.py: This is the code that the.feature file will execute.

- user.feature: A test that describes what the user endpoint functionality is in the application.

- application.py: The point at which the Flask app gets created and the server is started.

- views.py: This is the code that handles view registration and the response definition for the HTTP requests made to the view.

Creating a Flask Application

For this, you are going to create a web app built on Flask and, using the BDD approach, you will add features later. For now, you just need a basic app skeleton so go to the application.py file and add this code:

from flask import Flask

app = Flask(__name__)

if __name__ == "__main__":

   app.run()

All this code did was create the instance of Flask to begin the development server provided by Flask when the Python file is executed. Provided everything was installed as it should have been, you can open your command prompt, go to the project root and execute this command:

python app/application.py

If you see something like the following, the Flask app is running as it should be and you can continue:

$ python app/application.py

 * Running on http://127.0.0.1:5000/ (Press CTRL+C to quit)

Writing Your First BDD Test

Following BDD testing principles, you can begin by writing a test that provides a description of the basic functionality required in the app. As soon as you have the test in place and it is in failure, you will move on to writing the necessary code that will ensure the test passes.

The Feature File

Open the file called user.feature and add this as line 1:

Feature: Handle storing, retrieving and deleting customer details

All this first line is doing is documenting the functionality is covered by the situations in the file. So, add your first situation:

Situation: Retrieve a customer's details

Again, this is documenting the functionality this situation will test so now you need to add the body of the situation test:

Situation: Retrieve a customer's details

Given some users are in the system

When I retrieve the customer 'Jonathon01'

Then I should get a '200' response

And the following user details are returned:

| name |

This test is using a standard keyword set known as gherkin – Given, When, Then, And. The syntax is what gives your test its structure and it will usually follow this pattern:

- **Given** – initialization/setup of the test situation conditions. You could, for example, prime a few mocks so they return either an error response or a successful response. In the test detailed above, we are making sure that we have registered users so that the system can be queried.

- **When** – the action that is being tested, such as a GET request to the application endpoint.

- **Then** – the expectations you want from the test; you are, in the test above, for example, expecting to get a web app response of a 200 status code.

- **And** – lets you continue from the Then keyword. If the last statement started with the keyword When and the following line starts And, the And line is also going to be treated as a When.

There is one more important thing you need to note – the style the test is written in and the way that it reads. Your situations need to be as easy to read as possible and they must also be reusable. Anyone who reads them must be able to see exactly what this test is doing, what functionality is being tested and how it should behave. Your steps should be as reusable as they possibly can be, eliminating the need to keep rewriting code as well as maintaining consistency across the suite of tests.

You can now use Lettuce to execute the user.feature file and this is done from your project's root directory. This command is executed at the command prompt:

lettuce test/features

The output should be something like this:

$ lettuce test/features/

Feature: Handle storing, retrieving and deleting customer details # test/features/user.feature:1

  Situation: Retrieve a customer's details   #
  test/features/user.feature:3

    Given some users are in the system   #
    test/features/user.feature:4

    When I retrieve the customer 'Jonathon01'   #
    test/features/user.feature:5

    Then I should get a '200' response   #
    test/features/user.feature:6

    And the following user details are returned: #
    test/features/user.feature:7

      | name |

      | Jonathon Simpson |

1 feature (0 passed)

1 situation (0 passed)

4 steps (4 undefined, 0 passed)

Notice that the tests have failed but you should have expected no different; your code has not yet been written so the feature file has nothing to execute. Define the code for execution in steps and the Lettuce output does its best to put n the right path by providing a steps outline – all you need to do is complete the steps in executable Python code. Consider each of the steps to be an execution instruction to Lettuce and those steps will be matched by Lettuce to the proper code for execution.

Steps Definition

Beneath the feature file are the steps; these are nothing more than code written in Python along with some regular expressions that will give Lettuce what it needs to match the feature file lines with the step for execution. To start with, you need the steps.py file and you will add these Lettuce library imports:

from lettuce import step, world, before

from nose.tools import assert_equals

What you need to note are the Lettuce imports. These are what allow the steps to be defined, and the values for the steps stored on the object called world. You also need to note that the nose test library imports will allow you to make better assertions in the tests.

You now need to add what Lettuce calls a hook. This will be a step called @before.all and it will execute the given code before every situation. This code block will be used to create an instance of the test client built into Flask and this will let you put requests into your application just as if you were a proper client. So, open the steps.py file and input this code, not forgetting the import statement near to the top:

from app.application import app

@before.all

def before_all():

   world.app = app.test_client()

Now we have our test client sorted out, we can go ahead with the definition of the first step, the line that starts with "Given".

from app.views import USERS

@step(u'Given some users are in the system')

def given_some_users_are_in_the_system(step):

  USERS.update({'Jonathon01': {'name': 'Jonathon Simpson'}})

What this step is doing is adding a section of test data to the dictionary that is in memory. For your purposes, this dictionary will act as if it were a real system database. Note that you are importing code out of the application – this must now be added. An in-memory data store called USERS will act as a real application database so, now, you can add the code for USERS to our views file:

USERS = {}

Now that you have this, the next step can be defined. This step will call the application with the intention of retrieving user details. The response from the call will be stored in the Lettuce-provided object called world. The world object gives you the ability to save your variables and these are then accessible across the steps – without this object, this couldn't be done or, if it could, your code would end up very messy. Open steps.py and add this code:

@step(u'When I retrieve the customer \'(.)\'")*

def when_i_retrieve_the_customer_group1(step, username):

  world.response = world.app.get('/user/{}'.format(username))

With this definition, have you spotted that a capture group is used within the regular expression? This is how variables are passed in and also allows you to reuse the steps that were discussed earlier. This makes your behavior tests far more flexible and significantly more powerful. When capture groups are used, they are passed automatically by Lettuce as arguments to the method – in your code, this is named username. There are no limits on the number of variables in your definition.

The next thing to do is add the initial assertion step. This is going to check the application response for a status code and this code needs to be added to the steps.py file:

@step(u'Then I should get a \'(.)\' response')*

def then_i_should_get_a_group1_response_group2(step, expected_status_code):

  assert_equals(world.response.status_code, int(expected_status_code))

You are using the assertion that you imported from the assert_equals library from nosetests. This will take two arguments and will check them against one another to see if they are equal. Again, you are placing the status code you expect to get into a variable using a capture group. On this occasion, you should have an integer as your variable, so the type may be converted before the status code the application returned is compared to it.

Lastly, you must have a step to check that the returned data from the application is as it was expected to be. This definition is an excellent example of why there is support in Lettuce to pass data tables into the definitions – this is perfect for this example because you may end up a with a lot of data and using a table ensures that you can easily read what you expect to see. Open steps.py and add this last step:

@step(u'And the following user details are returned:')

def and_the_following_user_details(step):

  assert_equals(step.hashes, [json.loads(world.response.data)])

As you can see, when a data table is passed in, you can use the step object stored under hashes to access it. This is nothing more than a list of the dictionaries for each table row. A JSON string will be returned, a dictionary listing the name key to the name of the user. As such, your assertion will load a string into a dictionary; that is, the string returned by the application and then it is wrapped in a list making it equal to what is expected.

Execution

Now you have the steps you need, together produces a description of the functionality you expect your application to have, it's now time to execute your test; it should fail. As before, open the command prompt and execute this code:

lettuce test/features

We should see the following when the test fails, as it should do:

$ lettuce test/features/

Feature: Handle storing, retrieving and deleting customer details # test/features/user.feature:1

  Situation: Retrieve a customer's details   # test/features/user.feature:3

    Given some users are in the system   # test/features/steps.py:17

    When I retrieve the customer 'Jonathon01'   # test/features/steps.py:22

    Then I should get a '200' response   # test/features/steps.py:27

    Traceback (most recent call last):

      [SNIPPET REMOVED FOR READABILITY]

      raise self.failureException(msg)

AssertionError: 404!= 200

And the following user details are returned: #
test/features/steps.py:32

| name |

| Jonathon Simpson |

1 feature (0 passed)

1 situation (0 passed)

4 steps (1 failed, 1 skipped, 2 passed)

List of failed situations:

Situation: Retrieve a customer's details #
test/features/user.feature:3

Right now, you have a 404 Not Found error response and this is because you do not have the URL/user/<username> defined just yet; this is what the test wants to access and it can't. To make this right, to ensure that the test passes and you get what you expect, what was described in the behavior test, open views.py and add this code:

GET = 'GET'

@app.route("/user/<username>", methods=[GET])

def access_users(username):

```
if request.method == GET:

    user_details = USERS.get(username)

    if user_details:

        return jsonify(user_details)

    else:

        return Response(status=404)
```

First, the new URL is registered in /user/<username> - the <> are telling Flask that it should capture whatever comes after the / and put it into a variable with the name of username. The method is then defined to handle requests to the URL; in this, a statement is made that the only requests that can be made to the URL are GET requests. Next, check to see if the received request is a GET request and, if yes, attempt to get the username details as provided by the data store called USERS. If you find those details, the response is a status code of 200 and a JSON string listing the details of the user; if no, you get a 404 Not Found error response.

Go to your command prompt, execute your tests once more and they will all pass:

$ lettuce test/features/

Feature: Handle storing, retrieving and deleting customer details # test/features/user.feature:1

  Situation: Retrieve a customer's details   # test/features/user.feature:3

    Given some users are in the system   # test/features/steps.py:17

When I retrieve the customer 'Jonathon01'   #
test/features/steps.py:22

Then I should get a '200' response   # test/features/steps.py:27

And the following user details are returned: #
test/features/steps.py:32

| name |

| Jonathon Simpson |

1 feature (1 passed)

1 situation (1 passed)

4 steps (4 passed)

You now have the exact functionality that your behavior test described, and you can go to another situation; repeat these steps for each situation to ensure they all pass. This is, as you might have guessed, a cycle of iteration.

Behavior-driven development is one of the best testing procedures to follow, no matter whether you are part of a large enterprise working on an application or a single developer working on a smaller application. With BDD, you can make sure that your code does exactly what you want it to do before you write the actual code. With BDD, you also have the benefit of gaining what is called "living documentation" that is updated as your tests are maintained and new functionalities are delivered.

Pytest

Pytest is one of the easiest testing tools to use because it offers simplicity. In this section, we will acquaint you with the basics of pytest and you can then go on to do your own homework and learn how to use it for complex testing purposes, a task that pytest is more than capable of doing.

What You Need

You will need Python 3 and a virtualenv which you will create now using the support built-in to Python 3. Open your command prompt and run these commands:

mkdir pytest_project

cd pytest_project

python3 -m venv pytest-env

You now have a virtual environment with the name of pytest-env and it has been saved to your current working directory.

Now you must activate the virtual environment like this:

source pytest-env/bin/activate

Provided you have an active virtualenv working, any packages will be installed there rather than the Python installation. Begin by installing pytest:

pip install pytest

Basic Usage of Pytest

You are going to start by building a simple test. Python will want to find any tests that are written in files that start test_ or finish _test.py. The file you are going to create will be named test_capitalize.py and it will contain a function by the name of capital_case. The argument to this function must be a string and the return should be a version of that string in capitals. Alongside this, you will be writing a test called test_capital_case to make sure your function does what you want it to do. The test function is prefixed with test_ because pytest will expect this:

 # test_capitalize.py

```
def capital_case(x):

    return x.capitalize()
```

```
def test_capital_case():

    assert capital_case('semaphore') == 'Semaphore'
```

The first thing you should notice is that a vanilla assert statement is used by pytest – you can remember these a lot easier and you will find them very easy to use.

Running the test is done with the pytest command:

pytest

You should see a pass for the test.

Now, if you were really up on Python and knew your code back to front, you would have spotted something. You could end up with a bug in this code because there is nothing in place to check whether the argument type is a string as it should be. So, if a number were passed in as the function argument, an exception would be raised.

How is this handled? You do it inside the function and you raise a custom exception that shows a user a nice error message. Let's see if you can capture it in the test:

 # test_capitalize.py

import pytest

```
def test_capital_case():

    assert capital_case('semaphore') == 'Semaphore'


def test_raises_exception_on_non_string_arguments():

    with pytest.raises(TypeError):

        capital_case(9)
```

There is a big addition to this code – pytest.raises, which is a helper that will assert a TypeError is to be raised by the function should you have anything other than a string as the argument. Right now, running those tests should result in a fail with an error:

```
def capital_case(x):

    return x.capitalize()
```

E   AttributeError: 'int' object has no attribute 'capitalize'

You have already verified that this case has not been handled so you can do something about fixing it.

In the function called capital_case, you need to make sure that you have a string or, at the very least, a string subset as the argument before the capitalize function is called. If you don't have that string, a TypeError must be raised with your custom message:

```
# test_capitalize.py


def capital_case(x):

    if not isinstance(x, str):

        raise TypeError('Please provide a string argument')
```

return x.capitalize()

Now, when the tests are rerun, they should pass.

The first of your test functions uses the fixture called empty_wallet. This gives your test a wallet instance that has a 0 balance. The three tests that follow this are all given a wallet instance with equal balances of 20. And your last test is given the fixture called empty_wallet. This fixture is then used by your tests just as if the creation of the fixture had happened in the test function, just like before.

Now you can run your tests again and see if everything is working as it should be.

Using fixtures is a good way of reducing duplication of code. If you spot in any of your code a place where one piece of code is used over and over again in several tests, you could consider using a fixture.

Test Fixture Pointers

Look at a few pointers to use these text fixtures:

- Each of the tests is given a Wallet instance that is freshly initialized; they will never use an instance that has already been used elsewhere.

- Try, where you can, to give your fixtures docstrings. If you want to know what all the fixtures available are, run this command:

pytest --fixtures

Running this will give you a list of some of the pytest fixtures built into Python, as well as the custom fixtures that were created. You will see the docstrings as fixture descriptions:

- wallet – a wallet instance is returned with a value of 20 as the balance
- empty_wallet – a wallet instance is returned with a value of zero as the balance

Parametrized Test Functions

Now that you have run tests on the Wallet class method on an individual basis, you can move on and test several combinations of all the methods. This will answer some questions, like "If I start with a balance of 25, spend 15, add 75 and then add a further 50, what should my balance be?"

I'm sure you would agree that writing that as a test would not only be time-consuming, it would be somewhat tedious as well. That is where Python comes to the rescue with parametrized test functions.

If you wanted to capture something like the situation above, you would write your test like this:

```
# test_wallet.py


@pytest.mark.parametrize("earned,spent,expected", [

    (30, 10, 20),

    (20, 2, 18),

])

def test_transactions(earned, spent, expected):

    my_wallet = Wallet()

    my_wallet.add_cash(earned)

    my_wallet.spend_cash(spent)

    assert my_wallet.balance == expected
```

Using this test, you can test a number of different situations using just one function. The decorator called @pytest.mark.parametrize is used to specify the names of those arguments that the test function takes, along with the arguments that go with the names.

The test function that has the decorator then is run one time for each of the parameter sets. For example, the first time the test is run, there is an earned function with a value of 30, a spent parameter with a value of 10 and an expected parameter with a value of 20. On the second test, the second argument set is given to the parameters and then those parameters are used in the test function. This helps to capture your situation nicely:

- The wallet has an initial value of 0

- 30 cash units are added

- 10 cash units are spent

- The balance should now be 20

This is a nice way of testing multiple combinations without needing to write repetitive code.

Parametrized Test Functions and Test Fixtures Together

So that we can remove some of the repetitiveness from the tests, we can go even further and combine the parametrized test functions with the test fixtures. We can do this by taking the initialization code for the wallet out and putting in a test fixture, much like we *did earlier. The result will be:*

 # test_wallet.py

@pytest.fixture

def my_wallet():

   '''Returns a Wallet instance with a zero balance'''

   return Wallet()

```
@pytest.mark.parametrize("earned,spent,expected", [

    (30, 10, 20),

    (20, 2, 18),

])

def test_transactions(my_wallet, earned, spent, expected):

    my_wallet.add_cash(earned)

    my_wallet.spend_cash(spent)

    assert my_wallet.balance == expected
```

A new fixture with a name of my_wallet is created; this is identical to the earlier empty_wallet fixture. A wallet instance is returned with a 0 balance and to use the parametrized functions and the test fixtures together, the fixture is included as the initial argument, with the parameters as the other arguments.

We then perform the transactions on the function-provided wallet instance.

Now it's time to turn our attention to what we talked about earlier – automated testing.

Automated Testing

If you want to write software that is reliable and that works, you need to learn about automated testing. There really is only so far that you can go with manual testing and, to be fair, testing manually is never going to be as thorough as a machine can do it. We won't go into details about individual testing techniques or tool; rather we will try to get you into the mindset of thinking of automated testing as something that can be applied regardless of the project you are doing. We will attempt to give you a foundation you can work with when you need to move away from developing software and into broad automated testing, whether you are a solo developer or working for an organization.

So, what are automated tests for? In the same way as your manual tests, automated tests are designed to test that your software does exactly what it is meant to do. Okay, so this is a pretty vague definition, but it is reflective of just how many ways there are to verify what your software is doing:

- We can call functions on known inputs and use assert to see if the result is what we expect;
- We can set up a dummy website and make sure that the pages work as they should, that basic operations are performed properly and that the systems behind the website work;
- We can chuck loads of random data and inputs at the system to see what, if anything, will make it crash;
- We can compare our program behavior against that of reference implementations that are known to be good to make sure they behave the same way.

Did you spot anything there? We didn't mention integration or unit testing once! Why? Because on almost every occasion, neither of those will be your end goal. With automated testing, we want tests that will run automatically, to test the entire system, doing whatever is necessary, to see that it all works. Unit tests and integration tests are just one small part of the whole picture, just one tiny consideration in the ways we approach testing. Let's discuss these a bit more.

Unit Tests vs Integration Tests

When we work on automated tests there are three main arguments that always come to light:

- Are we writing integration tests or unit tests?
- Should we write integration tests or unit tests?
- How are integration tests and unit tests meant to be defined?

We could go on ad infinitum about how many correct ways there are to tell the difference between an integration test and a unit test and every way is different. There are rules, such as:

- A unit test must be done wholly within one process
- A unit test may not execute code from any more than one file and all imports should be mocked
- A unit test is any test that doesn't cross over the boundary between the client and server.

There is a real lack of perspective here. The reality is, the point where the line is drawn is arbitrary. Every system, every piece of code that you write is, in fact, a unit that is an integration of multiple smaller units:

- Clusters integrate several virtual or physical machines
- A physical or virtual machine integrates several different processes
- A process integrates several subprocesses, such as workers, databases, etc.
- Subprocesses integrate several modules
- Modules or packages integrate several small modules
- A module integrates functions that are all individual
- A function uses simple arithmetic to integrate primitives, i.e. Ints

Everything is a unit that can be tested, and every unit is an integration of multiple other units. That is the way all software can be broken down, now and in the future.

Automated testing is done to make sure your software behaves as it should; that software will contain code at every one of those hierarchical levels mentioned above. And every single piece of that code must be tested and verified by you.

To keep things simple, if a piece of code is low in that hierarchy, such as a function that integrates primitives, we will call it a unit test and, if it is higher, like the cluster that integrates the machines, we will call it an integration test. This is purely for the purposes of this part of the book – please don't take it that this is what they really are!

The most important thing is that you are aware of how your code breaks down in terms of that hierarchy and that you can have automated tests at each and every level. However, there is a distinction in the properties that each type of test has:

Unit Tests	Integration Tests
Low hierarchy	High hierarchy
Speedy	Not so fast
Reliable	A little more unreliable
Not much setup needed	Loads of setup!
Not many dependencies	A lot of dependencies
Not many modes for failure	Many more failure modes
Failure messages are specific	Failure messages are generic

In short:

- A unit test will be faster because there is less code to run
- A unit test will be more reliable because less code means fewer failures that can't be determined
- Unit tests don't need much setting up because they don't have so many dependencies
- When a unit test fails, it tends to be more specific and have fewer causes; with an integration test, you may get broad, generic failures that are pretty meaningless and have multiple causes.

So, as a person who is going to start writing tests, what does all of this mean?

What it really means is, it is down to you as the writer to define the distinction between integration and unit tests. Much depends on what the tests are for. For example, if you are testing a website, it will define unit and integration tests differently from, let's say, an algorithm library and this, in turn, will have a different definition than a system designed for cluster deployment.

- An algorithm library sees the unit tests as those that run a single function on the smallest of inputs while it may see the integration tests as using several functions to build algorithms.

- A website may see the unit tests as any test that doesn't go near the HTTP API while an integration test would.
- A website may also see a unit test as being any test that doesn't load a browser while the integration tests would open a browser and use Selenium for server interaction through JavaScript.
- A system for cluster deployment may see a unit test as any test that does not result in the physical creation of a virtual machine and that would include those that use database access or the HTTP API, while an integration test would be seen as one that uses a staging environment to open a cluster.

While there may be differences in speed, reliability, and so on, at the end of the day, all the different systems will use tests that may be more or wholly unit or more or wholly integration. As such, it is down to you to draw that line and then build your test practices using that line. In short, there is no real classification of what a unit or an integration test is because there is too wide a range of projects for classification to mean anything.

Hierarchical Testing

Each separate bit of software is written in a hierarchical manner as individual units integrating multiple small units. It is possible, at every level of that hierarchy, for a programmer to do something wrong. Ideally, whatever mistakes are made would be caught by an automated test. So, don't take any notice of the restrictive rules that state only integration tests or only unit tests should be written:

- You can't write only integration tests because, although the theory suggests it will work, if only because the code higher up in the hierarchy will exercise the lower code, you would require many integration tests to exercise enough cases. For example, if you needed to check the behavior of one function with 8 primitive argument sets, you would end up setting the application process up and tearing it all down no less than 8 times, a huge waste of time and resources.
- You can't write only unit tests because, regardless of how much you test a function, it won't matter if the functions are combined wrongly by the

module or if each module is used wrongly by the application process. Having a suite of tests is a good idea if each test is fast but if it misses the bugs that come in at the higher levels, it's of no use.

What you need is a test structure that mirrors as closely as possible the way your software is structured. You need to be able to test every level of the hierarchy in relation to how much code is there and the likelihood of it being wrong. Only then can you have some safeguard against errors being introduced.

Prioritizing Your Tests

With the automated tests, there are two purposes to serve – ensuring that you don't already have broken code that couldn't be detected through manual tests, and, ensuring the code that works cannot break in the future. The broken code may be a result of an implementation that wasn't complete; the reasons why a code may break in the future would be down to mistakes through the evolution of the codebase.

As such, there is no sense in having a set of automated tests for any code that is working (not broken), code where it is not important if it breaks, or code that is more likely to be long gone before anyone has the chance to break it.

It is far more of an art than it is science to determine the amount of testing needed on a specific code or system, but you could use these guidelines to help you:

- If something is important, it must be tested heavily. For example, if you have a system of passwords and authentication, it needs heavy tests to make sure bad passwords cannot be used, whereas some of the other random logic may not need so much testing.
- If something isn't quite so important, you must decide whether it needs little testing or even no testing. If it doesn't matter if a small part of your website doesn't get uploaded for a day or two, you could even consider small manual tests rather than the expense of automated testing.
- If you have code that is being actively developed, it must be tested over and over but if your code is no longer being developed, it won't need so

much testing. If you have a piece of code that has not been touched for some time, if it wasn't broken then, it isn't likely to break now. You might want to run a small test to make sure it hasn't broken but you won't need to run the tests that stop it breaking in the future.

- If an API is not going to disappear, it will need more testing than an API that has a chance of disappearing. Focus your real efforts on the parts of your interface that are stable; leave the unstable code until later or leave it alone altogether. Together with the previous guideline, you will see that the code that needs the most testing is undergoing development, but its API is stable.
- If your code is complex in odd places, such as browser-server, inter-process, etc., ensure that this logic is tested regardless of how awkward it may be. Don't stick with testing the easy stuff and ignoring the rest; it matters not if each function is through tested if the glue that holds them together doesn't work.

Tests Are Just Code

Writing a test is no different from writing a piece of code. Your testing suite is just a little bit of software that makes sure the main software works correctly. As such, test code is to be treated in the same way as any other software:

- You should refactor common testing logic into helpers. If you have a bug in any of this test logic, it is far better to fix it in just one place than have to keep going through loads of code to fix it.
- Your test code must be up to the same standard that your normal code has been written in; correct naming, correct formatting, comments added in, properly organized code, inline-docs, the correct style of coding and convention.
- In order to maintain the quality of the code, your tests must be refactored. All code has the potential to get a little bit messed up and, as it gets bigger, it will get harder to handle. As such you must refactor regularly, so that things stay neat, organized and follow the DRY principles (Don't Repeat Yourself) and the same applies to your test code.
- You must have a test suite that is flexible and agile. If you are testing an API that changes, your tests must be written in a way that they too can

change quickly. If some code is deleted, you should remove the corresponding test and, if you should rewrite a piece of code, you should be able to rewrite your tests accordingly. Using the correct fixtures, helpers, and abstractions will ensure that this becomes an easy job.

- And that leads to this – if those fixtures, abstractions and helpers themselves start to become complex, then they too must be tested, if only to a minimal level.

Not everyone is going to agree with all these; some may be of the opinion that tests are not the same as standard code. You may believe that it is better to have a type of copy and paste test code rather than using helpers and abstractions to follow the DRY principles. How you see things is entirely up to you but there is no denying one thing – when you write a test, you are writing computer code.

DRY Tests, Data-Driven

Because tests are just code, and code should always be DRY and must be factored so that we can only see the logic that is truly necessary; we also shouldn't have too much repetitive code. An example would be the definition of a test-helper that allows multiple test cases to be put through the testing suite to easily see which inputs are being tested. For example, look at this piece of test code:

// Sanity check the logic that runs when you press ENTER in the REPL and

// detects whether a set of input lines is...

//

// - Complete, and can be submitted without needing additional input

// - Incomplete, and thus needs additional lines of input from the user

def test1 = {

```scala
  val res = ammonite.interp.Parsers.split("{}")

  assert(res.isDefined)

}

def test2 = {

  val res = ammonite.interp.Parsers.split("foo.bar")

  assert(res.isDefined)

}

def test3 = {

  val res = ammonite.interp.Parsers.split("foo.bar // line comment")

  assert(res.isDefined)

}

def test4 = {

  val res = ammonite.interp.Parsers.split("foo.bar /* block comment */")

  assert(res.isDefined)

}

def test5 = {

  val res = ammonite.interp.Parsers.split(

    "val r = (1 until 1000).view.filter(n => n % 3 == 0 || n % 5 == 0).sum"

  )

  assert(res.isDefined)

}
```

```scala
def test6 = {

  val res = ammonite.interp.Parsers.split("{")

  assert(res.isEmpty)

}

def test7 = {

  val res = ammonite.interp.Parsers.split("foo.bar /* incomplete block
comment")

  assert(res.isEmpty)

}

def test8 = {

  val res = ammonite.interp.Parsers.split(

    "val r = (1 until 1000.view.filter(n => n % 3 == 0 || n % 5 == 0)"

  )

  assert(res.isEmpty)

}

def test9 = {

  val res = ammonite.interp.Parsers.split(

    "val r = (1 until 1000).view.filter(n => n % 3 == 0 || n % 5 == 0"

  )

  assert(res.isEmpty)

}
```

If you spotted, that piece of code is repeating itself continually; it should have been written like this:

```
// Sanity check the logic that runs when you press ENTER in the REPL and
// detects whether a set of input lines is...
//
// - Complete, and can be submitted without needing additional input
// - Incomplete, and thus needs additional lines of input from the user


def checkDefined(s: String) = {
  val res = ammonite.interp.Parsers.split(s)
  assert(res.isDefined)
}
def checkEmpty(s: String) = {
  val res = ammonite.interp.Parsers.split(s)
  assert(res.isEmpty)
}
def testDefined = {
  checkDefined("{}")
  checkDefined("foo.bar")
  checkDefined("foo.bar // line comment")
  checkDefined("foo.bar /* block comment */")
```

```scala
  checkDefined("val r = (1 until 1000).view.filter(n => n % 3 == 0 || n % 5 ==
0).sum")

}

def testEmpty = {

  checkEmpty("{")

  checkEmpty("foo.bar /* incomplete block comment")

  checkEmpty("val r = (1 until 1000.view.filter(n => n % 3 == 0 || n % 5 == 0)")

  checkEmpty("val r = (1 until 1000).view.filter(n => n % 3 == 0 || n % 5 == 0")

}
```

This kind of refactoring is normal, the kind that we would do on our code regardless of language. However, what it does is turns heavy repetitive code methods into something rather more elegant that follows DRY, allowing you to see instantly the inputs being tested and their output. You could do this in other ways, for example by defining the Empty cases within an array, the Defined cases within an array and then using asserts to loop over them:

```scala
def definedCases = Seq(

  "{}",

  "foo.bar",

  "foo.bar // line comment",

  "foo.bar /* block comment */",

  "val r = (1 until 1000).view.filter(n => n % 3 == 0 || n % 5 == 0).sum"

)
```

```
for(s <- definedCases){

  val res = ammonite.interp.Parsers.split(s)

  assert(res.isDefined)

}


def emptyCases = Seq(

  "{",

  "foo.bar /* incomplete block comment",

  "val r = (1 until 1000.view.filter(n => n % 3 == 0 || n % 5 == 0)",

  "val r = (1 until 1000).view.filter(n => n % 3 == 0 || n % 5 == 0"

)


for(s <- emptyCases){

  val res = ammonite.interp.Parsers.split(s)

  assert(res.isEmpty)

}
```

Both of these result in the exact same goal and are joined by many other ways; the style you opt for is entirely up to you. You will hear phrases such as "data-driven", "table-driven", and others with respect to the tests, but the basics are the same – your test cases must be concise and you must be able to see the behavior at a glance. Normal techniques for refactoring are more than capable of helping you to do this without you needing to use any other tools or techniques; that is something you should go into only after you have mastered manual and automated testing.

DSL's for Testing

There are several DSL's (Domain Specific Languages) available to help you to write tests in different ways than how you normally write code. General purpose DSLs should be avoided where possible although they do give a whole new way of writing tests. Take this situation, for example:

Ernie wants to use an ATM to take some money out of his bank account.

Given that he is in possession of a valid Debit or Credit card.

He has an account balance of $150.

When he puts his card into the ATM

And withdraws $50

The ATM should return $50

Leaving him with a balance of $100

Now the outline of that situation would be:

A user takes money from an ATM

Given <Name> is in possession of a valid Debit or credit card

They have an account balance of <OriginalBalance>

They put their card into the ATM

And withdraw >WithdrawalAmount>

The ATM should return <WithdrawalAmount>

Leaving the user with a balance of <NewBalance>

An example of this would be:

| Name | OriginalBalance | WithdrawalAmount | NewBalance |

Ernie	150	50	100	
Simon	175	25	150	
Billy	1500	500	1000	

While other DSLs will allow you to write the code as you would write normal code:

"An empty Set" should "have size 0" in {

  assert(Set.empty.size == 0)

}

"A Set" can {

  "empty" should {

    "have size 0" in {

      assert(Set.empty.size == 0)

    }

    "produce NoSuchElementException when head is invoked" in {

      intercept[NoSuchElementException] {

        Set.empty.head

      }

    }

  }

    "should be empty" ignore {

      assert(Set.empty.isEmpty)

```
        }

    }

}
```

val result = 8

result should equal (3) // By default, calls left == right, except for arrays

result should be (3)   // Calls left == right, except for arrays

result should === (3) // By default, calls left == right, except for arrays

val one = 1

one should be < 7   // works for any T when an implicit Ordered[T] exists

one should be <= 7

one should be >= 0

result shouldEqual 3   // Alternate forms for equal and be

result shouldBe 3   // that don't require parentheses

As a rule, these DSLs are often not worth using because they do nothing more than make things more complex and provide indirection. Both make it somewhat more difficult to work out what, exactly, is being tested by a test. The easiest way is just to use your normal for loops, helper methods, and asserts to write your tests. And you also have frameworks like PyTest to fall back on:

$ cat test_foo.py

def test_simple():

```
    result = 8

    assert result == 3
```

```
$ py.test test_foo.py
```

================================== FAILURES ==============================

_____ test_simple

_____

```
    def test_simple():

        result = 8

        assert result == 3

        assert 8 == 3
```

```
test_foo.py:3: AssertionError
```

========================== 1 failed in 0.03 seconds
==========================

Specialized DSLs

While the general DSLs may not be a good idea, there are specialized ones that
are. MyPy, for example, has a specialized syntax for defining the input and the
output of the test cases:

[case testNewSyntaxBasics]

```
# flags: --python-version 3.6

x: int

x = 5

y: int = 5


a: str

a = 5  # E: Incompatible types in assignment (expression has type "int",
variable has type "str")

b: str = 5  # E: Incompatible types in assignment (expression has type "int",
variable has type "str")


zzz: int

zzz: str  # E: Name 'zzz' already defined
```

The # E comments are nothing more than asserts; specific errors will be raised by the type checker at specific points when this file is checked.

Example Tests vs Bulk Tests

An example test is a test that takes your code through one example (in some cases, a few examples) using carefully placed asserts to make sure that the code does exactly what it should do. On the other hand, a bulk test is one that floods your code with loads of examples but not examining the behavior of each of the cases as thoroughly. All it really does is checks that your code isn't crashing and is behaving somewhat as it should.

As we saw with the unit and the integration testing, bulk and example tests are at opposite ends of a spectrum and most of the tests fall somewhere in between. For example, the DRY data tests we touched on earlier are in the middle somewhere because they covering multiple input data sets using just one check set.

Example Sets

An example test is exactly what most people think of as automated testing, especially those tests that make use of APIs in specific ways before checking results. One test like that is shown below, testing a trivial parser which will parse just one character:

```
import fastparse.all._

val parseA = P( "a" )


val Parsed.Success(value, successIndex) = parseA.parse("a")

assert(

  value == (),

  successIndex == 1

)


val failure = parseA.parse("b").asInstanceOf[Parsed.Failure]

assert(

  failure.lastParser == ("a": P0),

  failure.index == 0,

  failure.extra.traced.trace == """parseA:1:1 / "a":1:1..."b""""

)
```

As you see from this example, several steps are needed:

- The parser is defined.
- The parser is used for parsing strings that are different.
- The test checks to ensure that success or failure happens where it should.
- The test checks that what is in the success of failure are what is expected.

Example tests are an excellent form of good documentation. On most occasions, just from a couple of examples, you can see quite clearly what a module is doing and how it should be used. Example tests are also good to provide examples of success and failure cases, maybe those on which you already ran manual tests. What they cannot cover are the unexpected cases. You can use the DRY data-driven tests to cover multiple test cases for inputs and outputs but you will come up against a limit of what you can imagine in terms of examples and this is where we discuss bulk testing.

Bulk Tests

A bulk test is used to check a great deal more cases than manual testing alone can check. Instead of running one bit of code one time and seeing what it does, a bulk test will use hundreds, even thousands of outputs to run the code. This way, unexpected cases are covered, those you couldn't add into the example test or forgot about when you did the manual testing.

The nuts of bolts of bulk testing come down to this:

for i in range(0, 9999):

  for j in range(0, 9999):

    result = func(i, j)

    assert(sanity_check(result))

What we did here was to call func with an impressive 100,000,000 outputs. We used a sanity check function that has no idea of every output that could come from each of the inputs, but is able to check simple things like whether the output is negative or not. By the same token, we are also checking to see that func doesn't loop infinitely or throw exceptions on any input.

Bulk tests are used on such high input numbers that they are somewhat slower than example tests. Because of this, the cost of the tests is a good deal higher (more about this later) and that means they should be used carefully. However, when we are testing functionality with large input ranges, when it is hard to choose example tests manually to cover all the cases, bulk tests may well be worth it.

When we have such a large input set to deal with, we cannot define "correct" as being an expected output set of the same size. Instead, we define "correct" as the relationship that you expect as being true between the inputs and outputs, irrespective of the input.

Usually, we will do simple checks in bulk tests, checks that aren't quite as precise as those done in example tests. Running a file parser is not practical to do against a large dump to assert the many thousands of returned values will match exactly to a list of the values we expect. Errors are just as likely when your expected outputs are input as you are when writing the parser logic. However, there are some properties that, regardless of the values output by our program, will also be true. It is these properties that bulk tests are used for testing.

Quite apart from the large amount of data generated using the for loops, there is often quite a lot of useful, real-world data that you can use in your code. For example, a bulk test used to test a program that is designed to gain access to the source code in Python might look like this:

repos = [

   "dropbox/changes",

   "django/django",

```
    "mitsuhiko/flask",

    "zulip/zulip",

    "ansible/ansible",

    "kennethresitz/requests"

]

for repo in repos:

    clone_repo("https://github.com/" + repo)

    for file in os.walk(repo):

        if file.endswith(".py"):

            result = process_python_source(file)

            assert(sanity_check(result))
```

We know that bulk tests are not as fast as example tests; rather than milliseconds, they take seconds, and in some cases, minutes to run. Bulk tests are not quite as easy to read as an example test either; when you don't have many thousands of values being generated or you are not loading test inputs in the thousands from the internet, it won't always be very clear what inputs are cases and what ones are not very interesting.

Cost of Tests

We mentioned this earlier; testing does not come free. After all, they have to be written and, even after that, they will each impose some kind of cost on your testing suite. Each test you write will:

- Slow down your test suite
- Make your test suite less reliable

- Need to be maintained and must be updated as and when your code changes, it must be grepped through whenever you refactor your code, and so on.

You could parallelize the tests using many machines but, while this will speed up the testing, it will cost more in real-money terms, far more than running a test on one machine because each machine has a setup overhead.

If an automated test takes forever to run, isn't reliable, is far too difficult to keep maintained, then it may be considered as not being worth it. These tests can cause more harm than good, and shouldn't really be written; if they have been written they should be deleted.

Mocking

Mocking is a way of isolating certain bits of code that are under test conditions and replacing it with a 'dummy' piece of code. In this way, you can test how certain things are handled, like email responses, without actually receiving the emails in the application. Rather than calling the real implementation, the mock is called and assertions made about what is expected to happen.

The Benefits of Mocking

- Faster – Any test that runs fast is of benefit and this is especially true of functions that are resource-intensive. If you mocked that function it would reduce testing time by not using so many resources.

- No Bad Side-Effects – Let's say that you test a function that calls external APIs. You wouldn't want to make that API call in your tests because you would need to refactor your code whenever the API changed – mocking eliminates that need.

What You Need

Obviously you will need Python 3.x and a virtual environment. We'll set that up specifically for mocking so at your command prompt, type:

python3 -m venv mocking

And then run the following command to activate it:

source mocking/bin/activate

After that, create 2 files – main.py for the code and test.py for the tests

touch main.py test.py

Basic Mocking Usage

Let's imagine that we have a very simple class, something like:

class Calculator:

   def sum(self, a, b):

     return a + b

In this class, we are implementing a single method called sum. The 2 arguments this method takes are a and b, the numbers that are being added and the return should be a + b. So, we could build a very easy test case for this like this:

from unittest import TestCase

from main import Calculator

class TestCalculator(TestCase):

   def setUp(self):

     self.calc = Calculator()

```python
    def test_sum(self):

        answer = self.calc.sum(2, 4)

        self.assertEqual(answer, 6)
```

To run this test, you would use this command:

```
python -m unittest
```

And your output should look like this:

```
.



_____

_____



Ran 1 test in 0.003s



OK
```

Now that was fast but now think about what would happen if our code was more like this:

```python
import time


class Calculator:

    def sum(self, a, b):

        time.sleep(10) # long running process

        return a + b
```

Because we only have a simple example, we simulate a longer running time by using time.sleep(). We now get this output if we run it:

.

_____

Ran 1 test in 10.003s

OK

Doing that has slowed things down considerably so its clear that calling the sum method whenever we run a test is not the best idea. In this situation we could use mocking – this would make the test faster and also eliminate the unwanted side-effects.

Now we will refactor this so that, when the test is run, rather than having to call sum, we call a mock sum with behavior that is properly defined:

from unittest import TestCase

from unittest.mock import patch

class TestCalculator(TestCase):

   @patch('main.Calculator.sum', return_value=9)

   def test_sum(self, sum):

     self.assertEqual(sum(2,3), 9)

We imported a called patch form unittest.mock. This puts a mock function in place of the real sum function and the mock function does what we want it to do. In our case, that mock will always return a 9. If we run this, we get:

.

_____

_____

Ran 1 test in 0.001s

OK

You might think this is somewhat counter-intuitive but remember what mocking is all about faking a part of the implementation to give you more flexibility.

Another Example

This time, we are going to make our API calls using a library called requests. To get this, type the following at the command prompt:

pip install requests

The code in main.py will look like this:

import requests

class Blog:

   def __init__(self, name):

      self.name = name

```
def posts(self):

    response = requests.get("https://jsonplaceholder.typicode.com/posts")


    return response.json()


def __repr__(self):

    return '<Blog: {}>'.format(self.name)
```

We have defined a class called Blog and given it a method called Posts. When Posts is invoked on Blog, an API call is triggered to jsonplaceholder. What we want to do is mock the API call because it behaves unpredictably and ensures our test only makes sure that the Posts method of Blog will only return posts. To do that, all the posts methods in Blog need to be patched, like this:

```
from unittest import TestCase

from unittest.mock import patch, Mock



class TestBlog(TestCase):

    @patch('main.Blog')

    def test_blog_posts(self, MockBlog):

        blog = MockBlog()
```

```
blog.posts.return_value = [

    {

        'userId': 1,

        'id': 1,

        'title': 'Test Title',

        'body': 'Far out in the uncharted backwaters of the unfashionable end
of the western spiral arm of the Galaxy\ lies a small unregarded yellow sun.'

    }

]


response = blog.posts()

self.assertIsNotNone(response)

self.assertIsInstance(response[0], dict)
```

As you can see, test_blog_posts has been given the @patch decorator. When this is used to decorate a function, the return is a mock of the method, class or function that was passed to @patch and this is then passed to the decorated function as an argument.

In our case, we called @patch with the main_blog target and a Mock is returned and passed as MockBlog to our test function. Note that any target passed into @patch must be importable from the environment from which we invoke @patch. The main import Blog form should be resolved without any errors.

It is also worth noting that MockBlog is actually the name of a variable that is representing the mock created – we can call it whatever we want. When we call blog.posts on the mock, we get a return of the JSON we defined. All tests should now pass:

.

_____

Ran 1 test in 0.001s

OK

When we test a value that has been mocked rather than a real object, we can make additional assertions about the way the mock is used. For example, we could test the number of times the mock is called, which arguments were used and whether the mock even got called. We'll see some more examples next.

Other Assertions

Continuing with our example, there are some other assertions that we can make on our Mock object:

import main

from unittest import TestCase

from unittest.mock import patch

class TestBlog(TestCase):

  @patch('main.Blog')

  def test_blog_posts(self, MockBlog):

```python
blog = MockBlog()

blog.posts.return_value = [
    {
        'userId': 1,
        'id': 1,
        'title': 'Test Title',
        'body': 'Far out in the uncharted backwaters of the unfashionable end of the western spiral arm of the Galaxy\ lies a small unregarded yellow sun.'
    }
]

response = blog.posts()
self.assertIsNotNone(response)
self.assertIsInstance(response[0], dict)

# Additional assertions
assert MockBlog is main.Blog # The mock is equivalent to the original

assert MockBlog.called # The mock wasP called
```

blog.posts.assert_called_with() # We called the posts method with no arguments

blog.posts.assert_called_once_with() # We called the posts method once with no arguments

 # blog.posts.assert_called_with(1, 2, 3) - This assertion is False and will fail since we called blog.posts with no arguments

blog.reset_mock() # Reset the mock object

blog.posts.assert_not_called() # After resetting, posts has not been called.

Remember, we said that the mock object will let us test the way it was used by looking at how it was called and the arguments that were passed, rather than just checking the return value.

We can also reset a mock object to a state whereby it hasn't yet been called. This proves useful when we need to make several calls on the mock and each one needs a fresh mock instance on which to run.

Side-Effects

Side-effects are what we want to happen when we call our mock function, commonly, exceptions being raised or another function being called. Let's go back to the sum function from earlier. What would happen if, rather than hard-coding our value for return, we decided we wanted a custom sum function to run instead? The custom function mocks time.sleep() out and leaves us with the sum function that we really want to test. All we do is add a newly defined side_effect to the test:

```python
from unittest import TestCase

from unittest.mock import patch


def mock_sum(a, b):
    # mock sum function without the long running time.sleep
    return a + b


class TestCalculator(TestCase):
    @patch('main.Calculator.sum', side_effect=mock_sum)
    def test_sum(self, sum):
        self.assertEqual(sum(2,3), 5)
        self.assertEqual(sum(7,3), 10)
```

The tests should now pass:

.

———

Ran 1 test in 0.001s

OK

This was just a basic look at mocking, enough to give you the idea of what it is all about. You can take this much further if you wish; there is plenty of information to be found on the internet.

Chapter 19: Python Interview Questions

Have you found the job you have long sought? A job in Python? Not sure how you are going to get through the interview? We have 25 of the top questions asked in Python interviews as well as the answers. Keep in mind that every interview is going to be different, as will a job's scope.

These questions are split into two parts – Basic interview questions and Advanced questions:

Basic Questions

These are the very basic questions that you can expect to be asked at any Python interview:

1. What is Python and what are some of its key features?

Python is an interpretive computer programming language, both object-oriented and interactive, and used for scripting. It is designed as the most readable computer language in the world. Its key features are:

- It is interpretive which means you do not need to compile the program before you run it; it is interpreted at runtime by the interpreter, unlike other languages like C.
- It is a dynamically-typed language and this means there is no need to define datatypes for the variables you declare, or anything else for that matter. For example, a variable called x=10 can be declared, followed by x="Hello World" and, providing there are no errors, the datatype will be defined as per the value.
- Python functions are first-class objects.
- Python may be used for many applications, cross-platform, including web applications, big data applications, scientific models, and a whole lot more.

2. What is the difference between Python Lists and Tuples?

The single biggest difference between them is that a list is mutable, while a tuple is immutable. This means once a tuple has been created, the value cannot be edited or changed in any way; in a list, the value may be edited. The main differences are:

Tuples	Lists
Tuples are sequences of objects, immutable datatypes, mutable	Lists are very versatile
Parentheses are used for tuple syntax syntax	Square brackets are used for list
Tuples are fixed in length	Lists may be variable in length

3. What Operator Types Does Python Use?

Python uses the following types of operators:

Arithmetic Operators:

- Addition operator (+) for adding values
- Subtraction operator (-) for subtracting the value on the right from the value on the left
- Multiplication operator (*) for multiplying values
- Division operator (/) for dividing the left value by the right value
- Modulus operator (%) for dividing the left operand by the right operand and returning the remainder
- Exponent operator (**) for performing exponential value calculations

Relational Operators:

- == - if a pair of values are equal, the condition is true
- != - if two operand values are not equal, the condition is true
- <> - if a pair of values do not equal one another, the condition is true
- > - if the operand on the left is greater than the operand on the right, the condition is true

- < - if the operand on the left is less than the operand on the right, the condition is true
- >= - if the operand on the left is equal to or greater than the operand on the right, the condition is true
- <= - if the operand on the left is equal to or less than the operand on the right, the condition is true

Assignment Operators:

- = - Add
- += - Add And
- -= - Subtract And
- *= - Multiply And
- /= - Divide And
- %- -Modulus And
- **= - Exponent And

4. What is the maximum length a Python Identifier can be?

There isn't any maximum length because a Python identifier may be any length.

What do we mean by Python Decorators?

Python decorators are used for the modification or injection of code into classes or functions. By using a decorator, we can log calls and we can check to see what permissions are there.

5. What is a Python Dictionary?

A Python Dictionary is a list of the datatypes built-in to Python.

6. What is Python Memory Management?

Memory management in Python is carried out using the private heap space. Every data structure and every object in Python can be found in a private heap.

7. In one sentence, explain Python.

Python is one of the most powerful and modern of the interpreted computer languages, containing exceptions, modules, objects, threads, and with a memory management property.

8. Explain Python Interpretation

Python interpretation is nothing more complicated than the source code being used to run Python.

9. Explain the Python rules for global and local variables.

A local variable is one that has been assigned a value within the function while a global variable is one that has been defined externally to the function. A local variable can only be accessed from inside the function while a global variable can be accessed externally.

10. How are global values shared in Python?

To share a global variable, a config file is created and the variable to be shared is stored inside it.

11. How are Keyword or Optional Parameters passed between functions in Python?

To pass parameters we use the * specifier and the ** specifier from the parameter list attached to the function.

Advanced Questions

Now we move onto some of the more advanced questions you may be asked during an interview.

1. What are the different Python sequence types?

These are strings, lists, Unicode strings, xrange objects, buffers, and tuples.

2. What is the Python Lambda Form?

We use the Lambda keyword to create small functions that are anonymous, random, and can be thrown away.

3. What is Pickling?

Pickle is one of the standard Python modules used to serialize and de-serialize object structures.

4. How do we copy Python objects?

We can use two methods to copy objects in Python – shallow copy, which is where a compound object is constructed and object references placed into it, and deep copy, where a compound object is constructed and object copies are recursively inserted.

5. are Strings converted to Numbers?

Python contains many functions that we can use to convert datatypes and to convert strings to numbers and you would use the int or float functions.

6. How do we use a Python Script to send an email?

By importing the module called smtplib, an SMTP client-session object may be defined to send email using a script.

7. What command do we use to exit out of the Help command prompt?

We use the command called 'quit'

8. What do the Python Methods of sub(), subn() and split() do?

Split() uses its own regex pattern to split a specified string into a list. Sub() will find every substring that contains a match to the regex pattern and replaces the string. Subn() is much like sub(); the new string is returned with all the other replacements.

9. How do we display text content of a file in reverse order?

The file must first be converted into a list; reversed() is then used to reverse that list.

10. are the ODBS Modules?

The Python OBDS modules are:

- PythonWin ODBC
- MxODBC
- Pyodbc

11. What are the append() and extend() Python methods for?

The append() method is to add elements at the end while extend() will add the elements from a different list to the end.

12. What is TKlner?

TKlner is one of the Python libraries, a tool used for GUI development.

13. What is the difference between Python and Java?

The main difference is that Python datatypes are dynamically-typed while Java's are statically typed.

Hopefully these questions will give you a good head start when you attend your hard-fought-for Python interview.

Conclusion

Well, we finally reached the end of this guide and a long one it was too. But don't be disappointed when I tell you that we only really covered the basics as far as each subject is concerned. The idea behind the guide was to give you an overview in terms of learning the Python programming language and what you can do with it.

In Part 1, we started by looking at the Python language, going in-depth into data structure and algorithms. These are the fundamentals of Python and we learned how the two combine to help with Machine Learning. We also looked at Python variables, control structures and lists, along with objects and conditional statements. Data types followed that along with some internal modules before we moved on to the design of algorithms. Data structures followed that, primarily linked lists, stacks and queues. More algorithms came next, showing us the first steps in making sense out of vast amounts of data. This moved us neatly on to the next part.

In Part 2, we looked at Machine Learning. We learned what machine learning is and what the different types are. We looked at Sci-kit learn, the best Python machine learning toolkit you could ever have. We looked at classification and training, including training errors, moving on to preprocessing of data, clustering and the conversion of noisy text into a meaningful vector that could be clustered. We also learned about debugging classifiers, feature extraction and how they impact the performance of a classifier and we looked at several different algorithms.

In Part 3, we discussed Django and learned what it is and how to use it. We covered model-view-controller patterns and views and URL-confs before moving onto dynamic content. We looked at web templates, forms, content and dictionaries and then moved to tags and filters. Throughout this section, we built our first website using Django, learning how it all goes together and works seamlessly in the process.

Next we discussed ArcGIS and we learned what GIS is and how arcpy works. We learned about script execution and the developmental environments needed to create these scripts. Then we moved onto using the ArcGIS ModelBuilder, how to use it to create analyses and export scripts; we learned more about autogenerated code, how to generalize it and how to add functions that we can reuse elsewhere. We learned about model cursors, cursor parameters, and how to use geometry objects in arcpy. We looked at turning scripts into a permanent script tool that can be shared, before moving onto arcpy.mapping. We also learned how to create functions that can be reused and modules. We ended the section with a look at common ArcGIS for arcpy Desktop Advanced extensions.

We then discussed some of the different methods of testing, something that is vital to the success of your code, software or app. We discussed why testing was important, what TDD and BDD are, along with DSLs. We talked about automated testing, what it is used for and the differences between unit and integration testing. Finally, we went over some examples of using Mocking in Python as a way of making your tests more efficient.

Python is a great language to learn and I would suggest that if any of the sections in this guide particularly interest you that you take the time to learn more. There are plenty of online resources, books, and tutorials that you can use to learn more.

Remember, no matter what it is, practice really does make perfect and if you can grasp the fundamentals of all these areas of Python, you will be light years ahead of most people on the planet.

References

https://djangobook.com/

https://docs.djangoproject.com

https://interactivepython.org

https://pythonschool.net

https://medium.com

https://mathworks.com

https://towardsdatasience.com

https://arcgis.com

https://esri.com

https://pro.arcgis.com

https://agiledata.org

https://news.codeacademy.com

https://code.likeagirl.com

https://github.com/PacktPublishing/Python-Data-Structures-and-Algorithms

https://smartbear.com

https://realpython.com

https://semaphoreci.com

https://fullstackpython.com

https://jacobian.org

https://blog.fugue.co

http://pythontutor.com

Made in the USA
Lexington, KY
09 July 2019